Information Assurance and Security Ethics in Complex Systems:
Interdisciplinary Perspectives

Melissa Jane Dark
Purdue University, USA

Information Science REFERENCE

INFORMATION SCIENCE REFERENCE
Hershey · New York

Director of Editorial Content: Kristin Klinger
Director of Book Publications: Julia Mosemann
Acquisitions Editor: Lindsay Johnston
Development Editor: Joel Gamon
Publishing Assistant: Jamie Snavely
Typesetter: Michael Brehm
Production Editor: Jamie Snavely
Cover Design: Lisa Tosheff

Published in the United States of America by
Information Science Reference (an imprint of IGI Global)
701 E. Chocolate Avenue
Hershey PA 17033
Tel: 717-533-8845
Fax: 717-533-8661
E-mail: cust@igi-global.com
Web site: http://www.igi-global.com

Library of Congress Cataloging-in-Publication Data

Information assurance and security ethics in complex systems : interdisciplinary perspectives / Melissa Jane Dark, editor.
p. cm.
Includes bibliographical references and index. Summary: "This book offers insight into social and ethical challenges presented by modern technology covering the rapidly growing field of information assurance and security"--Provided by publisher. ISBN 978-1-61692-245-0 (hardcover) -- ISBN 978-1-61692-246-7 (ebook) 1. Computer security. 2. Data protection. 3. Privacy, Right of. 4. Information technology--Security measures. I. Dark, Melissa Jane, 1961-
QA76.9.A25I541435 2011
005.8--dc22

2010016494

British Cataloguing in Publication Data
A Cataloguing in Publication record for this book is available from the British Library.

Editorial Advisory Board

List of Reviewers

Table of Contents

Detailed Table of Contents

Chapter three builds on chapters one and two and caps the foundations section of the book. Chapter three is an ethical dilemma in action whereby a professional encounters an ethical dilemma. In a dialog with classic ethicists, the young professional explores the application of ethics to a modern day problem. By modeling this process for readers, chapter three aims to invite readers to join the conversation about information assurance and security ethics.

Chapter four is a research study that discusses the influence of culture on ethical attitudes and behavior. The chapter serves to remind readers that our only individual experiences are not the only filter we use in formulating judgments about right and wrong. The chapter confirms our expectation that many factors shape a person's interpretation of information assurance and security ethics, including partly culture.

Chapter five presents a polycentric view of the ethical challenges of peer-to-peer networks. The author clearly and concisely conveys the many parties with a stake in the peer-to-peer phenomenon, highlighting competing interests and demands from technical, economic, and policy vantage points.

In this fascinating chapter on pharmcogenomics, the authors discuss the basics of genetic testing as a way of introducing for the reader the importance of genomic information. The chapter offers a sound reasoning of the ethics of pharmcogenomic testing which serves as a useful model for readers wishing to reason through a macro-ethical dilemma. And while they conclude that for the most part pharmcogenomic testing is "ethical", they are cautious to remind us that there is much that is till not known.

Chapter 10 offers a case study of the costs and benefits of eGovernment in Sweden. While many of the benefits of e-Government services are appealing, this chapter highlights for readers that such advances come a need to continuously balance these benefits with a cost to privacy and increased vulnerability to fraud. The chapter concludes that because this cost-benefit is not easily calculated, the role of government officials who become the balancers of the cost and benefit is paramount.

Generally speaking, as technology becomes more fully integrated into our lives, social control of technology increases. Chapter 11 overviews this occurrence in information technology policy and focuses on the recent development of data breach disclosure laws in 45 of the states in the USA. Chapter 11 aims to help students in information assurance and security see the myriad of factors that influence public policy and highlights the challenges of policy solutions to polycentric social challenges commonly found in the information age.

Foreword

"There is more to life than increasing its speed." This aphorism by Mohandas K. Gandhi can be applied to computing technology as well as one's life: there is more value to it than simply increasing its speed. There are measures of worth other than those of speed and cost, and this book is an introduction to thinking about them, particularly in the context of security and privacy.

It is possible to view technologies as having multiple "waves" of development. The first such phase is to explore what may be accomplished with the new technological innovation. Whether we think about development of steam power, lasers, computing, or nanotechnology, there is a clear surge of effort by researchers and hobbyists to discover what might be done with the new technology. When some of the fundamental uses and bounds are discovered, a second wave begins as there are attempts to make the technology more reliable and consistent. This involves development of fault tolerance, standards, safety mechanisms, and understanding operational envelopes. Thereafter, a third phase is seen that is directed to making the technology more deployable: cheaper, smaller, and simpler to use, usually in a commercial context.

These three phases are visible when examining the history of almost any major technology. For instance, the airplane went from "we can fly" to "we can fly each time without crashing" to "we can mass-produce planes to use in commerce." Think about the evolution of transistors from a lab bench in Bell Labs, to integration into ICs, to quintillions of transistors on bits of silicon manufactured around the world. Or consider the transition of lasers from a room full of components to DVD players and presentation pointers, or the development of the automobile from first horseless carriage to modern hybrid vehicle. There is an evolution of each technology that includes these first three waves.

So too, computing has passed through these three phases. The first phase is still occurring but might have reached its peak in the 1970s through the 1990s as scientists and engineers explored what was possible to do with computing and information technology. We discovered foundations of operating systems, language grammars, networking, database, encryption, and more. From the 1980s through the near future we have been observing the second phase, as standards have been developed for protocols and interfaces, fault tolerant computing and storage (e.g., RAID) is explored, and new security mechanisms developed to "harden" the interfaces for internet commerce. There has been a near simultaneous third phase as new methods have been developed to reduce the size and cost of the technology, both hardware and software, to the point where the aggregate embedded computing in a modern kitchen or new automobile comprises more processing power and storage than was present in the entire world 50 years before — at a cost reduction of more than seven orders of magnitude.

We are now in a fourth phase of technology development, the one implied by the Mahatma's saying: the consideration of how the technology affects the quality of human life and dignity. Technology can change the way we live, alter economic and social balances, and change our abilities to achieve — but as sweeping as those changes may be, they do not necessarily occur without problems.

Computing and information technology can improve the world with increased access to information, better communication, and increased efficiency of large systems. We can enhance lives with on-line education and computer-controlled medical implants. However, we can also destroy privacy with unchecked data collection and correlation, and endanger whole economies with cyber attacks on critical infrastructure. For every bit of information that is gained to enhance our enforcement of laws we may also be reducing the privacy of those who are protected by those laws. New methods devised to protect a system from unauthorized use might also be used to suppress free speech and justified dissent.

It is important that those who are involved with the development and deployment of new cyber technologies understand these effects and tradeoffs. Science and the pursuit of knowledge may or may not be morally neutral, but the utilization of that knowledge in deployed technology has associated issues of ethics, policy, and law that the technologists ignore at their (and our) peril. The issues are more than science and engineering because people and societies are also involved: there are issues of law, of political science, of economics, of philosophy, of psychology, and more. The problems encountered in ensuring that systems are used appropriately are problems that cannot be solved with technology alone, but neither are they problems that can be addressed independent of the underlying computational fabric. Instead, they require an informed, multidisciplinary approach.

Nowhere is this approach more important than when considering issues of security, privacy, assurance, and crime. These are fundamental issues that computing and information technologies affect in overt (and sometimes, surprisingly subtle) manners. Recent history has shown how cyber crime and misuse can affect the world, both on the scale of nations and of individuals. Whether it is part of a military action against a country, such as Georgia, or the violation of a single individual's email privacy, computing technology can have a long-lasting and profound impact.

CERIAS (the Center for Education and Research in Information Assurance and Security) at Purdue University was founded in 1998 with the explicit mission of addressing these multidisciplinary issues in computing and information technologies. The editor of the book you are now reading, Professor Melissa Dark, has been an integral part of the Center from near its beginning, and she has a keen understanding of the need for a broad perspective on issues and approaches to addressing some of the fundamental challenges posed in this field. Guided by that experience, she has collected this volume of essays to expose some of the most important challenges — and approaches to their solutions — posed by the ever-increasing use of information technology.

No set of static readings can solve the total set of cyber security and privacy issues we face now and will face in the future. To really address those challenges will require ongoing efforts by a wide range of experts. Thus, it is critical that the computing experts, in particular, are familiar with the basic issues, understand some of the multidisciplinary nuances, and are able to engage the right communities in finding solutions to the most pressing problems. This book is intended to address that need for understanding. The material in this book should be considered as fundamental in any cyber curriculum as complexity bounds on algorithms and calculating throughput on a network; complexity bounds on algorithms and throughput analyses can increase the speed of our computing, but to paraphrase the Mahatma, there is much more to computing than increasing its speed. So, read these essays slowly and carefully, and consider, along with the authors, how computing should change the world for the better.

Eugene H. Spafford
Purdue University, USA

Eugene H. Spafford *has been working in computing for over 30 years, with activities in cyber security for most of that time. Spaf's (as he is known by many) current research interests are focused on issues of computer and network security, cyber-crime and ethics, and the social impact of computing. He is the founder and executive director of the Center for Education and Research in Information Assurance and Security (CERIAS) at Purdue University. This university-wide institute addresses the broader issues of information security and information assurance, and draws on expertise and research across all of the academic disciplines at Purdue. Spafford has received recognition and many honors for his research, teaching, and service, including being named as a Fellow of the ACM, of the AAAS, the IEEE, the (ISC)^2, and as a Distinguished Fellow of the ISSA.*

Preface

Often computers are viewed as machines that run algorithms. This view of computers covers a vast range of devices, from simple computers that perform limited and specific computations (for example, a computer found in a wristwatch) to supercomputers, which are groups of computers linked together in homogeneous and heterogeneous clusters and serving a vast array of computational needs. In between these extremes are a variety of machines from personal computers to embedded devices dedicated to serving a variety of functions. Let us call the perspective of computers as machines that run algorithms "mechanistic." Through the mechanistic lens, the computer is an artifact, coming from the Latin words *arte*, which means "skill" or "craft," and *facere,* which means to do or make. An artifact is that thing is skillfully or artfully made; and the computer, then, is a skillfully made machine for purposes of computation.

While the mechanistic view is irrefutable, it is also incomplete because it fails to consider contextual definitions of technology. One way of seeing the context of computing is to broaden the definition to consider the initial need for the innovation, as well as the consequent processes such as the conceptualization, design, development, implementation, use, diffusion, adaptation, evolution, maintenance, and disposal of computing. We will call this view the "social context influencing technology" perspective, shown in figure 1. This view assumes that such innovation processes arise from social needs and therefore positions computing as intrinsically social and humanistic. This view also suggests that technology occurs in a social milieu – a context – wherein the context is a set of interrelated conditions including social, cultural, and physical elements that form an environment, a circumstance, if you will. For example, in a society that where efficiency and productivity are highly valued norms, one would expect to see different technology innovations and adoptions in contrast to a society that is less concerned with efficiency and productivity (Bimber, 1990). The environment and its constituent elements in which technology is conceived, designed, developed, implemented, used, evolved, and so on, become factors that shapes how technology is conceived, designed, developed, implemented, used, evolved, etc.

An excellent example of how social context shapes technology innovation is provided in an article by Cowhey, Aronson and Richards (2009) that describes how political climate changed the US Information and Communication Technology Architecture. The social context that Cowhey, Aronson and Richards describe highlights how the division of powers, the majoritarian electoral system and federalism made it possible for a formulation of strong competition policy. The effects of this on the ICT architecture were threefold: (1) it enabled the architectural principle of "modularity" as multiple companies entered the marketplace making a "portion" of the goods that today comprise the Internet; (2) it created multiple network infrastructures for telecommunications, which is in contrast to other countries that either tried to retain a monopoly infrastructure or purposefully limit the number of competitors, and (3) it propelled both a particular architecture for computing (intelligence at the edge of the network) and the full realization of the potential benefits of the Internet (Cowhey, Aronson, and Richards, 2009).

Figure 1.

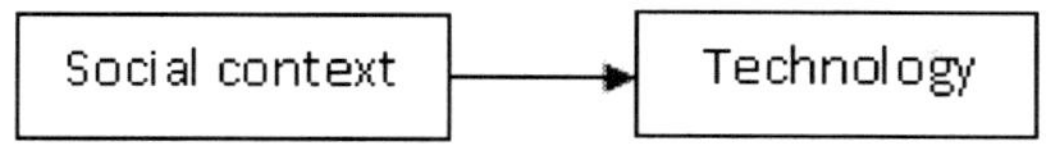

Figure 2.

In contrast to the "social context influencing technology" perspective is the view that technology shapes or influences social context. In this view (figure 2), technology is an agent that possesses active power, and perhaps even cause, and is capable of producing effects. The "technology influencing social context" perspective focuses on the manner in which technologies function as agencies in social functioning, change, and structure.

In an article ahead of its time, Moor (1985) offers an example of how technology can influence social context when he discusses how a program written to computerize airline reservations favored American Airlines by suggesting their flights first, even when the American Airline flight was not the best flight available. This example highlights how technology may affect social change in a manner that advantages American Airlines, but disadvantages the consumer. However, there are numerous examples where technology acts as a social agent for the betterment of human life. Take, for example, advances in health care. Today, information technology is being used to provide telecare and telehealth services to citizens in their homes. These technologically-mediated solutions promise many potential benefits including improved quality of life, cost savings, quality of service, and accessibility of service. Telecare, for example, offers elderly persons (1) the opportunity to age in place, which is widely known to be preferred by most older persons, (2) increased independence for the individual, and (3) an expansion of the possible care giving group to more easily include friends, family, and neighbors, as well as health care staff. Telecare also holds promise for a variety of cost savings, such as reduced travel costs for caregivers, where the time saved can be redirected toward offering improved care.

The quest for certainty blocks the search for meaning. Uncertainty is the very condition to impel man to unfold his powers.

—Erich Fromm, Psychologist

The perspectives in figures 1 and 2 are useful in helping us conceive our world. Using models such as these to partition and delineate relationships help us order and make sense of the world around us. These are sense making tools. Practically speaking, such delimitations are necessary so that the human mind can explore, define, and analyze phenomena. However, we need to be mindful that such partitions are artificial. Like technology, these boundaries are also artifacts. They do not reflect reality; rather they are conceptual boundaries that we impose (whether in our minds or on paper) due to our own limitations at comprehending totality. This book aims to cultivate awareness and questioning of these conceptual boundaries in readers' minds. Greater awareness should result in better preparation of the information assurance and security professional and consequently enable them to contribute to more socially robust and responsible endeavors.

This book is for students and practitioners in the rapidly growing field of information assurance and security. Early in the germination process, this book was going to catalogue the ethical issues that are of importance in today's online environment, e.g., privacy, access, ownership, security, cybercrime, and so on. However, several other books have taken this approach, focusing on 'what' the issues are and how they are exacerbated by the ubiquity and pervasiveness of information technologies (for example, see Johnson, 2000; Tavani, 2006). It was not my desire to duplicate what others already have done masterfully. Instead, this book will deliberate *some* of the ethical and social issues in information assurance and security. Chapters in this book address issues of privacy, access, safety, liability and reliability in a manner that asks readers to think about how the social context is shaping technology and how technology is shaping social context and, in so doing, to rethink conceptual boundaries.

This book assumes a complex adaptive systems' perspective regarding these ethical issues in information assurance and security by elucidating ways in which ethical issues (such as privacy, access, ownership) are at the intersection of information technology, policy, culture, and economics – all of which are systems with several associated subsystems. What this book aims to inculcate in the minds of readers is that issues of information assurance and security ethics are (1) co-constitutive, i.e., technology and social context co-adapt, (2) complex, which means there are actually several arrows, and (3) emergent, which suggests that these relationships are dynamic in uncertain ways.

Information assurance and security is inherently normative, dealing with weighty social and ethical issues. The core of information assurance and security ethics include questions such as these: What *ought* systems do in order to preserve privacy? To whom *should* access be granted? Who *should* be responsible for harm and risk of software security flaws? *Should* we have predictive insider threat monitoring? However, I need to be perfectly clear; this book will not offer answers to any of these questions. Not because answers are not desired. Rather because answers are not easy to come by. The social implications of questions such as these implicate deliberative participation, which occurs slowly. Social decisions about multiple goals calls for participatory control, which needs to occur transparently. Furthermore, in the large sense, what "ought to be" is akin to a journey without a destination. And while there is no preformulated state of balance, no foregone conclusion, the ideal of the common good and human flourishing are undeniable and ageless.

At the nexus of information assurance and security ethics are several complex systems. This book aims to reveal some of this complexity on the belief that more fully comprehending the problem space is more important than moving prematurely toward naïve solutions. This book asks readers to contemplate the role of existing norms in influencing what *should be* moving forward? This book extends beyond technical systems to include how, for example, political, cultural and economic systems shape and interact with technical systems and what this suggests for information assurance and security ethics. It is my hope that in reading this book, readers will question – and then question again – where system boundaries lie. I hope that readers come to understand, for example, that the responsibility for risk and harm of software security flaws is as much an economic challenge as a technical one. I hope that readers reflect on how peer-to-peer networks are acting as agents of social change in the intellectual property milieu and contemplate how the field of information assurance and security will change given advances in pharmacogenomics and personalized medicine. If at the end of this book, readers feel that information assurance and security ethics is messier and more vexing than originally perceived, then this book achieved its goal. If at the end of this book, readers feel more committed to *why* they chose information assurance and security as a field of study and their professional calling, then this book will have exceeded its goal.

As readers, you need to know that this book is grounded in constructivism, as opposed to rationalism or empiricism. What does this mean? Epistemologically, rationalists hold that knowledge is true or verifiable when what one knows corresponds to objective reality. For example, human beings breathe oxygen and exhale carbon dioxide. This is an objective reality. I can teach my child that humans breathe oxygen and exhale carbon dioxide and then test her knowledge thereof. If she knows this, then her knowledge reflects the world, ergo it is rational. Empiricism holds that knowledge is true when it can be observed through the senses. For example, my daughter is getting ready to start her seventh grade science fair project testing the effects of acid rain on aquatic plants. She will conduct her experiment by attempting to cultivate various aquatic plants in water with increasing doses of acid and observing the effects. The difference between rationalism and empiricism is in effect the degree to which sense experience is the source of knowing. Rationalists contend that some knowledge cannot be perceived through the senses, yet irrefutably exists.

The chapters in this book partly rely on rationalism and empiricism, yet, we all need to keep presence of mind that full knowledge of objective reality is unattainable – a key tenet of constructivism.

We love to overlook the boundaries which we do not wish to pass.

—Samuel Johnson, Writer

Constructivism recognizes that even the most elaborate theories of objective reality are through the mind's eye. As Piaget (1954, p. 400) noted, human "intelligence organizes the world by organizing itself." Our observations can never be independent of us. The interesting twists come when the observations we wish to make are observations about ourselves, what should be, and aspirations of one's contribution toward what should be. Here reality takes a different form; it is what we are working toward, not what is. This isn't to say that people do not work from experiences in formulating ideas about what should be – we do. It is just that our ideas about what should be can never fit reality – we humans are perpetually in the act of becoming. Here constructivism suggests that knowledge needs to be relevant and fitting to the context and circumstances, which are both external and internal. Questions of ethics require learning about our own ethics as context and circumstance, as well as the external context and circumstance. This book asks readers to engage in this reflection.

It might be useful for readers of this book to adopt a figure-ground practice with regard to their perception. You likely know of figure-ground phenomena; the concept of figure-ground is perhaps most well-known in the field of visual perception. In vision, figure-ground is a type of perceptual organization that involves assignment of edges to regions for purposes of shape determination, determination of depth across an edge, and the allocation of visual attention. One of the most well-known examples of figure-ground in vision is the faces-vase drawing popularized by Gestalt psychologist Edgar Rubin (see figure 3).

What is figural (either the faces or the vase) at any one moment depends on patterns of sensory stimulation and on the momentary interests of the perceiver. If the edges (the boundary) are perceived inward, then the perceiver sees a white vase against a black background. In contrast, if the edges are perceived outward, then the perceiver sees two black profiles against a white background. Both are valid.

Because they so aptly convey the human condition, figure-ground phenomena are also present in music and literature, including folklore. Consider this Russian joke; a guard at the factory gate saw a worker walking out with a wheelbarrow full of straw at the end of every work day. And every day the guard thoroughly searched the contents of the wheelbarrow, but never found anything but straw. One day

Figure 3.

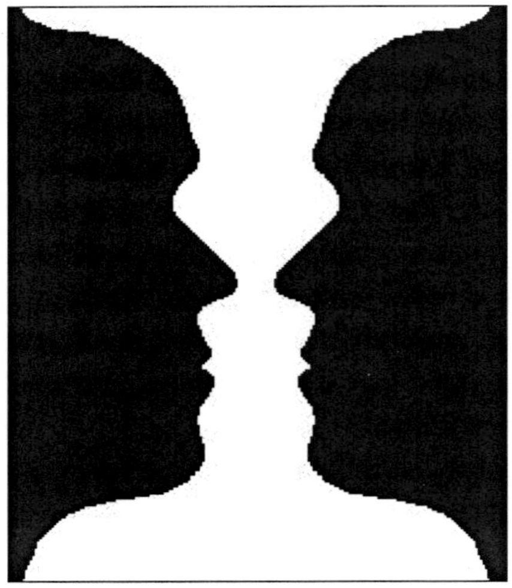

he asked the worker, "What do you gain by taking home all that straw?" and the worker replied, "The wheelbarrow." The illusion, you see, is that we are accustomed to thinking about the load of straw as the "figure." At first consideration, one assumes that the wheelbarrow is only an instrument and therefore it is relegated to the "ground" in the mind.

Figure-ground relationships are an important element of the way we organize reality in our awareness, which is at the heart of this book. This book then is about straw *and* wheelbarrows, about shifting attention from figure to ground or, rather, about turning into figure what is usually perceived as ground and then back again. Question your assumptions about figure and ground vigilantly – as they pertain to the world, to yourself, and to you in the world.

Chapter one of this book aims to help readers think about and develop a conceptual framework that serves the purpose of helping readers construe, question, and reconstrue their interpretive system about what *should be*. As chapter one positions questions of ethics in the individual mind, chapter two offers readers an historical view and in so doing serves to remind us all that ethics has a long and rich foundation from which one can build. Chapter three reinforces Harter's point in chapter two that while ethics is very old, it is forever new and invites readers to join the dialog.

Chapter four serves to remind readers that our own individual experiences are not the only filter we use in formulating judgments about right and wrong. In a study of international ethical attitudes and behaviors, Yates and Harris probe the role of culture in shaping perceptions about right and wrong use of information and information systems. While their findings are discussed in the context of information security policies for multi-national organizations, the second purpose of the chapter is to acknowledge that notions of right and wrong are often solidly grounded in group norms. Chapters five through nine present the following contemporary and emerging issues in information assurance and security: peer to peer networking, software security, predictive insider threat monitoring, behavioral advertising, and pharmocogenomic testing. Each chapter offers a critical analysis of ethical issues by looking at interplays of technology, policy, and economic systems.

Chapters 10 and 11offer two different glimpses of public sector involvement. Chapter 10 considers the competing interests of privacy versus public access to e-government services and public information. As information technology has become more ubiquitous and pervasive, assurance and security concerns have escalated; in response, we have seen noticeable growth in public policy aimed at bolstering cyber trust. With this growth in public policy, questions regarding the effectiveness of these policies arise. While public policy aims to ameliorate a social problem or need, public policy does not occur in a vacuum, it arises in a context which has implications for the policy outcomes we observe. Chapter 11 offers a retrospective and prospective look at data breach disclosure laws in the United States as a way of introducing readers to the broader context of public policy in information assurance and security.

I hope to create for readers a space where they reflect on the role of ethics in information assurance and security in the absence of certainty. This book asks the reader to engage in a conversation about the mutually adaptive roles of information and information technology to ethics, morality and emotional life, and to consider these entities in the context of their vitality to sustaining society. This book seeks to shed light on false, insufficient and/or useless distinctions between science and humanistic endeavors. Instead, the goal of this book is to provide a lens by which the adaptive relationships between information technology and human flourishing can be considered in meaningful and sustainable ways.

A final word, the subject of this book – information assurance and security ethics in complex systems – requires patience. Considering complex adaptive systems requires taking multiple vantage points and necessitates tolerance for uncertainty because adaptive systems are dynamic by nature – they vary, they evolve, and they emerge. For the reductionist or the rationalist, this can be frustrating. Impatience with messiness and imperfection has no seat at this table. Engaging in analysis of complex and adaptive systems does not reduce the number of questions one asks and attempts to answer. On the contrary, it produces more questions. The healthier mindset then is to abandon a quest for certainty and adopt a learning mentality, both at the individual and analytical levels, where the former is perhaps requisite to the latter. Knowing is an ongoing adaptive process in which objectivity and subjectivity emerge and continually evolve. The knower, like complexity itself, can be characterized as non-linear, sensitive to contextual conditions, and unpredictable. Your epistemology is not only a part of the complexity; it is also a part of the dynamic interactions. The nature of reality and its dynamics are complex and the knower is a part of that complexity. It is not the quest of this book to divorce subjectivity from objectivity in pursuit of the latter. As the essayist Henry David Thoreau said "Live your beliefs and you can turn the world around."

Melissa Dark
Purdue University, USA

REFERENCES

Bimber, B. (1990). Karl Marx and the three faces of technological determinism. *Social Studies of Science, 20*(2), 333-351.

Cowhey, P., Aronson, J., and Richards, J. (2009). Shaping the architecture of the U.S. information and communication technology architecture: A political economic analysis. *Review of Policy Research, 26*(1-2), 105-125.

Johnson, D. (2000). *Computer ethics.* Upper Saddle River, NJ: Prentice Hall.

Moor, J. (1985). What is computer ethics? *Metaphilosophy, 16*(4), 266-275.

Piaget, Jean. (1954). *The construction of reality in the child* (M. Cook, Trans.). New York: Ballantine.

Tavani, H. (2006). *Ethics and technology: Ethical issues in an age of information and communication technology.* Hoboken, NJ: Wiley.

Acknowledgment

Several individuals contributed to making this book come to fruition. I am grateful to the authors who worked with me through numerous drafts. I am indebted to the individuals who served on the editorial advisory board providing comments and suggestions throughout. I would especially like to thank Linda Morales, Richard Epstein, J. Ekstrom, Mario Garcia, Sydney Liles, John Springer, Cassio Goldschmidt, Katie Shilton, and Jeff Burke for their involvement throughout.

I am thankful for the graduate students in my Fall, 2009 Information Assurance and Security Ethics class who carefully read and deliberated most of these chapters. I learned from listening to them talk about the ideas and issues presented in these chapters. Not only did they give me feedback, they were a source of hope; I am confident that they will "pay it forward". So, I also thank them in advance for what they will do.

I am grateful to Purdue University and the Study in a Second Discipline program offered by the Provost's Office at Purdue. This support enabled me to take public policy and welfare economics classes that shaped my thinking in substantive ways. I am grateful to the College of Technology at Purdue University for allowing me the time and support to explore critical interfaces of technology and society.

I owe a unique thanks to Eugene Spafford and my other colleagues at the Center for Education and Research in Information Assurance and Security (CERIAS) at Purdue University. CERIAS is a vibrant and committed research and education center that is unique in its multidisciplinary approach to information assurance and security, ranging from purely technical issues (e.g., intrusion detection, network security, etc) to ethical, legal, educational, communicational, linguistic, and economic issues, and the subtle interactions and dependencies among them. I consider joining CERIAS in 2000 as one of the best (and luckiest) decisions I have made in my career.

I am also grateful for the partial support that I received for this book from the National Science Foundation program for Ethics Education in Science and Engineering and for the time and energy provided by my collaborators on this grant: Mario Garcia, Nathan Harter, and Linda Morales. This grant helped support meetings and workshops that provided invaluable input into the book.

Finally, thank you to the following colleagues who enthusiastically participated in a workshop deliberating the contents of this book, preparing to pilot test these materials, and helping write the discussion questions at the end of each chapter. These questions were the collective output of rich discussion among the following individuals (with some input from the chapter authors): Krishani Abeysekera, Jim Chen, John Chen, Barbara Endicott-Popovsky, Rosemary Fernholz, Mario Garcia, Hossain Heydari, Ming Ivory, Connie Justice, Michael Losavio, Linda Morales, Onook Oh, Sharon Perkins Hall, and Hal Sudborough.

Melissa J. Dark
Perdue University, USA

Section 1
Foundational Concepts and Joining the Conversation

Section 1
Introduction

Linda Morales
University of Houston Clear Lake, USA

How do we go about taking ethical positions on issues that affect us? How do we determine where we stand on questions of ethics? Often, the ethics of a situation is clear. For example, most individuals recognize that it is not right for a person to take credit for work that he or she has not done. It is rarely justified for an individual to infringe on someone else's privacy by reading e-mail, wiretapping, or eavesdropping in other ways. These judgments are easy to state, especially when one is not directly affected. But there are many situations where the ethical choice is not so clear. Suppose a supervisor orders a software team to meet an earlier deadline than previously planned. To do so, testing would be incomplete and inconclusive, and the resulting software could have serious flaws that might result in injury to users. The job market is bad and none of the team members can risk poor performance evaluations or being fired by their supervisor. They must keep their current jobs. Third party observers would probably say that the appropriate way to handle this situation is obvious. Of course the deadline must not be moved. Once the negative repercussions of the earlier deadline are explained, management will certainly agree that the team must be given adequate time to perform thorough testing. This opinion hardly requires a second thought. However, ethical choices are less facile for people who are directly affected by the outcomes. If a choice has to be made between losing one's income and cutting corners, which choice would a person make? If that person is the sole breadwinner of the family, or has financial obligations to meet, the decision gets even more difficult. It is easy for outside observers to make pronouncements about ethics. On the other hand, stakeholders by definition lack perspective and impartiality. It is much more difficult for them to make sound ethical analyses of situations that affect them. For stakeholders who lack a proper grounding in ethical theory, ethical decision making may well be impossible.

Sometimes ethical dilemmas, when they are mere intellectual exercises, seem easily solvable in the abstract. Turn them into real-life situations with personal repercussions and they become devilishly ambiguous, fiendishly bewildering. Reality and its complications have a way of turning the seemingly trivial into the complex, the obvious into the perplexing. Of course there are ethical dilemmas that are difficult to decide even in abstract. Take, for example, the biblical story of King Solomon and the two women (1 Kings 3:16-28, New International Version). Each woman was the mother of an infant. One infant died in the night, and both women claimed to be the mother of the live infant. Solomon ordered that the baby be cut in half with a sword, so that each mothers could have half of the baby. Upon hearing this order, one of the mothers asked Solomon to give the baby to the other woman to spare the baby's life. The other woman, however, agreed that the baby should be cut in half. Solomon deduced that the first woman must be the real mother and ruled that she should have the live baby.

This solution seems tidy and effective, though uncomfortably glib. It is also clearly unrealistic. No judge would ever propose cutting a baby in half! Well, let's put ourselves in Solomon's shoes and imagine having to decide such a case ourselves. Nowadays, DNA testing could be useful in determining parentage, but in earlier times before this tool was available, how would a judge or jury determine the real mother of an infant? It could be that no useful evidence is available, and that all there is to go on is one person's word against another's. With a child's welfare and his or her potential success as an adult at stake, the burden of a decision like this cannot be taken lightly. A just and ethical solution would be extremely difficult to arrive at, either by the jury for a real-life case, or by a student of ethics working on an abstract case study.

How then are we to improve our ethical thought process and sharpen our analytic skills? Chapters one and two suggest ways to do this. Chapter one discusses conceptual frameworks. The goal is to learn how to de-personalize ethical dilemmas so that we can inspect them from the outside, as if we have no stake in the outcomes. That is, we "render beliefs into ideas and then compare those ideas." In doing so, we hope to avoid getting fixed on a certain opinion before having carefully considered the alternatives. We must realize that dilemmas encountered in the Information Age (Toffler, 1981) tend to be complex and multi-faceted. "It is not one problem we face, but many entangled problems." Furthermore, in developing ethical responses to dilemmas we now face, we are, in a sense, influencing the future of the Information Age. This is a truly weighty responsibility, and there are many uncertainties. To throw up our hands as if deliberating an uncertain problem is a waste of time hardly seems admirable, yet we wrestle with the magnitude of the task before us.

Chapter two presents three classical ethical theories that have helped ethicists and other thinkers over the centuries to make sense of ethical muddles. Utilitarianism, deontological ethics and virtue ethics are discussed in detail. Our thought process benefits from being grounded in classical ethics and its analytical tools, which have been well tested over time. Chapter two observes that it is "by means of ethical behavior a profession earns trust from the community it serves." Trust is at the crux of many issues in the Information Age. It behooves us to understand what constitutes ethical behavior and how to practice it so that we, the systems we operate, and the services we offer, earn the trust of community. Furthermore, Chapter two points out that in situations when existing conventions and norms are inadequate, "(e)thical theory … becomes absolutely essential to thinking through and defending our choices. Otherwise, as a practical matter, defiance looks like incompetence or sheer willfulness."

Chapter three uses utilitarianism, deontological ethics and virtue ethics to analyze an ethical dilemma that any professional working in almost any high-technology field could easily encounter in the workplace. Chapter three illustrates in a concrete way how classical ethical theories might be used to examine a problem in order to formulate an ethical response. Chapter three offers a dialog that serves to invite readers to join the conversation about ethical issues in information assurance and security.

REFERENCES

Holy Bible, New International Version (1984). Grand Rapids, MI: Biblica.

Toffler, A. (1981). *The third wave.* New York: Bantam.

Chapter 1
On the Importance of Framing

Nathan Harter
Purdue University, USA

ABSTRACT

Forces have converged to produce stunning new technologies and the Information Age. As a result, we experience unanticipated consequences. Among the implications of this transition are a variety of ethical predicaments. This chapter introduces a process of conceptual framing. We classify this work as the inspection and consideration of our conceptual frameworks. We move from doubt about our current frameworks toward better ones. The way to make this transition is to render beliefs into ideas and then compare those ideas. Nevertheless, there is always an imperfect alignment of ideas with lived reality, so we must avoid dogmatic closure. The ethics predicaments we face are in actuality an ill-defined "mess" of multiple problems, the solutions to which affect one another. In response, we consider the processes of design for the future in the face of such ill-defined ethics problems.

INTRODUCTION

Every person has probably formed an opinion about being touched by information technology. Have the latest technological advances been generally good or bad? Could we have prepared ourselves better for them? Could we even have foreseen complications such as privacy infringement, identity theft, internet fraud, or failures with electronic voting devices? Now that we find ourselves beset by such complications, how do we navigate our way toward ethical responses?

In the last decades of the twentieth century, forces converged to produce stunning new technologies with far-reaching implications for human life—how we work and play, learn and think. It has truly become an Information Age (Toffler, 1981). As with any new technology of such power, we have also experienced plenty of unanticipated consequences. Familiar ways of life have been shifting. Novel threats to social order are emerging. Longstanding beliefs about

DOI: 10.4018/978-1-61692-245-0.ch001

the nature of our world and our place in it have given way to uncertainty.

There has always been such a rhythm to innovation (Dewar, 1998; Introna, 2007). Forces converge to produce some novelty, some widget or process, and over time the novelty becomes integrated into the larger array of systems we call society. This integration is subject to a variety of delays, as the prevailing systems attempt to adapt themselves. In these assorted time lags, people struggle to figure out what is going on and whether it is even a good thing. These struggles constitute a delay in the process of integration, while human beings try to make sense of the implications of their own innovations. Gradually, humanity comes to absorb the novelty, bringing it within the comprehending order, and moves on—though usually not without a period of disruption, sacrifice, and stress. In some instances, we replace the novelty with something better, or we simply reject it. Today, we find ourselves still trying to integrate the suite of novelties that goes by the collective name of Information Technology.

Among the many implications of this new age are a variety of perplexities we can refer to as ethical. As we assimilate or discard new technology, we struggle to understand and frame the meaning of ethics in the new context. These problems are the main focus of this book.

In order to develop tools for analyzing ethical issues, we turn to the work of several scholars who study the interplay of ideas, innovation, and ethics. In this chapter, we examine the ethical implications from various perspectives – to develop ways to formulate, conceptualize, and describe ethical dilemmas that arise from the Information Age. Only then can we hope to arrive at justifiable responses. Our hope is that through this preliminary work of *framing* information assurance and security ethics, we can advance our *understanding* of information assurance and security ethics.

The sections of this chapter build upon one another in the following way. The perspectives we present come from scholars of philosophy and organizational management from around the world. First, using the work of the Russian émigré, Isaiah Berlin, we consider the conceptual frameworks we use to think about ethics. Second, based on the work of an American, C.S. Peirce, we state as our goal the transition from doubt about our current frameworks to the adoption of superior ones. Third, relying on a seminal essay by the Spaniard José Ortega y Gasset, we argue that the way to make this transition is to remove our personal bias by rendering our beliefs and the beliefs of others into ideas and then comparing those ideas. Fourth, using advice in a cautionary note articulated by the Frenchman Henri Bergson, we recognize the imperfect alignment of ideas generally with lived reality, so that we might avoid dogmatic closure around any one idea to the exclusion of all others. Dogmatic closure would be unhelpful. Fifth, relying primarily on the work of management scholar Russell Ackoff, we try to describe the nature of the ethics problem of the Information Age and discover that it is what he calls an ill-defined "mess" of multiple problems, the solutions to which affect one another. It is not one problem we face, but many entangled problems. Sixth, we proceed to draw from the work of social scientist Herbert Simon on the processes of design for the future in the face of such ill-defined ethics problems as we seem to be facing.

BERLIN ON CONCEPTUAL FRAMEWORKS

Human beings at the current stage in the Information Age participate to a greater or lesser extent in conceptual delays as they try to make sense of its implications for ethics. They are trying, in the words of Isaiah Berlin, "to understand themselves and thus operate in the open, and not wildly, in the dark."[1] This effort to understand falls under the discipline of philosophy, as described in Berlin's essay on "The Purpose of Philosophy (2000)."

What does the classification of a "philosophical" endeavor mean, for the purposes of this book?

Berlin opened his essay by showing that when we have questions of the sort raised by the impact of new technology, many of them can be answered by either empirical or formal means. Empirical means are those determined by observation, measurement, and experimentation. Formal means are those determined by the axioms of a system and inferences from those axioms, as in logic or grammar. Deductions are then made by applying the rules. Plenty of uncertainties about living in the Information Age can be answered in one or both of these ways. For a range of questions, however, these methods will not suffice. We must look elsewhere for analytical tools. But where? For these questions, Berlin offers philosophy.

One of the practices of philosophy has to do with "questions that concern the very framework of concepts (2000, p. 28)". Frameworks are the mental models or schemata by which we understand the world. Berlin also referred to them as "patterns or categories or forms of experience..." (p.31). These frameworks, which are not altogether the products of empirical testing or formal deduction, matter a great deal in ethics. Berlin saw great evil in the world because human beings often operate by inadequate frameworks. He believed there is an ongoing ethical obligation to revisit our frameworks. We would certainly prefer to avoid any false or mistaken beliefs. A false or mistaken belief is bad enough, but an *incorrigible* false belief, impervious to persuasion of any kind, is the very definition of a delusion, and therefore is pathological (see Hillman, 1986, p. 5).

As a practical matter, different people can operate in the same environment using entirely different frameworks, almost like engineers from rival firms after a business merger who must now work together. Suppose they each used different software packages when designing equivalent products: how will they get along hereafter? Which software will they use? This lack of uniformity leads to confusion, conflict, and stress.[2] What can be done about that? In the absence of a single, uniform framework for thinking about the ethical implications of an Information Age, what can be done to understand the issues that empirical testing and formal deduction cannot resolve?

Philosophy offers, in the words of Berlin (2000):

To extricate and bring to light the hidden categories and models in which human beings think..., to reveal what is obscure or contradictory in them, to discern the conflicts between them that prevent the construction of more adequate ways of organizing and describing and explaining experience... (p. 33)

Toward the end of the essay, he offered as:

A reasonable hypothesis that one of the principle causes of confusion, misery and fear is...adherence to outworn notions, pathological suspicion of any form of critical self-examination, frantic efforts to prevent any degree of rational analysis of what we live by and for. (p. 34f)

It would follow that in order to avoid such a fate, we would be advised in our predicament to examine anew our underlying beliefs, the frameworks by which we perceive the world. But how is such a re-conceptualization accomplished? What is the process by which we might arrive at more adequate beliefs? Berlin did not offer an answer in this particular essay. One philosopher who had already begun to answer that question was C.S. Peirce.

PEIRCE ON TRANSFORMING DOUBT INTO BELIEF

Writing in *Popular Science Monthly* (November 1877), the American philosopher Charles Sanders Peirce wrote an influential article titled, "The Fixation of Belief." In it, Peirce explained the process by which a person who is not certain what to believe, comes to arrive at sufficient conclusions. His characterization of this phase describes what many of us are presently going through as we try to orient ourselves with unfamiliar, ethical predicaments associated with the Information Age.

At the time Peirce was writing his article, people did not yet know how to make sense of Darwinism. (Darwin's book, *The Descent of Man,* had just been published six years before.) We are, he wrote, "like a ship in the open sea, with no one on board who understands the rules of navigation" (p. 113). Peirce offers the following insights on how we work through such confusion: "there are such states of mind as doubt and belief—that a passage from one to the other is possible…" (p. 113). First, as to doubt: "Doubt is an uneasy and dissatisfied state from which we struggle to free ourselves and pass into the state of belief [not unlike] the irritation of a nerve and the reflex action produced thereby…" (p. 114). Belief, by way of contrast, "is a calm and satisfactory state in which we do not wish to avoid, or to change into a belief in anything else" (p. 114). Peirce added, "Our beliefs guide our desires and shape our actions….The feeling of believing is a more or less sure indication of there being established in our nature some habit which will determine our actions"(p. 114). He summarized in this way: "The irritation of doubt causes a struggle to attain a state of belief" (p. 114). What he was saying is that conceptual predicaments, such as the ethical predicaments of an Information Age, reveal the inadequacy of our habits of mind and stimulate the search for beliefs that will result in new habits.

Peirce did observe that many people resist the process altogether; and justify holding on to their beliefs by a method of tenacity (to borrow his phrase). With some scorn, Peirce called this "the instinctive dislike of an undecided state of mind, exaggerated into a vague dread, [making people] cling spasmodically to the views they already take" (p. 116). This response works only so long. Once doubt successfully insinuates itself into the mind, then it is not uncommon for many people to abandon habit and adopt a second method. Peirce called this second method Authority, by which we turn for answers to others we trust—whether credible individuals, such as experts or gurus, or credible institutions, such as the church. This method works for only so long. If enough members of a community adopt this method, it also fosters widespread ignorance and servility, let alone the potential for error, yet Peirce insists that this method is probably better than the method of tenacity.

In the same manner today, perhaps most participants in the Information Age cling to their beliefs in the teeth of novelty, and when they do experience doubt, they look to someone else for direction. They look to judges, legislators, professors, and professionals to alleviate their distress. They want someone else to have worked through the predicament and to have arrived at a satisfactory conclusion for them. "For the mass of mankind," observed Peirce, "there is perhaps no better method than this" (p. 118). For many people, however, neither method works. It certainly does not work for those on whom the rest of the community depends, because when they look around for someone to serve as their authority, they find only themselves. These people require a further method.

Peirce offered a third method of consensus for those who find themselves dissatisfied with the other two, a method that he described as "far more intellectual and respectable from the point of view of reason..." Its lowest form is to argue for that belief which most individuals will accept, almost like a consensus or common sense point of view. If we present alternatives and ask which one seems best to anyone who will listen, then perhaps we would discover superior beliefs that will also gain wide acceptance, until a more acceptable belief comes along. Peirce did not want to disparage this method. It has considerable advantages. Nevertheless, it guarantees nothing about the validity of those beliefs. Just because we tend to accept a belief does not make it the best belief. It might be relatively simple to take a vote or point out the lack of any voices of dissent. Nevertheless, we find ourselves right back at the old method of tenacity, tending to justify our present beliefs by an extra layer of spurious validation, namely that "everybody thinks in this way." Even if this claim were true as an empirical fact, "everybody" could be wrong. Any opinion, freely arrived at, can still be wrong—or at least doubtful.

What, then, is the higher form of this method? First, like the lower form, "the method must be such that the ultimate conclusion of every man [or woman] shall be the same" (p. 120). Second, however, is that conclusions must accord with the facts- those stubborn aspects of an external or paramount reality. This calls for a *scientific approach.* Through a scientific approach, we attempt to prove hypotheses by designing and conducting experiments, and arriving at conclusions based on experimental results. Happily, this approach is not so rare. Peirce even mentioned, "Everybody uses the scientific method about a great many things, and only ceases to use it when he does not know how it apply it" (p. 120). What the approach does, when applied stringently, is induce a state or condition of doubt, which we subsequently attempt to escape by reestablishing a state of belief. That might seem strange, namely to fix our beliefs by first entertaining doubt. But Peirce wrote that "a shade of *prima facie* doubt is cast upon every proposition which is considered essential to the security of society" (p. 122). Not to doubt—not to subject one's beliefs to some defensible standard—is itself, in his opinion, "as immoral as it is disadvantageous" (p. 123).[3]

We do not intend to describe or carry out the scientific method. Berlin had already warned us against relying too heavily on empirical or formal methods for trying to answer questions where the conceptual framework is not yet clear. Rather, it is sufficient to recognize that in his article, Peirce presented a part of this framework when he contrasted doubt with belief, depicting their relationship as an ongoing process of moving from some habit of the mind, through the experience of doubt, toward the fixation of superior beliefs that ultimately result in more successful habits of mind. As we proceed, we should also have before our minds Peirce's four methods for fixing belief: the method of tenacity, the method of authority, the method of consensus, and the method of subjecting beliefs to some external, independent standard in reality that anyone may consult, which we call the scientific method.

What we seek ultimately is some justifiable understanding of two things: (a) our situation at this moment without our conceptual delay and (b) what (if anything) we can do about our situation. And so we seek an adequate conceptual framework about the situation and well-grounded beliefs to give direction.

ON ORTEGA'S DISTINCTION BETWEEN IDEAS AND BELIEFS

Our focus on framing information ethics leads us to reflect on the role of our beliefs. To do so requires detachment; that is, we must render beliefs into ideas. In order to explain the important distinction between ideas and beliefs, we rely on a famous essay written by the Spaniard Jose Ortega y Gasset and translated by Jorge García-Gómez in 2002. In that essay, Ortega contrasted an *idea*, which we can be said to have, with a *belief*, to which we belong.

We take beliefs for granted and rely on them to conduct our lives (Gasset, 1984). However, until we reach that stage of intimacy with any given belief, it is at most an idea, not a belief, that we are simply considering. Ortega used the example that we avoid trying to walk through walls because we have come to *believe* in their solidity. There is no practical reason to doubt this. Beliefs are the basis for behavior. One might say that ideas occupy the surface of our minds, hovering across the cerebral cortex of our brains, as mere possibilities, whereas beliefs live like carbuncles deep within the core, at the center where one's sense of identity resides. We can imagine ideas auditioning to become beliefs. We *entertain* or *construct* ideas. We live according to beliefs.

Ortega went one step further. He hypothesized that ideas exist precisely where we lack belief, as though one must patch holes in the tent (Gasset, 1984). We would have no reason to consider an idea unless we were open to doubt on some question, even hypothetically. (For example, I might love my job, but that does not prevent me from fantasizing about other careers.) Once we do experience doubt, then we cast about for ideas to satisfy that doubt, and once we accept an idea that successfully quiets that doubt, it becomes part of our belief system. Thus, beliefs exist whether we are conscious of them or not—and usually we are not. Ideas, on the other hand, exist *only* because we are conscious of them, at some level. He summarized the difference this way.

To realize or be aware of something without counting on it is the most characteristic form of an idea; to count on something without realizing it, is the most characteristic form of a belief. Here, then, are two distinct modes of human comportment. (Gasset, 1984, p. 21)

In a sense, then, we *are* our beliefs. In Ortega's formulation, beliefs are ideas that we are. Ortega even referred to the "orthopedic nature of ideas..." (Gasset, 1984, p. 20; Gasset, 2002, p. 192). Our beliefs shape how we see the situation and also how we go about forming expectations and consequent action plans that project what we can do about our circumstances. In order to know who we are and not take this for granted, we must know our beliefs and make an object of them. By the same token, in order to know the world outside of ourselves, we must know our beliefs. And in order to conceive of a multi-dimensional and non-time bounded, co-constitutive relationship between ourselves and our situation, we must continue knowing our beliefs and their interrelations. Or, as Ortega was to put it elsewhere as a kind of slogan, "I am I plus my circumstances" (1961, p. 45).

The contrary, then, is also true. We cannot be said to be what we do *not* believe. So, it is equally essential for self-awareness, to know what we do not believe, inasmuch as disbelief is as defining as belief. The odd thing, of course, is that in order to contemplate either our beliefs or our disbeliefs, we must render them as ideas, holding them out at arm's length, returning them back to the surface for closer scrutiny. Ortega (2002) wrote, "that we only adequately understand what something is to us when it is not a reality to us but an idea..." (p. 197).

Perhaps a brief analogy will help make this point. There are two ways that a sculptor sculpts. He/she can sculpt by starting with raw materials and cumulatively add and modify through processes such as molding, casting and welding—building and building until the sculpture is formed. The other way that a sculptor can create is by starting with raw material and taking away; such is the case with carving—taking away and taking away until the sculpture is complete. In both cases, the result is three-dimensional artwork. However, in the first case, the dimension is formed by identifying what is, what needs to be, whereas in the second case, contour is a result of what is taken away. A belief system, like sculpture, is arrived at both by what we believe and by what we do not believe. And, as a result of saying this, certain logical questions follow.

- What do we already believe?
- What do we already disbelieve?
- How can we come to know what we already believe?
- How can we come to know what we already disbelieve?

Paradoxically, many of our beliefs are not really ours in the sense that we, as individuals, developed and adopted them for ourselves after a process of deliberation. Many of our beliefs came to us as a kind of inheritance, passed around the community as true, from one generation to the next, in a shared process of sensemaking (Ortega y Gasset, 1957, pp. 94-111). To be sure, each of us has arrived at a number of beliefs on our own, taking responsibility for the necessary labor of formulating and considering the value of certain beliefs, even if it turns out that we disagree with our friends and neighbors. But we also participate in collective beliefs, the sort of thing "everybody knows" to be true. We accept, for example, that the earth is not flat. Nevertheless, let me ask the following question: how many of us worked that out for ourselves, by means of logic or observation? Most of us see no reason to dispute many of the claims of science. We do not observe atoms, for example, yet we go about our daily lives supposing they exist. And it is not only science generating these widespread claims. Many of our shared beliefs even contradict science or have nothing to do with science.

The point is, that we must bring both kinds of belief to the surface, both the hard-won conclusion of the individual and the taken-for-granted opinion of the collective -- perhaps *especially* the widely held beliefs that we share with others, precisely because they enjoy a validity simply by virtue of their ubiquity. For, if the entire community seems puzzled or frustrated about the situation they find themselves in, then maybe we owe it to the community to diagnose where its collective reasoning seems to have gone wrong (Peirce, 1955, p. 13). That could be the case today during a conceptual delay as we try to make sense of the Information Age.

James Hillman is an American psychologist who has written on the deep power and importance of ideas. The 1995 book *Kinds of Power* (Currency Doubleday) developed his theme. During conversations and while reading books, a person is engaged in ideas. Between times, ideas can become almost like autonomous powers and shape human behavior. Ideas that have become "internalized" in this fashion – that is, ideas operating as beliefs – reside somewhere beyond conscious thought. We simply take them for granted. Now, despite the suspicion that what is not part of conscious thought is not conscious because it lies hidden away in dark recesses of the mind, Hillman (1995) pointed out that a person is least conscious of that which is, in his words, "most usual, most familiar, most everyday (p. 4)." It is out there, embodied in our daily life, almost too obvious to notice. The effects of what is not conscious are on display. And that, in itself, can be a problem, because once the habits of daily life prove to be dysfunctional in some respect, one would think the next step would be to reexamine the ideas on which those habits are based, yet we do not necessarily notice them. And so it does not occur to us to question them, to doubt their adequacy, which means they will likely persist until we do. That is the task set before us today.

For this reason, Hillman (1995) referred to the power of ideas – ideas that "trickle down into each act of making, serving, choosing, and keeping that we perform" (p. 6). He then wrote that "ideas determine our goals of action, our styles of art, our values of character, our religious practices and even our ways of loving" (p. 16). "Though we want ideas," Hillman continued, "we haven't learned how to handle them. We use them up too quickly. We get rid of them by immediately putting them into practice." (p. 18) Better to ponder them a while, play with them, rolling them over in our minds. There is a reason we are said to *entertain* ideas. No need to rush toward implementation.

An idea can be something one sees, like an image or form that is out there and enters the mind. "An idea came to me." "I see what you mean." It is also a way of seeing, like one's perspective, or as this book would have it: a conceptual framework – not just seeing something new but seeing something in a new way. This book is about seeing something new. Later chapters deliberate emergent socio-ethical dilemmas that arise in the context of complex, adaptive systems. These ethical dilemmas are unresolved and in many ways unresolvable. In addition, what this book is attempting to do is take one's perspective, one's way of seeing, and look directly at it. An idea is not just an image of the world out there. It can also reflect who you are. Rather than looking upward or forward, we must look inward.

A conceptual delay with regard to the ethics implications of the Information Age should, therefore, lead us inwardly to doubt certain beliefs (and disbeliefs) about technology, information, and the good, as we work toward even more adequate beliefs. Anyone who affirms the method of science especially, wrote Ortega (2002), "must constantly attempt to cast doubt on his or her own truths." (p. 201) We, too, must bring our beliefs and disbeliefs to the surface and treat them as ideas, which means that we must doubt, which in turn means that we must also consider alternative ideas, new ideas. We must engage in philosophy. And, as Berlin advised us in a previous section, the place to begin this process just might be the conceptual frameworks we are using to think about these issues. What we might ask ourselves, in other words, is how we already frame our problem.

BERGSON ON THE ROLE OF IDEAS

One might think that the objective at this point is to summon various ideas about the problems of ethics in an Information Age and compare them to each other, choosing the superior ones, and where possible, fitting them together into a comprehending system of ideas that approximates the reality we are trying to understand. By choosing better and better ideas—and by adding more and more of these better and better ideas—we might one day build an elaborate conceptual schema that will be adequate to the challenges we face. The French philosopher, Henri Bergson (1949, 1955), would caution us about such a plan.

In the previous section, which focused on the work of Ortega, we concluded by saying that the next task is to present ourselves with a variety of ideas about the problems we call information assurance and security ethics. Bergson understood this sort of project as analysis, and he acknowledged how natural and useful it is to do this sort of thing when confronted with a problem. It is not *wrong* to conduct an analysis. Nevertheless, for Bergson this is only one of two different ways of knowing. By means of analysis, we move around the phenomenon we are attempting to study, from an exterior point of view, looking at it this way and that, in the hopes that by accumulating multiple points of view we will ultimately know it completely. Because there are so many points of view, however, no one point of view is sufficient. By accumulating points of view, we might come to approximate complete knowledge. This, at least, is the ambition of science and the practical arts. And, because the possible points of view are literally infinite, this process of analysis never ends.

Bergson reminded us of a second way of knowing, however, and that is from the interior, which he referred to as intuition. These are experiences that we have directly, without reducing them to abstractions or symbols. A simple example would be a toothache. We can think about toothache, deriving endless conceptualizations, but that is not the same thing as having a toothache oneself. No matter how hard we try, we cannot, by means of analysis, know toothache in the same way that intuition knows.

For purposes of analysis, the process of abstraction actually helps. One must intellectually separate out something from the flux, paying attention to that and not to everything else. ("Paying attention" will become a significant project in any study of ethics.) Bergson gave the example of an artist in Paris who sketches the tower of Notre Dame. In order to render the tower, he has to omit or at least obscure two kinds of detail, namely the context for the tower (e.g. its streetscape) and the constituent parts of the tower (e.g. its individual stones). If the artist preferred to render the stones instead, he would have to engage in the same process of selective perception on a smaller scale, paying less attention to the stones' context and to the stones' constituent parts. Seen in this way, anything to which a person pays attention can serve as context, object, or constituent, depending on the magnitude at which one chooses to operate. These are examples of "points of view", even if the artist never leaves the same physical spot. Multiply these points of view from a single location by the infinite number of different locations in space around the tower. Point of view is an important consideration. While concentrating one's point of view is useful for analysis, one should be mindful that one's point of view is not reality.

We said that for analysis, abstraction helps. Nevertheless, it has its limits. Most significantly, analysis traffics in what Bergson referred to as immobility, like snapshots of a moving object. The brain tends to perceive the world as a series of discrete moments, discrete events, occupied by discrete things in relation to each other. Intuition on the other hand tells us otherwise. We live, in the words of Bergson, within a *moving* reality. It is all interconnected, and it is always changing, becoming. This world is better understood as a flux. We might be advised to pluck out portions for the purpose of noticing and examining them, which is what we mean by abstraction, but we should not conclude that the whole of reality is static and abstract.

At this point, you might be asking why anyone in our predicament should come to appreciate Bergson's insight. What does it add to our deliberations?

Elsewhere, Bergson (1962) referred to an idea as "the stable view taken of the instability of things ..." (p. 338). An idea is a representation or symbol bound to an immobilized view of the world — this is true even of the idea of a flux! The flux (like a river) is understood as an idea either of a unified stream or of a series of episodes; yet these are contrary. Neither really captures the *movement* inherent in a flux: they are two different crystallizations, whether of the whole or the parts, whereas reality flows, one thing shading imperceptibly into another. To entertain ideas is to work with an immobilized framework. So in that sense, we will be tempted toward inaccurate renderings of the reality we had hopes to understand. We will regard as fixed what is in reality in flux. That is one risk.

Left unchecked, analysis tends toward dogmatism in individuals who confuse their ideas about reality with reality itself, and think that by possessing an idea, they possess the truth. Then, by building idea upon idea into a comprehending system, we become ever more convinced of our knowledge and close our ears to alternatives—when, as we noticed earlier, there is no end to the possible points of views out there or to the possibility of an infinite set of entire systems. Thus, there is a *psychological* risk to engage in analysis, not a logical risk, and that risk is dogmatic closure. A person decides on an answer and refuses to consider the matter further. She has thought it through to her satisfaction and that's that.

Bergson claimed that by undertaking this task of analysis while successfully avoiding the risk of dogmatism, a person will remain open to new ideas, such that over time it is possible that he or she will be directed toward the experience of intuition, that "integral experience" qualifying as absolute, perfect. This movement toward understanding is, in Bergson's opinion, the purpose of philosophy, to transcend ideas—not so much to ignore them or reject them as to rise above them and treat them with a kind of equanimity. This is especially important because ideas—being immobilized and artificial—will ultimately present us with contraries, as though we must make a choice between A or B. Is the "flow" a single elongated thing or a series of discrete things? Analysis suggests that one must choose. Intuition allows a philosopher in this situation to engage in *recoupage*, seeing that despite the apparent differences between the rival ideas, they actually bear much in common. The philosopher is then in a position to detect the shared false assumption limiting each one and move on. (Kołakowski, 2001, p. 6) *Recoupage* permits "neither/nor" critiques of what amount to false dilemmas.

The problem, of course, is that any attempt to render an intuition is itself a kind of crystallization. No matter how one depicts the intuition—whether in mathematical symbols or poetry—he or she will have frozen in time that which by its very nature flows. It is always a kind of falsification of reality to communicate, even to oneself. Leszek Kołakowski (2001) mentioned this when he wrote: "Bergson's position is as awkward as that of any philosopher trying to speak of what is admittedly inexpressible" (p. 33). Nevertheless, it is unavoidable. As Bergson (1949, 1955) himself wrote, to render intuition in this way is "necessary to common sense, to language, to practical life, and even, in a certain sense, which we shall endeavor to determine, to positive science." (p. 50) This is because:

Intuition, once attained, must find a mode of expression and of application which conforms to the habits of our thought, and one which furnishes us, in the shape of well-defined concepts, with the solid points of support which we so greatly need. (1949, 1955, p. 53)

Thus, "intuition [,] when it is exposed to the rays of understanding [,] quickly turns into fixed, distinct, and immobile concepts." (1949, 1955, p. 55) It was for this reason that Bergson put such a great emphasis on openness as a virtue, i.e. a *perpetual willingness* to doubt one's own ideas and embrace the ineffable, the dynamic plenum within which we live and move and have our being. We could be wrong. We probably are wrong, to one degree or another. And even if we must engage in analysis (and obviously we must), we also retain the humility to remember that our ideas—no matter how apt or sweeping—are not the reality itself, and never justify the usual dogmatisms people suffer because of their favorite ideas.

We might say that reading Bergson coaxes us to gain some critical distance from our cherished beliefs, a critical distance which Peirce and Ortega had been encouraging in the first place. In other words, we are going to traffic in ideas, and it helps to keep in mind that this is all that they are. They are nothing more than ideas.

Having taken into consideration Bergson's cautionary note about our working with ideas, we can now return to the analysis of the problem we have called the ethics implications of an Information Age. How should we characterize these current day perplexities?

IS THIS AN ILL-DEFINED OR WICKED PROBLEM, OR IS IT REALLY A "MESS"?

At this point in the chapter, one might infer that our current beliefs about information assurance and security ethics are a problem, so that framing information assurance and security ethics is the search for a *solution* to that problem. But what exactly is the problem with our existing beliefs? Plenty of our daily beliefs are irrelevant, of course. By the same token, plenty of them might be relevant, but they do not appear, at first glance, to be problematic—and they may not be. It would seem that in order to *solve* a problem it would help to *define* the problem.

So, what in general is a problem? According to Roberts, Archer, and Baynes (1992) (in echoes of Peirce and Ortega), "A problem consists in a state of affairs, in which we feel some unease or discrepancy or incompatibility" (p. 38). This certainly seems to describe the situation we are in with regard to information assurance and security ethics. What makes it so difficult to solve? The problem itself is ill-defined, in the sense the "there is insufficient information available to enable [us] to arrive at solutions by transforming, optimizing, or superimposing the given information." (Romme, 2003, p. 563) Presumably, if we had such information, we would use it. But we cannot. And it is not so much that we can simply go get that information somewhere by sheer effort, either. The problem is ill-defined because we *cannot* obtain enough information, even though we are under obligation to proceed with decisions regardless. The information simply does not exist. Some of it may never exist. These possibilities do not excuse us from searching for some kind of resolution. We have a truly wicked problem.

Ackoff (1986) identifies four typical responses to problems. One is, in his words, to *absolve* the problem by ignoring it. Sometimes doing nothing is the best strategy. Another response would be to *resolve* the problem, meaning that our actions result in a satisfactory outcome. A third response is to *solve* the problem, meaning that our actions result in an *optimal* outcome. The fourth response is to *dissolve* the problem by redesigning the system so that the problem goes away; we would surpass an optimal solution by reaching an ideal future state where the problem never arises in the first place. Perhaps the following illustration will help.

Suppose a sprinter experiences a brief pain in her hamstring. It might be a soreness that comes with increased training, so that once a steady state of more training is reached, it will eventually go away. Early in any track season, this condition is not uncommon. In this way, the problem is *absolved.* But not every problem such as this can be ignored. The athlete might need to take a specific action to alleviate the pain, perhaps by stretching more, getting massages, and applying analgesic to the muscle. That might turn out to be entirely satisfactory for the time being. That would *resolve* the problem. But not all hamstring injuries are so easy to treat. In the case of a tear, for example, the athlete might have to stop training altogether, abruptly, in order to let the muscle heal. The season might come to a premature end. With a sufficient period of rest, the hamstring injury might quit nagging the athlete so she can return to running the next year. That layoff might fix things once and for all. In that case, the problem would have been *solved.* But as anyone who has experienced a hamstring injury will attest, even solutions of this sort do not always work indefinitely. Some injuries are recurring. Now, if the athlete finds that another activity such a bicycling does not stress the hamstring at all, she might switch sports. This response actually *dissolves* the problem.

Specifically with regard to the ethics implications of an Information Age, absolving every problem will not work. Occasionally, benign neglect is the smart move, but there would be no reason to ask the questions we have been asking if we were so confident that everything will fix itself without any effort on our part. Little by little, individuals, groups, and regimes have already decided they cannot ignore these issues indefinitely, so they are adapting as best they can. Because different groups or individuals act in different ways, they sometimes make matters worse for each other.

One might think that the objective of a book such as this is to arrive at a solution, an optimal response. In response to this expectation, we doubt that such a thing exists, or at least that we can recognize or characterize it during this period of conceptual delay. This is just as true for any attempt to dissolve the problems completely by transcending them. Modern day Luddites would encourage humankind to foreswear the digital technology on which the Information Age is based, and if as a species we were prepared to do this, many of the ethics implications would indeed dissolve; but that is just not possible.[4] Or perhaps it would be more accurate to say that removing the technology is infeasible and probably undesirable, even despite the ethics implications.

Russ Ackoff would argue that what we face is not a problem at all. It is what he would call a "mess." Understanding the difference is instructive. Ackoff (1981) defined a mess as a "set of two or more interdependent problems (p. 52)." "A mess," he went on to explain, "like any system, has properties that none of its parts have.... The solution to a mess depends on how the solutions to the parts *interact [emphasis provided]."* (p. 52). In other words, "messes must be [conceived] and understood holistically" (p. 246). We face not one problem, but many.

So, how do we go about thinking about such a thing as a mess? How do we frame it? Ackoff recommended extrapolating from the present into the future and comparing this default scenario to a more desirable outcome, identifying the threats and opportunities. Elsewhere (1981), he wrote that a mess "consists of the future that [our society] would have if it were to continue behaving as it does and if its environment were not to change or alter its direction in any significant way" (p. 79). This might appear to be an unreasonable premise from a logical point of view, since we know that change is inevitable, but Ackoff was not positing a static world that will not change at all. Rather, he was saying that we would be advised to project changes, predicting how the situation would change if nothing new were introduced into our trajectory. Even at that, Ackoff acknowledged that the resulting scenario is no forecast. That is not the point of it. He wrote in 1981, "We have to know where we are headed before we can take action to avoid getting there" (p. 52). How then does one solve a mess? According to Ackoff in a later work, you don't. He had misspoken. One does not "solve" messes.

As applied to our set of problems, we would be misguided to think there exists a single solution to the whole range of problems we have clustered together as the ethics implications in information assurance and security. That would be asking for too much...or for the wrong thing. Why is that?

One reason is that the nature of the problems we do face today will change so quickly that by the time we finally act, our solutions are obsolete. We would be solving yesterday's problems. That is one of the consequences of any conceptual delay. For another thing, solutions interact, so that one course of action to solve Problem A might make Problem B that much worse—or might create a new Problem C. The implementation phase requires constant attention and adjustments. At a more fundamental level, however, language of "solving" problems—alone or together—suggests that eventually the problems go away. That will not happen. It is an unrealistic expectation.

So, if Ackoff is correct, we find ourselves in a mess without the likelihood of finding one clear and final solution. Does that mean that our project is hopeless? By no means. Professionals respond to predicaments of this kind every day. Nobel Laureate Herbert Simon once described what we face as fairly typical, to which we can respond in typical ways. It is to Simon's work that we turn next.

SIMON ON PROGRAMS OF DESIGN

Many programs in the contemporary university are programs in design. The contemporary mass university interweaves three modes of engaging in research, namely Science, Humanities, and Design. These are different, yet complementary approaches to understanding and making a difference in the world.

Science tends to operate from an *exterior* perspective describing and analyzing as empirical objects that which exists, all that is out there in the physical world, seeking accurate representations and general patterns. The Humanities tend to operate from an *interior* perspective interpreting and reflecting upon human understanding as discourse, the meaning of things, seeking to appreciate the uniqueness and complexities of what lies within the inner world of individuals and communities. The third mode of engaging in research, Design, has an altogether different mission. The design mode creates and adapts systems that do not yet exist (or what Simon calls "artificial objects"), and does so according to pragmatic criteria about what actually serves human need. When you design something, what you do has to work. Unlike seeking generalizations and better models of phenomena (science) and expression (humanities), what a designer seeks is accomplishment. Design in its fullest recognizes that technical progress is not necessarily human progress, but that better design aims toward the latter.

Part of what makes this mode unique is its reliance on embedding these artificial objects (which can be thought of as possible future states) into existing systems, so that some familiarity with existing systems, as disclosed by the scientific mode, would be necessary. The home you design as an architect had better fit the terrain, the climate, the building code, the market, and so on. It has to find its way into the world, taking its place among all types of systems. Can it withstand an earthquake? Does it come within budget? Is it next door to a hog farm or an elementary school?

We could state this another way. During the process of design, students (and the professionals they become) are not seeking general patterns, as in science; instead, the design mode seeks to adapt science's general patterns to unique (and probably ill-defined) uses and circumstances. Romme (2003) refers to this mode "as the activity of changing existing situations into desired ones" and as "[devising] courses of action aimed at changing existing situations into preferred ones (p. 562)." Into this mode he places not only agriculture and engineering, but also medicine, management, and architecture.

We have already acknowledged how the mess we describe as ethics in an Information Age is ill-defined, standing in need of some kind of response. It has fallen to us to create the future, and the future is unknown. Even the present is volatile, uncertain, complex, and ambiguous. How can we proceed?

According to Herbert Simon (1987), we must proceed with caution. "It is time to take account… of the empirical limits on human rationality, of its finiteness in comparison with the complexities of the world with which it must cope" (p. 198). Elsewhere (1973), Simon wrote, "The number of alternatives that can be considered; the intricacy of the chains of consequences that can be traced—all of these are severely restricted by the limited capacities of the available processors" (p. 198)[5]. By "available processors" he means especially our brains. The sociologist Georg Simmel (1959) once wrote, "To see the whole as a unity, while giving equal consideration to each facet and direction of reality and to each possible interpretation, would require the power of a divine mind" (p. 303). We cannot begin any inquiry without unproven premises, and we cannot end with a completely encompassing framework. Whether you or I regard these realizations as the source of metaphysical horror or simple humility, the important point is not to seek *unwarranted* conclusions about ethics. Otherwise, there is little reason to engage in framing.

Does it matter that we are talking about multiple decision-makers, and not just one limited human being? Adding people to the project of working toward solutions to these problems is not necessarily an advantage. Groups can be wrong, and despite the expansion of knowledge and perspective that comes with collective deliberation, groups have a tendency to compound problems of bounded rationality, falling victims to such disabilities as groupthink, precisely because they operate as a group. Yet, the participatory nature of information technology coupled with its deep integration into our lives suggests that we cannot disregard the collective.

What we discover is a satisfactory approach that Simon (1973) referred to as "attention management"—which means that the "processing capacity must be allocated to specific decision tasks, and if the total capacity is not adequate to the totality of tasks, then priorities must be set so that the most important or critical tasks are attended to" (p. 270). What then is most important or critical? Simon (1981) asserted that it might be an exaggeration to say that "solving a problem simply means representing it so as to make the solution transparent"—yet he did urge "a deeper understanding of how representations are created and how they contribute to the solution of problems [as] an essential component in the future theory of design" (p. 153). We do not require some definitive representation—exhaustive, true, and final. That is not even possible. Instead, we need a conceptualization "that could be understood by all the participants and that would facilitate action rather than paralyze it" (1981, p. 166). Not surprisingly, we return to the task outlined earlier by Isaiah Berlin, namely to mind the way we frame our predicaments.

CONCLUSION

This book exists to represent the search for such a conceptualization of the ethics predicaments that we face in the information age. Whether we refer to frameworks, beliefs, ideas, conceptualizations, representations, the task before us is to apply the powers of our imagination and critical thinking to the reality on the ground and to the future we hope to realize. Much of the work waits until we frame the problems. As we undertake the task of framing information assurance and security ethics problem, we invite you to bear in mind the process. We inspect and examine our current frameworks, and as we uncover their limitations, we resolve to create better frameworks more suited to the current reality and our interests. In order to accomplish this, we must detach from our former beliefs by recognizing and examining them as ideas. We acknowledge that ideas are imperfect models of reality and that we may have to consider composites made up of several ideas – not unlike this chapter. We realize there isn't just one problem anyway, but many interrelated problems whose solutions are also interrelated. We consciously include historical precedence and the future in our consideration of the current mess.

REFERENCES

Ackoff, R. (1981). *Creating the corporate future*. New York: John Wiley & Sons.

Ackoff, R. (1986). *Management in small doses*. New York: John Wiley & Sons.

Bergson, H. (1949, 1955). *An introduction to metaphysics*. (T. Hulme, Trans.). Indianapolis, IN: Bobbs-Merrill.

Bergson, H. (1962). Time in the history of Western philosophy. In W. Barrett, & H. D. Aiken (Eds.), *Philosophy in the twentieth century* (A. Mitchell, Trans., Vol. 3, pp. 331-363). New York: Random House.

Berlin, I. (2000). The purpose of philosophy. In Berlin, I., & Hardy, H. (Eds.), *The power of ideas* (pp. 24–35). Princeton, NJ: Princeton University Press.

Dewar. (1998). *The information age and the printing press*. Santa Monica, CA: Rand

Gasset, J. O. (1984). *Historical reason* (Silver, P. W., Trans.). New York: W.W. Norton & Company.

Gasset, J. O. (2002). Ideas and beliefs. In J.O. Gasset, & J. Garcia-Gomez (Eds.). *What is knowledge* (J. Garcia-Gomez, Trans., pp. 175-203). Albany, NY: State University of New York Press.

Hillman, J. (1995). *Kinds of power: A guide to its intelligent uses*. New York: Currency Doubleday.

Introna, L. (2007). Maintaining the reversibility of foldings: Making the ethics (politics) of information technology visible. *Ethics and Information Technology*, *9*, 11–25. doi:10.1007/s10676-006-9133-z

Kim, D. (1999). *Introduction to systems thinking*. Waltham, MA: Pegasus Communications.

Kołakowski, L. (2001). *Bergson*. South Bend, IN: St. Augustine's Press.

Ortega y Gasset, J. (1957). *Man and people* (Trask, W., Trans.). New York: W.W. Norton & Co.

Ortega y Gasset, J. (1961). *Meditations on Quixote* (Rugg, E., & Marin, D., Trans.). New York: W.W. Norton & Company.

Peirce, C. S. (1955). *Philosophical writings of Peirce* (Buchler, J., Ed.). New York: Dover Publications, Inc.

Peirce, C. S. (1992). The fixation of belief. In Peirce, C. S., Houser, N., & Kloesel, C. (Eds.), *The essential Peirce* (*Vol. I*). Bloomington, IN: Indiana University Press. (Original work published 1877)

Roberts, P., Archer, B., & Baynes, K. (1992). *Modelling: The language of designing. Loughborough University of Technology, Department of Design and Technology*. Leicestershire, UK: Audio-Visual Services, Loughborough University.

Romme, A. G. (2003). Making a difference: Organization as design. *Organization Science*, *14*(5), 558–573. doi:10.1287/orsc.14.5.558.16769

Simmel, G. (1959). *Georg Simmel, 1858-1918* (Wolff, K. H., Trans.). Columbus, OH: Ohio State University Press.

Simon, H. (1973). Applying information technology to organization design. *Public Administration Review*, *33*(3), 268–278. doi:10.2307/974804

Simon, H. (1981). *The sciences of the artificial* (2nd ed.). Cambridge, MA: MIT Press.

Simon, H. (1987). *Models of man—social and rational*. New York: Garland Publishing, Inc.

Toffler, A. (1981). *The third wave*. New York: Bantam.

ADDITIONAL READING

Argyes, N. S. (1999, Mar/Apr). The impact of information technology on coordination. *Organization Science*, *10*(2), 162–180. doi:10.1287/orsc.10.2.162

Harter, N. (2007). Leadership as the promise of simplification. In Hazy, J., Goldstein, J., & Lichtenstein, B. (Eds.), *Complex systems leadership theory: New perspectives from complexity science on social and organizational effectiveness* (pp. 333–348). Mansfield, MA: ISCE Publishing.

Hillman, J. (1986). *On paranoia.* Dallas, TX: Spring Publications.

Kaczynski, T. (1995). *Special Section: Unabomber's Manifesto*. Retrieved January 6, 2008, from The Courier Electronic Edition: http://www.thecourier.com/manifest.htm.

Kegan, R. (1994). *In over our heads*. Cambridge, MA: Harvard University Press.

Simon, H. (2000). Bounded rationality in social science: Today and tomorrow. *Mind and Society*, *1*, 25–39. doi:10.1007/BF02512227

ENDNOTES

1 All quotations in this section appear in Berlin's essay titled "The Purpose of Philosophy" (originally published in 1962). Page numbers correspond to the essay's appearance in a collection of Berlin's work titled *The Power of Ideas* (2000).

2 For an example of this kind of problem in industry, see e.g. Argyes, 1999.

3 The process advised by Peirce is not without its psychological stresses, as described in Robert Kegan's 1994 book tilted *In Over Our Heads: The Mental Demands of Modern Life.* (Harvard University Press) What Kegan detected even then was the lack of a "fit" between the demands being placed on our minds and (in his words) "our mental capacity to meet these demands… (p. 9)" In such instances, we need a process to work through.

4 See e.g. Kaczynski, 1995. For a more detailed analysis of these possibilities as they pertain to leadership in complex systems, see Harter, 2007.

5 For a longer description of what Simon meant by "bounded rationality" and its historical usage in the social sciences, see Simon, Bounded Rationality in Social Science: Today and Tomorrow, 2000.

APPENDIX: DISCUSSION QUESTIONS

1. What is your working definition of ethics?
2. A mess of ethical predicaments.
   a. What, if any, are the "ethical predicaments" created by information assurance?
   b. Are these ethical predicaments genuinely novel or new, as proposed by the author, or are these old ethical predicaments?
   c. Please explain what the author means by the question "IS THIS AN ILL-DEFINED OR WICKED PROBLEM, OR IS IT REALLY A 'MESS'?"
   d. Why is information assurance and security a "messy" set of problems?
   e. How would you approach a messy problem in information assurance and security?
3. Whose ethics are we talking about?
   a. Do we have a common ground/common understanding of what ethics is?
   b. What are implications of not having a common ground?
   c. If we have conflicts, how do we live together?
   d. Can we create a common ground for us?
   e. How do we approach creating a common ground?
   f. To what extent is it valuable for you to expose yourself to different viewpoints?
4. Do you think we have ethical models for dealing with ethical challenges of the information age?
5. Framing.
   a. What is the process of framing?
   b. Why do we care about developing a framework in the first place?
   c. Would you agree that your ethical framework will evolve/change? Is that a good thing?
6. Ideas, beliefs, and doubts.
   a. What is the relationship between beliefs and ideas?
   b. Offer an example of ideas motivating some belief, for example: global warming, abortion, war, healthcare, intellectual property.
   c. What is the relationship between doubt and belief?
   d. Can you share a few examples of a time when you observed doubt turning into belief?
7. Truth and reality.
   a. What is the difference between truth and reality?
   b. Is it possible to have a common truth to describe reality?
   c. How does the changed reality (inter-connectedness and inter-dependence) affect our/your definition of security/privacy/information ethics in your class?
8. Living in the real world.
   a. What is your particular foundation for ethical thinking? How do you actually determine what is ethical or not? How would the analytical systems in chapter one apply here?
   b. What are the sources of ethical pressures that you face as a student/professional? What is the hierarchy of which is more important and why?
   c. When you employ technology in your activities within your peer group, do you perceive there may be consequences of your actions to society at large?
9. "Social engineering" is _______________. If social engineering offers us justification for false beliefs, how are we to recognize true ones?
10. Should professionals effectively control the direction of technology? If not, what should be their role?

Chapter 2
Toward What End?
Three Classical Theories

Nathan Harter
Purdue University, USA

ABSTRACT

Ethics as a distinct line of inquiry dates back to antiquity. Historically, the professions in particular have taken ethics seriously, since by means of ethical behavior a profession earns trust from the community it serves. The emerging profession of information assurance and security can engage in ethical deliberation using a variety of existing theories. The following chapter begins by answering whether there is really any point engaging in ethical theory. We argue there is such a purpose. Following this section, the chapter outlines three classic theories of Western ethics, namely utilitarian ethics, deontological ethics, and virtue ethics. We offer three of the most enduring theories for use in this book. Before we reach them, however, we must first explain why professionals in information assurance and security might want to learn them.

INTRODUCTION

The study of ethics is very old. The origin of ethics as a distinct line of inquiry dates back to the ancient Greeks. Since that time, the study of ethics has not been restricted to professional philosophers. Today, it permeates all cultures, from the most elaborate systems of ethical theory to bumper sticker slogans. The professions, in particular, have historically taken ethics seriously, since it is by means of ethical behavior that a profession earns trust from the community it serves. The emerging profession of information assurance and security is grappling with ethical dilemmas of all sorts as it comes of age. Rather than reinventing the wheel, practitioners and students can engage in ethical deliberation using a variety of existing theories, drawing from the wealth of ethics tradition from other professions and from classical ethical theory.

Not only would practitioners and students in information assurance and security learn something from what has already been said about ethics,

DOI: 10.4018/978-1-61692-245-0.ch002

they are also encouraged to contribute their unique point of view, based on their expertise. After all, information assurance and security affects society in profound and intimate ways. Professionals in this field are an important voice in an ongoing conversation on ethics. We stated that ethics is nothing new. However, given the innovative nature of technology—and humanity's eagerness to adopt it—it would be just as accurate to say that ethics is forever new.

In this chapter, we join a long and intricate conversation, going back for thousands of years – a conversation that persists because ethics is forever relevant to the issues of the day. We begin by answering a direct challenge to this premise. It responds to the question whether there is really any point engaging in ethical theory. We think there is such a purpose. In this chapter, we will investigate three of the most enduring classic theories of Western ethics, namely utilitarian ethics, deontological ethics, and virtue ethics. Certainly many other theories exist, but as a place to begin, these three will serve us well. They are typical and widely known. A basic understanding of these theories is a prerequisite for an informed discussion of ethics. Before we discuss them in detail, we must first explain why professionals in information assurance and security might want to learn them.

Why Engage in Ethical Theory?

Joseph Badaracco, Jr., writing in the "Harvard Business Review on Corporate Ethics" (2001/2003) once made a provocative claim. He wrote that "following the rules can be a moral cop-out.... [Quiet leaders] typically search for ways to bend the rules imaginatively (p. 11)." He continued by arguing that these leaders "try not to see situations as black-and-white tests of ethical principles (p. 11)." That way, they are not compromising their principles when they cut a deal. Otherwise, ethics might interfere with success. Badaracco's statements greatly resemble the moral advice of Nicolò Machiavelli (1532/1991), to the effect that sometimes it is best not to be moral. If we assume the contrary, that ethics means professionals do have binding ethics obligations, how would we discern what those obligations might be?

One might suppose that studying ethical theory would be prudent. Writing in the same periodical Laura Nash (1981/2003) found theoretical inquiry into ethics impractical, generally distracting from the common sense about workplace ethics. It was her opinion that a theoretical view of ethics is like a dinosaur – lumbering along and useless, incomprehensible to busy practitioners with urgent things to do. She was not alone feeling this way. Eight years later, writing in the same periodical on behalf of ethics, Kenneth Andrews (1989/2003) found a philosophical approach to be, in his words, remote and disengaged. Roger Crisp (1998/2003) wrote that he has heard this all before, about the perception that philosophical ethics is hopelessly abstract and impractical, to the extent a layperson can ever hope to understand its abstruse methods and jargon in the first place. And since philosophers cannot even agree among themselves, then why should busy practitioners look to them and their methods for guidance?

Aside from the objection to ethics generally, as voiced by Badaracco and Machiavelli, and aside from the objection to a *philosophical* approach to ethics, as voiced by Nash, Andrews, and Crisp, there is a more devastating critique that, though it accepts the importance of ethics as well as the importance of a philosophical approach to ethics, it casts doubt on the usefulness of a general ethical *theory*. It goes by the name of Particularism. According to particularism, the general principles arrived at by any ethical theory should be balanced, if not completely replaced on occasion, by a unique response to the particular and unique situation where you find yourself. Ramsey McNabb (2007) has offered hypothetical examples in which adhering to an ethical principle seems wrong. One such example is the old familiar question of refusing to tell a lie to a crazed killer who asks if you know where his intended victim hides. You know the answer to the madman's question, so does that mean you will tell, because you always tell the truth as a matter of principle? That response to the situation sounds wrong. McNabb (2007)wrote that from our perspective, at a quiet distance from any such extreme pressure, we might want to admit that every principle has an exception like this, but in the real world, these exceptions pop up with maddening regularity. And once you start making exceptions, the principle looks less and less like a principle.

McNabb (2007)is untroubled by this possibility. For him, principles are generalities with little binding force in particular instances. In fact, he wrote, we barely need them at all. Most of us know the right thing to do without engaging in elaborate theoretical discourse about the Good, and we would be hard pressed after the fact to explain in philosophically correct terms why it was the right thing to do. "It just was." There is perhaps a role for general principles, but are they binding, no matter what? McNabb (2007) denies that they are.

A writer by the name of John Cottingham (cited in Kegley, 1997) gave another concrete example in which a general principle calls for one response, yet our moral sense seems to reject it in favor of another response. In his case, the particularity in question has to do with partiality, i.e. preferring the interests of one group of persons over another. Cottingham (cited in Kegley, 1997) has explained that according to Particularism, it is morally correct to be partial – that is, to favor one's own goals and interests, as well as those persons closest to you. Because you happen to belong to a particular family, clan, business, or nation-state, you owe them special allegiances. We all often tend to agree when the issue is looking out for one's family or fighting wars on behalf of one's nation-state. We expect a certain degree of loyalty from our kin, our neighbors, and our friends. The novelist E. M. Forster (1951) once declared, "If I had to choose between betraying my country and betraying my friend, I hope I should have the guts to betray my country" (p. 78). Ethical theory, on the other hand, tends to call for an impartial perspective, as though working against privileging the individual's interests.

Let us summarize the objections: there is the objection to ethics when it interferes with achievement, the objection to philosophical ethics generally, and the objection to ethical theory per se. Students of applied ethics might find they share these troubling objections. We would respond in the following manner.

Professionals in information assurance and security are increasingly expected to be mindful of ethics by virtue of the increasing importance of their role in society. What will this mean in practice?

In many instances, expectations of ethical behavior have been identified and reduced to formal norms, such as legislation and codes of professional conduct. It is often the case that these expectations are general and vague, partly because of the relative ignorance of the general public about information assurance and security.[1] Their technical expertise is limited. Another reason, however, is the broad assumption that everyone in society is to behave ethically. Most people see no reason to elaborate the most basic norms, concerning honesty and integrity, for example. In ordinary situations, we have the implicit expectation of ethical behavior from our fellow humans. The norms are simply out there in the culture, unspoken, taken for granted.[2]

Often, the explicit norms of a group exist in their spoken form and are not necessarily written down anywhere. They weave an oral tradition that is already present in a complex structure before it ever becomes necessary to publish a code. The written form that does eventually emerge might not be seen to replace the oral tradition, so much as to codify or summarize it, so that these texts were never meant to *exhaust* the heritage that continues to reside in the stories and memories of group members.[3]

Behind these social expectations, both specific and general, there lies an implicit ethical theory. Whether people actually think about it or not, they operate from certain presuppositions about what is right and wrong, and why. We might refer to these implicit theories as street-level ethics -- not to denigrate them in any way, but instead to distinguish them from *explicit* ethical theory of the sort that arises formally in the field of philosophy.

Ethical theory, whether expressed or implied, serves as the basis for expectations. Ethical theory provides justification for expectations. It explains why a person has an expectation that another person behave in a certain way. People *rely on* ethical theory, whether they know it or not. That is the first reason for professionals in information assurance and security to take a closer look at ethical theory itself, namely to examine the basis for all of these expectations. It is our opinion that not only should professionals want to understand the basis of these expectations, as a simple matter of awareness, but soon they will become responsible for the ethics of their peers: for supervising other professionals in the workplace, training them, and assuming responsibility for the profession itself.

Professionals in information assurance and security are stewards of vast amounts of diverse information, which is valued for a wide variety of purposes, some of which conflict. Stewards have a special role in society in that they are entrusted to act as agents of others. Information technology is a combinatorial innovation. It allows possibilities that did not exist before. James Moor, in his seminal essay; "What is Computer Ethics?" (1985), noted that the computer revolution is revolutionary for a variety of reasons. Among these are increases in power, speed, and miniaturization coupled with the affordability and abundance of computers, which leads to the use in every sector of society as well as their integration into other products, such as power grids, pace makers, and cell phones. However, Moor notes that these are enabling conditions; the real essence of the revolution is the logical malleability of computers. Computers can be shaped and molded to do anything that can be defined in terms of inputs, outputs, and logical operations. Along with these innovations in processing, the communications infrastructure has advanced, so that the processed information can be integrated across business tiers, political processes, supply chains, and global economies; in essence, pervading everyday life. For professionals in information assurance and security, the study of ethical theory makes explicit what might have been implicit, raising it to the surface and justifying professional expectations.

Many professionals, in actual practice, first encounter expectations as they pertain to concrete situations, specifically as they pertain to predicaments or problems that turn up in the workplace. Day-to-day activities implicate ethics. There is, in other words, an ethics dimension to ordinary work. Because a true professional would want to be ethical, when these predicaments do arise he or she will want to refer to standards or guidelines. If an ethical response to a situation is clear, we hope that would be chosen. At the very least, we would hope that ethics are a factor in the solution to the problem. When there might be a moment's doubt, however, often a professional can simply consult his or her memory or ask a mentor or colleague. Or a professional might turn to written materials where these norms appear. In other words, perhaps a response can be looked up. At such moments, ethical theory probably has little or no place. There is scant reason to keep going back to the underlying philosophical arguments for routine activities. That would be tedious and wasteful. Nevertheless, at some point, the professional should understand and appreciate the theory that does serve as a foundation, if for no other reason than to be reassured there is a foundation to it all.

In some situations, however, the professional person might find that existing norms do not suffice. Perhaps even after reading a code of ethics and talking with peers, no clear, definitive answer can be found. It could be that norms come into conflict with each other. Sometimes, there are conflicts within specific codes, as one provision appears to speak directly against another. That can be a dilemma.[4] But sometimes there are conflicts between one code and another, as for example between legislative provisions in different jurisdictions, such as China and France, or between legislation (on the one hand) and the professional code (on the other). One norm might say to do a thing that another expressly prohibits. What then? These situations will become especially acute in a global environment where cultural norms frequently conflict with each other and also with global institutions such as multinational corporations. To complicate matters further, it is not uncommon for an employer to make demands that conflict with the profession's ethics code. That too presents an ethical dilemma. In short, there are many expectations on a professional from many sectors of society, and these expectations do not always agree (e.g. Hauptman, 1999)[5].

In any case, whether we are talking about conflicts *within* a code or conflicts *between* codes, when a professional must make a decision something will have to serve as the arbiter, as the basis for deciding between conflicting norms. This is one reason for studying ethical theory. John Stuart Mill (1861/2001) said as much when he wrote that "only in these cases of conflict between secondary principles is it requisite that first principles should be appealed to (p. 26)."

It could be that available norms require interpretation. Ethical theory offers the conscientious professional a way to interpret norms. This is a second reason for a professional to learn ethical theory. Norms might simply be vague, ambiguous, or otherwise unclear. Ethical theory may help by explaining why one version might make more sense than another. Theory has that kind of utility; in uncertain moments it offers a way for a person to work things through logically.

There are other occasions, in addition to those situations in which existing norms are in conflict or unclear, when these norms will not suffice. Occasionally a professional might find a vacuum or gap – a situation for which no norm presently exists (Johnson, 1985/2001, chap. 1). It might be a new predicament or at least a predicament new to the discipline of information assurance and security. When that happens, norms cannot help, since there are none that apply; so a professional is forced to go directly to ethical theory in order to craft a response. Norms have to come from *somewhere*. Historically, it is out of such occasions, when there was perceived to be a gap, that the existing norms have come to pass in the first place. There is no reason to think professional ethics will ever evolve to the extent that we would be entirely done with the project of crafting norms for the profession.

So far, we have said that a professional ought to become familiar with ethical theory for several reasons, namely that ethical theory serves as the basis of social expectations and can serve as a guide when existing norms are in conflict, unclear, or otherwise inadequate. We will take this one step further. Ethical theory gives a professional justification *to defy existing norms for the sake of a higher purpose*. Let us explain. There might be instances when existing norms are explicit, unambiguous, and clearly appropriate for a particular problem, yet it would be unethical to obey these norms. We do not advocate trying to practice our profession with reckless indifference to existing norms, much less in a constant state of rebellion against them. Nevertheless, there may be legitimate reasons in certain situations to reject them for a higher good. Soren Kierkegaard (1843/2006) referred to this as the teleological suspension of the ethical. Friedrich Nietzsche (1874/1980) once declared that a truly ethical person "must at some time rebel against secondhand thought, secondhand learning and imitation.... (p. 64)" Karl Jaspers (1936/1997) quotes Nietzsche thus: "The critique of morality represents a high stage of morality (p. 147)." Only in this way can he or she be authentic.

Ethical theory in such situations becomes absolutely essential to thinking through and defending our choices. Otherwise, as a practical matter, deviating from norms looks like incompetence or sheer willfulness.

We are willing to consider the possibility that in some rare situations, the most ethical course of action might be to ignore existing norms. Nevertheless, the burden of justification lies with the professional who chooses to do this. Others may ask, "How could you do that?" And, rarely will they accept an explanation such as: conformity "just doesn't feel right" or "offends my moral sense." Important people such as clients, employers, and judges usually require a more elaborate rationale. Without saying it in so many words, they expect you to make some kind of appeal to ethical theory. They expect a justification.

For these reasons, we concur with Richard Spinello (2003), who makes a succinct case for the importance of learning ethical theory. He writes: "Ethical theories present principles that will enable us to reach a justifiable normative judgment about the proper course of conduct (p. 4)."

Three Classic Ethical Theories

Just as it would be unnecessary to engage in theorizing about ethics when you already have a satisfactory answer to your predicament, so also, when you do engage in theorizing about ethics it would be unnecessary to "reinvent the wheel". There are many elaborate theories already fully developed by some of the most brilliant minds of all time. Underlying many, if not most, of the expectations put upon professionals is some combination of three classic ethical theories: utilitarian ethics, presented by John Stuart Mill in *Utilitarianism* (1861), deontological ethics, presented by Immanuel Kant in *Groundwork of the Metaphysics of Morals* (1785), virtue ethics, presented by Aristotle in the *Nicomachean Ethics* (dates unknown).

Each of these philosophers wrote numerous books, yet we rely on the representative texts. Even though many others have argued and elaborated these theories, making numerous refinements along the way, we focus especially on the original philosopher's exposition for each theory.

- Utilitarian ethics —John Stuart Mill (1806-1873)
- Deontological ethics —Immanuel Kant (1724-1804)
- Virtue ethics —Aristotle (384-322 B.C.)

If a person wants to think meaningfully about a subject, it pays to find out what the most important expositors have already written. Ethical theory in particular exhibits some of the most elaborate thinking about ethics by the greatest minds ever. In many ethics classes, the historical examples of such brilliance would be Aristotle, Kant, and J.S. Mill inasmuch as they represent three distinct traditions that resonate to this day. Ethically speaking, we are all, to one degree or another, descendants of these three traditions, and therefore of these three theories. Our interest in them is not idle curiosity. Instead, they articulate best, and in greatest detail, the theories that one finds implicit in everyday life.

Utilitarian Ethics

We begin with utilitarianism, the most recent of the three theories. It emphasizes that the justification for ethics resides in the *consequences* that one would expect to result from a given course of action. Internal dispositions, such as good intentions, are inadequate. What should interest us, according to Mill (1861/2001), are the actual consequences. Otherwise, what difference does it make whether we choose one action over another? An ethical person would anticipate the consequences of alternative courses of action; then choose the course that results in the best outcome. That is what determines whether a course of action would be considered ethical or not. For Mill, the best outcome would maximize human happiness, frequently referred to as the greatest good for the greatest number. It is a utilitarian's ambition to reduce ethics to calculation, a formula for decision-making, in which each person to be affected by a particular course of action would be identified and then the prospective impact on each person's happiness estimated and weighed. The course of action that generates the most happiness in the world stands as the most ethical choice.

Mill (1861/2001) summarized his ethics in this way: "The creed which accepts as the foundation of morals, utility, or the Greatest Happiness Principle, holds that actions are right in proportion as they tend to promote happiness, wrong as they tend to produce the reverse of happiness." He went on. "By happiness is intended pleasure, and the absence of pain; by unhappiness, pain, and the privation of pleasure (p. 7)."

For Mill (1861/2001), ethics is a matter of calculation roughly as follows. The actor recognizes that he or she has a decision to make. Decisions have consequences, so the actor should examine the likely consequences of alternative courses of action. How then to choose among the various alternatives, once these likely consequences have been examined? Ultimately, according to utilitarians, people want to be happy. That's the bottom line. To be happy, they pursue pleasure and avoid pain. What then is pleasure? Pleasure is some combination of "tranquillity and excitement (p. 13)." What the actor must ask is, How can I maximize happiness? Not my own happiness, but the sum total of happiness in the world? We all realize that the happiness of some persons will probably be sacrificed for the greater good, even to the extent that *our own* happiness must yield to the greater good. So the rest of the decision-making process is strictly a balance sheet of pleasures and pains that result from this one decision. Again, the final standard for choosing among available options is known as the greatest good for the greatest number.

If option A yields 4 units of happiness overall and option B yields 5 units of happiness – regardless *whose* happiness we mean – then option B is the ethical choice.

There are problems with this approach, of course, not the least of which is the nearly impossible task of identifying everyone potentially affected by a decision, figuring out how the decision will affect them, positively or negatively, and quantifying that impact. How do you know the ramifications of every decision you make, extending the ripple effect across the globe and over the passage of time? That is asking too much of a person. MacIntyre (1966) asserts that Mill eventually surrendered on this point, admitting that utilitarianism works only if you happen to know the consequences of a choice; if you do not know, then you cannot use utilitarianism. Even assuming you could do this, however, how do you measure happiness? Is there a way to compare one person's pleasure with another person's pleasure? I like Thai food. Thai food makes me happy. You might like Salsa dancing. It would be difficult, if not strange, to try to compare these two things according to a single measure, asking whether the happiness I get from Thai food is greater than the happiness you get from Salsa dancing. Besides, Mill (1886/2001)presupposes that all human beings are equal: their happiness is of equal value. Not everyone concurs (Popkin & Stroll, 1993).

Making matters worse, Mill (1861/2001) agreed that pleasures have different qualities, so that some pleasures are better than others for the same person. For example, if you like Thai food, but like warm weather even more. As Alasdair MacIntyre (1966) observed, "Mill abandons the view that the comparison between pleasures is or can be purely quantitative" (p. 235). Aside from these practical difficulties, the utilitarian approach permits the actual abuse of one person in order to make other people happy, so long as total happiness in the world increases, and this seems wrong. In addition, remarked MacIntyre (1966), human beings are so malleable they can be made to declare their happiness with paternalistic, totalitarian, or genocidal regimes, and there is something plainly deplorable about that.

Despite objections to this approach, we often resort to utilitarian arguments. We tend to take issue with people who interfere with our happiness, or those who ignore the happiness of others. Happiness does seem to be an important outcome for ethical reasoning. We would be hard pressed to argue that decisions resulting in unhappiness are ethical when the unhappiness could have been avoided (e.g. Mill, 1861/2001). Even short-term unhappiness such as receiving inoculations is often justified according to the long-term happiness that will result. This is a utilitarian approach. The approach also appears to be objective, satisfying the expectations of the modern temperament.

Writing "Philosophy Made Simple", Popkin and Stroll (1993) were concerned that "if we can never assess the rightness or wrongness of an act until we know all of its effects, we shall have to wait infinitely long before declaring an act to be right or wrong, since there may be an infinite number of effects" (p. 34). To be sure, Mill (1861/2001) had anticipated this objection. His version of the same objection goes like this: "there is not time, previous to action, for calculating and weighing the effects of any line of conduct on the general happiness" (p. 23).[6] Mill answered by arguing that such exertions would be necessary only rarely. Nevertheless, one way to avoid the headache of tabulating all of the likely consequences, and guessing at the rest, is to adopt a code of rules or secondary principles – rules that are *based* on utility – so that certain rules can be said to maximize happiness as a general principle. Rather than engage in the same tedious and exhaustive calculation of pleasure and pain, over and over, one can simply apply the rules that do this for you automatically.

Taking a giant step back, what would society look like if everyone were utilitarian? Despite occasional errors in calculation, happiness would supposedly abound. Some people might not be able to enjoy the benefits completely, but at least they would be deprived only when their sacrifice maximizes happiness overall.

Deontological Ethics

The language of ethics frequently appeals to some kind of obligation or duty that one person owes to another. According to Kant (1785/1997), a decision that happens to maximize happiness might be *good*, but that alone does not make it *moral*. Morality originates in a good will, regardless of the consequences. A duty is a duty. One does not get to claim the moral high ground by neglecting a duty because some calculation reveals that another course of action will lead to better results, as in utilitarian ethics. If that were the case, then duties mean nothing in and of themselves.

This deontological approach toward duty is based on a person's intentions, and not on the consequences of a given course of action. Kant (1785/1997) took the position that the only thing that is good, in and of itself, is a Good Will. What makes it good? A good will is good, not because of habit, feelings, personality, anticipated consequences, or compulsion. Kant denies that the consequences determine whether a decision or choice would have been moral or not. A good will must be based on duty. That is the key to deontological ethics: duty. What do you owe another person?

We all agree there are duties in life. In response, we might act *in defiance of* duty, which most people would consider wrong. We might act *under compulsion*, grudgingly, so that the duty is eventually carried out, but not willingly. This, says Kant, is non-moral. It is good, perhaps, to achieve compliance, but we do not want to praise the actor who did it only as a result of compulsion. Here is a third scenario: We might act *in accord with* duty, although not for the sake of duty, but instead for some other reason. It might be in our self interest to do our duty, for example. Kant does not want to praise that as moral, either. The course of action has no moral worth, even if the outcome is for the best. No, doing one's duty rises to the level of a moral action only when done *for the sake of* duty. This is difficult to accept, but it fits a very common view of ethics.

The trick, then, is knowing what might be one's duty in a given situation. On this, John Stuart Mill (1861/2001) agreed. He wrote, "It is the business of ethics to tell us what are our duties, or by what test we may know them" (p. 18). Here, Kant (1785/1997) refused to acknowledge the authority of any person, group, or tradition to define one's duty. Plenty of other people want to tell you what you must and must not do. Nevertheless, according to MacIntyre (1966), "external authority, even if divine, can provide no criterion for morality (p. 195)." Instead, one's duty must be discernible strictly by one's own reason, "the unassisted mind of man."

What standards shall one use to discern that duty? It must be a priori, which means it does not depend on any prior experience. It must be categorical, which means it would be conclusive, an end in itself, and not a means to some other end – such as happiness. It must be universalizable, which means that your choice would be the same as you would want any other rational creature to choose in the same circumstances. Kant (1785/1997) elaborated in different ways on his view of the duty that he called the categorical imperative. For example:

- "I ought never to act except in such a way that I could also will that my maxim should become a universal law' (p. 15).
- "Act only in accordance with that maxim through which you can at the same time will that it becomes a universal law" (p. 31).

In the same manner, one's duty must be reversible, which means largely what the Golden Rule prescribes: do unto others as you would have them do unto you.

How would you like to be treated? You want to be treated as important, unique, a complete person, and not like a fixture on the wall. Thus, the sum of one's duty, regardless of the particular circumstances at the moment, consists in this: Treat each person as an end in himself and not as a mere means to some other end. That is, don't use people. Remember that they have free will and reason, too, just as you do. They are to be regarded as having autonomy and dignity, unconditional value. Every human being is priceless.

Kant (1785/1997) is not without his detractors. MacIntyre (1966) noticed that the categorical imperative in Kant's writings offers no direction for what a person ought to do. Rather, it sets limits on what one may do. To that extent, it is not altogether helpful. MacIntyre (1966) also restates a familiar complaint that Kant's emphasis on duty can be construed as justification for conformity to legal authority, even the most heinous authority; so that convicted Nazis could cite Kant for the defense that they were only doing their duty. Simon Blackburn (2001) warned against oversimplifying Kant to mean that so long as I personally don't mind if you do something to me, such as whipping me to derive sexual gratification, then I can do it to you. That sounds awfully close to the reversibility standard associated with Kant, even though he would have been horrified by the idea. Popkin and Stroll (1993) repeated the additional objection that Kant's philosophy is not so useful when duties appear to conflict. What happens in those situations?

What sort of world would it be if everyone applied Kant's ethical theory? The ideal would be a union of free and rational people treating each other with respect, in a spirit of concord. For Kant (1785/1997), reason would inform the law and policies, which in turn would guarantee peace. To the extent the world is not ideal – and on this point Kant was no fool – one's duty is still one's duty, regardless. Do it anyway. God will reward the virtuous in the next life.

We are left with three dominant themes in Kantian ethics. First, perfect yourself, aligning yourself with duty. Second, serve others, inasmuch as this embodies the Golden Rule. Finally, respect everyone's rights, for the sake of the spirit of concord.

Virtue Ethics

Both utilitarian ethics and deontological ethics concentrate on some point at which, during the decision making process, one course of action or another can be established to be ethical. For these theories, ethics would be part of the process, so that ultimately what we would judge to be ethical or not is the *decision*, and the course of action flowing from that decision. For both of these theories, it makes sense to say, "Do the right thing." They simply disagree on how to decide what the right thing would be. Virtue ethics is different from both of these two theories – a fact that Mill (1861/2001) acknowledged.

According to virtue ethics, the central consideration is not some step in a process, but rather the character of the person. Is the individual a moral person? How so?[7]

Aristotle (trans. 2002) opens his most famous work on ethics with the following claim, "Every art and every inquiry, and likewise every action and choice, seems to aim at some good" (p. 1). What is the good that Aristotle refers to? Ethics is a field of inquiry that considers this question. What is good? Between good things, which is better? And which good is the best, the one good thing over all the rest? Aristotle, not unlike Mill (1861/2001) and the Utilitarians, asserted that the highest human good is happiness. To achieve the highest good, there are intermediate goods that must also be achieved, such as pleasure, honor, and contemplation. None of these is an end in itself, but they are all means to an end. The wise man figures out which intermediate goods to pursue at what time and in what manner. And to make this possible, an individual must cultivate virtue.

Life is a kind of motion toward fulfillment, realizing one's potential. It is in fulfillment that we ultimately achieve happiness. Virtue assists us in that motion. In order to achieve happiness, one ought to exemplify virtue. In order to obtain virtue, it must become a chosen habit, so that to become generous, one must elect to behave generously over time. Aristotle (trans. 2002) tended to believe that people already know roughly how to behave in an ethical manner; experience will refine our understanding, as we adopt these virtuous habits and practice them. Aristotle even wrote "we learn by doing" (p. 22).

How does a person learn from experience? In response to this question, Aristotle (trans. 2002) taught what is known as the "Doctrine of the Mean", by which a person learns to avoid both deficiency and excess. Thus, for example, bravery lies at the mean between cowardice (deficiency) and rashness (excess). Only by navigating between deficiency and excess can we figure out that bravery means intelligence in the face of danger. Each virtue can be found at the mean between some deficiency and excess.

After a lifetime of experience, we should be able to notice a hierarchy of goods, with happiness at the peak. Justice is the virtue associated with the right ordering of these virtues. From there, the process can be described as:

identify the end you seek;
deliberate about whether there is a better end to seek;
deliberate about the best means for achieving the best end;
then act on that deliberation; and finally;
if it does not work, be willing to change your habits.

Now, in Aristotle's estimation, ethics is not a field of inquiry that can be reduced to books, let alone codes, despite the fact that he wrote more than one himself. Books have their place, to be sure, but every person ultimately learns only by applying what might be found in books to each different set of circumstances. Here is an example. We usually find ourselves in different kinds of relationships, and these will make a difference as to the principles we would follow. In relationships of superiority, for example, when one person holds the dominant position rightfully, then *paternalism* would be called for. The superior one, like a parent, should protect and care for the inferior. This would not be true in relationships of interdependence, such as business transactions. In those cases, *fairness* ought to prevail, a fairness grounded in what individuals deserve. This would be different from a third type of relationship, namely relationships of *equality*, such as among business partners or citizens. In those cases, equality should prevail. Finally, in the highest type of relationship, which Aristotle identifies as friendship, simple *enjoyment* would be the governing principle.

An organization that took virtue ethics seriously would include individuals trying to improve themselves and live up to the highest standards, not only in their private lives, but in their relationships with each other and with the outside world. The organization itself would have a common purpose, a highest end of its own, which participants would hope to achieve, because in a perfect world, the organization's purpose aligns with the individual participants' personal purpose, and all of it fits together in harmony as we each strive to flourish, individually and in union.

CONCLUSION

Each of these three ethical theories survives in the workplace of the twenty-first century. You can hear veiled references to a consequentialist ethic in ordinary remarks about considering the interests of stakeholders and anticipating the impact of one's actions. "What if everyone did that?" Obviously, you hear a version of deontological ethics when somebody invokes a duty, such as obeying the law, keeping a promise, or performing under a contract. It also arises when somebody insists that you treat them as a human being. Appeals to a person's character and basic virtues, such as honesty and integrity, hearken back to Aristotle. All three of these theories influence present deliberations.

It is helpful to appreciate these theories in the field of information assurance and security. Not every expectation to behave ethically has been entered into some code of ethics simply to be followed. On some questions, the codes that do exist are silent or subject to interpretation or possibly in conflict with each other. In some rare cases, it might even be necessary to challenge a provision that does appear in a code of ethics. In any case, future professionals will need to understand the theoretical foundations of their profession's maturing norms whenever they seek to justify, apply, supply, or defy expectations.

REFERENCES

Andrews, K. (2003). *Ethics in practice. Harvard business review on corporate ethics*. Boston, MA: Harvard Business School Press. (Original work published 1989)

Aristotle,. (2002). *Nicomachean ethics* (Sachs, J., Trans.). Newburypoint, MA: Focus Publishing.

Badaracco, J. (2003). *We don't need another hero. Harvard business review on corporate ethics*. Boston, MA: Harvard Business School Press. (Original work published 2001)

Blackburn, S. (2001). *Being good: A short introduction to ethics*. New York: Oxford University Press.

Crisp, R. (2003). A defense of philosophical business ethics. In Shaw, W. (Ed.), *Ethics at work*. New York: Oxford University Press. (Original work published 1998)

Forster, E. M. (1951). *Two cheers for democracy*. New York, NY: Harcourt Brace and Company.

Hauptman, R. (1999). Ethics, information technology, and crisis. In Pourciau, L. (Ed.), *Ethics and electronic information in the twenty-first century*. West Lafayette, IN: Purdue University Press.

Jaspers, K. (1997). *Nietzsche: An introduction to the understanding of his philosophical activity* (Wallraff, C., & Schmitz, F., Trans.). Baltimore, MD: Johns Hopkins University Press. (Original work published 1936)

Johnson, D. (2001). *Computer ethics* (3rd ed.). Upper Saddle River, NJ: Prentice Hall. (Original work published 1985)

Kant, I. (1997). *Groundwork of the metaphysics of morals* (Gregor, M., Trans.). New York: Cambridge University Press. (Original work published 1785)

Kegley, J. (1997). *Genuine individuals and genuine communities*. Nashville, TN: Vanderbilt University Press.

Kierkegaard, S. (2006). *Fear and trembling (Cambridge Texts in the History of Philosophy)* (Walsh, S., Trans.). New York: Cambridge University Press. (Original work published 1843)

Machiavelli, N. (1991). *The prince* (Price, R., Trans.). New York: Cambridge University Press. (Original work published 1532)

MacIntyre, A. (1966). *A short history of ethics: A history of moral philosophy from the Homeric age to the twentieth century*. New York: Collier Books. doi:10.4324/9780203267523

McNabb, R. (2007, March/April). Why you shouldn't be a person of principle. *Philosophy Now, 60*, 26–29.

Mill, J. S. (2001). *Utilitarianism* (2nd ed.). Indianapolis, IN: Hackett. (Original work published 1861)

Moor, J. (1985). What is computer ethics? *Metaphilosophy, 16*(4), 266–275. doi:10.1111/j.1467-9973.1985.tb00173.x

Nash, L. (2003). *Ethics without the sermon. Harvard business review on corporate ethics*. Boston, MA: Harvard Business School Press. (Original work published 1981)

Nietzsche, F. (1980). *On the advantage and disadvantage of history for life* (Preuss, P., Trans.). Indianapolis, IN: Hackett Publishing. (Original work published 1874)

Popkin, R., & Stroll, A. (1993). *Philosophy made simple* (2nd ed.). New York: Doubleday.

Spinello, R. (2003). *Case studies in information technology ethics* (2nd ed.). Upper Saddle River, NJ: Prentice Hall.

ADDITIONAL READING

Berlin, I. (2001). *The power of ideas* (Hardy, H., Ed.). Princeton, NJ: Princeton University Press.

Kant, I. (1991). *The metaphysics of morals* (Gregor, M., Trans.). New York: Cambridge University Press. (Original work published 1797)

Ortega y Gasset, J. (1957). *Man and people* (Trask, W., Trans.). New York: W.W. Norton & Co., Inc. (Original work published 1952)

Ortega y Gasset, J. (1958). *Man and crisis* (Adams, M., Trans.). New York: W.W. Norton & Co., Inc. (Original work published 1933)

Pelikan, J. (2005). *Whose Bible is it?* New York: Penguin.

Schneier, B. (2000). *Secrets and lies*. Indianapolis, IN: Wiley.

ENDNOTES

1 Most people wouldn't know exactly how to regulate their professionals, despite a broad interest in their ethics. Though laymen rarely understand what professionals do, this does not mean they do not care how professionals behave. Their ignorance requires them to trust (see e.g. Schneier, 2000, chap. 17). They may say, for example, that they expect

professionals to be honest, which is a perfectly natural thing to expect, but they have little or no idea what that means in practical terms and how it might arise on the job.

2 José Ortega y Gasset (1958) wrote that "ordinarily we live installed, too safely installed, within the security of our habitual, inherited, topical ideas.... (p.78)" These are part of the environment one simply finds. Yet if we let the opinions of other people unduly influence us, then we cease to be authentic. We become false. In solitude, wrote Ortega (1957), a person will "come to terms with himself and define what it is that he believes, what he truly esteems and what he truly detests (p. 16)." In the absence of this activity, a person fails to exercise the powers unique to humanity and (if we may put it this way) ceases to be human.

3 We would note a similar approach to the interpretation of legal rulings and sacred writings, where the plain text was never intended to replace an entire tradition (Pelikan, 2005).

4 Theorists such as Isaiah Berlin (2001) claim that these dilemmas are inherent in any attempt to codify ethics, since the goods that a code exists to realize are themselves incompatible. A typical example would be freedom and equality: one cannot sustain both simultaneously. At some point, these incompatible goods will need to be balanced.

5 We might characterize this situation as a kind of pluralism: i.e. the existence of multiple, independent systems of norms.

6 Kant (1785/1997) had foreseen this objection as well, noting that no one can determine "with complete certainty what would make him truly happy, because for this omniscience would be required (p. 29)." How much more difficult to anticipate the happiness of *everyone else in the universe* who is potentially affected by your actions?

7 Kant (1797/1991) treated virtue extensively in a section of *The Metaphysics of Morals* titled "Metaphysical First Principles of the Doctrine of Virtue."

APPENDIX: DISCUSSION QUESTIONS

1. How many people have died through the ages deciding what is right and wrong? Name one.
2. Who is responsible for injecting a "good" technological perspective?
3. Who has more responsibility? Designers or users?
4. As an IAS student, why is it important to know ethical models?
5. Why should we maintain ethical theories?
6. Do we expect that we will all fall into a specific ethical model?
7. To what extent are ethical theories useful? Why should people follow rules?
8. What are the three classical ethical theories?
9. Which ethical model do you think is most relevant and why?
10. What are the major problems with each of the ethical models in chapter two?
11. How can the three classical ethical theories be applied to IAS?
    a. Apply one of the three ethical theories in a concrete situation and discuss what is working and what is not working.
    b. What are the consequences of each approach?
    c. What would Kant/Mill/Aristotle teach us, for example, about developing penetration testing/hacking tools?
    d. Compare ethical dilemmas of developing nuclear bomb, and compare it with Google filtering. Can you analyze both cases using the three ethical models introduced in this chapter?
    e. Consider government defined filters on search engines. What is the ethical dilemma? How would you analyze it using each of three ethical models?
    f. Analyze a case using these three ethics models and compare results. Possible examples include:
        - RIAA suing college students
        - SPAM
        - Global warming
        - Abortion
        - A disgruntled employee
        - Malware
12. Culture and ethics.
    a. Compare and contrast the ethical theories discussed in the chapter with the ethical framework of another cultural background.
    b. How might cultural differences affect the outcome of these three classical theories?
    c. How do different cultures bring in different perspectives in the use of ethical theories?
13. What is new about information technology that can't be addressed by the three ethical models?
14. Does the new age of information technology warrant new ethical theories; said differently, are the classical ones obsolete?
15. Discuss a case in which different ethical theories agree/disagree.
16. Discuss a case in which part of different theories apply.
17. Virtue.
    a. What are examples of virtues?
    b. Who do you think is virtuous? List the attributes that make them virtuous in your eyes.

c. How do some of the virtues discussed by Aristotle compare with your person?
d. Are virtues different now than as they were listed by Aristotle?
e. Can an institution, corporation, country be virtuous?

18. Can a Kantian use people and still be ethical?

Chapter 3
Balancing Policies, Principles, and Philosophy in Information Assurance

Val D. Hawks
Brigham Young University, USA

Joseph J. Ekstrom
Brigham Young University, USA

ABSTRACT

Laws, codes, and rules are essential for any community and society, public or private, to operate in an orderly and productive manner. Without laws and codes, anarchy and chaos abound and the purpose and role of the organization is lost. However, there is a potential for serious long-term problems when individuals or organizations become so focused on rules, laws, and policies that basic principles are ignored. We discuss the purpose of laws, rules, and codes, how these can be helpful to, but not substitute for, an understanding of basic principles of ethics and integrity. We also examine how such an understanding can increase in the level of ethical and moral behavior without imposing increasingly detailed rules.

INTRODUCTION

Technology seems to move ahead of the legal framework and social customs that surround it. In the past, copyright infringement was relatively difficult to accomplish. It was always possible, but generally impractical to manually "copy" a book using pen and ink into a notebook. Then the copy machine made it possible to obtain a duplicate copy of a book without the purchase of a copy from the publisher. However, it was still not cost effective enough to make an issue from a copyright infringement perspective, because a published book was still less expensive and provided better quality. Today, digital media and high-speed networks have totally changed the publishing landscape. Making a digital copy can actually improve the quality of the printed material. The copy is totally portable and millions of illegal copies can be distributed quickly with very little effort.

While the legal system is still trying to address these issues, the social norm in some segments of the population seems to be acceptance of clear violations of the intent of copyright law. The ethical conflict has become even more apparent

DOI: 10.4018/978-1-61692-245-0.ch003

in the case of digital music. Many consider the tactics of the Recording Industry Association of America (RIAA) to be the heavy handed and intrusive (EFF, 2007; Beckerman, 2008). This coalition of large recording companies has used scare tactics and gamed the legal system to the point that judges have become adversarial (Beckerman, 2008). The press has sensationalized the lawsuits against people who simply settle out of court to avoid legal fees (Beckerman, 2008). This has led to some people behaving in ways they would normally consider unethical just to spite the 'bullies' (Yankovic, 2006). In addition to the RIAA's attempts to recover damages through sometimes less than ethical approaches, Sony and BMI, two large record companies, created a public relations nightmare by illegally compromising the security of their customers' machines while trying to protect their CD's from digital duplication. Sony's actions were found to be illegal in additional to being unethical and intrusive. The unethical antics of these companies fuels a sense of renewed justification to unethical file downloading of the very material they have been trying to protect (Felten & Halderman, 2006). Because it is clearly fair use of purchased material to rip a song from a CD to play on a personal listening device, and it is also illegal to share that same file without additional compensation to the copyright owners, both sides of the issue have used the other's unethical behavior as an excuse for their own descent into illegal actions. There is clearly no technical or legal solution to the problem since any technical solution that allows fair use can be compromised by a technical attack. If you can hear the song, you can make an illegal copy.

Geographical distance has become irrelevant thanks to increasingly powerful communications technology. The amount of information now available, and the speed at which it can be communicated, requires a high degree of integrity from those who use the information and the technology. Even more important is the requirement of uncompromising integrity of those who design, build, and control information systems and technology. Misuse of information about individuals and organizations has become as least as serious an issue as the misuse of funds. It would seem that the policies and laws that govern the use of information must be well-founded and complete. However, establishing a complete and sound set of policies and laws is impractical when the technology that drives information systems is changing at such a rapid pace.

Laws, codes, and rules are essential for any community or society, public or private, to operate in an orderly and productive fashion. Without laws and codes, anarchy and chaos abound and the purpose and stabilizing role of society is lost in a whirlwind of selfishness and lawlessness. However, there is a potential for serious long-term problems when individuals or organizations become so focused on rules, laws, and policies that basic principles of integrity and honesty are ignored. In fact, individuals, groups, and organizations can become policy-bound and unable to "think" ethically if policies and rules become too specific.

This chapter discusses the benefits and drawbacks of policy-based versus principle-based ethical codes and systems as they relate to technology, their role in society, and the men and women who design, implement, manage, and control them. Through a case study and an imaginary discussion with some well-know philosophers, we illustrate that as helpful and important as rules, codes, policies and laws are, they cannot substitute for personal and organizational behavior based on time-honored principles of integrity.

BACKGROUND

The basic principles of ethical and moral behavior are the same for every discipline (though the application of the principles may vary slightly with the nature of the particular discipline). The rapid change in information technology and computing allows for uses never considered previously, at speeds never before imagined, and across geographical and political boundaries as if they were invisible. Still this does not change the fact that honesty is still the best policy and respect for human dignity is a primary value. Rapid change complicates matters by providing convenient opportunities to compromise not only prudence, but one's own values by offering tempting circumstances for violation of sound principles of ethical and moral behavior.

Similarly, information assurance crosses most of the boundaries of discipline, geography, culture, and politics. Widespread acceptance of digital representations of information allows behaviors whose ethics are questionable, such as stealing and misuse of personal or organizational information, or pirating software or music downloads. It does not take long to realize that it is nearly impossible to describe all the ways one can commit an ethically questionable act in a world of digital media. It follows logically that it would be even more difficult to establish a law or rule to prohibit each of those acts. Therefore, as helpful as laws and policies might be, they are, at best, guidelines for proper behavior. Real protection from dishonesty comes from the ethical and moral principles held by individual, groups, and organizations. If society relies on rules and laws as the primary way to govern ethical and moral behavior, we may soon face an overload of policies and rules.

We already know that legislation cannot keep up with technological advancement. The negative impact of the delay could be mitigated if more people were governed by time-tested and deeply held principles of integrity. Consider what Isocrates shared regarding this condition:

Where there is a multitude of specific laws, it is a sign that the state is badly governed; for it is in the attempt to build dikes against the spread of crime that men in such a state feel constrained to multiply laws. Those who are rightly governed, on the other hand, do not need to fill their porticoes with written statutes, but only cherish justice in their souls; for it is not legislation, but by morals, that states are well directed, since men who are badly reared will venture to transgress even laws which are drawn up with minute exactness, whereas those who are well brought up will be willing to respect even a simple code. (Isocrates, trans. 1929)

It is not our position to do away with codes and rules, such would lead to anarchy. We must have legal boundaries if for no other reason than protection against malicious violators. It is our position that real ethical behavior in a dynamic environment must be based on principles, not simply laws, policies, rules, and enforcement.

Apparent Tension Between Policy and Principle

When people require laws and rules as the primary governance of their behavior, there is a tendency their inherent sense of conscience to be diminished. When conscience is diminished, laws and rules must become increasingly specific to try to keep order in the organization and society. Hyman, citing Jones said, "Setting out detailed rules in an attempt to cover all conceivable situations creates . . . a tendency to substitute rules for judgment. The hidden danger is the temptation to use the absence of a direct rule as a reason for plunging ahead even when one's conscience says 'no' " (Hyman et al., 1990, p. 15). However, having no, or an overly general a code, can lead to danger as well. Such a situation leaves people without guidance in unclear situations and without protection from those who don't care if they are honest or not. The questions then become: (1) why do we need rules and laws; and (2) what is the balance between principle vs. formal rules and regulations? Referring back to the statement of Isocrates it is apparent if a group (company, club, society, etc.) consists of ideal situation in which all "cherish justice in their souls" then virtually no law would be necessary. A biblical injunction states that "the law is not made for a righteous man but for the lawless and disobedient" (1 Timothy 1:9, King James Version).

Laws and rules do have purpose. One is to protect the public against those who would inappropriately take advantage of others (the lawless). Another is that laws and rules serve as guidelines for determining correct behavior until an intuitive or internal sense can be developed that would guide decisions and render rules and laws less necessary. What if the rules or policies that governs action conflict with what one feels one should do, or with what one wants to do? Or what if there is no apparent rule or policy that covers the situation or dilemma at hand? How then does one act? This possible tension and how to resolve it, is an important element of this chapter. The exercise of considering the ethics and morality of situations is crucial, because no one lives professional, personal or community life without having to occasionally address some sort of moral dilemma. In addition, such dilemmas help sharpen and prove the principles we cherish.

It is not the purpose, or the promise of this chapter to provide an easy resolution of difficult situations and ethical dilemmas, for this may not be possible. Some situations in life are difficult, especially those that concern our values. Instead, the intent of this chapter is to provide a perspective, and offer an approach for dealing with these difficult issues by showing how to use laws and codes as a guide, how to follow one's principles in ambiguous situations, and how to find and refine guiding principles when they are not clear.

Sources of Ethical Theory

The quest for valid principles to govern behavior, regardless of the context, is not new. It is what truth seekers have sought through the ages. Plato, in his debates with Thrasymachus, Polemarchus, Glaucon and others, claimed that justice is the principle by which one lives a moral life (Plato, trans. 2000). Aristotle described the Golden Mean as the principle for just living (Aristotle, trans. 1998). Though more subjective than other definitions, Aristotle saw this as a way to provide solutions to a broad range of problems that avoids the messiness of specific laws and rules in resolution of conflicts and dilemmas. Kant argued that the key to a just life is the application of the Categorical Imperative (Kant, trans. 1993), a form of Golden Rule Mill, the utilitarian, held that a reasonable creed for decisions "holds that actions are right in proportion as they tend to promote happiness (which is pleasure and the absence of pain); wrong as they tend to produce the reverse of happiness." (Mill, 1979 version, p. 7) Although these theories differ in their approach, they all seek the same end: to find a principle, or set of principles, to guide behavior because rules and policies are frequently insufficient. The advantage of living by principles is that principles provide a basis from which to operate regardless of specific situations; principles are applicable to a wide variety of circumstances, and principles, unlike policies, do not multiply in complex environments and systems. However, living by principles requires a more thoughtful and self-disciplined approach to life than does governance simply by adherence to specific rules and laws.

In summary, principles are more fundamentally sound and more broadly applied than ethical codes of conduct and rules, though codes and rules can provide intimation as to what the principle(s) may be. Through that seeking to understand and live by fundamental principles, behavior will improve. Fundamental principles are founded on truth that is independent of and beyond us as individuals. Our role is not to define it, but to seek to comprehend it.

Practical Philosophy

We all face ethical situations in professional settings that require thoughtful and principled action. The following vignette will help stimulate thought about varying views of a dilemma from a philosophical approach. It presents ethical theories and philosophical ideas from well-known philosophers in a dialogue setting with the intent of: (1) showing that though the great philosophers agreed is some respects, they also had varying points of view, and (2) modeling for readers how such a dialog might ensue. All of the views stem from the idea that honorable living is based on more than just adhering to rules and laws. In this vignette, David, a young professional, comes to his former professor seeking advice regarding a decision he previously made. During the discussion they encounter a gathering of famous philosophers who offer their views of David's dilemma. The story depicts the application of ethical theories to an actual ethical dilemma faced by a professional. Our goal is to provide a basic understanding of the similarities and differences between ethical theories, and a framework that technical professionals can use to consider how to apply philosophical ethical theories.

Readers should note that double quotes indicate use of a direct quote from the citation indicated. Single quotes are used to show where the author has paraphrased or "put words in the mouth" of the character. Where double quotes are used with no citation, it is a conversation between the main characters of the story.

Part One: The Problem

A Scene Moving from the Professor's Office to the University Garden[1]

David, a former student, knocks on the door; I invite him in; he walks into my office and sits down. By his somber demeanor I immediately know something is amiss. He doesn't say anything for a moment, then quietly states: "I think I made a mistake." He doesn't say anything more for a few moments.

As David described it, he found himself at a concert in the local community outdoor shell. While waiting with his wife for the concert to start, he overheard two men behind him talking about a work situation. Within a few moments he realized that the men were employees of a firm that was a competitor of the company he works for. It became apparent to David that they were talking about a product that was in direct competition with one of his own company. In fact, David leads the design team in his company, with responsibility for key aspects of the product. He was having some technical problems that were holding up further progress on the design. He knew this project was proprietary and that information about the product, for both companies, was very sensitive. The first to market with this product, according to the trade literature, would take over leadership in the industry. A lot was riding on this design. Though he had not yet heard any critical information, David also knew, through the industry grapevine, that the other company's product was weeks, possibly months, ahead of his. They had reportedly been able to solve the main technical problem that David and his company still faced.

When David first started describing the dilemma to me, it seemed relatively minor. He was in a public place and he had a right to be there as much as they did. They were the ones who chose to talk about proprietary information in a public place. It was they who were breaking company policy, not David. Still David seemed very bothered. I asked why.

"Well," he began, "If I was the one talking about proprietary material, I think I would like to have someone stop me. I questioned whether it was right to get information this way - it didn't seem right to sit there and listen." He paused before he continued, carefully choosing his words, obviously having given this much thought and worry. "In my company we take very seriously the Codes of Ethics advocated by the Institute of Electrical and Electronics Engineers (IEEE), the Association for Computing Machinery (ACM) and other professional groups. You first introduced it in our ethics class. For example, the ACM Code of

Ethics states that we should, "honor confidentiality." And, element 4.1 instructs us to "uphold and promote the principles of this Code [of Ethics.]." The Software Engineering Code of Ethics and Professional Practice simply states that we should be, "fair, and avoid deception." The Professional Engineers Code of Ethics, Canon 6, states that professionals are to, "conduct themselves honorably, responsibly, ethically, and lawfully so as to enhance the honor, reputation, and usefulness of the profession." David looked at me again, this time with a look of confidence, "I am not sure where the problem I faced would fall in terms of legality. That doesn't really matter. It is clear that if I am to live by the intention of these canons, and to promote the honor and reputation of the profession, I should not use what I am confident is proprietary information from another company to further my own career and work."

He paused again while he thought, then continued, voicing the thoughts that had already crossed my mind. "As I told you, this could lead me to the break that I need to get our project back on track. I think I know where the problem lies, but I am still at least a couple of weeks away, probably longer, from a solution. Any additional information I get could be a great help toward completing this project, and," he continued with some fervor, "this one could be a BIG money maker. The company that gets this product out first owns the market." He was emphatic.

"What were your alternatives?" I ask.

"As I see, I had three options. One, I could have left my seat and waited for the concert to start; by that time they would probably have finished talking. Second, I could have just stayed where I was. Whether I listened closely or not or even tried to ignore them is not relevant as staying there, which meant I was very likely going to hear something. The last alternative is perhaps the hardest. I could have told them that I work for their competition and it seems they are discussing proprietary information. Then let them decide what to do."

After considering his words, I offer a suggestion. "David, sometimes when I need to ponder hard questions, I go to the Philosophers Centurium in the University Garden. Being surrounded by the statues of great thinkers in a quiet setting helps me clarify my thoughts. Would you like to take a walk?" David smiles as he stands up.

The campus garden is a relaxing place, secluded by trees and foliage; and, for the most part, treated respectfully by visitors. It is quiet, with walking paths and an occasional bench throughout. At one end of the garden is a gazebo. This is the Philosophers Centurium. Here statues of twelve of the great thinkers of the ages including Socrates, Hume, Plato, Mill, Kant, Erasmus, Aristotle and others surround six marble benches.

As we walk toward the garden I ask David to once again review the events that led to his dilemma. As he finished re-telling the story we came to the path that led to the Centurium. Both of us are quiet as we turn to walk into the Centurium when a voice of someone, who had evidently been following closely behind us, breaks our silence.

'May I offer a view?' We turned to see a thin-faced, dark-haired man dressed in what appeared to be Renaissance attire. David, looking inquisitive, asks. "And you are?"

'Oh, forgive me.' He bowed slightly as he spoke with a slight Italian accent, 'My name is Niccolo Machiavelli of Florence. Though I am not familiar with the technical aspects of your situation, I believe I have the most expedient answer to your question. May I proceed?'

We look at this thin man in awe, taken aback by what we see before us; a figure from 500 years ago. Machiavelli, without waiting for our response, continues. "We see here extraordinary and unexampled proofs of Divine favour... What remains to be done must be done by you; since in order not to deprive us of our free will and such share of glory as belongs to us, God will not do everything himself"(Machiavelli, trans.1992, p. 69).

While I ponder this modern application of what I recognize as being a passage from his book,

The Prince, David, still in awe, stumbles with his words. "I'm not sure I understand. Are you saying that providence brought me to such a situation, and thus, I must grasp the benefit it might offer regardless if it is right or not? Many an event may occur just by chance, and just because it occurs does not mean it is what you call 'Divine favour.' To act only in self-interest, it would seem to me, can bring much trouble."

Machiavelli replies, "I believe that he will prosper most whose mode of acting best adapts itself to the character of the times; and conversely that he will be unprosperous, with whose mode of acting the times do not accord" (Machiavelli, trans. 1992, p. 67). He peers at David intently as he speaks, but David says nothing. Instead he waits for Machiavelli to continue, which he finally does. 'Most certainly, your views may appear noble and desirous to cause no damage to others, but certainly you can see, as you have aptly described yourself, if you do not take advantage of your fortune and acquire all the information you can, with little regard for how, it will be you, not your opponent that will be unprosperous. What's more my young friend, you are breaking no law by remaining still. Surely this proves that providence has smiled upon you most graciously, does it not?'

Smiling, Machiavelli, appears more confident. "It is essential, . . . for a prince who desires to maintain his position, to have learned how to be other than good, and to use or not to use his goodness as necessity requires. . . For if he will consider the whole matter, he will find that there be a line of conduct having the appearance of virtue, to follow which would be his ruin, and that there may be another course having the appearance of vice, by following which his safety and well-being are secured" (Machiavelli, trans. 1992, p. 40).

I now feel it appropriate to add my thoughts, for to this point I have been silent. "Then, Niccolo, it is not what is good or not good that matters, but what maintains your power and position. For example, you suggest that necessity requires David to take advantage of this situation because his company is behind in the design of the product, and without the information they will likely fall behind in the market, thereby giving the market to their competition. Thus, though David is concerned about the correctness of the action, he should not be unless it serves his interest or that of his company. To not to take advantage of the opportunity that fortune, as you have described it, has placed before him would be foolish, regardless of its correctness. If the appearance of virtue does the trick then so be it, but if cruelty is what is needed, then so act. Do I reflect your thoughts accurately?"

'Very nearly so, because,' he responds, "attainment depends not wholly on merit, nor wholly on good fortune, but rather on what may be termed fortunate astuteness" (Machiavelli, trans. 1992, p. 24). Machiavelli then leans forward and in a quieter, but confident voice says, 'And astuteness requires you to use the knowledge that, by good fortune, has come your way.'

While talking, we had been gradually moving toward the Philosophers Centurium and were now upon it. We are so intent in our conversation and stating our respective positions, we don't notice another person standing just before us inside the Centurium until he speaks.

His question, is plain and without judgment. 'But is such just?'

Machiavelli looks at him as if he vaguely recognizes him but cannot place the name, and puts forth his answer. 'What is just unless it is "to do what is good to our friends and ourselves and harm to our enemies?" (Plato, trans. 2000, p. 9). Can anything but this position be just? It must be so, if we are to keep harm from ourselves.'

Suddenly we see the light of recognition in Machiavelli's eyes as, just louder than a whisper, he continues. 'Would you think, esteemed Plato, that it could be otherwise?'

David and I stand in disbelief at what is before us. We stand at the entrance of the Centurium and see before us, not statues, but live men. Some were in Greek togas, others in various attire of the ages.

Plato, who had just joined the conversation, is standing just inside the Centurium. Aristotle stands behind him, arms folded, observing carefully and listening intently. Two more, whom I believe to be John Stuart Mill and Immanuel Kant, are both seated on marble benches nearby. Socrates is in the center of the Centurium, arms folded behind him, slightly smiling as he observes his student in discourse. Others are also nearby all looking at the exchange that is taking place and appearing very interested.

Part Two: Dialogue with Philosophers

A Scene at the Centurium

As we enter the Centurium we have obviously interrupted a discussion that was taking place among these great thinkers. They silently acknowledge our presence and politely wait for Plato to continue the discussion, which he does.

'It is evident from what I overheard of your conversation that you have found yourself in a dilemma.' Plato looks around at the gathering and continues. 'Perhaps we may be of service. Though you may be weary of explaining your situation, may I implore you to do so once more that we all may hear?'

David nods in agreement and describes his situation. At the end of the explanation, Plato speaks again. 'Our guest has given such a case that I believe some here may question why our young friend is concerned. In fact, upon my first hearing of his case, he was being advised by Machiavelli.' Plato looks toward Machiavelli as he speaks. 'Do you wish to restate your advice to our guest?'

Pleased at the attention, Machiavelli takes a small step forward. 'My position is simply that the prudent man will act quickly as to grasp the benefit presented him. He breaks no law, has a chance to gain position in his organization, and increase prosperity. There is no negative to his choice to gaining the advantage this case offers him.' He pauses for a moment, measuring the others' reaction to his position. "Moreover, I believe that he will prosper most whose mode of acting best adapts itself to the character of the times; and conversely that he will be unprosperous, with whose mode of acting the times do not accord" (Machiavelli, trans. 1992, p. 67).

He looks at David as he continues. 'As you have all heard from David's description, he finds himself in a situation with great competition and it behooves him, and the many who depend on him, to use this information to advance himself, his organization, and all in it. If the situation were opposite, would not his competition very likely do as I suggest?' It is quiet for a moment while all consider this argument. Then the one who was leaning against the marble pillar asks, 'May I offer a view?' He is looking at Plato who has taken the role of moderator of sorts. 'We would be honored to hear your view Mr. Mill.' As I had supposed, this is John Stuart Mill.

He begins. 'It may be expedient for David to do as you have stated, but there are many other issues and people to consider before he can determine its correctness. What about the happiness or well-being of others? Has that been evaluated? A reasonable creed for decisions "holds that actions are right in proportion as they tend to promote happiness; wrong as they tend to produce the reverse of happiness. By happiness is intended pleasure and the absence of pain; by unhappiness, pain and the privation of pleasure" (Mill, 1979 version, p. 7). Thus, if David is to do the right thing, he must first determine what will be of the greatest good for all affected.'

David, who has been listening carefully, now looks at Mill and asks, "How do I determine what is best for all? Is it the greatest good for me? What kind of good is counted? Should I consider only financial benefit and improved position, or does peace of mind count also? What about the good of the other company? It is a young, new company, only about a fifth of the size of our company. By virtue of number of people who would benefit by that measure, it would be right to acquire the information. But who knows what good they may do if they are successful? There are so many issues to consider. Is it possible to do so?"

'Your questions address good for you and good for others, both in quantity and quality and the value of all of these.' Mill responds. "It is quite compatible with the principle of utility to recognize the fact that some kinds of pleasure are more desirable and more valuable than others. It would be absurd that, while in estimating all other things quality is considered as well as quantity, the estimation of pleasure should be supposed to depend on quantity alone" (Mill, 1979 version, p .8). Certainly you must consider the numbers involved, for example the size of your company being significantly larger than the other. You must also consider the good, such as monetary benefit and excitement for their work, which comes to your employees if you acquire this much needed information. You must, however, also consider the bad, or the pain, that may be incurred if you fail to take advantage of this fortuitous situation. It is this pain that must be avoided as much as possible.'

David sighs. "I know I have heard that before from co-workers who told me I hurt them all by not using whatever advantage might come my way."

Mill nods slightly then continues. 'And this should not be taken lightly, for even in expressing your own concerns, as well as those with whom you are employed, you have begun to ascribe a very high value to it. You should not feel shame in the concern for money. For money, is "a means to happiness, [thus] it has come to itself a principal ingredient of the individual's conception of happiness. The same may be said of the majority of the great objects of human life: power for example, or fame. . ." Thus money, or power or fame all have value in our attainment of happiness, not due only to the attainment of them alone, but also because in the acquisition of them "is the immense aid they give in the attainment of other wishes" (Mill, 1979 version, p. 36).

Plato has now slowly moved closer to Mill and David. 'What of the peace of mind of which our quest has inquired. Is this not a higher value and thus to be more seriously considered?'

Mill turns toward Plato to acknowledge his question; then back to David. 'When, my good man, you spoke of peace of mind, may I ask more specifically, what was your meaning?'

David looks at Plato, then me, then back to Mill. He pauses for a few seconds before he speaks. "My reference to peace of mind is to conscience. We all have a conscience to which we must account, and I know from experience that when the conscience is unsatisfied, the 'pain', as you would call it, is not insignificant."

Mill responds immediately. 'There are numerous sanctions on our actions, both external and internal. The external sanctions for your situation, in terms of legality, appear non-existent. However, other sanctions, such as the disapproval of friends or the behaviors expected by your professional code of ethics, do exist. Even so, "the ultimate sanction, therefore, of all morality (external motives apart) [is] a subjective feelings in our own minds" (Mill, 1979, p. 28). Though many attempt to attribute such feelings to other sources, such as' "subjective religious feelings, . . . if a person is able to say to himself, "that which is restraining me and which is called my conscience is only a feeling in my own mind" he may possibly draw the conclusion that when the feeling ceases the obligation ceases, and that if he find the feeling inconvenient, he may disregard it and endeavor to get rid of it" (Mill, p. 29).

Kant stands. 'I must object to your explanation.'

Mill smiles, 'I would be surprised and disappointed if you did not.'

Kant steps closer as he speaks, while I see Plato raising his hand as if in support and say. 'I must as well, though perhaps not on the same grounds.' Then he defers. 'But please, Mr. Kant, proceed.' Kant bows slightly; then does so.

'Thank you, I shall. It seems, Mr. Mill, you have reduced David's sense of conscience to whims of the moment or, perhaps better stated, inclinations driven by a very temporary perspective. What you refer to as internal sanctions (Mill, 1979 version, p. 27) are perhaps driven by adherence to his code of ethics, as he has described, or one could call duty to a greater good, and offer the only real hope for resolution based on constant principles, especially in time of confusion. Here we have seen that a powerful inclination for acting contrary to duty is the inclination for money. "It is on the level with such actions as arise from other inclinations e.g., the inclination for honor, which if fortunately directed to what is in praise and encouragement but not esteem; for its maxim lacks the moral content of an action done not from inclination but from duty" (Kant, trans. 1993, p.11). "But when there is a conflict between duty and inclination, duty should always be followed" (Kant, p.11 notes). Kant pauses for a few moments as if to allow time for his words to sink in. Then he continues. 'It is on this that which is called the categorical imperative is based.'

David quickly interrupts. "And, the categorical imperative, as I recall from my philosophy class, states that "I should never act except in such a way that I can also will that my maxim should become a universal law" (Kant, trans. 1993, p. 14). Is that correct?"

Kant smiles and replies, 'It is.'

"Then," David continues, "Your position, according to the imperative would be that not only should I not use the information, but I should address, and correct, the men. Is this true?"

Kant continues, 'Well said, but still perhaps this is simply your desire. Consider also, is it your duty? Does this choice have a moral sense that makes it right? Does it treat the others, as well as yourself as an end not means? For "[you] must in all [your] actions, whether directed to [your] self or to other rational beings, always be regarded at the same time as an end".' (Kant, trans. 1993, p. 35)

David has been looking intently at Mr. Kant as he speaks and it is as if he is answering the questions in his mind as Kant recites them. Finally, David replies. "Yes, I believe the action I described meets those conditions."

'Then you are correct, it is the course I would declare as the correct one.' Kant still looking at David then hears Mill respond.

'But Mr. Kant, is not David's duty to act in the best interest of all involved? And as for the moral sense of which you speak, it seems you are still attempting to appeal to some subjective feeling that, if disregarded, he could employ the more tangible considerations offered by utility.'

Kant turns again to face Mill. 'It may seem so to you Mr. Mill, but in fact, you have contradicted your own theory by suggesting David' disregard his sense of conscience. You say his conscience, which tells him to act contrary to what may be perceived as the good of the whole, is simply a feeling of restraint in his own mind and will cease if ignored. How then, can you not also say that thoughts of what is best for the whole are also simply feelings of restraint in his own mind and will also cease if sufficiently ignored? By suggesting his conscience is simply a weak inclination to be ignored, do you not uncover a fallacy in your theory as well by suggesting any thoughts should be similarly disregarded?'

Mill responds. 'I do not, for the basis of my point is that the greatest good for the greatest number is measurable by David and others. In fact, I propose that my theory supersedes your principle that one should "so act that the rule on which thou actest would admit of being adopted as a law by all rational beings" (Mill, 1979 version, p. 4). Because "when [you] begin to deduce from this precept any of the actual duties of morality, [you] fail, almost grotesquely, to show that there would be any contradiction; any logical (not to say physical) impossibility, in the adoption by all rational beings of the most outrageously immoral rules of conduct. All [you] show is that the consequences of their universal adoption would be such as no one would choose to incur" Mill, p. 4). Thus, is not this imperative that you describe, based on the greatest good for the greatest number and therefore encompassed within the utilitarian view?'

Kant's reply is immediate. 'By so stating Mr. Mill, you suggest that we, as humans, would both be "rational beings" and still adopt "the most outrageously immoral conduct." Such is contradictory. "Everything in nature works according to laws. Only a rational being has the power to act according to his conception of laws, i.e., according to principles, and . . . . the derivation of actions from laws requires reason" (Kant, trans. 1993, p. 23) or an inclination to moral sense, prudence, duty and virtue (Kant, pp. 47, 26, 13). Thus we as humans are protected from irrationality by our inclination to good, virtue and law unless one accepts your encouragement to disregard such sagacity until it ceases.'

Plato, as if acting as moderator, interrupts the debate and turns toward Mill. 'Then Mr. Mill, what action would you suggest David take in this situation?'

Mill is clear and definite in his response. 'The only sure course of action, verified by the young man's own description, is to use the opportunity presented to him. The information, not illegal nor deceitfully obtained I might add, should be used for his company's benefit, and to secure for himself and his company greater good and happiness.'

Kant, who has been listening intently, counters, 'I do not agree. Your premise is that what brings happiness is what is right. I disagree simply with your root. It is not happiness that defines rightness. Right must be defined by an ideal, and happiness is derived by living accordingly, not the opposite. "To secure one's own happiness is a duty (at least indirectly); for discontent with one's condition under many pressing cares and amid unsatisfied wants might easily become a great temptation to transgress one's duties" (Kant, trans. 1993, p. 12). 'Therefore, amidst the unsatisfied wants and pressing cares one can easily misconstrue what would, in reality, bring true happiness. In short, it is by living right that we become deserving of happiness. It is this point that we must more deeply consider.'

Mill's response is again immediate. 'Utility does not ignore the longer view; in fact, this is part of the equation' (Mill, 1979 version, pp. 22-23).

Plato answers. 'Mr. Mill, by your way of thinking, societies have discovered what is just because they were happy. This progression does not follow logic or reason. I propose they have learned well because they were just, and thus have obtained happiness. In this I agree with Mr. Kant.' "Must we not acknowledge . . . that in each of us there are the same principles and habits which are in the State; and that from the individual they pass into the state? – how else would they come there?" (Plato, trans. 2000, p. 105). Therefore, it would seem that happiness, an emotion or state of being, must be the result of an action; even a just action. And, to be just means that virtue, even that beyond law, must decide the action.'

Aristotle, observant and quiet to this point, now adds, "Again, every Virtue is either produced or destroyed by the very same circumstances: art 'may give an example'; "it is by playing the harp that both the good and the bad harp-players are formed; and similarly builders and all the rest; by building well men will become good builders; by doing it badly, bad ones" (Aristotle, trans. 1998, p. 21).

Kant adds, 'and the development of habit is certainly different than the reason or principle on which decisions are made. And, the categorical imperative provides a test for each case that may arise, irrespective of the inclination, case, or person, thus maintaining "moral content" and insuring the habit developed is also good' (Kant, trans. 1979, pp. 10-11).

Plato adds. 'I must agree with Mr. Kant on this point, and further explain the purpose of the virtues.' First looking at Mill, then Aristotle, Plato continues. 'Virtue itself is not produced by the doing of the action, nor is it destroyed by the not doing. Virtue stands as the light and its' brightness is not dependent on whether you or I chose to act virtuously. It is only our own brightness that is thusly dimmed or enhanced. Virtue remains the beacon.' (Plato, trans. 2000, pp. 52-53)

'It is Virtue that is concerned with feelings and actions,' Continues Aristotle. "For instance, to feel the emotions of fear, confidence, lust, anger, compassion, and pleasure and pain generally, too much or too little, and in either case wrongly; but to feel them we ought, on what occasions, towards whom, why, and as, we should do, is the mean, or in other words the best state, and this is the property of Virtue" (Aristotle, trans. 1998, p. 27). 'Virtue then is "a state apt to exercise deliberate choice, being in the relative mean, determined by reason, and as the man of practical wisdom would determine" ' (Aristotle, p. 27).

'In theory this is well,' Kant continues. "But there cannot with certainty be at all inferred from this that some secret impulse of self-love, merely appearing as the idea of duty was not the actual determining cause of the will. We like to flatter ourselves with the false claim to a more noble motive; but in fact we can never, even by the strictest examination, completely plumb the depths of the secret incentives of our actions. For when moral value is being considered, the concern is not with the actions, which are seen, but rather with their inner principles, which are not seen" (Kant, trans. 1993, p. 19).

Aristotle, not fazed by Kant's disagreement, continues introducing his theory of the Golden Mean. 'David, let us examine your situation. You stated one distress of your case was fear to speak out, was it not?'

David nods in agreement.

'This being the case, you would want to act in such a way as to exhibit sufficient courage to perform the right act, would you not? Not overly brash, yet not cowardly either.'

David agrees but adds. "You are referring to your ideas as described by the Golden Mean are you not?"

Aristotle explains. 'I am, for "the mean state is Courage: men may exceed, of course, either in absence of fear or in positive confidence: the former has no name (which is a common case), the latter is called rash: again, the man who has too much fear and too little confidence is called a coward" ' (Aristotle, trans. 1998, p. 28).

Aristotle pauses allowing David to ponder for a moment. Gradually a look of understanding lightens; then David says, "If I am correct, it may be explained this way. If I act in every case as if I must exhibit clear courage, I could, in reality, become very imprudent, or as you more accurately describe it, rash. If I exhibit only fear I am accurately demonstrating cowardice. Is this the case?"

Aristotle smiles, 'Indeed it is. Likewise, you have spoken of honor for yourself and profession; a noble concern. With honor "the mean state [is] Greatness of Soul, the excess which may be called braggadocios, and the defect Littleness of Soul." (Aristotle, trans. 1998, p. 29)

David continues. "If I understand you then, I must honestly evaluate my motivations, feelings, and actions. For example, I earlier expressed concern for the well-being of my fellow engineers who were sharing information they should not, and therefore, the lack of respect they, and others, may have for their actions. The mean, as you call it, for this concern may be described as disappointment in their action. The excess may be exhibited as a feeling of envy or jealousy, the defect as spite or anger. Is this correct?"

'Tis so, my young friend. I hasten to add, however, that an exception to the description of the mean is the quality of Virtue itself. "Viewing it in respect of its essence and definition, Virtue is a mean state; but in reference to the chief good and to excellence it is the highest state possible" (Aristotle, trans. 1998, p. 27).

'Let me explain further.' Aristotle sits down near David and motions for him to do the same. 'For the ultimate good to be satisfied four ends must be realized. The first is the good must be realized by doing. That is, it must have an action that is an end in itself. It must also be final, not the means to another end. A further condition is the action must be sufficient in itself, that is, that it can be taken alone. Lastly, it must be the most choice-worthy of the actions presented (Aristotle, trans. 1998, pp. 7-9)'.

'Yes,' Aristotle replies. 'But also, "the situation must dictate the action." For, just as "he that tastes of every pleasure and abstains from none comes to lose all self-control; while he who avoids all, as do the dull and clownish, comes as it were to lose his faculties of perception; that is to say, the habits of Self-Mastery and Courage are spoiled by the excess and defect, but by the mean state are preserved." (Aristotle, trans. 1998, p. 22). Likewise, if you act rashly in every such case, or cowardly in every case the mean states of temperance and truthfulness are lost.'

"Then, if I understand you correctly, prudence may call for me to neither speak out, nor to remain seated; as speaking out may be rash or boastful and to remain seated is to be cowardly or deceitful. Thus the mean state of the two extremes suggests I leave my seat. Is this correct?" David asks.

'The action you have described embarrasses neither you nor the gentlemen, and meets the conditions you have well described. It seems to me you have found a suitable answer for your situation.' Aristotle leans back again as if completed.

Plato steps closer and speaks. 'My student has become my teacher in very many things, but it seems one thing is lacking.' 'I sense,' Aristotle says, 'you wish to return us to a discussion of what is just. Am I correct?'

Plato smiles and pauses; thinking for a moment. 'You are. For though your solution, on the surface, seems to harm no one, it breaks no law, allows all to continue on their way seemingly unscathed, and seems temperate and prudent; it lacks the courage and justness of a virtuous person.' (Plato, trans. 2000, p. 99-100)

'What do you mean it lacks courage?' Aristotle asks. 'Though he did not speak, he took courage and left the scene. Is this not enough? What is courage, if not this?'

"I mean that courage is a kind of salvation . . . respecting things to be feared, what they are and of what nature, which the law implants through education; and I mean . . . to intimate that in pleasure or in pain, or under influence of desire or fear, a man preserves and does not lose his opinion" (Plato, trans. 2000, p. 99). 'If David speaks not, he does so out of fear and thus is not courageous.' Plato's words seem to strike David deeply. He looks at Plato with an expression of deep thought and admiration.

"And what of justice?" I ask.

Plato turns to look at me, then the others, as if to speak a closing remark. 'And what of justice?' He pauses again, and then carefully chooses his words, "Why, my good sir, at the beginning of our inquiry, ages ago, there was justice tumbling out at our feet, and we never saw her; nothing could be more ridiculous. Like people who go about looking for what they have in their hands – that was the way with us – we looked not at what we were seeking, but at what was afar off in the distance; and therefore I suppose we missed her" (Plato, trans. 2000, p. 102).

"What do you mean?" David asks.

Plato continues. 'In describing the problem you faced, did you not express desire to follow the canons set forth by your society to "act as [a] faithful agent." Also, to "avoid deceptive acts" and conduct yourself honorably?'

"I did." David answers.

Plato continues. 'And even more, did you not express to us that you wished to do what was right, as it seemed in your nature to do so? And even with very many views which have been expressed, is it not your nature to act honorably, even divinely as the gods would have your act?'

"I am not sure I can speak for the gods, but I desire it to be my nature to act as you have described." David responds.

"That one man should practice one thing only, . . . to which his nature was best adapted; -- now justice is this principle or part of it" (Plato, trans. 2000, p. 102). 'And that practicing comes largely through the decisions of life, just as you have faced here and, I believe acted justly.' Plato continues, 'The contradiction you have felt push and pull within you, is justice and virtue seeking to enlighten your soul. Consider this, "might a man be thirsty, and yet unwilling to drink? . . . And in such case what is one to say? Would you not say that there was something in the soul bidding a man to drink, and something else forbidding him, which is other and stronger than the principle which bids him?" ' (Plato, p. 109)

David voices my thoughts and asks, "Then in this pushing and pulling what should rule my action? How do I proceed?"

"Everyone," Plato replies, "had better be ruled by divine wisdom dwelling within him; or if this be impossible, then by an external authority, in order that we may be all, as far as possible, under the same government. . . .And this is clearly seen to be the intention of the law, as is seen in the authority which we exercise over children, and the refusal to let them be free until we have established in them a constitution analogous to the constitution of a state, and by cultivation of this higher element have set up in their hears a guardian." (Plato, trans. 2000, p. 250) 'Justice is that guardian.'

I ask, "And how is this done?"

Plato replies, 'As my colleague Isocrates has said, "Virtue is not advanced by written laws but by the habits of everyday life." (Isocrates, trans. 1929) He smiles and simply says, and remember, "to be just is always better than to be unjust." ' (Plato, trans. 2000, p. 30)

No one speaks more as they begin to make their way toward the pedestals. David and I sense the need for our departure and leave the Centurium.

Epilogue

This dialogue between the philosophers illustrates some of the different fundamental philosophies by which proper behavior is defined by some of the great thinkers of the ages. However, it also illustrates one very important point summed up by Herberg wherein he explains that "The philosophers sought to ground the truth, in its objectivity and transcendence, in the rational nature of things. The Hebrew prophets sought the truth in the revealed word of God. But despite the differences between these two approaches, basic and irreconcilable as they are at some points, Greek philosopher and Hebrew prophet were one at least on this, that the truth by which man lived was something independent of him, beyond and above him, expressing itself in norms and standards to which he must conform if he was to live a truly human life" (Herberg, 1967, p. 7).

AN OVERVIEW OF POLICY-BASED VS. PRINCIPLE-BASED ETHICAL SYSTEMS

In a discussion about laws and principles it is important to differentiate between fundamental law, which is akin to principles, and operational laws, which by necessity, become more specific to address detailed situations. For example, Constitutional law is the study of the foundational laws and principles that govern a nation or organization. It is the description and definition of principles of governance extracted from more fundamental natural law and foundational principles of truth of which we wish to gain greater understanding. The Constitution of the United States declares its primary purpose and in a brief document lays down the guiding principles by which the nation will be governed, who has authority to govern and to what degree.

It is beyond the scope of this discussion to address this important aspect in more detail, but we readily acknowledge the role of constitutional and other fundamental law as instrumental in defining an overall environment of integrity and ethics as well as other aspects of moral action. Operational laws then become more specific to address individual cases and situations. This is where the main point of this chapter comes into play, that is, at what point is the number of laws or the detail of control detrimental to the cause of ethics and integrity. As a general rule, too much is worse than not enough.

When the ethics and morality of a community become enmeshed in specific laws and regulations, it indicates that the community has resorted to laws and regulations as the primary method of governance. However, as was previously pointed out, it is impossible to define every unethical act, therefore also impossible to define a rule to prohibit the same. This contradiction between attempting to legislate all action and the impossibility of being able to do so results in a state of increasing legislation, yet declining morality. Recent events in politics and business have illustrated the shallowness of those who use specificity of a written rule or law to guide their actions as well as to excuse their behavior. It also demonstrates the superficiality and fleeting nature of their defense when fear and punishment is the primary mode of operation rather than adherence to deeply and personally held values and principles.

Rules do serve a purpose. A sense of conscience, inherent in every person (though it seems to a greater degree in some than others), should preclude a rule. However, sometimes situations arise that are, for a variety of reasons, confusing. When confusion, a lack of knowledge, or insufficient experience cause uncertainty, rules provide acceptable parameters of action and protect against inappropriate behavior. This is a very important purpose for rules, codes, and laws. Guidance about how to act in situations in which we are new, or lack a sense of direction, is very helpful in protecting both individuals and organizations. Rules and codes set bounds on behavior. These bounds protect the operating principles of the organization and point to better behavior as one comes to understand the basic principles upon which any reasonable rule or law is based. It is similar to having a set of tolerances or specifications which set the outer bounds of acceptability of a product, but in-and-of-themselves, rules do not define the optimum. The optimum, however, is found within the specifications and can be achieved through disciplined process and continuous improvement. Citing again Isocrates, "Virtue is not advanced by written laws but by the habits of everyday life."

Another important purpose of laws is to prohibit inappropriate or dangerous behavior of one individual against another. Some people, though (hopefully) a minority, lack a sense of right and wrong and seek to satisfy their own wishes at the expense of others, and will break the law. In these cases it is important to have rules and laws to protect society. For example, there are laws against stealing and a punishment affixed if one does, because, unfortunately some people will try to steal anyway.

It is impossible to define the many ways unethical or improper acts could be committed. Therefore, if one will be governed only by what they can't do, as opposed to using a set of basic standards for what they should do, then there is really no way to govern at all, except by restricting their actions. Thus, with those lacking personal responsibility, and though restrictions will be found inadequate, they must be governed by specific laws and regulations. It is true that such governance is seriously impaired and lacks equity, yet the irresponsible can be governed by nothing else.

Thus, if organizations are focused only on the specifications to guide them, they will inevitably fall victim to volumes of specific laws and rules that must undergo constant modification and addition to try to enforce some semblance of order and proper behavior. At the same time, behavior worsens and many spend their time trying to find ways around the rules at best, or even worse, gradually loosen rules and policies in an attempt to reduce violations. When an organization or society feels compelled to eliminate laws or rules because they have lost the ability, through disobedience of the masses (as opposed to a thoughtful legislative process which considers deeply the flaws of the laws such as racially biased laws or policies), to have the law obeyed, one may rest assured the overall integrity of the organization or society is diminished. The seriousness of this situation means the eventual loss of the organization as described by Adams who worried, "When public virtue is gone, when the national spirit is fled . . . the republic is lost in essence, though it may still exist in form." The existence in form is a result of some momentum, which is eventually overcome by the lack of organizational or societal integrity.

DEVELOPING A FOCUS ON PRINCIPLES

Being ethical is not just a matter of what one (individual or organization) does, but who or what they are. It is usually fairly easy to be able to get a "take" on the values of an organization or person within a few minutes of interaction with them. This "take" is a sense of the culture and values that guide them. It emerges from the people in the organization and what they sense is most important as projected by the leadership of the organization. Organizationally, it has to do with three fundamental questions, easy to ask, harder to answer, and requiring constancy of purpose to implement. These three questions are: (1) is acting with integrity and honesty expected by all in the organization; (2) do we treat all stakeholders, be they employees, customers, suppliers, or others with fairness and respect; and (3) are integrity, honesty, respect and other virtues, evident in not just what we do as an organization, but who we are?

These questions, applied here to organizations, can be boiled down to three similar questions that we as individuals can ask in nearly every ethical question or dilemma. Blanchard and Peale (1991) describe the three as: Is it legal? Is it balanced? And how would it make me feel about myself? Answering affirmatively to all three without reservation may provide assurance that a right decision has been made.

We will use them to check the situation that David faced, in our story. Obviously the first check is legality. If it is not legal, don't do it. This is compatible with the organizational expectation that all act with integrity. This is the lowest level of ethical expectation. David would have passed this test as he was not doing anything illegal. Next, is it balanced? That is, is the decision fair or will it heavily favor one party over the other. If it is not balanced, then serious consideration should be given as to the correctness of the action. This is one of the things that David, keyed in on. If he decided to listen without disclosure (meaning doing so in hiding, so to speak), he was heavily favored. Lastly, how would it make me feel about myself? This is a similar approach to those who ask "If what I did came out in the newspaper the next day, would I be happy with the decision I made?" Or others who ask, "If my children or grandchildren became aware of the decision I made, would they be proud of me?" David was clearly very concerned about this as he expressed more than once the "feeling" that he shouldn't listen, and the concern he had about "peace of mind."

Occasionally, we come across those who violate rule one (Is it legal?), and yet suggest they feel fine (how would it make me feel about myself) about violating the policy. When this happens there is clearly a gap that exists in the ethical sense or training of that person. It is these situations that will increase laws and rules and decree the ethical sense of the community.

Consider a few other examples with these rules in mind to determine if the scenarios below are ethical behavior for your organization.

1. Your organization has paid for 8 licenses of a particular software package and you find that almost 20 are in use.
2. You have been hired to manage medical information for a new hospital. You know you can't give out any medical information (the law), but your curiosity tempts to you to

just look at medical records for some well-know politicians in the area. You won't tell anyone.

3. In searching for a new hardware vendor you are given numerous opportunities to enjoy sporting events, dinners, and other benefits from vendors.

People and organizations guided by basic principles learn to live in a way that is not dictated by specific laws and regulations, yet the laws and rules are almost always followed because that is what principled people do. When acting according to the principle, their actions will generally fall within the bounds of the rules or laws. When these people do clash with laws, it is often the case that they expose poorly described or ill-founded laws. Gandhi's civil disobedience and Rosa Parks' refusal to sit in the back of the bus illustrate this point. Important in the example of both of these people that even though both "broke" rules and laws, their motivation for doing so and the result of their action did not violate their principles. Both acted on the belief that all people are equal; that one race is not better than another. Furthermore, they acted so as to not inflict violence on others, but accepted it themselves. In other words, though the laws and rules violated dignity and morality, the behavior of those battling them did not. They had the integrity and influence to be part of the eventual identification of unjust laws and the modification of them as necessary. This is an important aspect of principle-based behavior.

In the process of gaining greater understanding of morality and truth, a deeper sense of conscience, or intuition about correct behavior, will also develop. In addition, there are some things that can be done to increase and heighten this sense of correctness in understanding and determining principles. One must search for greater understanding of the fundamental purpose of the rule or law, and identify what kind of behavior would not only satisfy the rule, but also yield better behavior according to the intent of the rule. The search can be aided by studying the lives of individuals who have practiced and lived by deeply held principles and by discussing dilemmas with well-meaning and deep-thinking people. These topics should be part of the on-going dialog in a principle-driven organization.

Everyday life offers many opportunities to act on what we know to be right and thereby increase our knowledge and uncover what we still must learn. It is by choosing correctly in daily actions that we gain knowledge and strength so that when a significant ethical event or moral dilemma does occur, the correct choice is clearer and the decisions easier to make. Though the issues often get clouded by extraneous facts, falsehoods, worries, and projections of failure, none of these change the reality that every decision requires choice and, as Plato claimed, there is intrinsic value in choosing what is just and right. It is this value that is of greatest good for it comes from living "a just life according to the four great virtues." Likewise, even though it takes constant time and effort, we must give serious consideration to Aristotle's declaration that "men must do just actions to become just, and those of self-mastery to acquire the habit of self-mastery." Through study, practice, experience, and consultation, we can make better decisions that are ever closer to what is ethical in any situation. Just as a strong rope is made up of hundreds or thousands of small strands, so is a strong organization made up of consistent responsible daily actions and choices by its members. We can never define enough detail into policies, procedures, or laws to cover all circumstances in a rapidly changing environment. We must engender a shared understanding of the principles that govern acceptable behavior.

REFERENCES

Adams, J., & Rush, B. (2001). *The spur of fame: Dialogue of John Adams and Benjamin Rush, 1805 – 1813*. Indianapolis, IN: Liberty Fund. Aristotle,. (1998). *Nicomachean ethics* (Chase, D. P., Trans.). Mineola, NY: Dover Publications, Inc.

Beckerman, R. (2008), Large Recording Companies v. The Defenseless: Some common sense solutions to the challenges of the RIAA litigations. *The Judges' Journal, 47*(3).

Blanchard, K., & Peale, N. V. (1991). *The power of ethical management*. New York: Fawcett Books.

EFF (Electronic Frontier Foundation). (2007). RIAA v. The People: Four years later. *Electronic Publication.* Retrieved August 2009 from http://w2.eff.org/IP/P2P/riaa_at_four.pdf

Felten, E. W., & Halderman, J. A. (2006). Digital rights management, spyware, and security. *Security & Privacy, IEEE, 4*(1). Retrieved from http://ieeexplore.ieee.org/stamp/stamp.jsp?arnumber=1588821&isnumber=33481

Herberg, W. (1986). *What is the moral crisis of our time?*The Intercollegiate Review.

Hyman, M., Skipper, R., & Tansey, R. (1990). Ethical codes are not enough. *Business Horizons, 33*(2), 15–22. doi:10.1016/0007-6813(90)90004-UIsocrates,. (1929). *Isocrates II: On the peace. Areopagiticus. Against the Sophists. Antidosis. Panathenaicus* (Norlin, G., Trans.). Cambridge, MA: Harvard University Press.

Kant, I. (1993). *Grounding for the metaphysics of morals* (3rd ed.). (Ellington, J. W., Trans.). Indianapolis, IN: Hackett Publishing Company.

(1979). *King James Version Bible*. Salt Lake City, Utah: Published by The Church of Jesus Christ of Latter-Day Saints.

Machiavelli, N. (1992). *The prince* (Thompson, N. H., Trans.). New York: Courier Dover Publications.

Mill, J. S. (1979). *Utilitarianism* (Sher, G., Ed.). Indianapolis, IN: Hackett Publishing Company.

Plato,. (2000). *The republic* (Jowett, B., Trans.). New York: Dover Publications.

Yankovic, A. M. (2006). *Don't Download this Song. On Straight Outta Lynwood* [CD]. Volcano.

ENDNOTE

1 Similar dialogs can be found in literature across time; one further example is the writing of Peter Kreeft.

APPENDIX: DISCUSSION QUESTIONS

1. Can you give an example of how this philosophic dialog could be used in a different ethical situation (context)?
2. Describe David's conceptual framework including components of such a framework discussed in chapter one.
3. How do you think your conceptual framework is affecting what you think David should do?
4. Suppose you are a student in the coffee line and you overhear two students discussing an exam they just took. You in a different section of the same class and scheduled to take the test tomorrow. How is this similar to or different from David's situation? What would Machiavelli, Aristotle, Plato, Mills, Kant say?
5. Why do you think David was in a quandary? Was the lack of a specific rule/law an issue in his mind?
6. David describes three options for solving his ethical dilemma on page 5, which one would you chose and why?
7. What would you do in such a situation?
8. In your opinion, is there any underlying bias in the article? If so, what?
9. Who do you consider as an ethical representative and what would their advice be in such a situation?
10. There are some ethical scenarios given on page 16, have you come across or have been in any such ethical dilemma/scenarios? Can you come up with more scenarios like these? What might be the reaction of the philosophers mentioned in this chapter to such scenarios?
11. Do you have any perspectives regarding the ethics of the people whom David overheard?
12. Would the parameters change if David knew that it is covered by a patent? How?
13. What do you think David did?
14. In this chapter, Gandhi and Rosa Parks' case was mentioned, where the activities were illegal/unethical, yet considered ethical. Do you consider their actions ethical? Why or why not? Do you know of other such examples?

Section 2
Private Sector

Section 2
Introduction

Linda Morales
University of Houston Clear Lake, USA

The Information Age is a powerful agent for change in the lives of individuals and for the global community as a whole. Along with the benefits offered by the Information Age come a multitude of complications. Responses seem to fall into one of two extremes. The first is that the very foundations of ethical norms that have anchored us for years seem to tremble under the paradigm shifts taking place. Our sense of trust and security is shaken by every new ethical challenge that crops up. The sense is one of profound discomfort and uneasiness that accompanies rapid change, even if few of us would be able to describe the extent of the impact or to be able to enumerate the ways in which our lives and relationships have been affected. Perhaps it is precisely that we do not know the extent that makes the discomfort so unsettling. We are even less successful at being able imagine future products and services that emerge as the Information Age evolves, or to predict future impacts and future ethical challenges that may result.

The second is a sense of casual dismissiveness. The sense is that man has and will continually encounter challenges and strife; in this regard, there is nothing new here, nothing to get overwrought about. At first glance, this seems like a dose of realism and reason. Perhaps it well is. However, at some level, we all recognize that choosing to not to act is also a choice. And it is not hard to think of examples where, in hindsight, the effects of choosing to do nothing range from unpleasant to tragic.

How do we get our bearings in such a mixed-up world? How do we re-orient our ethical compass? How do we restore some sense of order to this ethical mess? This question should sound familiar. Chapter 1 observed that the ethical "problem is ill-defined because we *cannot* obtain enough information, even though we are under obligation to proceed with decisions regardless. The information simply does not exist. Some of it may never exist. These possibilities do not excuse us from searching for some kind of resolution. We have a truly wicked problem. " (p. 10)

The Information Age extends the benefits of technology to the far reaches of the globe, bringing people of diverse cultures virtually face-to-face as never before. Not surprisingly, cultural differences complicate the ethical analysis of problems. Chapter four examines these differences. Through a survey of 599 students from five different countries the chapter probes opinions on ethical questions concerning data, software and hardware usage. The chapter confirms our expectation that "(m)any factors can influence a person's interpretation (of information security policy and ethics), including user expectations, user experiences, and culture." Policy makers should be cognizant of differences in attitudes and behaviors of people from different cultures.

Chapter five discusses the ethical challenges posed by peer-to-peer networks. Several factions are represented in this battle, all struggling to protect their interests. Users want to download and share content at a minimum cost to themselves. Content owners wish to protect their copyrights and their royalties. Internet service providers want to optimize bandwidth utilization, which at times might mean limiting bandwidth available to peer-to-peer networks. Consumer electronics manufacturers generate profit by providing state-of-the-art hardware for fast downloads. Their profit margin depends on consumer desire for faster downloads, which in turn requires high bandwidth. Software providers know the financial benefit of offering free (or low cost) software for downloading content. They generate revenue by charging for content downloaded using their products, or by selling advertisements which they host at their download portal. Multiple players have multiple conflicting incentives, which bring multiple problems. It is through careful analysis of these issues and we begin to appreciate the messiness (Ackoff (1981).

System complexity is not a linear function. Systems are made up of subsystems, which do not behave as independent entities. The complexity of the composite system is not simply the sum of the complexities of the individual components. Subsystems interact and often produce side effects that cannot easily be foreseen. Subsystems affect each others' behavior creating a composite system whose behavior is very hard to model. This is true even if the behavior of the subsystems is well-understood (which, by the way, is unlikely). This phenomenon is observed in weather systems, systems of plants and animals, systems of humans, systems of cultures, systems of conflict and war. It is observed in virtually every scenario where subsystems interact.

The phenomenon is also evident when we study the security vulnerabilities of composite systems. This topic is not well understood. Software is imperfect. Software flaws are a fact of life. Chapter six discusses the topic of responsibility for software security flaws. During the software development process, what steps do software vendors and software adopters to secure software? What issues might influence their policies and procedures for securing software? Once software is released to the public, the nature of responsibility for software vulnerabilities changes. Software security vulnerabilities expose consumers and providers to serious problems, such as identity theft, fraud, service disruptions, and may other issues. To what extent are providers legally or ethically bound to disclose vulnerabilities to their customers and to the public at large? To what extent are consumers responsible, since they tend to prefer feature-rich systems, and vendors, needing profits, may choose to devote resources to feature development rather than vulnerability testing. These are thorny questions. The remedies offered by the private sector have often been unsatisfactory, and have left consumers with little recourse but to appeal for help from legislators. In reaction, state governments have enacted laws and the result has been a hodge-podge of legal mandates. The chapter explores the role of legislation in developing and enforcing policy in this area.

Security attacks are often mounted from the outside, by the exploitation of system vulnerabilities. There is the other side of the coin as well. Security attacks can also come from the inside of an organization. Organizations are concerned about insider threat, and wish to prevent or mitigate it by using various predictive techniques to identify potential perpetrators or to detect attacks. Employees and privacy watchdog groups are concerned about protecting the privacy of people being monitored. Chapter seven focuses on predictive insider threat monitoring. It describes the data used for monitoring and predicting insider threat and the tools for analyzing the data. It discusses privacy law at it applies to insider threat monitoring and considers ethical implications. It then presents a model for predictive insider threat monitoring using a combination of physical and psychosocial information that incorporates ethical safeguards and privacy legislation.

Privacy concerns are also raised in the use of behavioral advertising. Market research has been used by companies for decades to identify potential customers. Market research ethics has developed over the years to include codes of conduct and consumer rights. Chapter eight describes consumer rights as follows: "These rights are four-fold: the right to choose, the right to safety, the right to be informed, and the right to provide feedback and be heard." (Ch 8 p. 11). The chapter analyzes the ethics of various methods of behavioral advertising, including cookies, web bugs, local shared objects (also known as flash cookies) and deep packet inspection, from the context of codes of conduct and consumer rights and legality. Areas of future research include the possibility of providing users with a way to control deep packet inspection, further analysis of legal remedies, including the use of the Fourth Amendment to protect users' privacy, and broader research to investigate the effects of behavioral advertising on other civil liberties (besides the right to privacy).

The free-market doctrine seems to encourage an unequal expectation of ethical behavior from the public sector vs. the private sector. In many situations, the government is expected to abide by a more stringent ethical code, one that demands transparency, integrity, accountability, and many other qualities. Corporations are allowed much more leeway; in truth, perhaps they demand it. The implicit message is that the fruits of a free market economy (e.g. profit and market share) are sacred, and deserve more protection than individual civil liberties and public safety. What now exists is a weird and unequal state of affairs in which corporations often seem to be above reproach and the profit motive is the loftier ideal to strive for. Mere ethics should not stand in the way.

Is this justified? Does this make ethical sense? Is this what we want? Perhaps we would be well served to evaluate privacy policies such as those discussed in these chapters using the Fair Information Principles (FIPs) described in Chapter 11 (see also http://www.privacyrights.org/ar/fairinfo.htm). The public sector as well is grappling with ethical dilemmas in the Information Age. There is no doubt about this. Perhaps the time has come to use the same microscope to inspect both sectors of society. Similar ethical behavior should be expected from both entities.

Chapter 4

International Ethical Attitudes and Behaviors:
Implications for Organizational Information Security Policy

Dave Yates
University of Maryland, USA

Albert L. Harris
Appalachian State University, USA

ABSTRACT

Organizational information security policy must incorporate organizational, societal, and individual level factors. For organizations that operate across national borders, cultural differences in these factors, particularly the ethical attitudes and behaviors of individuals, will impact the effectiveness of these policies. This research looks at the differences in attitudes and behaviors that exist among five different countries and the implications of similarities and differences in these attitudes for organizations formulating information security policies. Building on existing ethical frameworks, we developed a set of ethics scenarios concerning data access, data manipulation, software use, programming abuse, and hardware use. Using survey results from 599 students in five countries, results show that cultural factors are indicative of the differences we expected, but that the similarities and differences among cultures that should be taken into account are complex. We conclude with implications for how organizational policy makers should account for these effects with some specific examples based on our results.

INTRODUCTION

Increasing numbers of organizations are operating multi-nationally, if not globally. Some of these organizations employ workers in locations across the globe; others serve global markets. In either case, these organizations face unique challenges implementing information policy – their stated goals and procedures for managing and securing internal and external information and the systems for storing, transferring, and processing that information. While information security policy deals with every aspect of protecting information, one of the most vulnerable areas of information security is the unethical decisions made by agents of an

DOI: 10.4018/978-1-61692-245-0.ch004

organization who were trusted to act otherwise, such as employees and sometimes customers. In information security, this is known as the insider threat. Sometimes information security challenges stem from conflicting technological standards, but more often are due to a lack of awareness of different ethical and social norms from one location to another (Lu, Rose, & Blodgett, 1999; Volkema, 2004). For multi-national companies, cultural differences could be a relevant factor when considering insider threats and information security policy.

The importance of both cultural differences and ethical attitudes for information security was recently recognized by world organizations as being highly influential for maintaining information security. Recently, the United Nations Education, Science, and Cultural Organization (UNESCO) has taken as a priority the discussion of what it calls "info-ethics" and the challenges of understanding ethical technology use in different regions of the world, such as Africa, Latin America, and Europe (http://www.unesco.org/webworld). A prominent example is the copying of software outside of licensing agreements, which in some cultures is not seen as unethical, but in others is deemed unethical and illegal. Another example shows that married couples and members of collectivist communities such as Australian aboriginal groups routinely share confidential passwords and personal identification numbers (PINs), despite bank warnings that such information must be kept private (Singh, Cabraal, Demosthenous, Astbrink, & Furlong, 2007). A third example is the Maori people of New Zealand. The Maori have the concept of kaitiakitanga—guardianship and care of data about Maori. Kaitiakitanga introduces the concept of tiaki. Tiaki means to look after and guard, wherein, the emphasis is placed on collective ownership in order to serve purposes of improvement and benefit for all first and foremost. For the Maori, rights of data ownership and intellectual property are subsets, not supersets, of the broader ethic of collective ownership (Kamira, 2007). Cultural differences do not just span countries. Take, for example, the conflicting records management practices in the United States with so-called "sunshine laws". Florida and Ohio (Sitton, 2006) mandate open access to records that contain personally identifying information, compared to states such as Texas and Iowa that more tightly control government records disclosure.

Laws come from ethics, not the other way around. Cultural norms and laws of a country co-evolve; they influence each other, and both are intimately reflective of the relevant ethics. It is our belief however, that while organizations must take local laws into account when formulating and implementing information security policies, they do not always take into account local cultural differences. This is problematic. Understanding laws is only part of the picture; understanding cultural differences is a critical piece of the puzzle. Because the internet operates as one, large and globally interconnected system, the information security practices in one country have implications worldwide. When cultural norms conflict, or are misunderstood, it is difficult to guarantee that information security policies generated in the context of a given cultural norm (such as in the United States) will be effective elsewhere.

Organizations crossing boundaries must not only be sensitive to local laws, but must institute policies that will allow them to successfully interface with local populations. Often laws alone cannot help organizations shape these policies and identify differences, but a better understanding of the needs and expectations of users (internal, such as employees, and external, such as customers) might provide needed insight (Mitrakas, 2006; Sitton, 2006). The significance of this research then is based on the premise that organizations will be able to better formulate information security policies given enhanced understanding of differences in cultural norms specific to information security.

In most organizations - commercial, private, or public - information security policy is a necessity.

It falls to information security professionals to formulate this policy. However, these professionals are often challenged with understanding how the ethical implications of using information and technology in different geographical and cultural areas have an impact on policies.

BACKGROUND

Beyond laws, primary social mechanisms for promoting ethics include codes of conduct, codes of ethics, and generally accepted industry standards and guidelines. Within the information systems (IS) profession, professional societies such as the Association for Computing Machinery (ACM), the Association of Information Technology Professionals (AITP), and the Institute of Electrical and Electronics Engineers (IEEE) have established codes of ethics for their members. The Computer Ethics Institute has a Ten Commandments of Computer Ethics. In addition to professional associations, companies that operate internationally have created codes of ethics for the business as a whole and within the IS function. For example, the Bank of America has a Code of Ethics for all employees; Microsoft has a Code of Ethics for all employees in the company and for global partners for intellectual property; and Google has a "Code of Conduct" that applies to all employees worldwide. One can look at almost any company and find a "Code" that outlines ethical behavior, whether it is called a Code of Ethics, Code of Conduct, or has some other name. In each case, these Codes of Ethics are meant to apply to employees worldwide and in a variety of cultures. The concern though is that these codes attempt to normalize cultural differences and assume that a code of ethics is universal.

Similarly, standards and guidelines are used to shape organizational policy. For example, the Sans Institute (www.sans.org) offers information security policy templates for dealing with any number of different technologies (e.g. passwords, mobile devices, and removable media). These are widely used as guidelines by organizations, yet these templates make no attempt at incorporating culture. The International Standards Organization (ISO) (www.iso.org) 27002 Information Security Standard is a guidance document for making information security policy). However, ISO 27002 makes no mention of culture, except for noting that differences exist in *organizational* culture. Instead they promote one universal standard for evaluating security and formulating policies. While organizational culture is important when implementing information security policy, organizational culture is partially shaped by broader cultural influences.

These approaches might lead policy makers to believe policies will be universally successful in any culture, which is not necessarily the case. Thus, while we acknowledge that there is a place for such "organizational" codes of conduct/ethics, we also believe that a wide variety of practitioners, policy makers, and professionals would benefit by understanding how cultural differences might shape ethical decision making.

Other researchers have also noted that cultural differences are an important issue when developing information security policy (Conger & Loch, 1995; Thorne & Saunders, 2002; Vitell, Paolillo, & Thomas, 2003). Yet to date there has been no research on how strong or weak these differences are, how these differences shape the motives and actions of users, how knowledge of these differences might be used to transform organizational approaches to information security, and the conditions under which such differences are salient. One challenge we face in improving understanding of the role of culture on information security is that information security breaches experienced by organizations are often covered up, making detection of unethical behavior, its consequences, and correlation to culture problematic. Another challenge is that information security problems that occur in one country or culture are often attributed to causes other than cultural differences, such as economic climate or criminal activity like organized crime, even when one consistent security policy is in effect for two or more cultural areas. Unless cultural differences are accounted for, this mindset will not change.

If we can account for cultural differences with respect to how people think and act in ethical situations regarding information security, it will help in two distinct ways. First, those responsible for information security will have a more realistic outlook on the provision of information security policies in different cultural areas. If one consistent security policy will be effective, they can employ this strategy. If specific policies for such things as software licensing and installation are needed for each culture where an organization operates, then this also can be expressed. Second, understanding cultural differences can help organizations better enforce the information security policy they have. For example, a policy that relies on workers to report potential security problems to managers might not be effective in a culture that shuns subordinates taking responsibility for failure; in such a culture, more active technological measures, such as regular system scans, may be needed to enforce data security. However in countries that encourage individual initiative, a simple reward mechanism (like a $100 gift card for identifying security gaps) may be the best strategy.

Culture and Ethical Decision Making

Cultural norms are the particular ways of thinking and acting unique to a certain nation or ethnic group based on shared history, language, and beliefs. Culture impacts every aspect of ethical decision making (Rest, 1994; Thorne & Saunders, 2002). First, culture impacts what we recognize as a moral issue. For example, in some cultures software piracy or illegal downloading of copyright songs is not considered wrong. Second, culture establishes how we make a moral judgment. In some cultures, copyright is recognized in the laws, but not enforced in society. Although someone might recognize software piracy or illegal downloading of copyright songs as a moral issue, they might make the moral judgment that it is acceptable in their culture to proceed to the next step. Third, culture becomes a basis for the establishment of moral intent. Not surprisingly, individuals' intentions to act are often based on how they have seen others around them act. Culture and social norms are often assumed to be right as they have shaped the interactions and expectations among one's primary referent group. Therefore, it is common for individuals to perceive their culture as "right" and "moral"; and conversely to perceive other cultures as less "right" and "moral". For example, Asian countries such as China and Malaysia have a history of supporting copyright infringement of software and videos (Yar, 2005). Despite World Intellectual Property Organization (WIPO) agreements that now outlaw this infringement, people who are accustomed to black market materials being available are not likely to view this practice as unethical or criminal. Finally, culture can become an incentive to engage (or not to engage) in what one has determined as moral behavior. For example, those who live in a poor, developing country are incentivized to use all resources to their fullest to better achieve parity with the developed world. This rationale could justify the reuse of software on many computers instead of just one. If culturally acceptable, this would not necessarily be thought of as unethical behavior.

Understanding National Cultural Differences

In his seminal work, Hofstede (1980, 1991) defined national culture as a set of mental programs that control an individual's responses in a given context. Erez and Earley (1993) further defined national culture as the shared values of a particular group of people. Hofstede (1980) performed one of the most well known studies about cultural differences, based on how people from different cultures act towards each other when faced with difficult situations. Using a wealth of data, Hofstede (1980, 1991) systematically identified four dimensions that can be used to describe and classify different cultures: power distance, individualism, masculinity, and uncertainty avoidance[1]. Each cultural dimension was quantified on a scale from 1-120, based on survey and observation scores, to illustrate countries' relative differences. Interested readers are encouraged to visit Geert Hofstede's website (http://www.geert-hofstede.com/) where these values were available as of the date of publication of this book. Other information systems researchers have also found the Hofstede dimensions useful for evaluating cultural differences with respect to information technology (Dinev, Goo, Hu & Nam, 2009). We briefly describe these cultural dimensions below.

The first dimension Hofstede (1980, 1991) studied is power distance. Power distance describes the degree to which the less powerful individuals in a culture accept that power is unequally distributed. Cultures with high power distance, such as Mexico, have come to expect that power is continually held by the 'haves' and thus the 'have nots' have less of an ability to make a difference in their society. Power distance as a cultural dimension may affect ethical decisions, according to Thorne and Saunders (2002). For example, in high power distance cultures individuals are more likely to look to formal sources of authority for guidance on how to act than in societies where they would be more likely to rely on their own or friends' counsel (for better, or for worse).

The second dimension is individualism (Hofstede, 1980, 1991). Highly individualistic cultures promote the distinctiveness of individuals and individual rights as opposed to the tendency to form and rely on strong, integrated communities such as family or religious groups, which is characteristic of collectivist cultures. The United States and Australia are very high on individualism, whereas many Middle Eastern and South American countries are relatively high in collectivism. The degree of individualism might impact someone's moral intent to act; for example, persons lower in individualism (and therefore higher in collectivism) may be more likely to forego their own self-interests for the sake of their community. Thorne and Saunders (2002) predict that in more collectivist cultures, individuals feel more obligated to reciprocate. Thus an individual might be more willing to share a copy of software obtained from work with friends, even if they personally knew it was wrong, if the friends had done the same for them in the past.

The third Hofstede (1980, 1991) dimension is masculinity vs. femininity. This dimension describes the value a society places on assertiveness and achievement vs. caring and quality of life. While the labels are obviously biased, the cultural distinction is valid. Organizational research shows that managers in more masculine cultures, i.e., those valuing assertiveness and achievement, have been less sensitive to personal dilemmas of employees and more likely to make corporate goals most important in ethical situations (Vitell, Paolillo, & Thomas, 2003). By contrast, in cultures that place more emphasis on caring and quality of life, i.e., the feminine orientation, such as many of the Scandinavian countries, society seems to reward a more equitable balance of work and life (Thorne & Saunders, 2002). Thus for more masculine countries, a policy that better aligns information security goals with personal success in the corporate is more appropriate; in more feminine countries, information security policy might instead emphasize employees responsibilities to conduct work as they conduct their family life, i.e. with concern for helping others make the right security choices.

The fourth dimension is uncertainty avoidance. This dimension refers to the extent to which a culture expects and shapes its members to feel comfortable in situations that are uncertain, novel, and unclear. This dimension reflects the tolerance a culture has for ambiguity and uncertainty, or alternatively, the extent of a culture's reliance on firm policies and rules. Greece and Portugal

Table 1. Hofstede's index values for countries in the study (Source:www.geert-hofstede.com).

	USA	Spain	Ireland	Italy	Portugal	World Average
Power Distance	40	57	28	50	63	55
Individualism	91	51	70	76	27	43
Masculinity	62	42	68	70	31	50
Uncertainty Avoidance	46	86	35	75	104	64

have the highest uncertainty avoidance reported in Hofstede's study (1980, 1991), while Singapore has the lowest. We might expect someone from a culture with high uncertainty avoidance to rely more strictly on rules and policies, when established, than someone from a low uncertainty avoidance culture when making ethical decisions. High uncertainty avoidance cultures therefore expect information security policy to be clearly and exactly explained, so that the rules, responsibilities, and remediation are clear. Low uncertainty avoidance cultures by contrast might come to resent such exacting information security guidelines as too formal or restrictive.

Using Hofstede's Dimensions

Some researchers have noted that when research questions are focused on different cultural groups within or across different nations, it may not be appropriate to segment the population by nationality. The appropriateness of country as a unit of analysis directly relates to the research questions. In this study, we compare the culture of Ireland, Italy, Portugal, Spain, and the United States. We picked these different nations because they for the most part are distinct cultures with little cultural overlap. However despite their cultural differences, the United States and the European Union countries studied have similar laws for intellectual property protection and computer security. They also have roughly the same level of technological sophistication. The selection of countries with similar laws and technical sophistication was purposeful to allow us to see cultural differences if they exist.

It should be noted that the history of laws toward computer security as well as level of technology sophistication may be just as important for information security policy as cultural differences. For instance, India only recently passed the Information Technology Act Amendment (ITAA) of 2008 to specify penalties for cybercrimes (Moily, 2009). Prior to 2008, the previous 2000 Information Technology Act was largely concerned with electronic commerce and data security for Indians working with multinational firms. As laws are implemented and enforced, cultural norms regarding acceptable behavior relative to information technology will slowly change over time.

In other words, there is both a time and space dimension at play. Research studies that investigate cultural differences can focus on different cultures at a point in time, one culture across time, or different cultures across time. This chapter focuses on cross cultural differences at a point in time and assumes that culture is usually interrelated with how laws and technology infrastructure have been implemented.

Table 1 shows the index values for each of Hofstede's dimensions for these five countries selected for this study.

What we may infer from Table 1 is how cultures differ among countries, as well as how the culture associated with each country may be characterized. Consider the power distance dimension. The United States, Ireland, and Italy are below the world average measured for power distance.

Given an overall level of more social equality, the less powerful individuals in these countries have a higher expectation for cooperative interaction across power levels. We might expect that people in Ireland (with a score of 28) and the United States (with a score of 40) especially would be more accepting of peer influences than established authority; or put more precisely, in these countries formal leaders must rely on more than just the virtue of their position to ensure compliance with information security policy.

There is more variability among our sample countries when it comes to Individualism. Compared to other countries, the United States has one of the highest individualism scores in the world, as does Italy. But all of our countries are above average, except for Portugal. Thus, we might expect that an approach emphasizing collectivism, such as peer review or group-level incentives to protect data, would be more successful in a country like Portugal. We can make similar types of expectations concerning the dimensions of masculinity and uncertainty avoidance. Of our countries, Portugal is extremely low on the masculinity scale but extremely high on uncertainty avoidance (Spain is similar but with more moderate scores). The United States and Ireland are similar with relatively high masculinity and low uncertainty avoidance. From a purely cultural perspective, therefore, we might expect some consistency in ethical attitudes in information security within these respective country pairs.

RESEARCH QUESTIONS

Given that there are known differences that appear among cultures, this study probed how these different may be manifest in individuals' attitudes and actions with regard to information security. Because the state of information security is highly dependent on human behavior (it is individuals who must implement information security policy and, alternatively, who have the capacity to circumvent it for unethical/criminal purposes), studying human behaviors and attitudes toward information security is timely and relevant. The research questions for this study were as follows:

- Do individuals' personal experiences in ethical situations regarding information security differ among cultures? If so, how do they differ?
- Do individuals' ethical attitudes toward information security differ among cultures? And if so, how do they differ?
- If there are differences, can these differences inform us as to how organizations and information security specialists should formulate information security policy across cultures?

METHODS AND PROCEDURES

To address these questions, we conducted a survey of ethical behaviors and attitudes among students from five different nations. Students were selected as the sample for several reasons. Students are ideally positioned to discuss ethical decision making because colleges and universities throughout the world have led the way in establishing information policies regarding ethics for their IS professionals, faculty, and students (Ben-Jacob, 2005; Fleischmann, Robbins & Wallace, 2009; Harris, 2000). Most colleges and universities require employees and students to acknowledge and agree to comply with the policies before users are allowed to access the computing resources. In addition, libraries, various academic departments, and business departments have Codes of Ethics. Finally, students have access to information technologies and the capacity to make mental judgments, and are generally active participants in the information society of their particular culture or nation.

In order to find the most consistent base of respondents possible across five different nations, we relied on students enrolled in major undergraduate institutions in each country as our respondent pool. A total of 599 students completed the survey between August 2005 and May 2007. Surveys were administered in waves since specific classes at each institution participated (most geared toward information systems and/or international business) rather than the whole institution. However, the waves overlapped significantly; only in one country (Spain) did all respondents complete the survey before it was initiated in Italy and Portugal. The survey was administered to all participants in English, because in each country the students' classroom instruction was in English. Respondents were able to indicate any problems understanding the language or context of the survey in a free-form comment section. No respondent reported difficulty comprehending or completing the survey.

The data were collected using a survey that included demographic information followed by two main parts: the ethical profile and the ethical scenarios. Regarding demographic information, we asked respondents their age and gender, factors previously shown to impact responses to ethical situations (Harris, 2000), as well as respondent's knowledge of computers (1=very little or no knowledge, 5=extremely knowledgeable).

It should be noted that observation would be the ideal instrument for collecting data about ethical actions. However, observing ethical dilemmas in real life, particularly on a large scale, is infeasible given that most people encounter these situations surreptitiously and often when they are alone or in private. Even if observation were possible, it is likely that social desirability bias (behaving in a way that makes the person look more favorable, even if the answers are false) would skew the results. Therefore, we employed an anonymous survey methodology.

Ethical Profile

This study investigated whether individuals' personal experiences in information security differ among cultures. An ethical profile was used to collect information on respondents' actual experiences in potentially unethical or illegal situations. We asked participants to respond yes or no to a series of 8 questions about past and present activities such as illegal use of shareware, changing data, knowingly releasing viruses, and downloading music without paying for it. Respondents indicated either 'yes' they had done that activity in the past, or 'no' they had not, which allowed us to build an ethical profile for each participant. The list of ethical profile questions is shown in Table 2. Each yes response was given a score of 1 and each no response was given a score of 0.

Table 2. Ethical profile questions (Responses indicated as Yes or No).

1. Have you ever used or sold shareware illegally (without registering it)?
2. Have you ever purchased a legal copy of software and given the old version to someone else'?
3. Have you ever changed data that that someone else will rely on?
4. Have you ever used software in an illegal manner?
5. Have you ever given someone unauthorized access to a computer?
6. Have you ever knowingly released a virus or worm into any system?
7. Have you ever made an illegal copy of software?
8. Have you ever downloaded songs or DVDs from the Web without paying for them?

We summed the responses to create an *individual ethical profile*. We were concerned about social desirability bias, that is, if respondents would not report unethical/illegal activities even though the survey was anonymous, so we asked the same set of questions (presented in table 2) again but asked "do you know anyone..." instead of "have you..." We summed these responses into an *associative ethical profile*, given that it reflects respondents' knowledge of unethical or illegal activities from their close associates. Each profile has a potential response range of 0 (no unethical/ illegal activity reported) to 8 (respondent has done,

Table 3. Summary of ethics scenarios from survey. Respondents rated participant's actions as: 1= Ethical, 2= Acceptable, 3= Questionable, 4= Unethical, or 5= Illegal.

Data Access Scenarios – 5 scenarios total
The Data Access scenarios presented various situations where employees access company data without authorization, visit websites prohibited by organizational information security policy, give company data to outsiders, and download music from a file sharing site and use it to make and sell DVDs.
Data Manipulation Scenarios – 3 scenarios total
The Data Manipulation scenarios concerned a bank employee who temporarily changes his account balance so that a check won't bounce (then fixes it back) and also a student competition where one student alters the files needed by other teams and enters incorrect data. The third scenario concerns releasing a program that destroys users' data.
Software Use Scenarios – 6 scenarios total
Software Use scenarios presented situations where employees download, make copies of, or transfer software to others in violation of licensing agreements (which typically state software may be loaded on one machine only). Other scenarios concerned improper use of email, and an IT operator who finds a substantial software bug but fails to report it.
Hardware Use Scenarios – 3 scenarios total
Hardware Use scenarios related situations involving unauthorized access to organizational computers or networks by others, or concerned employees misusing computers and networks.
Programming Abuse Scenarios – 5 scenarios total
Programming Abuse scenarios referenced creating a virus, creating a program to hide information from auditors, sending SPAM email messages, and using false trademarks on a website.

or associates with those who have done, all of the activities listed). A higher profile score indicates a history of greater unethical or illegal behavior.

Ethical Scenarios

The second part of the survey used ethical scenarios to measure respondents' ethical attitudes toward information security. The scenario approach is widely used in ethics research (Fleischmann and Wallace, 2005; Harris, 2000; Paradice, 1990), and, in higher education, corporate, and government ethics training (Ben-Jacob, 2005; Robbins, Fleischmann and Wallace, 2008). In each scenario of our survey, the participant evaluated whether the individuals and organizations involved responded (a) ethically, (b) acceptably but not strictly ethically, (c) questionably, (d) unethically, or (e) illegally (broke the law). Responses were given a value of 1 to 5 with 1 being ethical and 5 being illegal.

We employed the set of 16 ethical scenarios concerned with information assurance adapted from Harris (2000), and expanded the survey to 22 scenarios overall to reflect advances in technology use. These included peer to peer networking and file sharing, third party verification such as privacy seals, and widespread SPAM. The survey was originally designed to map Mason's (1986) ethical issues of information privacy, information accuracy, information ownership, and information accessibility into computer use scenarios. Five types of scenarios were employed: data access, data manipulation, software use, programming abuse, and hardware use. Some scenarios concerned gray areas of law or policy where it was not clear that the action was illegal, or even unethical. Other scenarios were designed to represent events that were illegal, either by specifically stating in the scenario that an illegal action was taken, or, by presenting a de jure illegal action. A summary of the 22 scenarios is listed in Table 3 and the complete scenarios are listed in the Appendix.

For each scenario, respondents rated the action of one or more involved scenario participants (such as employee/manager) or respondents rated multiple participant actions (such as downloading

Table 4. Background characteristics of respondents by country of origin

Country	Number of Responses	Average Age (Years)	Gender	Average Computer Knowledge
USA	261	20.9	64% (M) 36% (F)	3.07
Spain	135	21.1	35% (M) 65% (F)	3.04
Ireland	43	20.8	60% (M) 40% (F)	3.60
Italy	19	26.0	53% (M) 47% (F)	3.11
Portugal	141	23.1	55% (M) 45% (F)	3.22

Computer Knowledge: 1=Very little/no knowledge; 2=Somewhat knowledgeable; 3=Knowledgeable; 4=Very knowledgeable; 5=Extremely knowledgeable

music vs. making and selling DVDs with that music). We chose the impersonal approach in which scenarios represent the actions of others (Paradice 1990; Wood 1993) rather than the personal approach (i.e. "you steal another user's password...") to allow for multiple participant roles in certain scenarios and to avoid self-relevant bias from participants imagining themselves in these situations (Reis & Gable, 2000).

We tallied the responses by individual scenario and also combined the responses by scenario type to look at broader trends within each of the five areas: data access, data manipulation, software use, programming abuse, and hardware use.

RESULTS

We now provide a summary of the results, first reviewing the demographic and computer knowledge findings, followed by the ethical profile findings, and then the ethical scenario findings.

Table 4 shows summary statistics for the background characteristics from the survey respondents, organized by country of origin, along with the number of respondents from each country.

We ran a country-wise comparison of the background characteristics to determine if these factors were significantly different from one country to another. This was done in case these factors might account for the differences we were looking for in our analysis of the scenario and ethical profile responses, instead of culture being responsible for these differences. We compared age, gender, and computer knowledge using country as a grouping variable. For age, our respondents from both Italy and Portugal were significantly older than respondents from the USA ($p < 0.01$ and $p < 0.001$ respectively), Ireland ($p < 0.01$ and $p < 0.001$ respectively), and Spain ($p < 0.01$ and $p < 0.001$ respectively)[2]. We found that the 65% female response rate from Spain was significantly greater than the percentage of female respondents from the USA, Ireland, and Portugal ($p < 0.001$, $p < 0.01$, $p < 0.001$ respectively). Finally, we found that respondents from Ireland reported significantly greater computer knowledge than respondents from the USA, Spain, and Portugal ($p < 0.001$, $p < 0.001$, $p < 0.01$ respectively). Because of these differences we included age, gender, and computer knowledge as covariates in our analysis of both the ethical profile and the ethical scenario results.

We next analyzed responses to our ethical profile questions to determine if respondents' ethical behaviors vary by culture and if so, how. Table 5 lists the average values for Individual Ethical Profile and Associative Ethical Profile for the full sample and by country, on a scale from 0 to 8. For both the Individual Ethical Profile and Associative Ethical Profile measures, a HIGH score suggests greater familiarity with unethical or illegal activities, while a LOW score indicates less familiarity with these activities. Interestingly,

Table 5. Individual ethical profile and associative ethical profile by country, average values

Country	Individual Ethical Profile	Associative Ethical Profile
USA	3.20	4.28
Spain	3.75	4.46
Ireland	3.63	4.67
Italy	3.21	4.11
Portugal	3.55	4.33
Entire Sample	3.44	4.35

Table 6. Regression results: Age, gender, and computer knowledge on individual ethical profile (Table lists standardized regression coefficients and associated p values).

Country	Age	Gender	Computer Knowledge
USA	-0.16**	0.18***	0.16**
Spain	-0.29***	0.25**	0.28**
Ireland	0.13	0.07	0.01
Italy	-0.19	0.38	0.19
Portugal	-0.20*	0.38***	0.11

* $p < 0.05$ ** $p < 0.01$ *** $p < 0.001$

we found that ethical profiles vary only slightly between respondents of the five countries studied; only one significant difference was found in individual ethical profile between Spain (the highest at 3.75) and the USA (the lowest at 3.20, $p < 0.01$). None of the associative ethical profiles were significantly different among the five countries, although for each country the associative ethical profiles were greater than the individual ethical profiles.

Because we were more interested in our respondents' personal ethical profile than the associative ethical profile, we continued our analysis with individual ethical profile results. Using multiple regression, we analyzed the effect of age, gender, and computer knowledge on their individual ethical profile. We found that none of these factors played a role in the results for respondents from Ireland and Italy. However, there were significant effects for the other three countries, as shown in Table 6. We found that older respondents reported fewer incidents of unethical behavior in the United States, Spain, and Portugal. Conversely, males reported more unethical behavior in Spain and Portugal (Italy also, although this was not a significant result, perhaps due to the small sample size for Italy). Finally, those with more computer knowledge in the United States and Spain reported more unethical activity.

Table 7 lists the responses for each individual question in the ethical profile. The last column provides the responses for the entire sample. As can be seen, "yes" responses for the entire sample to our ethical profile questions varied greatly; for example, 71% of respondents indicated they had downloaded songs or DVDs from the web without paying for them, but only 5% had every knowingly released a virus or worm into a system.

We examined responses to each of the individual profile questions and compared them by country. Using independent sample t-tests we made country-wise comparisons on the mean of the individual ethical profile questions. Results indicated a number of significant differences (all

Table 7. Personal ethical profile question responses by country (Significant differences discussed in the text are highlighted in gray).

Ethical Profile Question ("Have you ever..." Respondents answered Y or N)	Percentage[3] of affirmative responses					
	USA	Spain	Ireland	Italy	Portugal	Entire Sample
E1: Used or sold shareware illegally (without registering it)	41%	44%	35%	26%	46%	42%
E2: Purchased a legal copy of software and given the old version to someone else	31%	27%	37%	42%	22%	29%
E3: Changed data that someone else will rely on	08%	14%	00%	11%	13%	10%
E4: Used software in an illegal manner	38%	56%	47%	42%	56%	47%
E5: Given someone unauthorized access to a computer	18%	33%	53%	11%	20%	24%
E6: Knowingly released a virus or worm into a system	03%	07%	00%	05%	06%	05%
E7: Made an illegal copy of software	41%	50%	58%	53%	62%	49%
E8: Downloaded songs or DVDs from the Web without paying for them	78%	76%	60%	68%	60%	71%

Table 8. Summary of Significant Differences by Country for Individual Profile Questions

Activity with which individuals have more experience	Countries associated with this activity
Changed data in an information system (Question 3)	Spain and Portugal
Used software illegally (Question 4)	Spain and Portugal
Grant unauthorized access to computer (Question 5)	Ireland and Spain
Make an illegal copy of software (Question 7)	Ireland and Portugal
Download music without paying (Question 8)	United States and Spain

at the $p<0.01$ or $p<0.001$ level), though the small sample size with Italy again impinged on our ability to discern differences among Italy and the other countries.

Respondents from Spain and Portugal were significantly more likely to have changed data in an information system (question 3) than were respondents in the USA ($p< 0.01$ level) or Ireland ($p<0.001$ level). Similarly, respondents from Spain and Portugal were significantly more likely to have used software illegally (question 4) than were US respondents ($p<0.001$). The most telling difference was with our question concerning giving unauthorized access to a computer (question 5). Irish respondents were much more likely to give unauthorized access than respondents from Spain ($p<0.01$), and both groups (Ireland and Spain) were significantly more likely to do so than in the other three countries ($p<0.001$). Respondents from Ireland and Portugal were significantly more likely to make an illegal copy of software (question 7) than USA respondents ($p<0.001$). Finally, respondents from the USA and Spain were significantly more likely to download songs without paying (question 8) than were respondents from Ireland or Portugal ($p<0.01$). Thus when evaluating specific user experiences, we start to see a clearer picture of differences among cultural groups. We summarize these findings in Table 8.

Next, we examined responses to the 22 scenario questions to determine if ethical attitudes vary by culture and if so, how. Table 9 lists the average responses by country for each scenario question. Note that for some questions, respondents rated the actions of employees and a manager, or an insider or an outsider. For the sce-

Table 9. Scenario question responses by country on a 5 point scale where 1=ethical, 5=computer crime (significant differences discussed in the text are highlighted in gray).

	Response (mean)					
Scenario Questions by Scenario Type	**USA**	**Spain**	**Ireland**	**Italy**	**Portugal**	**Entire Sample**
Data Access						
Q1: Manager Accesses Employee Email	2.24	2.90	2.79	3.26	2.70	2.57
Q1b: Employee Sends Improper Emails	2.95	3.24	2.77	3.21	3.35	3.10
Q14: Employee Accesses Payroll Records	3.75	3.29	3.86	3.26	3.70	3.63
Q16: Creates Database of Others Personal Information	2.92	3.35	3.44	3.53	3.38	3.18
Q18a: Manager Monitors Web Traffic	2.51	3.15	3.05	3.26	2.80	2.79
Q18b: Employee Accesses Improper Website	3.60	3.51	3.70	3.53	3.72	3.61
Q21a: Outsider Accesses Proprietary Code	4.14	3.91	3.93	3.53	3.70	3.95
Q21b: Insider Grants Access to Code	4.16	4.02	4.14	3.63	3.98	4.07
Data Manipulation						
Q2: Employee Alters Data to Avoid Payment	3.72	3.13	4.16	3.95	3.70	3.62
Q5: Student Changes Data Others Utilized	3.98	4.10	4.28	4.00	4.10	4.06
Q13: Creates Program to Destroy Data	4.33	4.13	4.79	4.42	4.31	4.32
Software Use						
Q3: Does Not Register Software	3.72	3.45	3.53	3.16	3.66	3.62
Q4: Gives Old Version of Program to Other	3.20	2.51	3.00	2.42	3.09	2.98
Q6: Copies Software for Backup Only	2.53	2.35	2.26	2.05	2.87	2.53
Q11: Fails to Report Error in Program	3.97	4.14	4.23	3.95	3.90	4.01
Q12: Loads Program Onto Two Computers	2.95	2.70	2.60	2.26	3.34	2.94
Q22a: Download Music from P2P Network	3.45	3.03	3.33	3.05	3.38	3.32
Q22b: Makes DVD of Pirated Music	3.62	3.30	3.63	3.05	3.66	3.54
Q22c: Sells DVD of Pirated Music	4.35	4.29	4.51	4.21	4.55	4.39
Programming Abuse						
Q8: Releases a Non-destructive Virus	3.26	2.85	3.37	3.42	3.30	3.19
Q9a: Programmer Writes Program w/ Inaccurate Data	3.48	3.10	3.35	3.21	3.13	3.30
Q9b: Manager Directs Program w/ Inaccurate Data	4.23	4.24	4.58	4.47	3.86	4.18
Q10a: Employee Misuses Email to Send Spam	3.45	3.29	3.79	3.84	3.60	3.48
Q10b: Manager Misuses Email to Spy on Employees	3.02	3.38	3.33	3.21	3.13	3.16
Q17: Programmer Creates Advertising Spam	3.72	3.88	4.26	3.84	3.84	3.83
Q20: Designer Misrepresents Seals of Authenticity on Website	4.52	4.71	4.74	4.53	4.21	4.51
Hardware Use						
Q7a: Authorized User Gives Access to Computer to Outsider	3.34	3.28	3.02	3.00	3.41	3.31
Q7b: Outsider Receives Unauthorized Access to Computer	3.57	3.64	3.35	3.58	3.81	3.63
Q15: Use Work Computer for Private Business	3.47	3.44	3.23	3.26	3.55	3.46
Q19: Use Work Computer for Illegal Gambling	3.31	4.13	3.70	4.21	4.11	3.74

nario responses, a high score indicates low tolerance for unethical or illegal behavior, and conversely a low score indicates a high tolerance (i.e., that the respondent finds a particular behavior acceptable). For each scenario type we ran country-wise comparisons to identify significant differences among the five countries. We found that age, gender, and computer knowledge were not influential factors for the scenario responses like they were for the individual ethical profile responses; in only a handful of cases was a significant correlation found between any of these factors and the scenario questions; and, even in those situations the correlations were extremely low (i.e., less than.15). Thus, we do not include age, gender, and computer knowledge in our presentation of the scenario question results, below.

Within the Data Access scenarios there were numerous significant differences among the five countries' respondents. Respondents from the United States thought that reading employee email, creating a database of personal information, and monitoring web traffic (questions 1, 16, and 18a) were more acceptable than did respondents in other countries ($p<0.001$), but conversely they thought someone illicitly accessing source code (question 21a) was clearly unethical while other respondents found it more of a questionable activity ($p<0.01$). Spanish and Portuguese respondents thought sending improper email (question 1b) was more unethical than did other respondents ($p<0.01$ for both cases), but conversely Spanish and Italian respondents thought accessing employee records (question 14) was less of an ethical problem than did other respondents ($p<0.001$ for both). Finally, granting insider access to code (question 21b) was more acceptable to Italian respondents than the others ($p<0.01$).

For the Data Manipulation questions, there were only two significant differences. Respondents from Spain found that changing data (question 2) was more acceptable than did other respondents ($p<0.01$), while respondents from Ireland reported that creating a program to destroy data (question 13) was essentially computer crime whereas on average other countries' respondents reported it as unethical, but not criminal ($p<0.001$).

For the Software Use scenarios, we found that in three instances respondents from Italy rated the scenario as more acceptable than other countries (all significant at the $p<0.001$ level). These were for scenarios concerning not registering software (question 3), giving an old version of software to someone else (question 4), and making DVDs of pirated music (question 22b). Respondents from Spain also rated questions 4 ($p<0.001$) and 22b ($p<0.01$) as more acceptable than others, and both Spain and Ireland rated question 11, failing to report an error in a software program, as more unethical than did other countries ($p<0.01$). Respondents from Portugal, however, rated scenarios concerning making backup copies of software (question 6, $p<0.01$), loading a program onto multiple computers (question 12, $p<0.01$), and selling DVDs of pirated music (question 22c, $p<0.001$) as less acceptable than the other countries.

In the area of Programming Abuse, respondents from Spain found releasing a non-destructive virus (question 8) as more acceptable than others ($p<0.001$) as well as Question 10a, misusing email to send spam ($p<0.01$). Respondents from Portugal reported two other scenarios as more acceptable than did respondents from other countries – A manager directing a program that generates inaccurate data (question 9b, $p<0.01$) and a web designer misrepresenting seals of authenticity (question 20, $p<0.01$). The only other significant difference found was for Irish respondents, who reported that writing a program to create advertising spam (question 17) was more unethical ($p<0.001$) than other countries' assessments.

Finally, in the area of hardware use, United States respondents found illegal online gambling from work (question 19) as more acceptable than other countries ($p<0.001$), while respondents from Ireland rated unauthorized access to another's computer account (question 7b) as more accept-

Table 10. Ranking of individual ethical profiles by country (1= most unethical, 5=most ethical)

Ethical Profile Question: "Have you ever..."	USA	Spain	Ireland	Italy	Portugal
E1: Used or sold shareware illegally (without registering it)	3	2	4	5	1
E2: Purchased a legal copy of software and given the old version to someone else	3	4	2	1	5
E3: Changed data that someone else will rely on	4	1	5	3	2
E4: Used software in an illegal manner	4	1	2	3	1
E5: Given someone unauthorized access to a computer	4	2	1	5	3
E6: Knowingly released a virus or worm into a system	4	1	5	3	2
E7: Made an illegal copy of software	5	4	2	3	1
E8: Downloaded songs or DVDs from the Web without paying for them	1	2	4	3	4

able than did respondents from other countries ($p<0.01$). For the other hardware use scenarios the respondents' ratings were consistent across all five countries.

DISCUSSION

This study investigated whether personal experiences in ethical situations regarding information security and ethical attitudes toward information security differ among cultures. The results from this descriptive study indicate that there are some notable similarities and differences, but that characterizing ethical attitudes by culture is complex. We discuss our findings more fully in the context of our research questions.

Do Individuals' Personal Experiences in Ethical Situations Regarding Information Security Differ among Cultures?

We expected that individual ethical profile would tell us something about the differences among the five countries, but unexpectedly our composite scores for both individual and associative ethical profile were very similar across the countries. As expected, associative ethical profiles were greater than individual profiles for each country, likely due to one of two factors. First, respondents may have been more hesitant to answer affirmatively regarding their own illicit behaviors, but were perhaps less reluctant when discussing the behavior of their peers. Thus a type of social desirability bias may account for the difference. However, since the survey was anonymous, it is more likely that the associative profiles are higher because respondents drew on their knowledge of several peers, and that as a group, the peers' illicit experiences were more frequent than the respondent's alone.

When we rank ordered the proportion of respondents by country for each ethical profile question, we found a few interesting differences. Using the data provided in Table 7, the rank order of those percentages by question on the ethical profile is provided in Table 10. In Table 10, ranking first means that the country had the highest number of respondents reporting engagement in this unethical act. Unlike other tables in this chapter, a high ranking here means a relatively higher level of unethical behavior. For question 4, Spain and Portugal both ranked first. For question 8, Ireland and Portugal both ranked fourth.

As can be seen, Spain and Portugal rank first or second in the percentage of respondents indicating engagement in unethical or illegal actions regarding information security more often than the USA, Ireland, and Italy do. This is somewhat interesting. This trend suggests that culture might play a part in how individuals from these respective countries act when faced with opportunities to, for example, change data, or use software illegally. As shown in Table 1, Spain and Portugal, compared to the other countries, exhibit a culture higher in power distance (more likely to look to formal sources of authority for guidance), collectivism (rely on strong integrated communities), uncertainty avoidance (more reliance on rules and policies), and lower in masculinity (emphasis on caring and quality of life). Thus it could be that more feminine and collectivist cultures, coupled with high power distance and uncertainty avoidance, have a higher tendency to try different activities that are viewed as unethical in other cultures.

While the similarity between Spain and Portugal is interesting, so are the differences among Spain and Portugal, and Ireland. Compared to Spain and Portugal, Ireland scores low on measures of power distance and uncertainty avoidance. Yet, when looking at the ethical profile results (Table 7), we see noticeable similarities between Ireland and Portugal and Ireland and Spain on a few items. For example, respondents from Ireland and Portugal were the highest to report making an illegal copy of software (question E7) and that this was significantly higher than USA respondents ($p<0.001$). Furthermore, respondents from Ireland and Spain were the highest to report giving unauthorized access to a computer (question E5). Irish respondents were much more likely to give unauthorized access than respondents from Spain ($p<0.01$), and both groups (Ireland and Spain) were significantly more likely to do so than in the other three countries ($p<0.001$).

One way to view these findings is to remember that the United States and Ireland, which are culturally similar, are the most culturally different from Spain and Portugal (which also, as a pair, are similar). Mostly, those two pairs of countries had similar responses with each other, and yet occasionally the greater similarities were between Spain and Ireland, or the United States and Spain as was the case of downloading songs (question 8). It is possible that the relationship between national culture and information security behavior is explained by other contextual factors that interact with and elicit or counteract culture as an explanatory variable. It is also possible that cultural dimensions may be highly influential in the case of one particular behavior, but less influential for other behaviors. Ireland is a good example of this. Irish culture is the lowest of our group of countries in power distance, which may reflect a disregard for authority that explains why responses for using software illegally and granting others unauthorized access was so high. However, the same logic doesn't apply to other behaviors, such as changing data others use and releasing a virus, for which a disregard for authority might also be an explanation. In fact, none of the Irish respondents reported these behaviors.

Thus overall, we found that there were differences in individual ethical profile, some of which are more easily explained by cultural factors than others. Let us turn to the results from the ethical scenarios to see if we can provide a more in-depth explanation of these differences.

Do Individuals' Ethical Attitudes toward Information Security Differ among Cultures?

Again, we aggregated findings to determine if there were trends. We took results from each scenario and created a composite score and then rank-ordered the responses within each country. Table 11 shows the rank order of scenario categories within country. This offers a glimpse of which type of ethical scenario was most problematic in each country.

The table shows some obvious similarities across cultures. For example, for all five countries the scenarios from the data manipulation category were rated as the most unethical. The destructive and unrecoverable nature of this type of situation may have played a role in this consistency. This suggests that, across cultures, some information security breaches may be commonly recognized as significantly harmful thus policies to

Table 11. Rank order of scenario categories within each country (1= least unethical, 5= most unethical) as rated by country respondents.

	USA	Spain	Ireland	Italy	Portugal
Data Access	1	2	3	2	1
Data Manipulation	5	5	5	5	5
Software Use	3	1	2	1	2
Programming Abuse	4	4	4	4	3
Hardware Use	2	3	1	3	4

Table 12. Rank order of scenario categories within each country (1= least unethical, 5= most unethical) as rated by country respondents

	USA	Spain	Ireland	Italy	Portugal
Data Access	1	4	5	2	3
Data Manipulation	2	1	5	4	3
Software Use	4	2	3	1	5
Programming Abuse	3	2	5	4	1
Hardware Use	2	4	1	3	5

mitigate these actions could be consistently applied. Similarly, programming abuse was ranked as the next most unethical category in all countries except one, Portugal, again showing come convergence.

Countries varied significantly however on which category represented the least unethical (or most acceptable) activities. For the United States and Portugal, it was unauthorized access to data. For Spain and Italy, it was software (mis)use. And for Ireland, it was hardware use. In the Ireland case, it may be that the combination of low power distance (these resources belong to me as much as the boss), high masculinity and low uncertainty avoidance (the rules on this kind of misuse are vague, so why not further my own goals) are more aligned with misusing hardware resources (which has little long-term consequences). MacFarlane, Murphy and Clerkin (2006) also note that Ireland is in the midst of information modernization in areas such as telemedicine, which might reflect greater awareness of data security and integrity as a societal concern. Because culture changes slowly, it is difficult to find specific causal links between changes like this and cultural attitudes toward information security; however this suggests that culture might play an additional role as a secondary factor (i.e., certain cultures experience technological change, which influences attitudes towards security).

We also ranked the scenario categories, but this time across countries. For each scenario category, which country found it the most unethical is presented in Table 12. Surprisingly, 3 of the 5 categories were found most unethical by respondents from Ireland. Interestingly, the Irish respondents had the second highest ethical profile score, on average, indicating more experience in unethical situations. Ireland also ranks lowest in our set of five countries on power distance and uncertainty avoidance. This begs the question. What is the relationship between power distance, uncertainty avoidance, perception of unethical behavior, and unethical behavior?

The two other categories were reported as the most unethical by Portugal. If we look at the cultural dimensions for Portugal, we find that Portugal is lowest overall in individualism and masculinity, and highest in uncertainty avoidance and power distance. Do these dimensions help explain the results? A collectivist culture might be more sympathetic to software sharing, like Spain, but unlike Portugal. However, a culture that avoids uncertainty like Portugal might find hardware misuse (unauthorized access to and use of computers) as a major problem, since access rules (e.g., passwords, usernames, and physical access) are usually explicitly tied to security policy.

Limitations

The small sample for Italy was a limitation for this study. Compared to the other countries in this study, Italy ranked highest on the cultural trait of masculinity, i.e., the value that society places on assertiveness and achievement. In contrast, Spain and Portugal ranked low on masculinity, which means they value caring and quality of life more. It is possible that this dimension has explanatory power that we were not able to detect. While rankings used in Tables 10, 11 and 12 are useful for interpretive purposes, it is important to bear in mind that the absolute differences in respondents' ratings were fairly low. A larger sample size and a more sensitive instrument for data collection of ethical behaviors may help us better discern absolute differences.

As discussed earlier, this study shows that the effect of culture on ethical behavior and ethical attitudes is complex. It is possible that cultural dimensions co-vary, i.e., it is the unique combination of the dimensions for a given culture that shapes ethical attitudes and behaviors in information security. In order to study this, researchers will need not only a larger sample size, but also raw data on cultural dimensions. Early in this chapter, we referred to the Rest model for ethical decision making. Rest found that ethical decision making is comprised of four distinct components: (1) recognizing a moral issue; (2) making a moral judgment; (3) establishing moral intent; (4) and engaging in moral behavior (1986, 1994). It is quite possible that the influence of culture functions differently in the different phases of ethical decision making.

In summary, we have identified both some strong similarities and strong differences; although in the majority the differences are minor among cultures. This result leads us to conclude that our initial premise is correct, namely that cultural differences must be at least acknowledge if not accounted for with unique policies by information security specialists; however, the problem is not as grave as we had suspected. A balanced approach is needed, as we explain in our discussion of the third research question, below.

Can Similarities and Differences Be Used to Inform Information Security Policy?

The implications of the specific results of our research for information security policy are threefold. First, we suspected that culture would mediate behavior and attitude toward ethical actions in information security. This study showed that individuals' ethical profiles are often correlated with their reactions to ethical scenarios about information and technology use, and that the strength of this relationship is different for the five nations studied.

Second, we were able to delve deeply into different scenarios in an attempt to discern points of convergence and divergence across cultures. Points of convergence are areas where policies need less customization based on cultural differences. Points of divergence need more investigation as discussed earlier. We also believe that the descriptive results of this study have utility for policy makers. Readers may find based on high incident rates of an undesirable behavior to allocate resources toward education and ethics training as they deem appropriate. For example, respondents across the five countries studied were very homogeneous in their opinion of the ethics of downloading several hundred copyrighted songs from a file sharing website (Question 22a), which suggests that this behavior is both universal and of equal concern in varying cultures. However responses differed quite a bit when we asked about the ethics of putting those songs on DVDs so they could be enjoyed by others (Question 22b). Policy makers concerned with illegal music sharing may find that educating music sharers on the ethics of how they use their music rather than how they obtain it will be more effective in some countries.

Finally, we provide a springboard for studying how cultural differences might shape differences in ethical attitudes and behaviors toward emergent or future technologies or toward existing technologies, but in other countries besides those we studied. Marshall (1999) notes that information security and privacy policy creation typically lags information technology advances, causing critical ethical and social problems. Our research shows that this problem has another dimension. As information technologies diffuse throughout the world simultaneously, individuals in different countries will experience unique ethical and social problems related to the same technologies. Our results are a valuable litmus test both for policy makers and organizational practitioners charged with assuring and securing information and information technology.

FUTURE RESEARCH DIRECTIONS

Future research should investigate more specifically the types of information security incidents that occur around the world and how those have developed differently depending on the culture. Unfortunately, more and more organizations are reporting these types of problems worldwide, but this at least means researchers will have more solid information on which to test their models.

Information and communications technologies have created a business world where every company can be a global company. As companies cross country boundaries, information assurance and security become critical areas. Information security policies must encompass technical areas and must be applied to a variety of situations in numerous countries around the world. The problem is that not everyone interprets policies the same. As researchers investigate the effectiveness of information security policy, we suggest looking at the many factors that can influence a person's interpretation, including user expectations, user experiences, and culture.

Earlier we mentioned the need for research that looks at the influence of culture on different components of ethical decision making. Questions such as these seem relevant. Do cultural values shape one component of ethical decision making more than another? If so, how? How might that propagate to other components of ethical decision making? And what are the implications for information security policy?

Companies are continuing to become more global in nature. The development of new information and communications technologies has accelerated this trend. Emerging markets are becoming global opportunities for expansion. What is the impact of this trend on a company's information assurance and security policy? The large area of information assurance and security policy development is a rich one for research, but one that seems to lack substantial effort. How can effective policies be developed that span countries? What impacts peoples' interpretation of these policies? How will Web 2.0 technologies (wikis, blogs, social networks, etc.) impact these policies? All of these areas are open to researchers.

This chapter and the research reported in it is a beginning effort to look at the impact of culture on information ethics. We are in the process of expanding this study to include Asian and Oceanic countries. We have plans to extend the study to Arab, Africa, and other possible regions in the world. We invite other researchers to join us in this line of research.

CONCLUSION

We are becoming a global economy. Companies are connected with each other via global trade, information and communication technologies, products/services that span countries and cultures, and keen interests of knowing and working with others who live around the world. Information is particularly important for the successful operations of a multinational enterprise. The geographical nature of business creates differences in culture, expectations, business norms, educational systems, legal systems, and ethical values in the global economy. It is vital for a multinational organization to understand these differences when formulating global information assurance and security policies. Information assurance and security professionals are often tasked with designing, implementing, and enforcing information security policies for inter and intra-organizational purposes. It is our hope these they will be better able to take into account cultural differences in so doing.

REFERENCES

Ben-Jacob, M. G. (2005). Integrating computer ethics across the curriculum: A case study. *Journal of Educational Technology & Society*, *8*(4), 198–204.

Conger, S., & Loch, K. D. (1995). Ethics and computer use. *Communications of the ACM*, *38*(12), 30–32. doi:10.1145/219663.219676

Dinev, T., Goo, J., Hu, Q., & Nam, K. (2009). User behavior towards protective information technologies: the role of national cultural differences. *Information Systems Journal*, *19*, 391–412. doi:10.1111/j.1365-2575.2007.00289.x

Erez, M., & Earley, P. C. (1993). *Culture, self-identity,and work*. New York: Oxford University Press.

Fleischmann, K. R., Robbins, R. W., & Wallace, W. A. (2009). Designing educational cases for intercultural information ethics: The importance of diversity, perspectives, palues, and Pluralism. *Journal of Education for Library and Information Science*, *50*(1), 4–14.

Fleischmann, K. R., & Wallace, W. A. (2005). A covenant with transparency: Opening the black box of models. *Communications of the ACM*, *48*(5), 93–97. doi:10.1145/1060710.1060715

Harris, A. L. (2000). IS ethical attitudes among college students: A comparatives. In D. Colton, J. Caouette, B. Raggad (Eds.), *Proceedings of the Information Systems Education Conference 2000*: Vol. 17,§801. Retrieved from http://proc.isecon.org/2000/801/ISECON.2000.Harris.pdf

Hofstede, G. (1980). *Culture's consequences: International differences in work-related values*. Newbury Park, CA: Sage.

Hofstede, G. (1991). *Cultures and organizations: Software of the mind*. London: McGraw-Hill.

Kamira, R. (2007). Kaitiakitanga and health informatics: Introducing useful indigeneous concepts of governance in the health sector. In Dyson, L., Hendricks, M., & Grant, S. (Eds.), *Information technology and indigenous people*. Hershey, PA: Information Science Publishing.

Lu, L.-C., Rose, G. M., & Blodgett, J. G. (1999). The effects of cultural dimensions on ethical decision making in marketing: An exploratory study. *Journal of Business Ethics*, *18*, 91–105. doi:10.1023/A:1006038012256

MacFarlane, A., Murphy, A. W., & Clerkin, P. (2006). Telemedicine services in the Republic of Ireland: An evolving policy context. *Health Policy (Amsterdam)*, *76*, 245–258. doi:10.1016/j.healthpol.2005.06.006

Marshall, K. P. (1999). Has technology introduced new ethical problems? *Journal of Business Ethics*, *19*, 81–90. doi:10.1023/A:1006154023743

Mason, R. O. (1986). Four ethical issues of the information age. *Management Information Systems Quarterly*, *10*(1), 4–12. doi:10.2307/248873

Mitrakas, A. (2006). Information security and law in Europe: Risks checked? *Information & Communications Technology Law*, *15*(1), 33–53. doi:10.1080/13600830600557984

Moily, V. (2009). IT act will be amended to tackle cyber crime. *The Times of India.* Retrieved from http://timesofindia.indiatimes.com/news/india/IT-Act-will-be-amended-to-tackle-cyber-crime-Moily/articleshow/5048201.cms

Paradice, D. B. (1990). Ethical attitudes of entry-level MIS personnel. *Information & Management*, *18*, 143–151. doi:10.1016/0378-7206(90)90068-S

Reis, H. T., & Gable, S. L. (2000). Event-sampling and other methods for studying everyday experience. In Reis, H. T., & Judd, C. M. (Eds.), *Handbook of research methods in social and personality psychology* (pp. 190–222). Cambridge, MA: Cambridge University Press.

Rest, J. (1994). Background theory and research. In Rest, J., & Narvaez, D. (Eds.), *Moral development in the professions* (pp. 1–26). Hillsdale, NJ: Lawrence Erlbaum Associates.

Rest, J. R. (1986). *Moral development: Advances in research and theory.* New York: Praeger.

Robbins, R. W., Fleischmann, K. R., & Wallace, W. A. (2008). Computing and Information Ethics: Challenges, Education, and Research. In Luppicini, R., & Adell, R. (Eds.), *Handbook of research on technoethics* (pp. 391–408). Hershey, PA: IGI Global.

Singh, S., Cabraal, A., Demosthenous, C., Astbrink, G., & Furlong, M. (2007). Password sharing: Implications for security design based on social practice. In *CHI Proceedings 2007,* San Jose, CA.

Sitton, J. V. (2006). When the right to know and the right to privacy collide. *The Information Management Journal*, *40*(5), 76–80.

Thorne, L., & Saunders, S. (2002). The socio-cultural embeddedness of individuals' ethical reasonin in organizations. *Journal of Business Ethics*, *35*(1), 1–14. doi:10.1023/A:1012679026061

Vitell, S. J., Paolillo, J. G. P., & Thomas, J. L. (2003). The perceived role of ethics and social responsibility: A study of marketing professionals. *Business Ethics Quarterly*, *13*(1), 63–86.

Volkema, R. (2004). Demographic, cultural, and economic predictors of perceived ethicality of negotiated behavior: A nine-country analysis. *Journal of Business Research*, *57*, 69–78. doi:10.1016/S0148-2963(02)00286-2

Wood, W. A. (1993). Computer ethics and years of computer use. *Journal of Computer Information Systems*, *23*(4), 23–27.

Yar, M. (2005). The global 'epidemic' of movie 'piracy': crime-wave or social construction? *Media Culture & Society*, *27*(5), 677–696. doi:10.1177/0163443705055723

ADDITIONAL READING

Baumer, D. L., Earp, J. B., & Poindexter, J. C. (2004). Internet privacy law: A comparison between the United States and the European Union. *Computers & Security*, *23*, 400–412. doi:10.1016/j.cose.2003.11.001

Berleur, J., & Avgerou, C. (Eds.). (2005). *Perspectives and policies on ICT in society.* New York: Springer. doi:10.1007/b135654

Bowyer, K. (2001). *Ethics and computing*. New York: IEEE Press/John Wiley Press.

Brunnstein, K., & Berleur, J. (Eds.). (1996). *Ethics of computing – Codes, spaces for discussion and law*. London: Chapman & Hall.

Christians, C., & Traber, M. (Eds.). (1997). *Communications ethics and universal values*. London: Sage.

D'Arcy, J., & Hovav, A. (2009). Does one size fit all? Examining the differential effects of IS security countermeasures. *Journal of Business Ethics*, *89*, 59–71. doi:10.1007/s10551-008-9909-7

De George, R. T. (2000). Business ethics and the challenge of the information age. *Business Ethics Quarterly*, *10*(1), 63–72. doi:10.2307/3857695

De George, R. T. (2003). *The ethics of information technology and business*. Oxford: Wiley-Blackwell. doi:10.1002/9780470774144

Earp, J. B., Anton, A. I., Aiman-Smith, L., & Stufflebeam, W. H. (2005). Examining internet privacy policies within the context of user privacy values. *IEEE Transactions on Engineering Management*, *52*(2), 227–237. doi:10.1109/TEM.2005.844927

Gopal, R. D., & Sanders, G. L. (2000). Global software piracy: You can't get blood out of a turnip. *Communications of the ACM*, *43*(9), 83–89. doi:10.1145/348941.349002

Herath, T., & Rao, H. R. (2009). Encouraging information security behaviors in organizations: Roles of penalties, pressures, and perceived effectiveness. *Decision Support Systems*, *47*(2), 154–165. doi:10.1016/j.dss.2009.02.005

Himma, K. E., & Tavani, H. T. (2008). *The handbook of information and computer ethics*. Hoboken, NJ: Wiley. doi:10.1002/9780470281819

Hone, K., & Eloff, J. H. P. (2002). Information security policy – what do international information security standards say? *Computers & Security*, *21*(5), 402–409. doi:10.1016/S0167-4048(02)00504-7

Iacovino, L., & Todd, M. (2007). The long-term preservation of identifiable personal data: a comparative archival perspective on privacy regulatory models in the European Union, Australia, Canada, and the United States. *Archival Science*, *7*, 107–127. doi:10.1007/s10502-007-9055-5

Jensen, C., & Potts, C. (2004). Privacy policies as decision-making tools: An evaluation of online privacy notices. In *CHI Proceedings 2004*, Vienna, Austria.

Kadam, A. (2007). Information security policy development and implementation. *Information Systems Security*, *16*(5), 246–256. doi:10.1080/10658980701744861

Karyda, M., Mitrou, E., & Quirchmayr, G. (2006). A framework for outsourcing IS/IT security services. *Information Management & Computer Security*, *14*(5), 402–415. doi:10.1108/09685220610707421

Kizza, J. M. (2007). *Ethical and social issues in the information age*. London: Springer-Verlag.

Korba, L., Song, R., & Yee, G. (2007). Privacy rights management: Implementation scenarios. *Information Resources Management Journal*, *20*(1), 14–27.

Moghe, V. (2003). Privacy management – a new era in the Australian business environment. *Information Management & Computer Security*, *11*(2/3), 60–66. doi:10.1108/09685220310468600

Peslak, A. R. (2006). Internet privacy policies of the largest international companies. *Journal of Electronic Commerce in Organizations*, *4*(3), 46–62.

Pottie, G. J. (2004). Privacy in the global e-village. *Communications of the ACM, 47*(2), 21–23. doi:10.1145/966389.966407

Quigley, M. (2005). *Information security and ethics: social and organizational issues*. Hershey, PA: IRM Press.

Quinn, M. J. (2005). *Ethics for the information age* (2nd ed.). Boston, MA: Addison Wesley.

Wood, C. (2008). *Information security policies made easy* (10th ed.). Houston, TX: Information Shield, Inc.

Workman, M., & Gathegi, J. (2007). Punishment and ethics deterrents: A study of insider security contravention. *Journal of the American Society for Information Science and Technology, 58*(2), 212–222. doi:10.1002/asi.20474

KEY TERMS AND DEFINITIONS

Computer Crime: Actions which violate international, national, state, or locality law concerning the use of computer or networking technology or information stored or transferred with that technology.

Cultural Dimension: One of five classifiers created by the research Geert Hofstede to describe differences in culture between nations. The classifiers are Power Distance Index, Individualism, Masculinity, Uncertainty Avoidance, and Long-Term Orientation.

Ethical Attitudes and Behaviors: How individuals think about and act on their personal morals and values in different situations.

Ethical Profile: A composite of responses to a series of questions about an individual's past activities in the area of information security. A lower score indicates less experience with unethical or illegal activities.

Ethical Scenario: A short vignette describing a possibly unethical or illegal activity, often used in ethics training. Scenarios can be written as to place the reader into the scenario (i.e. "You take home sensitive information…") or relate the activities of a third party (i.e. "John takes home sensitive information…").

Information Ethics: Moral issues and values concerning the use of information and information technology, for example the public disclosure of personally identifying information. Information ethics also deals with the ethical implications of living in an information society, such as network neutrality.

Information Policy: An organization's stated goals and procedures for managing internal and external information and the systems for storing, transferring, and processing that information. This context differs slightly from government information policy which is typically a formalized framework which guides legislation.

ENDNOTES

1. Hofstede later added a fifth dimension to his model, long-term orientation. Since long-term orientation data was not available for all the countries we studied we excluded this dimension.
2. P value is an indication that the result is statistically significant – generally p values less than 0.05 are considered acceptable.
3. Percentages presented in the table are rounded.

APPENDIX: SCENARIO QUESTIONS

Summary of ethics scenarios from survey. Respondents rated participant's actions as: 1= Ethical, 2= Acceptable, 3= Questionable, 4= Unethical, or 5= Computer crime.

Data Access Scenarios
1. A manager enters the company's E-Mail system and reviews messages sent by various subordinates to ensure that the E-Mail system is not being used for private purposes, against policy. Two employees have sent messages to other company employees critical of management. The manager subsequently reprimands them. *The manager's actions are... The employee's actions are...*
14. A salesperson accesses payroll records on the main computer. She reviews the pay of the other salespeople and the sales manager and concludes that she is getting paid appropriately. No other use of the information was made. *The salesperson's action is...*
16. A police department has a database of persons who have been charged (but not necessarily convicted) with a crime. t would be accessible by 1500 people in the city for various purposes. The data would be maintained for the life of the person. *The department's action is...*
18. A company allows its employees to use the Web for limited personal use but unknowingly monitors the web addresses visited. Two employees have visited pornographic sites and the general manager fires them. *The manager's action is... The employee's actions are...*
21. Samantha thinks that technology patented by Company.com could be used by her newly created website. Alfred, a friend who has access to the source code for the new technology, has offered to give it to Samantha. Samantha's gets the technology from Alfred and integrates the technology into her company's web site. *Samantha's action is... Alfred's action is...*
Data Manipulation Scenarios
2. A bank employee has accidentally overdrawn his checking account and realizes three checks will "bounce." He changes the account status of his checking account so that no overdrawn check charges will be assessed, and as soon as he makes a deposit that will make his balance positive again, he changes the account status back. *The employee's actions are...*
5. A finance class has an investment competition and the winning team gets an A. John changes data in a files needed in the competition. The other teams process their investments using the changed data. Just before the results are due to the professor, John changes the data back to its original values and his team wins. *John's action is...*
13. Jim is a shareware programmer who has created a solitaire game free to use 25 times. To force users to register, Jim creates a virus that will be released anytime someone plays the game more than 50 times without registering. The virus, when released, will start randomly destroying data stored on the user's computer. Jim is doing this in an attempt to stop illegal use of software and encourage users to register shareware. *Jim's actions are...*
Software Use Scenarios
3. Jose downloads a shareware program from the internet. Shareware requires anyone using the software to register and pay a small fee for continued use of the program after a 14 day trial and cannot be sold by anyone except the author. Jose uses the program he downloaded every day. He decides not to register his use since no one will ever know. *Jose's use of the software is...*
4. Jane has a legal copy of a word processing program. Jane purchases an upgrade version and the upgrade license says that the old version is to be discarded or kept only for backup purposes. Jane loads the old version into her secretary's computer for her to use. *Jane's actions are...*
6. Sue buys a copy of the latest spreadsheet software. The license agreement clearly states that no copies of the CD-ROM can be made for any reason. Sue makes a backup CD-ROM for use if something happens to the original copy. *Sue's action is...*
11. Howard is a programmer for a loan company. He finds an error in the program that computes interest that adds 25 to 50 cents to the bill of each borrower each month. Since the amount of the error is so small and he has so much to do, Howard decides not to report the error to management. *Howard's action is...*
12. Felicia's company just purchased a spreadsheet package for her to use on the job. The license agreement says that this particular program is licensed to her machine. She knows that she can't make copies of the program and give to her peers, but she does make a copy and loads it on her machine at home. Felicia doesn't feel guilty because she knows she will never be using both programs at the same time. *Felicia's action is...*
22. Susan downloads music from file sharing sites to her PC using someone else's account. She then uses her DVD burner to make albums for her friends, for which she charges $5 a DVD. *Susan's actions in downloading music are... Susan's action making DVDs is... Susan's action selling DVDs is...*

continued on following page

Programming Abuse Scenarios
8. Jill is working on a research paper about the effects of computer viruses. She creates a short program that releases a PEACE message through E-mail. The message does not corrupt receiver's data, but does interrupt their screen. Jill is doing this as a test to see how fast a simple, non-destructive virus can spread. *Jill's action is...*
9. A programmer is asked to write a program to generate inaccurate information for external auditors. The manager tells him he must write the program or be reassigned to the maintenance staff. He writes the program. *The programmer's action is... His manager's action is...*
10. There is no company policy on the use of E-mail. A manager reviews messages sent by various subordinates to ensure that the E-Mail system is not being used for private purposes. One employee sent hundreds of SPAM type E-mail messages to political donors. The manager subsequently reprimands him. *The employee's actions are... The manager's actions are...*
17. A company asks a designer to build a web site to collect name, address, and e-mail addresses from internet surfers. The company sells the data to advertisers for a profit. The advertisers will use the information to send SPAM and sexually explicit mailings to the unwitting people. Despite this, the designer builds the site. *The designer's actions are...*
20. Gary created a new website to sell a new line of hand-made toys To increase the number of visits to your website you use a seal that says, "Approved by the United Nations Commission on Children" and the "Fisher-Price" trademark. Neither the United Nations nor Fisher-price has given Gary permission to use their names, seals, or trademarks. *Gary's action is...*
Hardware Use Scenarios
7. A friend of Jacob's who is not a student asks to use the school's computer, so Jacob gives him his password. The unauthorized friend uses several hours of computer time a week over the summer to play computer games. *Jacob's action is... The unauthorized friend's action is...*
15. Jack works in the IT Department and has started doing some part-time consulting work for small businesses that would like to set up their own databases. Working after hours and without obtaining permission to use the company's computer system, Jack uses the company's computer to create databases for his clients. *Jack's actions are...*
19. Gambling is illegal in the state or country where you are located. A coworker, Jackson, uses his computer at work to access an off-shore gambling web site. *Jackson's action is...*

APPENDIX: DISCUSSION QUESTIONS

1. Discuss the various ways that cultural differences contribute to ethical dilemmas in information assurance and security? What do the authors say on this point and what do you think?
2. How does the role of culture contribute to the "messiness" of information assurance and security problems?
3. How does culture influence individual notions of right and wrong? What is the authors' position on the role of culture and information security policy? Do you agree with them? Why or why not?
4. From your own perspective and culture, answer the personal and associative ethical profile questions and the ethical scenario questions given in the chapter. Compute your scores in the way described for Tables 7 and 9. (Since you can't compute a mean score, compute your raw score instead). Which country are your scores closest to? Can you deduce your Hofstede score using analysis techniques similar to those used by the authors? Do you agree or disagree with your Hofstede score?
5. In your opinion, is the Hofstede score useful as a predictor of the behavior of a given cultural group when faced with an ethical dilemma? Discuss the use of the Hofstede score for this purpose.
6. Suggest other cultural dimensions to augment the four described by Hofstede. Discuss their meaning and give examples of behavior that illustrate these cultural dimensions.
7. Read Google's "Code of Conduct". Which of the chapter's ethical scenarios or ethical profile questions are addressed? Discuss how they are addressed. For any that are not addressed, discuss if the Code of Conduct can be modified to address these concerns. Should additional ethical issues be addressed by the code of conduct?

8. Several banks and credit card companies have outsourced their customer service call center operations to a third world country. You have been asked to prepare an ethics training program for call center employees. In order to ensure that the training program addresses potential ethical issues, you have been advised to get a sense of the ethical attitudes of potential employees. Develop at least 10 ethical profile questions that you would ask in order to gather information as a basis for designing the training program.
9. Your grandmother is quite forgetful and, as her legal guardian, you have the authority to access her bank account to pay her bills. She has quite a bit of money in her savings account. Would it be OK to deduct a small "service fee" from her account for your services? Why or why not? Discuss the ethics of this situation.
10. Using the scenario described in the previous question, you have a temporary need for $500 to pay your credit card bill. You should be able to repay the loan when you get paid next month. Would it be OK to borrow the money from your grandmother's account? Why or why not? Discuss the ethics of this situation. Since your grandmother is so forgetful, you feel that there's no point in asking her permission – you expect that she would probably say yes, anyway.
11. Suppose you have discovered the username and pin for your neighbor's bank account. Would it be OK to check the account balance? Should you tell your neighbor that he or she should change his pin? Discuss the ethics of this situation.

Chapter 5
Peer-to-Peer Networks:
Interdisciplinary Challenges for Interconnected Systems

Nicolas Christin
Carnegie Mellon University, USA

ABSTRACT

Peer-to-peer networks are one of the main sources of Internet traffic, and yet remain very controversial. On the one hand, they have a number of extremely beneficial uses, such as open source software distribution, and censorship resilience. On the other hand, peer-to-peer networks pose considerable ethical and legal challenges, for instance allowing exchanges of large volumes of copyrighted materials. This chapter argues that the ethical quandaries posed by peer-to-peer networks are rooted in a conflicting set of incentives among several entities ranging from end-users to consumer electronics manufacturers. The discussion then turns to the legal, economic, and technological remedies that have been proposed, and the difficulties faced in applying them. The last part of the chapter expands the scope of ethical issues linked to peer-to-peer networks, and examines whether existing laws and technology can mitigate new threats such as inadvertent confidential information leaks in peer-to-peer networks.

INTRODUCTION

Since their inception in 1999 with the Napster file-sharing service, peer-to-peer networks have grown to become a predominant source of Internet traffic (Karagiannis et al., 2005; Basher et al., 2008). One of the reasons behind the success of peer-to-peer networks is that they have many uses. For instance, in contrast to a centralized server that would have to bear over a awarm of hosts, peer-to-peer networks facilitate information dissemination by spreading the load, thereby reducing infrastructure costs. Applications that take advantage of the cost reduction offered by peer-to-peer infrastructures include software distribution, for example open-source software such as the Linux kernel,[1] or proprietary software such as World of Warcraft patches.[2]

As another societal benefit, peer-to-peer systems offer increased censorship-resilience thanks

DOI: 10.4018/978-1-61692-245-0.ch005

to their decentralized organization. Once a file is in a peer-to-peer network, it is extremely difficult, if not impossible, to completely remove that file from the network, due to both the sheer number of machines in the network that may host a copy, and the rate at which users join and leave the network.

For all their advantages, peer-to-peer systems pose considerable ethical and legal challenges, which stem from a conflicting set of incentives among the different network participants. As a case in point, a significant share of peer-to-peer traffic has historically consisted of copyrighted materials. Indeed, for end users, the ability to download "free" content often proves tempting, particularly when considering that most consumers are either unaware of, or have a basic misunderstanding of copyright law. As a response, copyright holders, most notably the music and movie industries, have been aggressively investigating legal and technological means to reduce, disrupt, or even abolish peer-to-peer network traffic.

To add further confusion, Internet service providers (ISPs) have adopted a more ambiguous position, due to the economic conundrum they face. On the one hand, peer-to-peer applications are a driver for consumers to purchase higher levels of broadband connectivity, which translates into higher revenue for ISPs. On the other hand, the explosion of peer-to-peer traffic puts a severe strain on network infrastructure, which results in increased costs for ISPs. Consequently, some service providers have been known to treat peer-to-peer traffic as undesirable, e.g., by downgrading its priority when it enters their network, without necessarily advertising this fact to their customers.

In this chapter, we will first examine in greater detail the incentive misalignment among the actors in peer-to-peer networks. We will then briefly summarize the legal issues associated with peer-to-peer networks, especially the questions of contributory infringement and vicarious liability. In this context, we will provide an overview of the legal and economic remedies that the content industry and service providers have entertained to tackle challenges posed by peer-to-peer networks.

In the third part of the chapter, we will describe the technological arsenal that content industry and Internet service providers have been using to limit peer-to-peer traffic, as a complement to legal recourse. We will present "interdiction technologies" for which patent applications have been filed. We will distinguish between methods that target content (i.e., files) from those that target peer-to-peer hosts (i.e., actual machines). We will use this distinction to inform our discussion on the ethical and legal dilemmas that the application of these interdiction technologies presents.

In the fourth, and final, section, we will explain how the problem of controlling information flow in peer-to-peer networks far exceeds the mere realm of copyright enforcement. We will show that the assumption that the content present in the network is voluntarily introduced by end-users may be flawed. Studies indeed document that private data (e.g., credit card numbers) are often accidentally leaked due to end-user misconfiguration. Even more perniciously, recent viruses and worms have been seen to exploit peer-to-peer infrastructures to leak and disseminate private information on a large scale.

We will conclude by discussing whether or not existing interdiction technologies can mitigate these new threats. We will use these recent developments to highlight the modern ethical challenges that society faces in dealing with peer-to-peer networks.

THE ROOT OF THE PROBLEM: CONFLICTING INCENTIVES

We argue that the root causes of the rapid rise of peer-to-peer filesharing of copyrighted materials belong more to the economic realm, than to the technical realm. To be sure, technology has acted as a primary catalyst in the development of peer-to-peer filesharing – but, far from being slanted toward nefarious purposes, digital technology has also facilitated economies of scale on the content provider side. In other words, technology has been agnostic, in that it has favored both sides equally. Conversely, economic tensions between end-users, software manufacturers, Internet Service Providers (ISPs) and content providers have given rise to current conflicts.

Technology as a Facilitator

It may be useful to recall what has fueled the massive dissemination of information we see today. First, digital storage has become extremely cheap: a 4 GB USB drive, which can roughly contain a full movie in DVD format, today sells for less than U.S. $15; optical storage, e.g., DVD, is about 100 times cheaper – $20 for 100 blank 4.7 GB DVDs was a common price at the time of this writing.

Second, replication and compression technologies have benefited from massive improvements in computing power and technology over the last decades. Average processor speeds have jumped from 100 MHz in the mid 1990s to 2-3 GHz in the late 2000s, an increase over 20-fold. At the same time, the development of compression technologies, such as MPEG Layer 3 (MP3) and MPEG-4 (and its derivatives such as the DivX or Xvid codecs), have made it possible to quickly transcode, compress, and store digital content using commodity hardware. For instance, compressing a full DVD into DivX format and storing the resulting video on a CD-ROM can now be done in mere hours using off-the-shelf hardware. Added to this, network access speeds have increased – another important factor that we will discuss in more detail later – and indeed, copying and transmitting content, including copyrighted content, has never been as easy as it is today.

Content providers have also benefited from these technological advances. Industry consortia indeed encouraged the digitization of most musical and video content. The Compact Disc format, which signaled a departure from more than a hundred years of analog recordings, was pushed to the forefront by consumer electronics manufacturers, and was enthusiastically adopted by content providers due to the potential economies of scale they could realize in the manufacturing process. In 2009, replicating 1,000 records (LPs) currently costs about $1,850; producing 1,000 CDs is about half as costly,[3] and these estimates likely include digitization of part of the process even in the case of LP pressing. Likewise, DVDs are considerably cheaper to produce than videotapes, yet are being sold at comparatively higher prices (even when adjusting for inflation) thanks to the inclusion of bonus contents and special features, made possible by the additional storage available on the medium.

In short, the development of new technology to copy, store, and transmit information rapidly has had economic benefits for all parties involved, by reducing content providers' manufacturing costs, and making it more practical for consumers to create data back-ups.

Digital Replication and the Change in the Rules of Engagement

While digitizing media and replicating digital content has become possible for the average user since the mid- to late-1990s, it could be argued that, at that point, nothing had changed much since the days of the Sony Betamax recorder. The Betamax allowed individuals to record programs of their choosing and replay them at a later time, presaging the considerable development of VCR devices.

Initially, the content industry was strongly opposed to Betamax technology, and in fact went all the way to the U.S. Supreme Court to make the case that the technology was a vital threat to their revenue model (Boyle, 2008). However, the U.S. Supreme Court disagreed, the Betamax paved the way for VCRs, and the content industry eventually realized that, far from threatening its business model, improved replication technology could in fact lead to new revenues, i.e., by creating a secondary market for movies through their video releases. In 2009, the size of the home video market is estimated to be about $7.5 billion,[4] down from about $9.2 billion in 2001 (Dana & Spier, 2001), but still considerable. On the other hand, the risk posed by the increased ease of unauthorized replication of content proved considerably exaggerated and was estimated by the industry itself at around $100 million in the 1980s.[5] This number is significant but it is small compared to the size of the whole industry, even when accounting for inflation and for the differences in the market size between the late 1980s and the early 2000s.

Thus, one would think that the development of digitization and peer-to-peer technology would be more warmly received by the content industry, which could certainly take advantage of novel revenue opportunities the way it took advantage of the ubiquity of VCRs in the 1990s. However, this has not been the case, and, as we will discuss later in the chapter, peer-to-peer technology in particular has been at the center stage of a number of legal battles. The key reason is that, while digitization in itself did not fundamentally change the rules of the game,[6] the advent of the Internet provided a massive distribution channel that did not exist before.

At the time of the Betamax recorder, copyright infringement was extremely limited in scale. While replicating a movie or a TV program was made much easier, *mass diffusion* of the replica was impractical for all but the most determined people. Sending copies of a movie for instance, required a person to manually replicate the movie, and then to either send the replicas by mail, or to sell them "under the table." Mailing the copies was costly and time consuming. Selling them under the table posed non-negligible risks such as police raids and easy prosecution. By providing a way to interconnect millions of computer systems, the Internet lowered these diffusion costs to zero. What was missing was a technology that could harness this ubiquitous connectivity and turn it into a massive diffusion channel for digital content; which is precisely what peer-to-peer software provided.

The Modern Five-Way Tussle

With replication *and* distribution costs of content nearing zero even for the average user, the content industry perceived a threat to its existing business model. Industry set out to eliminate this threat, both by fiercely combating the development of peer-to-peer technology in courts (and, as collateral effect, changing social norms), and by trying to limit its impact through technology. To paraphrase Clark et al. (2005), peer-to-peer filesharing technology set the ground for one of the major "tussles in cyberspace" between the different actors involved.

It would, however, be a mistake to reduce the peer-to-peer tussle to a tension only between content providers standing to lose their business revenue, and unscrupulous end users interested in obtaining free content. Specifically, the tussle taking place involves at least five actors, all with different incentives: content providers and end users, as noted earlier, but also consumer electronics manufacturers, software manufacturers, and Internet service providers.

End users have, in general, a fairly simple objective. They want to obtain the content they are interested in, at the smallest cost possible. Cost, here, however, does not solely mean pure monetary cost. For instance, obtaining a movie for free, but having to wait for 10 weeks for the download to complete may be much less satisfactory than paying a nominal price in order to obtain the same movie immediately, a phenomenon economists call "instant gratification."

As a case in point, in Europe and Asia, a large portion of peer-to-peer traffic consists of popular U.S. television shows: These shows are available on peer-to-peer networks the day after they are broadcasted, but, outside of the United States, are not available for legal downloading for several months. Rather than wait for the legal alternative, a large number of users prefer immediate downloads at the potential expense of copyright infringement.

To summarize, most users' preferences appear to be driven by a combination of monetary factors and convenience.[7] Economists and technologists have been trying to express user preferences through utility functions, which formalize how users value different situations. Precisely characterizing utility functions for peer-to-peer users may be quite challenging (Golle et al., 2001; Feldman et al., 2004; Christin & Chuang, 2005), but understanding what determines the evolution of the utility function may be all that is needed for a business to be economically successful. Indeed, adapting to the end-users' utility function proved successful in the past. At a time where sales of VHS recordings were prohibitively expensive for most (about $40-45 on average in the early 1980s), video rental stores emerged and were extremely successful thanks to their affordability and convenient service.

Particularly relevant to the discussion in this book is the question of ethical behavior as opposed to, or in intersection with, utility. Most users generally refrain from engaging in unethical activities, which rules out a large number of possible strategies. In particular, despite the potential for instant gratification and low cost, very few people walk out of a video store with stolen DVDs. On the other hand, most users do not view it as necessarily wrong to download music or movies from a peer-to-peer network. While the recording and movie industry have been arguing that downloading copyrighted materials is akin to stealing from a store, a large number of users have a different perception (Shang et al., 2008) – and instead view peer-to-peer downloads as closer to recording contents from a radio program or a TV program (Easley, 2005). As a result, users do not rule out downloading as a possible strategy in evaluating their own utility. Why do some users perceive walking out of a store with a DVD as stealing, but downloading a movie from a peer-to-peer network as acceptable?

Content providers such as movie studios or the recording industry argue that the rapid rise of peer-to-peer software combined with the ubiquity of digital media results in massive infringement, which in itself yields staggering revenue losses, evaluated in the vicinity of U.S. $1 billion per year by Liebowitz (2006). However, this estimate needs to be viewed with caution. First, others, such as Oberholzer-Gee and Strumpf (2007) reach different conclusions that do not seem to support the existence of sizeable losses. Second, even if we accept the premise of considerable losses, loss calculations are based on business models currently in place, and do not factor in new revenue streams made possible by the development of peer-to-peer technology. As a less controversial proposition, we postulate that, regardless of the magnitude of the realized losses, there is a certain perceived risk to the revenue stream of content providers, caused by the significant economic shift that peer-to-peer infrastructure has induced. The recent development of new business models, such as iTunes, which harness new diffusion capabilities, has been spearheaded by consumer electronics manufacturers like Apple and software companies such as RealNetworks or Microsoft, not by the content industry. The content industry still worries about the risks associated with a change in business model, and there is, in fact, still some reluctance from content providers to embrace such new business models, as evidenced by the much-publicized rift between Apple and Universal.[8]

The plot thickens when we consider *consumer electronics manufacturers*. These companies, which, as we mentioned, were opposing the content industry in the Sony Corp. v. Universal City studios "Betamax case," actually have a much more conflicted set of incentives. On the one hand, they fully stand to benefit from digitization and peer-to-peer networks. Indeed, digital replication requires faster computers and more disk space; at the same time it provides content, which makes portable hardware such as portable MP3 players useful. In that respect, the incentives of consumer electronics manufacturers and *software manufacturers* are aligned. As a particularly striking example, Apple's commercials ("Rip, mix, burn") put digitization as the new "killer" application to sell more software; but this software itself demands state-of-the-art hardware. In this particular case, the consumer electronics manufacturer and the software manufacturer are one and the same company, but more generally there may be a certain level of collusion (voluntary or not) between both entities. At the same time, hardware manufacturers cannot antagonize the content industry completely. Content is indeed, as discussed above, what most consumers want in the end. Hardware without content is of little interest to most segments of the population, and as such, hardware that does not support enough content is doomed to fail, regardless of its intrinsic qualities. Examples abound, but, perhaps ironically, a good example is the Betamax system itself, which was edged out of the market by the VHS standard, as soon as content providers decided to primarily use VHS.

Software manufacturers have a similarly complex set of incentives. We define peer-to-peer software in a large sense, comprising both programs running on personal computers, and indexing services running on remote servers, such as offered by YouTube, MiniNova or The Pirate Bay. Peer-to-peer software has value to customers, as it can reduce the cost of obtaining content (copyrighted or not) and that makes it a "must-have" program for end users as shown in surveys (Good et al., 2005). As such, peer-to-peer software can be relatively easily monetized. Indexing services can be made accessible through paying subscriptions, or can derive revenue for online advertising. Likewise, software programs can be sold (but then, at the risk of itself ending up being copied and distributed over peer-to-peer networks), or can produce advertising revenue to its manufacturer, as was, for instance, the case of the KaZaA peer-to-peer system. While a "free" version of KaZaA existed, it came with bundled software, including adware, whose providers paid Sharman Networks, the company that developed KaZaA, a fee to tie their programs to KaZaA. Interestingly enough, KaZaA itself showed that software, much like hardware, is only viable if content is available. As soon as content started to be difficult to access in KaZaA (due both to the legal threats, and the technological countermeasures, which we will discuss later), users switched to different peer-to-peer systems. To sum up the incentives of software manufacturers, content brings visibility; visibility can then foster business models even if the software or service itself is free. Outside the peer-to-peer realm, Google is the primary example of a service that has been immensely successful in generating derived revenue despite offering its core search service free of charge.

Finally, *Internet Service Providers* (ISP) have an even more ambiguous position. Peer-to-peer software requires consequent network capacity to be useful, particularly in the case of applications, such as BitTorrent, that reward contributions to the network. The situation was different in earlier decades. Relatively low bandwidth applications such as web access and email made up the bulk of Internet traffic. Higher bandwidth broadband connections like DSL and cable were in general not necessary for web or email, so that, by the end of the 1990s, Internet Service Providers had a hard time driving their customers to purchase broadband connectivity. Hence, although video compression technology was available, the lack of access network capacity led to very poor quality at the end-hosts, which in turn, hindered the development of a market for Internet-based video content.

Peer-to-peer networking changed the game as people bought increased network access in order to be able to download peer-to-peer content. As a matter of fact, the ability to download movies and multimedia content was heavily advertised. While stopping short of encouraging users to participate in copyright infringement, ISP advertisements have been, at the very least, ambiguous; encouraging users to sign up for "fast downloads," including access to "movies and music."[9]

As we will discuss in the next section, the content industry felt that Internet Service Providers were actually partly responsible for copyright violations, and tried to hold them liable for it. While attempting to hold Internet Service Providers liable for copyright violations only had mixed success in court, one outcome was clear. It made ISPs aware that an unconditional support of peer-to-peer infrastructures would essentially alienate the content industry.

In addition, from an economic standpoint, peer-to-peer systems are not necessarily lucrative for Internet Service Providers. If, indeed, peer-to-peer partly fostered the adoption of faster access links, this adoption finally allowed video services (e.g., YouTube) and other multimedia applications (particularly photo sharing) to soar, and led to a greater demand for access capacity from end users. In other words, peer-to-peer systems were great as a *bootstrapping* mechanism to initially drive the demand for bandwidth, but their impact on bandwidth demand is no longer as predominant as it once was. Furthermore, a profitable ISP is an ISP that sells access capacity that is not used. Assume that a given ISP sells 100 Mbps access to 100 customers. If all users transmit simultaneously up to the promised rate, the ISP needs 10 Gbps of capacity. If, however, most users are idle most of the time, the ISP is able to multiplex and significantly reduce its infrastructure costs. If customers use, on average 10% of their access capacity, the ISP should be able to only provision a 1 Gbps link. Web traffic lends itself well to multiplexing, because it consists mostly of short bursts of data transfers. On the other hand, peer-to-peer traffic, which typically consists of large file transfers[10], tends to heavy and prolonged usage. This is partly due to the TCP congestion control protocol, which tends to grant larger shares of network capacity to long-lived flows (Katabi et al., 2002). So, while peer-to-peer systems might have played an interesting role to attract new customers, their extensive use actually hurts the economic bottomline of Internet Service Providers, because the bandwidth usage of peer-to-peer networks does not fit the provisioning model used by ISPs for network planning.

To add to the ambiguity, recent years have seen a blurring of the roles of content providers and Internet Service Providers. For instance, consider the case of an entity that is both a cable service provider, as well as a broadband service provider. As an ISP, this entity stands to gain from the promise of free content offered by peer-to-peer systems; yet, if the content in question includes popular TV series, the cable division is at risk of losing customers. Such a situation is far from unique due to the increased integration of data services: Comcast in the United States, Orange in Europe, and Virgin Media in the UK are among the many operators that offer both services.[11]

With their complex incentive structure and possible conflicts of interest, it is not surprising that ISPs' positions have not generally been transparent to customers. In a well-publicized incident (Eckersley et al., 2007), it was discovered that Comcast was aggressively filtering BitTorrent traffic without having previously informed its customers. Worse, Comcast was using strategies akin to denial-of-service attacks. Public outrage persuaded Comcast to eventually relent. Other ISPs (e.g., Verizon) have been forced to turn over names of potential copyright infringers to law enforcement agencies despite fighting court injunctions to do so. In these cases, end users felt betrayed by the ISP, whom they thought was "on their side" when in fact the reality was markedly different.

A BRIEF REVIEW OF LEGAL ISSUES AND REMEDIES IN P2P NETWORKS

In the five-way tussle just described, all participants try to tip the scale in their favor using different strategies. Of particular interest to the discussion in this chapter, are the strategies employed by the content industry to achieve its goals. Defensive strategies against the perceived threat of peer-to-peer networks can be categorized into economic, legal, and technological strategies. Economic defenses are often overlooked as an old saying goes, "You can't beat free." That is, if content replication and diffusion has a negligible cost to end users, it will be difficult for the content industry to provide economic incentives against copyright infringement. While such propositions neglect the possibility that new business models, such as models in which revenue comes from advertising derived from content, they have colored the perception of the content industry that legal and technological recourse are the most promising avenues to win the tussle. In this section, we provide a brief summary of copyright law, and discuss the liability issues at hand, before summarizing the legal actions pursued by the content industry. We point out that this section is heavily colored with U.S. law. Other countries present differences that, in the interest of brevity, we do not discuss here. For an abridged treatment of international copyright laws, we refer the interested reader to Gassner (2005).

Relevant Elements of U.S. Copyright Law

In the United States, the Copyright Act of 1976 defines copyright. Copyright applies to works of authorship, such as literary works, including software, which is considered as literary work in this context, pictorial work (e.g., movies, photographs), and musical works. The copyright owner is usually the author of the work, with the caveat that the employer of the author may be entitled to copyright as well, if the work has been performed "for hire." In the United States, copyright automatically applies, by default, to any work of authorship that is (1) an original work, and that is (2) fixed in a tangible medium. However, authors must register to be able to sue. Copyright owners are, among other things, granted exclusive rights to prepare derivative works (including translations), and to publicly perform, display or broadcast the work. Directly related to the discussion in this chapter, copyright owners are also granted *exclusive rights to reproduce work in copies and to distribute copies to the public*. Furthermore, copyright owners are also provided with some rights to control the acts of those who facilitate or contribute to copyright infringement.

The Digital Millennium Copyright Act does not fundamentally change the rights of the copyright holders, but amends the Copyright Act of 1976 to (1) criminalize production and dissemination of technology that can circumvent measures taken to protect copyright (e.g., it becomes illegal to defeat copy-protection mechanisms for instance) and to (2) heighten the penalties for copyright infringement on the Internet.

Limitations and Fair Use Doctrine

There are limitations on the set of exclusive rights granted to copyright owners. These include personal backup copies and library-archival copying along with specific exceptions such as the right to play a radio in a restaurant without it being considered a "public performance." Most importantly, the concept of "fair use" defines a large category of exceptions to copyright. The main challenge is that what constitutes fair use is relatively open to interpretation. Indeed, prior to the Copyright Act of 1976, fair use was only defined by common law in the United States. The Copyright Act of 1976 made the definition a bit clearer, by requiring a balancing test consisting of at least the following four criteria to determine whether a specific usage of a work characterizes as fair use:

1. the purpose and character of the use, including whether such use is of a commercial
2. nature or is for nonprofit educational purposes;
3. the nature of the copyrighted work;
4. the amount and substantiality of the portion used in relation to the copyrighted work as a whole; and
5. the effect of the use upon the potential market for or value of the copyrighted work. (Copyright Act of 1976, p. 107)

In general, fair use applies primarily to scholastic citations for reference or critique. The last criterion proves particularly interesting to our discussion, because it ties in economic value to the notion of copyright.

Primary and Secondary Liability

Most important to the issue at hand in this chapter is the question of liability. When a copyrighted work is illegitimately distributed over the Internet, who is legally responsible? While this question, as a whole, remains an open problem as argued by Taipale (2003), it is useful to distinguish between two classes of liability in copyright infringement: primary liability, where the perpetrator directly violates one of the exclusive rights granted to the copyright holder; and secondary liability, where the perpetrator does not directly abuse these rights, but either facilitates infringement by providing active support to the person infringing (*contributory infringement*), or indirectly exerts benefits, e.g., obtains monetary rewards, from infringement (*vicarious infringement*).

This distinction raises an ethical problem. As our brief economic discussion showed, one can make the case that, to some extent, a large number of parties indirectly benefit from peer-to-peer traffic and could therefore be liable for secondary infringement. Unfortunately, the law only imperfectly specifies whether punishment is needed, who should be punished, and to which extent.

Liability and P2P File-Sharing

Copyright holders have two legal remedies at their disposal: (a) going after the primary infringers, i.e., the end users who exchange copyrighted material over peer-to-peer networks in violation of the exclusive rights of the copyright holders, and/or (b) going after entities that can be held liable under secondary liability criteria. These include software manufacturers (including designers of online content indexing services such as The Pirate Bay, MiniNova, YouTube), consumer electronics manufacturers, and Internet Service Providers.

At first glance, it seems that identifying primary infringers is relatively easy. After all, end users downloading or uploading music to peer-to-peer networks do so without authorization, and could easily be held liable for it. However, the issue is not as simple.

First of all, some, including Charles Nesson, a Harvard Law School professor, have argued that peer-to-peer filesharing essentially falls under fair use, as the four criteria are only illustrative and not a complete test.[12] This argument has been used in defense of Joel Tenenbaum, a student who was sued for sharing 30 songs on the KaZaA network. This defense has gained little traction, and has been ultimately unsuccessful – Tenenbaum was convicted and fined $675,000,[13]and reportedly plans to appeal the verdict.

A much thornier issue lies in the notion of control, i.e., whether willful infringement can be proven easily. On the uploading side, suppose a user participates in a peer-to-peer network, and mistakenly shares a portion of his or her hard drive where legitimately purchased music is stored. Should the user be held liable? As we will discuss in a subsequent section, misconfigurations are far from being an exception, as users frequently share data unknowingly, as shown by Good & Krekelberg (2003). If we allow the premise that users may not be held liable for configuration mistakes, the question becomes one of showing active intent to share data – which is considerably more difficult to prove.

If, on the other hand, we consider that users should be in complete control of their systems at all times, we then make users responsible for all possible security vulnerabilities present on their machines, as a single security vulnerability can give full access to the system to a remote unauthorized party. However, most security vulnerabilities are due to faulty software, rather than user mistakes, and liability is, here too, difficult to assess. If Software A is exploitable, e.g., because no software patch exists or because installing a patch is beyond the expertise of most casual users, is it the user's responsibility to ensure Software A does not run on their computer? What if Software A is actually a critical piece of software, e.g., the operating system?

On the downloading side, one could think that the responsibility should be clearer. After all, downloaders are copying work that they do not own. Yet, the same issues of control that apply to uploading entities can apply to downloading entities. That is, it is very difficult to prove with absolute certainty that a specific user was indeed in control of the machine when a download took place. For example, one can easily show that a machine on Bob's computer network downloaded a song – but that does not necessarily mean that Bob was the person downloading the song. It could as well have been Alice, his wife, using Bob's computer, Mallory, a malicious third-party who gained unauthorized access to Bob's computer, e.g., through a virus, or even Eve, a neighbor who simply took a free ride on Bob's unprotected wireless network, and made it look like, from the outside world, Bob was actually downloading the file. Actually proving that Bob was responsible for the download is considerably difficult.

In the context of secondary liability, the discussion is even more complex. Consumer electronics manufacturers have, thus far, by and large escaped the ire of content producers in the context of peer-to-peer networks. They argue, for instance, that it is difficult to say that a vendor of MP3 players vicariously benefits from peer-to-peer systems, as there are plenty of other, legal, sources of MP3 music, including personal backups of CDs and online music stores. On the other hand, Internet Service Providers and software manufacturers have faced legal pressures from the content industry. Both have been accused of contributory and vicarious infringement. As discussed in our section on incentives, ISPs profit to some extent from peer-to-peer networks by enticing users to purchase additional broadband connectivity. Peer-to-peer software manufacturers stand to gain from the use of their software or service. And, as we have mentioned before, content is the main driver for use. Here again, however, showing actual intent to benefit or contribute to infringement is relatively difficult, and has not always been successful.

Legal Strategies against Peer-to-Peer Networks

The content industry initially focused its legal strategies against the peer-to-peer software providers. Shortly after the Napster service was started in 1999, several companies, including A&M Records, sued Napster on grounds of vicarious and contributory infringement. Napster was eventually shut down following the decision of the 9th Circuit Court of Appeals.[14]

Subsequently, various content providers sued software companies that were providing peer-to-peer software. Some of these cases gained extreme visibility. MGM v. Grokster/Streamcast,[15] went all the way to the United States Supreme Court. In Universal Music Australia v. Sharman Networks,[16] about thirty copyright holders sued the makers of the KaZaA software. The Federal Court of Australia ultimately decided the case.

The main lessons are that, the courts have generally sided with copyright holders, and have held software manufacturers responsible for secondary infringement. However, the court decisions have also outlined the difficulties of rendering judgment in these cases. For instance, the MGM vs. Grokster decision rejected the fair use argument from Grokster and its allies, stating "We hold that one who distributes a device with the object of promoting its use to infringe copyright, as shown by the clear expression or other affirmative steps taken to foster infringement, is liable for the resulting acts of infringement by third parties."[17] Rather than bringing finality to the debate, this decision actually shifted the problem to defining "clear expression" and "affirmative steps." If Streamcast and Grokster had been less aggressive in their marketing, would the outcome have been the same?

Also, courts have repeatedly refused to declare any specific piece of software illegal. That is, the use of a peer-to-peer system may be illegal, and may in fact cause the designer of the peer-to-peer system to be held liable for secondary copyright infringement in some cases (e.g., if they have taken the "affirmative steps" to promote infringement), but writing peer-to-peer software, in itself, is not illegal. Thus, when faced with decentralized networks supported by free software like eMule or Gnutella, the content industry could not simply sue the individuals that had contributed to the software (many of whom are outside U.S. jurisdiction). They instead applied legal pressure on the other two actors in the tussle: ISPs and end users.

In the United States, ISPs are conditionally protected from secondary liability by a safe harbor clause (17 U.S.C. § 512, 1998); namely, they cannot be held liable for data that merely pass through their networks, as long as they do not make a profit from it, are unaware of the violation before being notified, and respond immediately to "take-down" notices. We note that this law predates the rise of peer-to-peer systems, and was intended to target services where, for instance, an ISP providing web hosting had some of its customers post copyrighted materials on their webpages. In the context of peer-to-peer networks, this law has led the content industry to send take-down notices to ISPs, asking them to provide a list of infringers. Indeed, the only information available publicly about infringers is their IP addresses. Mapping an IP address to an actual individual is not possible without the help of the ISP that owns the IP address. In many cases, ISPs have fought off such requests, citing privacy concerns, but most have been forced to comply.

Armed with lists of potential infringers, copyright holders have then taken steps to directly sue individuals as primary infringers. This strategy is interesting, in that it is more of an economic strategy than a legal one. Indeed, the key idea is to impose significant monetary damages on infringers in order to deter them from using peer-to-peer software. For instance, Universal requested that Marie Lindor pay $750 in punitive damages per track she downloaded, when the actual damages were estimated at about 70 cents per song.[18] Most of the cases were settled out-of-court for a few thousand dollars in total. Among the cases that did in fact go to court, was that of Jammie Thomas, who was fined $222,000 for sharing over 1,500 tracks on the KaZaA network. The judgment was later overturned and a mistrial declared. The new trial, finally held in June 2009 resulted in an increase of the penalty to U.S. $1.92 million, or about $80,000 per song.[19] Thomas has appealed. Both Thomas and Tenenbaum, whom we mentioned earlier, face bankruptcy if the penalties are held on appeal.

While the magnitude of the potential fines has had a deterrent effect on some users, Bhattacharjee et al. (2006) question the actual effectiveness of the deterrent on users sharing small numbers of files. They claim that legal action had overall no noticeable impact on file availability. In addition, the content industry also suffered tremendously from bad publicity linked to suing "grandmothers,"[20] and has, so far, only won two court cases (the aforementioned Thomas and Tenenbaum cases), whose appeals were pending at the time of this writing.

Finally, a more recent line of legal attack has been to put pressure on owners of websites, such as The Pirate Bay,[21] that support searches for peer-to-peer networks. We grouped these content indexing service providers with software manufacturers earlier, but while legal action against program designers has diminished, content indexing services have been increasingly targeted. The problem with this strategy is that such websites can be replaced relatively easily, and suing the owners, as in the case of The Pirate Bay can actually turn into a public relations nightmare. As a case in point, in response to the lawsuit against The Pirate Bay, a "Pirate Party" was created in Sweden and ran in the 2009 European Parliamentary Elections on a platform advocating copyright and patent law reform.

Having a political party solely running on a copyright reform platform outlines one key concern with the legal issues outlined thus far: the ethical dilemma they present. First, users are still not convinced that downloading copyrighted materials off the Internet is "wrong." In fact, whether the strategy of suing individuals for primary copyright infringement has been a success is open to interpretation, as peer-to-peer transfers have not slowed down much (Kargiannis et al., 2004), and the legal strategy came at a public relations cost. The fact that peer-to-peer activity persists despite the increased legal threats to users, and repeated attempts at education through commercials and advertisements, shows that the public does not perceive copyright infringement as a serious crime (Easley, 2005), and that social norms are actually not playing in favor of copyright holders. This ethical question is the primary reason behind the rise of the Pirate Party and similar movements that argue that, instead, it is the law that is "wrong" and must be changed. Second, as discussed above, many different parties can technically be held liable to some extent. The law does not distinguish between the different degrees of liability, so it is up to the copyright holders and the courts to decide whom to punish, and to which extent. Compared to the legal argument of what constitutes infringement, both ethical discussions of where the responsibilities lie, and to which extent should each party be held responsible, have received little attention. We do argue, however, that, in absence of stronger social norms, the situation is unlikely to change. That is, only the most risk-averse users will refrain from exchanging copyrighted materials over peer-to-peer networks; others will run a simple cost/benefit analysis as described before, and may not even necessarily be convinced that the activities in which they are engaging are of questionable legality.

Using Technology to Mitigate the P2P "THREAT"

Well aware of the limits of a defensive strategy resting on pure legal grounds, copyright holders have also been aggressively pushing technology to alleviate the perceived threat posed by peer-to-peer networks. Here, the objective is to prevent the diffusion from copyrighted materials already present in the network by either making content difficult to find, or difficult to download.

We purposely do not discuss Digital Rights Management technologies aiming at preventing content from being copied in the first place. Indeed, such technologies are generally flawed, in that no DRM technology is 100% effective. As argued by Felten[22], all DRM technologies are vulnerable to the fact that content has to be decoded at some point to be usable, and that decoded content can be replicated. However, with the advent of peer-to-peer technology, DRM has to be foolproof to be viable as a protection mechanism for copyright holders, as a single copy can be propagated to millions of users immediately. As a result, while content providers have been using DRM technologies in an effort to reduce copyright infringement, they have been relatively unsuccessful thus far, and have, by and large, combined any DRM protection with defenses directly targeted at peer-to-peer infrastructures.

There are two major components to any peer-to-peer infrastructure: indexing, which tells peers where desired content is located, and transmission, which is the mechanism by which peers acquire content once it has been located. As illustrated by the Napster episode, compromising either of the components (in Napster's case, the indexing infrastructure) can result in a quick demise of a given peer-to-peer network.

In this section, we first discuss technologies that primarily aim to incapacitate specific hosts, in charge of indexing or serving data that can violate copyrights. The interesting aspect of this group of techniques is that some implementations are essentially a form of denial-of-service (DoS) attack, whose legality is itself suspect, as we discuss in more details below.

We then look at an alternative proposal, also in use, which targets search mechanisms by making content hard to find, but without assaulting specific hosts. This technique, called "poisoning", and studied in depth by Christin et al. (2005), relies on drowning peer-to-peer searches in a large amount of useless information. Rather than compromising network participants, poisoning is usually done by voluntarily injecting extraneous data in the peer-to-peer network. As such, poisoning may circumvent some of the legal doubts surrounding denial-of-service, and can additionally permit selective targeting (e.g., of a specific artist, song, or movie), but it comes at the expense of potential overload in the network.

A Primer on Peer-to-Peer Structure

Before we delve into the technical details of interdiction technologies, it may be useful to recall how most peer-to-peer services operate. As discussed in Christin et al. (2005), a large number of popular peer-to-peer networks, including Gnutella, eDonkey, and FastTrack, use two-tiered hierarchical topologies. In these hierarchies, nodes are split between leaf nodes and hubs – called "ultrapeers" in Gnutella, "supernodes" in FastTrack, and "servers" in eDonkey. Leaf nodes only maintain connections to a handful of hubs, while hubs maintain connections with hundreds or thousands of leaves, and with many other hubs.

Figure 1 shows the relationship between hubs and leaves. Each hub node serves as a centralized index for the leaf nodes to which it is connected. Whenever a leaf node issues a query, the leaf node first sends the query to the hub(s) to which the leaf node is connected. If the item requested is not present in the index maintained by the hub(s), the hub forwards the query to other hubs. BitTorrent, which was not studied in Christin et al. (2005), has a similar two-tiered structure, where hubs are referred to as "trackers." Originally, BitTorrent supported a centralized tracker, which was hosted on a single machine. The more recent versions of the BitTorrent protocol support "decentralized trackers," which spread the tracking tasks over several hosts that communicate with each other.

Most current peer-to-peer networks use this kind of two-level hierarchy. A notable exception are peer-to-peer networks solely based on distributed hash tables (DHT), such as Kademlia (Maymounkov & Mazières, 2002). DHT networks are decentralized, flat networks, which rely on a hashing function associating each item (e.g., search term, file) to a hash value. Items are then stored over one or several nodes according to their hash values, which greatly increases the efficiency of look-up and indexing. The specifics of the hashing and repartition functions used depend on the specific network under consideration, and have as an objective to provide better load balancing and faster search compared to hierarchical networks. An example of a DHT network is the Overnet network, but, interestingly, Overnet shares content with the eDonkey network so that the hierarchical indexing is indirectly used in Overnet as well.

Figure 1. Peer-to-peer network structure

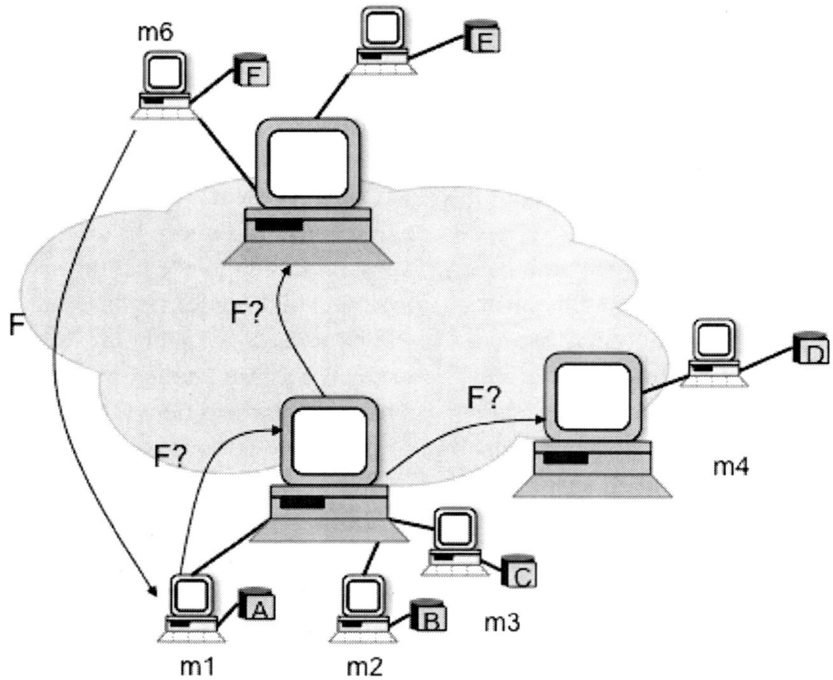

Proposed Interdiction Technologies

Among the many companies engaging in "interdiction" methods, Macrovision Corporation submitted a number of interdiction technologies to the U.S. patent office (Moore et al., 2004, Levin & Disher, 2004). Rather than disserting on the merits or originality of the patent applications, we point out that the interesting feature of these documents is that they formally express what many users suspected was taking place, without having firm evidence of it actually happening. We summarize the technical content of these patent applications briefly considering the potential impact of the described techniques on existing peer-to-peer networks.

We can categorize the proposed mechanisms using the three types of attacks they implement: man-in-the-middle attack, a poisoning attack, similar to what Christin et al. (2005) and Liang et al. (2005) described in their academic works, and a partitioning attack. These terms are borrowed from the network security jargon, and are not used *as is* in the patent applications.

Man-in-the-Middle Attack

A man-in-the-middle attack is an attack on two entities communicating, whereby an intruder independently makes connections with both entities, and impersonates the other entity to both communicants. A similar principle is behind the first set of mechanisms proposed to control peer-to-peer traffic. The key idea here is to infiltrate the network with malicious nodes, which reroute query traffic to a third-party controlled server and database. When responses to a query match a record indicating a protected (copyrighted) item in the database, the server can modify the query results to:

- point to invalid peers, which can be either non-existent IP addresses, or IP addresses of hosts not participating in the network, or
- point to incorrect files, that is, either decoys hosted by the server, or files present in the network, which do not match the requested content; e.g., someone trying to download a song by Madonna could end up receiving a picture of a dog instead.

Details on how, in practice, traffic can be rerouted unbeknownst to the users are discussed in a related patent application (Levin & Disher, 2004).

Partitioning Attack

A second set of mechanisms aims to isolate nodes that serve infringing content, by surrounding them with malicious nodes in the peer-to-peer topology. The malicious nodes can then "quarantine" each offending node by, for instance, dropping all query traffic coming to that node, which results in making the infringing content unavailable to the rest of the network.

The interesting aspect of this attack lies in the implementation details the patent application discloses. In practice, one has to first disconnect existing connections between peers to insert malicious nodes at the appropriate locations in the network. For the disconnection phase, the partitioning attack includes techniques such as (Moore et al., 2004):

- "overwhelming the capacity of [the targeted] node[…]'s connection to [its neighbor] by bombarding it with messages or requests it must parse", or
- "eliminating or disconnecting N1 [a node adjacent to the targeted node] […] by exploiting a known defect in the client software application."

While the specific techniques used to achieve these goals are not disclosed in the patent application, they implement what is commonly known as a denial-of-service attack. For instance, the former could, in practice, be implemented by techniques such as TCP SYN flooding similar to those described in Lemon (2002). It is quite surprising to find such statements in a U.S. patent application, as they seem to be in violation of U.S. law. More precisely, the Computer Fraud and Abuse Act (CFAA, 18 U.S.C. § 1030 (1984)) makes it an offense to "intentionally access a protected computer without authorization, and as a result of such conduct, cause damage," which makes the first technique of flooding a host with unsolicited requests illegal. The CFAA also makes it illegal to "knowingly cause […] the transmission of a program, information, code, or command, and as a result of such conduct, intentionally cause […] damage without authorization, to a protected computer," (CFAA, section (a)(5)(A)) which seemingly makes the second technique equally illegal.

If the peer happens to be in the United States, both of the techniques described above would therefore appear to be in violation of CFAA. Perhaps more puzzlingly, peers might not have to serve infringing files to be targeted, according to the description of the attack. Being "in the wrong place, at the wrong time," i.e., too close topologically to an infringing peer is sufficient.

Poisoning Attack

A third category of mechanisms detailed in the patent application implements poisoning attacks. A poisoning attack is characterized by nodes serving bogus, synthesized decoys whose metadata matches the description of infringing content, but which contain unsuitable data (e.g., white noise). Such attacks were first proposed in a different patent (Hale & Manes, 2004).

Whether the poisoning attack discussed is really new, especially compared to the technique discussed in (Hale & Manes, 2004), is unclear, but some of the proposed variants are interesting:

- "File transfer attenuation" consists of malicious nodes serving (potentially correct) files with a transmission speed decreasing as a function of time, ultimately halting completely right before the whole file has been uploaded. Here, the goal is obviously to maximize user frustration.
- "Hash spoofing" consists of advertising files (or file chunks) with a hash corresponding to a valid file, when in fact the file (or file chunk) is corrupted, or contains bogus content. Contrary to a common misconception, hash spoofing does not necessarily require breaking strong cryptographic primitives. In most peer-to-peer networks, the hash is indeed merely advertised along with the metadata of the file. Hence, simply advertising fake metadata suffices to implement hash spoofing. Since the advertised and the actual hash do not match, hash spoofing generally results in a peer-to-peer client inferring that a network error occurred during transmission of the file. In the case of a naive implementation, hash spoofing can lead the client to request the corrupted file again, with the same results. Here again, the primary goal is to maximize user frustration.

Comments

Most of the mechanisms described in Moore et al. (2004) rely on the ability to infiltrate the peer-to-peer network with malicious hubs, in order to manipulate the results peers obtain in response to search queries. In highly distributed peer-to-peer filesharing systems (e.g., KaZaA/FastTrack, and Gnutella), where promotion to hub is relatively frequent and generally not monitored, the proposed interdiction mechanisms could be particularly effective.

However, man-in-the-middle attacks are much more difficult to carry out in more centralized networks, such as eDonkey, which rely only on a few dozens of supernodes ("servers"). Indeed, the modest number of servers makes newcomers particularly obvious, and network infiltration problematic. In contrast to FastTrack and Gnutella, effectively infiltrating networks like eDonkey is further complicated by the fact that users can manually choose to which server(s) their peers connect.

Likewise, setting up partitioning attacks in a highly centralized network reduces to launching a denial-of-service attack on the infringing node or the server to which it connects. In the extreme, in a peer-to-peer filesharing system such as BitTorrent, where a centralized tracker is in charge of coordinating the progress of all transfers, taking down the tracker might be the most effective strategy.

On the other hand, it is interesting to note that some of the mechanisms we classified as "poisoning attacks" (file transfer attenuation and hash spoofing) can apply to most (if not all) existing peer-to-peer networks. Their effectiveness, however, once again depends on the ability of the poisoning entity to infiltrate the peer-to-peer network.

Also, except for mentioning that malicious nodes avoid expulsion from the network by frequently changing IP addresses, the patent application (Moore et al., 2004) contains very little detail concerning the defenses that malicious peers need to implement to evade detection. With the proliferation of automated blacklists of peers known to be malicious, and ever improving distributed reputation systems used to rate the integrity of other peers and the contents they transmit, e.g., (Walsh & Gün Sirer, 2006), one may wonder for how long the techniques presented in this patent application will be effective.

Finally, the proposed technological defenses also present considerable ethical dilemmas. Even setting aside the questionable legality of some of the defenses presented here, how do we ensure that these defenses are used only to target "undesirable" traffic? More specifically, what defines "undesirable" traffic? Our discussion so far has mostly revolved around copyright issues, but the techniques presented here can apply to any kind of peer-to-peer traffic. Defining which traffic is "undesirable" is likely to be based on social norms and legal grounds, which differ from one country to the next, while on the other hand peer-to-peer networks are usually not contained within geopolitical borders.[23] For instance, contents considered subversive in China may be protected under the First Amendment in the United States. So, is it legitimate for a Chinese computer to poison networks hosted in the United States? Likewise, copyright laws in the United States may protect some materials that are not protected in some other countries, or whose protection has a much narrower scope. Is it then legitimate for a U.S. based entity to attack hosts situated in a different country on grounds that they are facilitating infringement on U.S. soil?

Beyond Copyright Enforcement

Peer-to-peer networks are not limited to exchanging copyrighted materials. As we discussed in the introduction to this chapter, they have many beneficial uses, including promoting free speech, or reducing infrastructure costs for software providers.

But, beyond copyright infringement issues, peer-to-peer systems also create puzzling challenges for the community. With so many hosts connected to each other, information leaks can propagate at extremely high speed. Indeed, in Japan for instance, nuclear plant floor maps or databases of crime victims ended up on the Winny peer-to-peer network,[24] after a virus targeting the Winny software was found to upload the victims' entire hard drive on the network.[25] Similarly, Good & Krekelberg (2003) showed that inadvertent information sharing on peer-to-peer networks was very common, with some peer-to-peer users' credit card statements or mortgage documents being shared on the KaZaA network.

Unfortunately, once data start being replicated on a peer-to-peer network, it is all but impossible to "take it back." Thus, the only possible defense is to limit its diffusion as much as possible. On the bright side, most users of peer-to-peer networks have no interest in accessing such confidential data, so that propagation on the peer-to-peer network is relatively limited even in the absence of counter-measures.[26] As a result, techniques like the poisoning techniques discussed above may be particularly effective to further impede the diffusion of confidential data.

CONCLUSION

In this chapter, we have discussed how economic incentives led to the establishment of a "tussle" between the different actors involved in peer-to-peer networks. We have shown that, to try to win the tussle, the content industry has used a pretty extensive legal arsenal, with relatively limited success thus far. We have also shown some of the technological countermeasures in place to attempt to limit dissemination of copyrighted materials in peer-to-peer networks. We have shown, however, that some of these technologies appear themselves to break the law. In addition, the proposed countermeasures may work to some extent, but are likely most applicable when targeted at specific items with small propagation (e.g., private information leakages) rather than widely distributed movies or songs.

While we have tried to paint a picture of the tussle as neutral as possible, our conclusion is that the tussle probably will not come to a resolution without the intervention of legislators. None of the legal or technological remedies against copyright infringement appear to be working satisfactorily. Peer-to-peer traffic is more predominant than ever on the Internet, driven by the widespread availability of hardware and network connectivity. Copyright reform seems necessary and could lead to new business models, in the same way the "legalization" of the Betamax technology paved the way for the home video industry.

On June 7, 2009, the Pirate Party of Sweden gained 7% of the votes in the European Parliamentary elections and will have one representative seated in Brussels. More significantly, 19% of the voters younger than 30 years old cast a vote in favor of the Pirate Party.[27] While the name of the party may elicit a smile, these new developments show that the issue of copyright reform has now been put in the spotlight more than ever. Likewise, the surprising initial rejection by the French National Assembly of the Hadopi law, which advocates "gradual response" against copyright infringers culminating in a loss of right to use the Internet, grabbed the headlines. While the law was eventually adopted, these events again demonstrated the importance to society of the debate about copyright reform.

Besides copyright reform, the emergence of peer-to-peer networks presents us with considerable ethical challenges. Defining acceptable use, assigning liabilities, and establishing acceptable punishments for misuse all pose legal and ethical questions that we need to answer. Given the large amount of peer-to-peer traffic that is infringing copyright, there seems to be a large disconnect between acceptable social norms and legal behavior. The content industry is trying to reduce this disconnect through aggressive advertising campaigns, including messages on DVD informing customers that illegal downloads are a crime. But the fact that peer-to-peer traffic persists tends to show this education strategy is not successful, as most users remain unconvinced that copyright infringement is a serious offense (Easley, 2005). Even if we agree that copyright infringement is a criminal offense, we have shown that peer-to-peer networks involve a large number of actors, besides end users, that stand to indirectly profit from infringement. Who should then be held liable? And last, in terms of punishment, both the legal and technological remedies invite reflection. As far as legal sanctions are concerned, appropriately quantifying the amount of monetary losses suffered and fairly defining the punitive damages are both challenging. Is it acceptable to use large monetary punishments for the sake of deterrence? From a technological standpoint, is it ever acceptable to launch denial-of-service attacks against some users? Is suspected copyright infringement enough of a justification? When considering leaks of private or sensitive data in peer-to-peer networks, should we consider the level of confidentiality of the information in our decision to deploy countermeasures? Can we authorize such attacks while at the same time guaranteeing freedom of speech may not be threatened?

We do not claim to have answers to these questions, at this stage. While we can point out the conditions in which certain technical countermeasures may be more effective than others (Christin et al., 2005), we firmly believe that the issue of information flow control that has been posed by the emergence of peer-to-peer networks, will require considerable thought, and will be one of the more important technological challenges of the 21st century.

ACKNOWLEDGMENT

This chapter greatly benefited from the feedback and suggestions of several anonymous reviewers, and from discussions with John Chuang, Andreas Weigend, Alexandre Mateus, Joe Hall, Jens Grossklags, Keiji Takeda, and the students at Carnegie Mellon CyLab Japan, among many others. Part of this presentation is derived from notes the author contributed to the blog of Pam Samuleson's peer-to-peer seminar at UC Berkeley, which was held in the Spring of 2005.

REFERENCES

Act, C. (1976). 17 U.S.C. § 101-122. *Pub., L*, 94–553.

Basher, N., Mahanti, A., Mahanti, A., Williamson, C., & Arlitt, M. (2008). A comparative analysis of web and peer-to-peer traffic. In *Proceedings of the 2008 WWW Conference*. Beijing, China.

Bhattacharjee, S., Lertwachara, K., Gopal, R., & Marsden, J. (2006). Impact of legal threats on online music sharing activity: An analysis of music industry legal actions. *The Journal of Law & Economics*, *49*(1), 91–114. doi:10.1086/501085

Boyle, J. (2008). *The public domain: Enclosing the commons of the mind*. New Haven, CT: Yale University Press.

Christin, N., & Chuang, J. (2005). A cost-based analysis of overlay routing geometries. In *Proceedings of IEEE INFOCOM'05* (Vol. 4., pp. 2566-2577). Miami, FL.

Christin, N., Weigend, A., & Chuang, J. (2005) Content availability, pollution, and poisoning in peer-to-peer file sharing networks. In *Proceedings of the Sixth ACM Conference on Electronic Commerce* (pp. 68-77). Vancouver, BC, Canada.

Clark, D., Wroclawski, J., Sollins, K., & Braden R. (2005). Tussle in cyberspace: Defining tomorrow's internet. *IEEE/ACM Transactions on Networking, 13*(3), 462-475.

Computer Fraud and Abuse Act, 18 U.S.C. §1030 (1984).

Dana, J., & Spier, K. (2001). Revenue sharing and vertical control in the video rental industry. *The Journal of Industrial Economics*, *49*(3), 223–245.

Easley, R. (2005). Ethical issues in the music industry response to innovation and piracy. *Journal of Business Ethics*, *62*, 163–168. doi:10.1007/s10551-005-0187-3

Eckersley, P., von Lohmann, F., & Schoen, S. (2007). Packet forgery by ISPs: A report on the Comcast affair. Electronic Frontier Foundation online report. Retrieved from http://www.eff.org/wp/packet-forgery-isps-report-comcast-affair.

Feldman, M., Lai, K., Stoica, I., & Chuang, J. (2004). Robust incentive techniques for peer-to-peer networks. In Proceedings of the *Fifth ACM Conference on Electronic Commerce (EC'04)* (pp. 102-111). New York, NY.

Gassner, U. (2005). Copyright and digital media in a post-Napster world: International Supplement. Retrieved from SSRN: http://ssrn.com/abstract=655391 or DOI: 10.2139/ssrn.655391

Golle, P., Leyton-Brown, K., Mironov, I., & Lillibridge, M. (2001). Incentives for sharing in peer-to-peer networks. In *Proceedings of the Second International Workshop on Electronic Commerce*. L. Fiege, G. Mühl, and U. G. Wilhelm (Eds.), Lecture Notes in Computer Science, Vol. 2232. (pp. 75-87). Springer-Verlag, London.

Good, N., Dhamija, R., Grossklags, J., Thaw, D., Aronowitz, S., Mulligan, D., & Konstan, J. (2005). Stopping spyware at the gate: A user study of privacy, notice and spyware. In *Proceedings of the First Symposium on Usable Privacy and Security (SOUPS)*. Pittsburgh, PA, USA.

Good, N., & Krekelberg, A. (2003). Usability and privacy: A study of Kazaa P2P file-sharing. In *Proceedings of the ACM Symposium on Human Computer Interaction (CHI)*. Fort Lauderdale, FL, U.S.A.

Hale, J., & Manes, G. (2004) Method to inhibit the identification and retrieval of proprietary media via automated search engines. U.S. Patent number: 6732180. Filing date: Aug 8, 2000. Issue date: May 4, 2004

Karagiannis, T., Broido, A., Brownlee, N., Claffy, K. C., & Faloutsos, M. (2004). Is P2P dying or just hiding? In *Proceedings of IEEE Globecom 2004*. Dallas, TX, USA.

Karagiannis, T., Rodriguez, P., & Papagiannaki, K. (2005). Should internet service providers fear peer-assisted content distributions? In *Proceedings of the 2005 ACM/USENIX Internet Measurement Conference*. Berkeley, CA, USA

Katabi, D., Handley, M., & Rohrs, C. (2002). Congestion control for high bandwidth-delay product networks. In *Proceedings of the 2002 ACM SIGCOMM Conference.* Pittsburgh, PA, USA

Lemon, J. (2002) Resisting SYN flood DoS attacks with a SYN cache. In *Proceedings of USENIX BSDCON 2002*. San Francisco, CA.

Levin, S., & Disher, J. (2004). System and methods for communicating over the Internet with geographically distributed devices of a decentralized network using transparent asymmetric return paths. U.S. Patent Application number 10/869,208, publication number 2005/0089014.

Liang, J., Kumar, R., Xi, Y., & Ross, K. (2005) Pollution in P2P filesharing systems. In *Proceedings of IEEE INFOCOM'05*, Miami, FL.

Liebowitz, S. (2006). File-sharing: Creative destruction or just plain destruction? Center for the Analysis of Property Rights Working Paper No. 04-03. Retrieved from SSRN: http://ssrn.com/abstract=646943 or DOI: 10.2139/ssrn.646943

Limitations on liability relating to material online. 17 U.S.C. § 512 (1998).

Maymounkov, P., & Mazières, D. (2002) Kademlia: A peer-to-peer information system based on the XOR metric. In *Proceedings of the International Workshop on Peer-to-Peer Systems (IPTPS)*. Cambridge, MA.

Millennium Copyright Act, D. (1998). 17 U.S.C. §§ 512, 1201–1205, 1301–1332; 28 U.S.C. § 4001. *Pub., L*, 105–304.

Moore, J., Bland, W., Francis, S., King, N., Patterson, J., Srinivasan, U., & Widden, P. (2004) Interdiction of unauthorized copying in a decentralized network. U.S. Patent Application number 10/803,784, publication number 2005/0091167.

Oberholzer-Gee, F., & Strumpf, K. (2007). The effect of file sharing on record sales: An empirical analysis. *The Journal of Political Economy*, *115*(1), 1–42. doi:10.1086/511995

Shang, R. A., Chen, Y. C., & Chen, P. C. (2008). Ethical decisions about sharing music files in the P2P environment. *Journal of Business Ethics*, *80*(2), 349–365. doi:10.1007/s10551-007-9424-2

Taipale, K. (2003) Secondary liability on the internet: Towards a performative standard for constitutive responsibility. Center for Advanced Studies Working Paper No. 04-2003. Available at SSRN: http://ssrn.com/abstract=712101

Walsh, K., & Gün Sirer, E. (2006). Experience with an object reputation system for peer-to-peer filesharing. In *Proceedings of the Symposium on Networked System Design and Implementation*. San Jose, CA, USA.

ENDNOTES

1 See for instance http://www.slackware.com/torrents/, last accessed June 9, 2009.

2 See http://www.blizzard.com/us/legal-bfd.html, last accessed June 9, 2009.

3 From http://www.dynamicsun.com/, last accessed June 2, 2009.

4 See http://www.enterprisenews.com/archive/x1225086200/MASS-MARKET-Nostalgia-alone-won-t-keep-movie-rental-stores-afloat, last accessed June 8, 2009.

5 See "Disc Piracy: it costs more than you think," by Dan Daley, http://www.linkdata.dk/linkpress/TDB-pir.htm, last accessed June 8, 2009.

6 An exception worth noting is that in Asia, sales of illegitimate copies of movies on VCD and CD-ROMs have soared using traditional distribution channels (e.g., brick and mortar video stores) and have been made solely

possible by the shift from analog to digital media.

7 Formally, convenience can be formulated in monetary terms, e.g., by estimating how users value their time. Formal economic modeling of actors' incentives, however, is beyond the scope of the discussion in this chapter.

8 See http://www.nytimes.com/2007/07/02/business/media/02universal.html, last accessed June 8, 2009.

9 See for instance http://www.plus.net/support/broadband/products/archive/bbyw/features.shtml, last accessed June 9, 2009.

10 Even if complete file transfers are broken down in smaller pieces, they remain generally much longer than typical web connections.

11 It is worth noting that the risk of cannibalization of one's own business is not limited to peer-to-peer vs. digital TV, for these operators. Internet telephony, which is another "killer application" driving the demand for more bandwidth, essentially competes with traditional telephone access which are offered by the same service providers. A desire to avoid self-cannibalization has lead to the emergence of "triple play" offerings – discounts aimed at securing users' patronage in all services simultaneously.

12 See http://arstechnica.com/tech-policy/news/2009/05/harvard-prof-tells-judge-that-p2p-filesharing-is-fair-use.ars, last accessed June 8, 2009

13 See http://tech.yahoo.com/blogs/null/146827, last accessed August 7, 2009.

14 See A&M RECORDS, Inc. v. NAPSTER, INC., 239 F.3d 1004 (9th Cir. 2001).

15 See MGM Studios, Inc. v. Grokster, Ltd. 545 U.S. 913.

16 See Universal Music Australia Pty Ltd v. Sharman License Holdings Ltd. FCA 1242 (2005).

17 See MGM Studios, Inc. v. Grokster, Ltd. 545 U.S. 913.

18 See http://www.betanews.com/article/RIAA-Piracy-Damages-Questioned-in-Ruling/1163182272, last accessed June 9, 2009.

19 See http://arstechnica.com/tech-policy/news/2009/06/jammie-thomas-retrial-verdict.ars, last accessed July 28, 2009.

20 See http://www.sfgate.com/cgi-bin/article.cgi?file=/chronicle/archive/2003/09/25/BUGJC1TO2D1.DTL&type=business, last accessed June 9, 2009.

21 See http://thepiratebay.org/, last accessed June 9, 2009.

22 See http://www.freedom-to-tinker.com/blog/felten/why-unbreakable-codes-dont-make-unbreakable-drm, last accessed June 8, 2009.

23 Some of them may, however, be somewhat contained within linguistic and cultural borders, due to the type of contents they are hosting. The next section discusses one such example with the Winny network.

24 Winny is one of the most popular peer-to-peer networks in Japan.

25 See Nihon Asahi Shimbun, "Leaks spur splurge for new SDF computers," March 8, 2006.

26 "Security and privacy in file-sharing networks", presentation given by Nicolas Christin at Tokyo University, June 18, 2007.

27 See http://www.thelocal.se/19928/20090607/, last accessed June 9, 2009.

APPENDIX: DISCUSSION QUESTIONS

1. For what purpose are you using P2P software?
2. What is the copyright law and what is the purpose of copyright law?
3. Who are stakeholders of copyright law?
4. How can each different stakeholder (including you) change the copyright law to their maximum benefits?
5. Assuming that copyright law is intended to produce a collectively creative society, are there any other ways to achieve the same goal? If so, how might P2P networking play a role in this?
6. Are there ethical issues pertaining to P2P network? If so, what are they?
7. If a large percent of the P2P uses are copyright infringing, and only a small percent of uses are not infringing, how can we manipulate technology to differentiate those two uses? If so, how?
8. Is it an ethical countermeasure of content providers to inject poisoned files to protect their contents against illegal file sharing of P2P network users?
9. Under which conditions would new copyright law be accepted by all stakeholders?
10. What role does a business model play in the ethics of sharing songs, videos, books, and other copyrighted material? Should you consider ethics when creating your business model?
11. Describe the different ethical perspectives of recording companies, artists, and music consumers.
12. Consumers who purchase music feel that they should own the product they purchased. Describe in detail an ethical argument supporting this statement.
13. Analyze the DMCA's anti-circumvention arguments (or some other argument made in the DMCA) using utilitarianism, deontological ethics, and virtue ethics.
14. Discuss the DMCA from the perspective of end-users, content creators, ISPs, content publishers, and software manufacturers.
15. Describe a possible alternative to using copyright, such as subscription or compulsory licensing services. How do the ethics change for the stakeholders involved?
16. The original duration of copyrights in the United States was 28 years. Currently, copyrights are valid for the life of the author plus 70 years. Construct an ethical argument supporting this change and an ethical argument against this change.
17. An orphan work is a copyrighted work where it is difficult or impossible to identify or contact the copyright owner. Describe the ethics involved in violating the copyright of an orphaned work. Do these ethics differ from violation of non-orphaned copyrighted works?
18. Is there an ethical difference between stealing a physical DVD from a brick and mortar store and downloading a digital copy of a DVD from a file sharing network?
19. When a copyrighted work is illegally distributed over the Internet, assign a percentage of legal responsibility to each of the following groups: end-users, content creators, ISPs, content publishers, and software manufacturers?
20. Do you agree with Charles Nesson, a Harvard Law Professor, who believes that peer-to-peer file sharing is essentially fair use?
21. Suppose a person who participates in a peer-to-peer network accidentally shares a portion of their hard drive that is legally protected by copyright. Should this user be held liable?
22. What impact does copyright violation have on a young musician who is beginning his/her career? What is the impact of a young musician who is just starting out when the distribution channels are controlled by a select number of highly influential companies?

23. The stakeholders in this chapter include end users, content providers, consumer electronics manufacturers, software manufacturers and Internet Service Providers. What are the costs (harms) and benefits to each?
24. Use utilitarianism, deontological ethics and virtue ethics and discuss what of the five stakeholders groups (end users, software manufacturers, content providers, hardware manufacturers, and Internet Service Providers) should do and why.
25. How might a "contraband" model for copyright infringing materials change this analysis?
26. Is compulsory licensing based on bandwidth tiers the solution? How would distribution be handled?
27. Should copyright law be changed? If so, how?
28. How might cultural differences impact ethical perspectives from different members on the network?
29. How might wealth differences impact ethical perspectives from different members across the network?

Chapter 6
Responsibility for the Harm and Risk of Software Security Flaws

Cassio Goldschmidt
Symantec, Corp., USA

Melissa J. Dark
Purdue University, USA

Hina Chaudhry
Purdue University, USA

ABSTRACT

Software vulnerabilities are a vexing problem for the state of information assurance and security. Who is responsible for the risk and harm of software security is controversial. Deliberation of the responsibility for harm and risk due to software security flaws requires considering how incentives (and disincentives) and network effects shape the practices of vendors and adopters, and the consequent effects on the state of software security. This chapter looks at these factors in more detail in the context of private markets and public welfare.

INTRODUCTION

This chapter describes the current landscape of the responsibility for the harm and risk of software security flaws. We focus on software vulnerabilities for several reasons. Software assurance is critically important to information assurance and security and we believe it will be important for some time to come. While improvements in software security will be made, these will be incremental at best. Getting software right is still an art. No practical, formal methods exist to prove application security nor does a definitive authority exist to assert the absence of vulnerabilities. Small coding errors can lead to fatal flaws due to interactions among different components of complex software. The first portion of this chapter outlines who vendors are, their current practices to securing software, and overviews the forces that impinge on vendors' software security practices.

DOI: 10.4018/978-1-61692-245-0.ch006

While software is developed by vendors, it is deployed, operated, and sometimes adapted, by a myriad of adopters. Numerous decisions that adopters make have implications for the state of software security, for example, installation with default settings or patching practices. Given the interdependent nature of information systems, the role of adopters, their practices, and the forces that constrain their software security practices are also discussed. Special attention is given to how current practices in patch availability and deployment affect software security.

Despite best effort to build, deploy, and govern secure software, some portion of software vulnerability is inevitable, which brings us to the role of vulnerability disclosure. Vulnerability disclosure is about the sharing of vulnerability information: relevant issues include how, when, with whom, and how often vulnerability information is shared. This chapter discusses the role of vulnerability disclosure on the responsibility for harm and risk of software insecurity with a focus on how disclosure enables and constrains software security practices.

Producing robust software that is able to withstand attacks, work around hardware limitations, and even inform users about the potential security risks related to their choices is no longer seen by society as nice to have, it has become a requirement. Enacting this mandate, however, is far from clear. Improving software security is as much about economics, public policy, and social welfare as it is about abuse cases, error conditions, and testing methodologies. Who should be responsible for the harm and risk caused by security flaws?

BACKGROUND

One of the challenges in understanding who should ultimately be responsible for the harm and risk caused by security flaws is our lack of a full understanding of the nature of information technology risk. "As systems become more complex and interconnected, emergent behavior (i.e., unanticipated, complex behavior caused by unpredictable interactions between systems) of global systems exposes emergent vulnerabilities" (Computing Research Association, 2003, pg. 21). This complexity and emergence make risk assessment hard. Our existing mathematical/statistical risk models are based on independent failures, where "a component failure in one part of the system does not affect the failure of another similar component in another part of the system. This leads to especially beautiful and useful models of system failure that are effectively applied thousands of times a day by working engineers" (Computing Research Association, 2003, pg. 21). Unfortunately, these models are not transferrable to networked systems where failures are interdependent, not independent.

We need models that can account for dependencies between system components in a manner that sheds light on how the behaviors of system components interact to lead to system failure. Progress in interdependent risk measurement will enhance the effective management of investment. "Without an effective model, decision-makers will either over-invest in security measures that do not pay off or will under-invest and risk devastating consequences" (Computing Research Association, 2003, pg. 21). Interdependencies also pose considerable challenges when it comes to assigning liability, and formulating reasonable policy and associated compliance.

Despite our lack of understanding of the nature of interdependent risk, it is widely acknowledged that we are interlinked and the risk interdependent. Interdependent risk necessitates interdependent responsibility. In the words of Jane Addams (1910), "the good we secure for ourselves is precarious and uncertain, is floating in mid-air, until it is secured for all of us and incorporated into our common life" (pg. 116). Addams was awarded the Nobel Peace Prize in 1931 for her unwavering commitment to social improvement through cooperative efforts.

The relevance of her words today is in conceiving solutions for how self-interested individuals and groups collectively and cooperatively work toward improved software security. Rational choice suggests that humans, individually, and in groups, act in their own best interest. The logic of collective action states that large groups with a common interest will not act collectively in the absence of individual incentive or compulsion (Olson, 1971). When the good to be provided is a public (shared) good, by definition, the good is of benefit to a group larger than those who are providers of the good. Any individual or group will only get a portion of the benefit of any expenditure made to obtain the good. When circumstances are such that the gain to an individual (or small group) could be disproportionate to the immediate losses or costs, there will be a failure to take collective action as each individual perceives the possibility of losing more than individually gained (as well as perceiving that someone else gained at lesser cost). The result will be a failure to provide the public good. Given the premise of self-interest, the individual or group will seek to discontinue the expenditure before the optimal good for the group has been obtained.

This suggests that the question of the responsibility for harm and risk from software security flaws requires looking at the groups involved and their respective interests. It also requires that we consider the dual private good/public good nature of software. While software has been privatized, software vulnerabilities have largely been treated as externalities; which means that the costs of software security are borne by those who are not involved in the transaction. Given these challenges, questions such as who should be responsible for the provision of public goods, to what degree, and how, become, in part, the purview of government. This chapter considers the responsibility for harm and risk of software security flaws in the context of collective action, competing private interests, and public welfare.

The Common Good

While an exhaustive definition is beyond the scope of this chapter, a working definition of philosophical notions of the common good is in order, as well as discussion of the relationship of common good, public policy, and economics. This foundation should serve as a framework so that when we discuss current issue in software assurance and software vulnerabilities, we can go beyond recounting current debates to consider theoretical underpinnings providing an analytical basis from which we can discuss the consequent implications.

In the abstract, a good is a common good when the causes are also the ends. That is, the internal order is a good in and of itself, and is also an instrumental good that serves as a means to other ends. The "common" is comprised of particulars, where particulars are entities or functions that correlate to the whole. For example, an individual is part of a family, a family is part of a community, a community part of a city, a city part of a state, and a state part of a nation. The whole to which they correlate though is not merely the sum of these parts and their utilities. Common goods are more than a collection of particular goods; the whole of the common good is more than the sum of its parts. The goodness of the whole exists independent of the goodness of each part, yet the goodness of the whole also exists to enable the goodness of constituent parts so that the parts can in turn constitute the whole.

The 'common good' can be traced to the early foundations of political theory. In Aristotle's Politics, Aristotle considers what form of community is best for all to realize the ideal of their life. According to Aristotle (Aristotle, 350 BC), a common good state concerns itself with the relative equality of outcomes where all citizens can flourish. Aristotle's proposed that the *polis* (city in Greek; the modern day equivalent would be the nation state) should be a context in which citizens deliberate about the common good in a manner that it, in and of itself, is a common good. The ideal is that the polity should be a common good itself as well as exist to ensure that other goods are realized by the *communis* (Latin for public) to include both shared and individual resources for collectives and individuals. The polity includes the actions, practices, and institutions that regulate social and political life such that these actions, practices and institutions serve the good of all its citizens and not only the good of some. The polity includes social systems, institutions, and environments on which we all depend and work in a manner that benefits all people. For example, the systems might include the public health care system, the public safety and security system, the legal and political system, and the economic system.

While the notion - the ideal - of the common good is transcendent, how the material and manifest work of the common good are worked out is a matter of collective action, including the action of particular groups and the collective action of the totality of the groups. It is through this lens that we will consider responsibility for harm and risk of software security flaws. As we explore the contours of software assurance, we consider three constituent parts, vendors, adopters, and vulnerability disclosure, as well as the sum of those parts.

Welfare Economics

Welfare economics is a branch of economics that looks at economic welfare theory with regard to public policy questions, which are by definition questions of the common good. The objective of welfare economics is to help society make better choices with regard to the use of resources. Better choices alludes to the criteria for how goods and services produced in an economy should be distributed among individuals and considers issues of liberty, justice, and equity from political, moral and economic perspectives. Welfare economics focuses on using the scarce resources optimally such that the maximum well-being of individuals in society is realized.

Welfare economics seeks to define social welfare (the total well-being of the entire society) in economic terms that describe the activities of individuals and collectives. However, because the welfare of individuals and collectives cannot be directly observed, an abstract measure of welfare, called a utility function, is used. The utility function in welfare economics can be understood by contrasting it to the notion of profit maximization in microeconomics. Whereas microeconomics is concerned with how businesses provide goods and services to maximize profit, utility maximization is concerned with what resources should be allocated to maximize "satisfaction" or "happiness" within a society and how. The idea is that utility within a society can be increased and decreased; and, those shifts can be represented in economic terms as social welfare gains or losses.

Utility within a society includes goods and services that can be purchased in the marketplace as well as goods and services that private markets will typically not provide, which are referred to as common goods (also known as public goods and collective goods in economics) and club goods. In this chapter, we call them public goods so as to not confuse them with "the common good". A public "good" refers to a thing, a commodity, a state, or a service. Examples of public goods are roads, defense, law enforcement, air, and information goods, such as software. By calling something a public good, we are not implying that it is "worthy", "desirable", or "satisfactory". Public goods can actually be "bad". For example, pollutants are public goods. However, the reciprocal – pollution abatement – can be called the public "good" in both senses, the thing and the value.

A good is considered a public good when the cost of providing the good to another user is effectively zero, that is, there are no marginal costs. Public goods are also defined as goods that are non-rivaled and non-excludable. A non-rivaled good means that a person can benefit from the good without denying another person the opportunity to benefit from the same good. So, in the case of roads, my getting to drive on a well-kept road is a benefit. It does not cost any more to provide this good to you and me than it does to provide the good to only me (marginal costs are zero). And my opportunity to benefit from this good does not deny you of the same benefit (the good is non-rivalrous). Non-excludable means that no one can be excluded from using the good or service regardless of whether or not they pay for the service. For example, a street light is non-excludable. If I invest money to install a street light outside my house for safety purposes, I cannot prevent my neighbor from the safety benefit of the light. The cost of my neighbor having light is no more than the cost of me having light. This is where the case of software becomes interesting. The marginal costs in producing software are effectively zero. It is possible for a software vendor to provide me with a piece of software and provide you the same piece of software at no additional costs. However, digital rights protection is often applied to make software rivalrous. Just as the process of converting source code into binary code makes it excludable.

Public goods are sometimes thought of as market failures. In a market system, goods, services, and information are exchanged forming part of the economy. This exchange of goods and services for money is called a transaction. Transactions are sources of information; they tell us what consumers pay for products at given quantities, and the price for which producers sell given quantities of products. Markets enable tradable items to be evaluated and priced. The two fundamental forces of a market are supply and demand. A market that is in equilibrium produces a good/service at a price where the quantity demanded by consumers equals the quantity supplied by producers. Such a market is considered to be in equilibrium and efficient.

A market failure refers to circumstances when market-like behavior fails to produce efficient results; such instances are commonly referred to as externalities. Externalities arise when the well-being of a consumer or the production possibilities of a producer are affected by the action of another decision maker in the economy and this interaction is not attributable to changes in price. Public goods, then, can be thought of as externalities – public goods (or "bads") arise in situations where a competitive market fails to allocate resources efficiently. The primary reason we see market failures of public goods stems from their non-excludable nature. When it is not possible or overly costly to make a good excludable, people will free ride. Free riders are individuals who have access to consume the good, but will not pay for it. Because free riders decrease private firm profits, private markets fail to produce public goods at socially optimal levels. When a market fails to produce a public good at the level desired, other mechanisms are used to reach socially optimal production levels. These include civic responsibility, volunteerism, private donation, and public provision (policy). Throughout this chapter we discuss the ways that market failures affect the responsibility for harm and risk of software security flaws.

The traditional means of addressing externalities through public provision are mechanisms such as taxation and quotas. Positive taxes impose a cost on the producer for producing the externality or a consumption tax on the consumer, both of which aim to decrease the externality. Negative taxes, also called subsidies, seek to subsidize the provision of a public good in the private market by incentivizing the producer to produce less or the consumer to consume more of the externality. Later in this chapter we talk about policies for providing incentives for software patching, two of which are patching rebates (a subsidy) and usage tax.

One of the most widely used theoretical concepts (though not undisputed) in welfare economics is the "Pareto Criterion", proposed by Vilfredo

Pareto in 1896 (Just, Hueth, & Schmitz, 2005). The idea of the Pareto Criterion is that a situation is socially desirable when it is possible to make a change to make one (or some) person(s) better off while no one is made worse off. A policy change that makes at least one person better off by moving them from state A to state B while also ensuring that no one is made worse off would be a *pareto improvement*[1]. This does not mean that no one loses consumption or access to goods and services. Some portion of the population could experience loss, but through compensatory mechanisms their loss could be offset so that, in effect, overall welfare remains unchanged. If two alternatives exist to the status quo, the alternative that produces the most social gain is considered *pareto superior*. While a thorough discussion of the idea of *pareto optimality* and criticisms thereof are beyond the scope of this chapter (interested readers should have no problem finding additional resources), as we shall see throughout this chapter, questions of pareto improvements and pareto superiority, whether explicitly or only implicitly, are at the core of the debate regarding responsibility for risk and harm of software security flaws.

We turn now to discussion of the software assurance milieu. We look at the players; their roles, and their practices in the context of public good; incentives and disincentives; and externalities in an effort to shed light on the complexity of responsibility for harm and risk of software security flaws. Given that there are no easy answers and that scrutiny frequently produces more questions before it produces any answers, we conclude with a list of questions that we think will be important in the future.

Vendors

Generally speaking, software vendors are companies that specialize in making software. Most of us are familiar with large software companies, such as Google and Microsoft. However, there are countless companies that produce software for a myriad of diverse purposes; administering medication, controlling inventory levels, routing packages, and scheduling and coordinating air transportation are just a few. All of these entities are software vendors.

Vendor Practices Regarding Software Security

As the creators of software applications, vendors generally bear accountability for the safety and functionality of their products. A generally accepted practice is for software vendors to stay abreast of common attacks against software applications and actively design products that reasonably withstand and mitigate the impact of such attacks. However, the difficulty - and considerable uncertainty - comes from the fact that it could be the poor operation of software that causes harm; in which case the vendor should not be responsible for the misuse of an artifact they developed. In some ways, that would be like holding automobile manufacturers responsible for people's driving habits. A software-related computer failure has several parties who may be partially responsible: the software vendor, the computer vendor, the network vendor, the user, possibly another hacker, and so on (Schneier, 2008). To date, models of partial responsibility in this area have been elusive.

Despite uncertainty about what it means for a vendor to "bear accountability" for a software application, there are best practices that vendors can, and do, use to improve software security. A systematic engineering methodology can improve the overall quality of the product and reduce security risk. Best practices prescribe that security should commence when product ideas are conceived and be an intrinsic part of the software development process. Threat analysis should be performed early in the development lifecycle to highlight problems that are more architectural in nature. During threat analysis, seasoned engineers step into the shoes of attackers to construct threat models. The software architecture is then analyzed and scrutinized to search for possible abuse cases. The data flow diagrams created in this phase of the development serve as the basis for security test cases later performed during the development lifecycle.

Because poor coding practices can result in software that is vulnerable to cyber attacks, another best practice of vendors is the utilization of well-defined policies for their coding efforts. Programming library functions that have been rendered obsolete due to safety, but are still supported for compatibility reasons, should not be utilized when crafting new code. Whenever possible, these functions, also known as deprecated functions, should also be replaced with the new and safer counterparts. Developers are also encouraged to avoid "reinventing the wheel" and instead make use of security patterns, which are well-understood solutions to a recurring information security problem. Vendors should utilize new programming languages and compilers that significantly simplify the developer's task of writing secure code by providing sophisticated memory management capabilities and built-in mitigations against common attacks. Vendors should avail themselves of the current state of the art in static and dynamic source code analysis tools to scan source code for security flaws and partially automate vulnerability testing. Static source code analysis can be performed without the need to execute programs. In most cases the analysis is performed on some version of the source code and in the other cases it is performed on some form of the object code. In contrast, dynamic source code analysis identifies vulnerabilities in a runtime environment.

However, because neither static nor dynamic analysis can recognize sophisticated attack patterns or business logic flaws, another best practice among security conscious vendors is to perform manual code reviews. Many vendors go beyond the use of automated tools and engage security experts to perform a special type of security assessment called penetration testing. In these assessments, security experts simulate hacker attacks against the target system to find security flaws. In some cases, vendors hire third parties to conduct the penetration testing in order to obtain unbiased assessment of their products.

Software is developed by people and frequently inspected by people. When it is not inspected by people, it is inspected by automated software tools that are developed by people. Software is produced in teams and companies that are comprised of and run by people. The common denominator, i.e., the human element, is critical to advancing software security. When hiring software developers, vendors should perform background checks. Hiring candidates with appropriate security certifications can help assure a certain level of security knowledge and expertise. Once hired, ongoing training of all personnel must be an essential component of any strategy to build secure applications. Developers must be required to know how to write secure code. Quality assurance professionals must be trained to test software for security vulnerabilities. Management needs to understand how to ensure that security is integrated into every step of the development lifecycle. It would be best practice to continually educate everyone involved with product development on common attack patterns and how to protect against them. Some of the well-known sources of common attack patterns that vendors can use are the "OWASP Top 10" (Open Web application Security Project), "SANS/CWE Top 25 most dangerous programming flaws", the "OSVDB" (which is the Open Source Vulnerability DataBase, and the "CVE" (Common Vulnerability and Exposures) project by MITRE. Armed with these lists, vendors can both focus their educational and remediation efforts to address the most prominent threats. Due to the dynamic nature of the information security field, such lists have to be regularly updated. The OWASP Top 10, for example, is updated every two or three years. Although the list varies with time, many attacks remain on the list year after year.

Forces that Constrain Vendors' Software Security Practices

Complexity and Cost

Considering that even the best security professionals struggle to spot complex coding flaws when reviewing only a few lines of code (Howard and LeBlanc, 2003), the task gets considerably more difficult when millions of lines of code need to be reviewed, redesigned, and fixed. Quality assurance personnel must test the fixes and perform regression tests to ascertain that no product functionality has been lost in the process of correcting flaws.

A development methodology that includes the aforementioned activities, coupled with diligent risk mitigation, inevitably increases the time and resources spent on a project. Experience suggests that there is a direct relationship between the number of features introduced on a project and the number of developers needed. The chance of having a vulnerability introduced to the codebase is directly related to the knowledge and care of the sloppiest developer on a team (Anderson & Moore, 2006): if the number of developers in a team increases, the chance of having a sloppy developer on the team also increases. (Anderson & Moore, 2006) On the other hand, the application security assessment and testing usually depends on the sum of a team's effort as there are several touch points in the development lifecycle where a group of individuals is responsible to review the work. Putting a premium in hiring fewer, better, and more expensive developers, and, keeping them educated while increasing the number of testers in the organization raises the software production cost and diminishes the number of features added to a new release.

Quality assurance is expensive for producers. It has been estimated that almost 50% of development costs are due to testing (Myers, 1979). While software testing is recommended as a best practice for removing software defects, little is known about how to use these resources devoted to testing in the most cost effective way (Wagner, 2005). A recent study by Zheng, Williams, Nagappan, Snipes, Hudepohl and Vouk (2006) examined whether an organization can economically improve the quality of software products using automated static analysis. Their findings show mixed results. While the cost of automated static analysis is roughly equivalent to the cost of inspection and testing, the benefits are less conclusive. Zheng et. al. (2006) found no conclusive results regarding an increase in overall product quality as a result of using automated static analysis; and, found that defect removal using automated static analysis was equivalent to results obtained using inspection and testing. Because most software projects are led by companies and companies are profit maximizers (Wagner, 2007), software quality needs to be approached using measures such as Net Present Value (NPV) and Internal Rate of Return (IRR). While it is possible that such measures have been used within a company, these measures have not been widely used in the research literature. Advances in this area could help vendors adopt more efficient and effective testing methods. As testing efficiency improves, more resources can be devoted to secure development and testing.

Other Market Forces

Because customers seem to find value in new features, as evidenced by purchasing trends, software makers have the incentive to create them. Software vendors, like most producers, want to get to market early to capture market share; a delay in the time to market can be costly. While some industry sectors can increase production by increasing personnel, this is not a particularly effective strategy in software development. Having more developers frequently means additional coordination, which often results in time delays (Arora, Caulkins & Telang, 2004).

The "first to market" advantage makes some vendors rush to launch their products at the expense of overall product quality and security. Coupled with the fact that, in the software industry, vendors have the ability to fix bugs later, this leads to a scenario where software vendors launch a product early, then release corrections later as a software update. The study by Arora, Caulkins and Telang (2004) found that patching investments and time of entry to the market are strategic complements. Identifying a bug and writing and testing code to fix it is mostly 'fixed cost' in nature, which allows vendors to reasonably build patching into their product costs. A predictable future investment in patching coupled with the need to enter the market early incentivizes vendors to release buggier products earlier and patch them later.

Many customers adopt market dominant applications because of synergy and interoperability created by using the same application others are already using. This phenomenon is known as the bandwagon effect. To foster a larger network of users, vendors create an ecosystem or a platform that appeals to makers of complementary products. Platform adopters desire openness and straightforward interfaces as this represents more product opportunities and lower prototyping costs. More often than not, both attributes are at odds with security. Vendors who spend the time and resources developing a secure architecture for system extensibility may incur the risk of stifling platform innovation as security requirements could get in the way and make life harder for the complementers. Platform vendors tend to ignore security in the first releases until they build a market position (Anderson, 2001). It is generally accepted that security is treated as an add-on. Based on the above discussion, it seems that market forces may be partly responsible for security being considered and add-on.

Unfortunately, most customers lack the ability to distinguish secure from insecure software. A situation where the vendor knows more about the quality of the product than the consumer is considered to be one of asymmetric information. Akerlof (1970), an American Economist, called this the "Market for Lemons". As a result of insufficient information about product quality, consumers cannot discern what level of quality they are getting for their money. In the absence of information, consumers assume that they will only get average quality and therefore are only willing to pay average prices. The effect over time is that producers will only produce average quality product given that is what sells. Because high quality products are driven out, the market is called "a market for lemons".

While one might think that the presence of vulnerabilities would suggest product inferiority to customers, research shows that software customers believe that software in a uniquely complex product that is bound to have defects (Cusumano, 2004). Therefore, it could be that software customers are more willing to accept software defects than would be accepted in other product markets. And, contrary to what one might expect, it is possible that the presence of vulnerabilities actually leads consumers to perceive that the vulnerable software product is superior. Let's take Microsoft for example. Microsoft is widely known for its vulnerabilities. Many believe that it is Microsoft's large market share that makes it an appealing target. If hackers want notoriety for their exploits, a large attack target is likely to offer more notoriety. The consequence of this is that it signals product superiority, not inferiority, to customers.

Moving Forward

A possible solution path to the problem of the high cost of creating secure software is to enact legislation that provides incentives to software makers who invest in practices such as training and automation. However, relying on policy to ensure software assurance is not a fool proof solution. Past attempts at standardization, such as the Payment Card Industry Data Security Standard (PCI) made companies race to become compliant but not necessarily secure, diverting corporations to focus solely on compliance. The Common Criteria motivated vendors to shop around for evaluators who would give their products the 'easiest ride', for example, by asking fewer questions, charging less money, taking the least time, or all of the above.

Others have suggested that penalties for egregious vendors are needed. For example, taxing vendors who have high vulnerability rates has been suggested. Earlier we noted that many vulnerabilities are known about Microsoft products, in part because Microsoft is an attractive target for hackers. Is Microsoft an egregious vendor or a large target? One challenge with this approach then is in identifying what constitutes egregious behavior. Stiff financial penalties against vendors could also create barriers for newcomers entering the market. With fewer market entrants, the goal of "greater consumer choice" becomes a dream. Homegrown software is developed either by internal developers or by outside contractors, neither of which have the necessary resources to go through the same level of scrutiny that large vendors such as Microsoft can apply to product development. These groups have more insecure development processes than just about any major software vendor. Should financial penalties be levied against vendors, these groups could suffer the most.

Another action that could raise the tide of software security is to grant read access to source code. Advocates assert that this approach will finally treat software as what it truly is – a common good. By allowing read access, consumers and citizens can truly signal what they demand in terms of software security and at what cost. Furthermore, such an approach is in the best interest of society as the technical means of today are too powerful to be in the hands of the few. Advocates note that if citizens are to influence their own future, they must know enough about technology to fulfill their role as citizens; they must be in a position to speak from a position of enlightenment and knowledge regarding technical means. If they are not speaking from this position, they are speaking from a position of ignorance, which is always a position of subservience. Critics note that while the access granted to all consumers and citizens might be the same, the resources for each consumer and citizen to participate will still be asymmetric. Those with resources will be able to participate more fully at the risk of further discrimination to those who cannot. Other critics contend that the motivation to report vulnerabilities will still vary. Suppose a military agency of a government discovers a flaw in a widely used software application. If this flaw is reported to the vendor, who then corrects the flaw, all users (including adversaries) will benefit from improved security. If the agency remains quiet, it could take measures of its own to mitigate the vulnerability, while at the same time, exploit the flaw to attack adversaries.

Summary

Vendors are the creators of the software and have responsibility for creating secure software. Vendors can follow a number of best practices to enhance the security of their code. However, there will never be perfectly written code. The complexity of code and code development in combination with competing interests among consumer choice, barriers to entry, price, and security continue to challenge progress toward the common good of the development of more secure software. While vendors are creators of code, adopters are also important in the software security equation, which we turn to next.

Adopters

Adopters are organizations and individuals who use software. This includes both legal and illegal users (i.e., pirates). For our purposes here, legitimate adopters are organizations and individuals who use software in accordance with current copyright laws. This includes a wide variety of for profit businesses, nonprofit businesses, organizations, associations, government agencies, institutions, and users. These entities range in size and location to include small, locally owned or operated entities (e.g., a local food cooperative, the local school district, and a community credit union) to large national and multinational entities (e.g., the Department of Treasury, Chase Bank, Wal-Mart Stores, Nestle, Royal Dutch Shell and Bayer Group).

Illegal users are those who do not act in accord with current copyright laws when using software. Illegal users range from individual users who share a copy of a piece of software with a friend to organized groups and nation states. Increasingly, groups are organizing and challenging existing copyright practices. Take, for example, the Pirate Party, which was founded in Sweden in 2006. One of the foremost goals of the Pirate Party is to reform copyright law. Specifically the party is seeking (1) modification of copy right law so that all non-commercial copying of software is free, and (2) a complete ban on digital rights management technologies (The Pirate Party, 2009). On a larger scale, the World Trade Organization (WTO) was established in 1995 to deal with rules of trade between nations. The WTO has outlined rules on the intellectual property protection and enforcement for the multilateral trading system (World Trade Organization, 2009). However, several countries where software piracy is rampant are not members of the WTO and do not acknowledge these rules. And in some cases, countries that are members still fail to abide by the agreement.

The relative recency of the WTO ruling and the development of the Pirate Party show that issues of software ownership are anything but resolved. As these issues play out, it makes the contributions of the myriad of adopters to the state of secure software use anything but clear. There are multiple competing interests, and ineffective and incomplete practices that merit a closer look, not so much for providing a full characterization, but to at least approximate some of the systemic challenges.

Adopter Practices Regarding Software Security

Across organizations of all sizes, type, and locale, one trend seems clear - the responsibility for information security within organizations is evolving. In the past, information security was relegated to the information technology department and primarily viewed as a technical and system concern. Today, information security is increasingly being regarded as a matter of governance within organizations where the focus is on strategic alignment of information security to business objectives and value delivery, as well as attention to risk, resource, and performance management. According to the IT Governance Institute (2006), information technology governance has the following goals:

- Increase share value for organizations that practice good governance
- Increase predictability and reduced uncertainty of business operations by lowering information security-related risks to definable and acceptable levels
- Reduce potential for civil or legal liability as a result of information inaccuracy or the absence of due care
- Enhance the structure and framework to optimize allocation of limited security resources
- Improve assurance of effective information security policy and policy compliance
- Fortify the foundation for efficient and effective risk management, process improvement, and timely incident response related to securing information
- Increase the level of assurance that critical decisions are not based on faulty information
- Increase accountability for safeguarding information during critical business activities, such as mergers and acquisitions,

> business process recovery, and regulatory response (pg. 13).

As information technology governance evolves, one best practice is for organizations to adopt a cost benefit model to manage the return of their security investment. Costs are the programs and initiatives instituted to reduce risk. Costs can be categorized in four broad categories: transitory, long term, tangible, and intangible (Cavusoglu, Mishra, & Raghunathan, 2004). Transitory costs include things such as lost business and decreased productivity as a result of system downtime, as well as costs to detect, contain, repair, and restore the system, and costs to prosecute and notify customers and the public. In contrast are long term costs such as customer loss (both customers who leave as a result of the breach, as well as the loss of potential new customers), potential increases in insurance, and higher capital costs in debt and equity markets. Costs such as lost sales, material and increased insurance are calculable and therefore tangible, while costs associated with decreased trust, such as loss of potential new customers, are more intangible (Cavusoglu et. al., 2004).

Using a cost benefit approach, reduction of information security risk can be treated as the intended benefit. Organizations that adopt a cost benefit approach will need to think purposefully about how to measure the benefit. Research has shown a relationship between the announcement of information security breaches and loss of market value. Ranges on market devaluation following an information security breach have been reported from 2.1 percent of market value within two days of announcement (Cavusoglu, Mishra, & Raghunathan, 2004) to 5.6 percent over a three day period following breach disclosure (Garg, Curtis, & Halper, 2003). An expected benefit of reducing information security risk would be to preempt the possibility for this type of market devaluation. Another way for assessing information security risk would be the Risk Management Guide for Information Technology Systems published by the National Institute for Standards and Technology (Stonebruner, Goguen & Feringa, 2002). By using this framework to measure information security risk, adopters can develop a risk baseline. Then, as security investments are made, risk can be assessed again. Reductions in risk can serve an indicator of benefits of the program. While business analysts can clearly articulate the need for a cost benefit approach to software security, operationalizing such studies is still a challenge due to the interdependent nature of risk in this area as mentioned earlier.

Errors in system administration, configuration, and maintenance are often reported by the media as causes of security breaches in large enterprises (Greenemeier, 2007). Hence, there are a variety of adopter best practices regarding system administration, configuration, and maintenance. Responsible use of software starts with choosing the right solution. Due to the high incidence of new security attacks, patching becomes an essential ongoing activity to keep the software secure. Patching needs to be augmented with other key operational tasks. For example, no system is secure without addressing physical security. Large institutions often run internal pilot tests of products before deployment. The goal of pilot programs is to make sure the software runs as expected in the company's unique environment and that no vulnerabilities are introduced to this environment. Software must be configured properly. Applications should encrypt sensitive data in storage and in transit. The use of firewalls, antivirus software, and intrusion detection is essential to provide defense in depth. Strong physical security at data centers is critical. Systems entrusted with sensitive data must be isolated both physically, using different hardware, and logically, using isolated networks and access controls. Whenever possible, a company's financial and HR system must not be directly accessible by external networks such as the internet.

Patch management is an important part of every IT administrator's responsibilities. By ensuring that the latest security patches are installed, the company mitigates the risk of exploitation of vulnerabilities that may exist within the organization's network. Worm and virus attacks such as Nimda and Code Red caused significant downtime for numerous companies and exposed the necessity of effective patch management and patch deployment on all computers on the network. Activities related to patching go beyond a single deployment. Organizations must monitor the success of patch deployments on all of their computers. Employees' machines must be monitored to ensure that all receive patches. For instance, laptops of employees who travel may not receive patches. New machine builds must include the latest patch. In addition, contractors must only be granted permission to access the network if their machines are in compliance with the company's patch policy.

Software security patches must be up-to-date for all adopted software; and, all unnecessary system functionality needs to be removed. Restricting user access and limiting accessibility to applications reduces the attack surface and therefore, the vulnerability (Howard & Lipner, 2006). Access control must be carefully planned to ensure that users do not receive more privileges than necessary to perform their work. Access to servers must be logged on a separate machine for a potential audit. Strong password policies must be enforced to mitigate brute force attacks, including frequent password change and prevention of password reuse.

Forces that Constrain Adopters' Software Security Practices

Operational Challenges

Clearly, there are always risks associated with choosing products. In the case of an enterprise, the team entrusted with this responsibility must be held accountable for selecting the products that best fit a company's needs. Too often, business motives conflict with security concerns. For example, the people testing new products or the individuals responsible for the decisions are not the same individuals who will support and pay for the consequences when the product fails. Incentives for the ultimate decision of purchasing a product over another may be related to a generous discount offered to customers who buy a product bundle with another product offering, extended or premium support, or a strategic business partnership. Managers who opt to go with well known brand names often don't get fired, even if the product proved to be inadequate as they chose the market leader. Companies may allow security maintenance to take a back seat during critical periods such as end of quarter deadlines.

Despite vendor's best efforts and guidance at installation, complex systems often communicate with other in-house applications that may not adhere to the same security standards. This potentially poisons the system with tainted data or forces companies to use the lowest common denominator to exchange data, which is often insecure.

The trend of outsourcing IT infrastructure and services goes against the principles of having strict control over data access. Although outsourcing may bring higher profits and convenience to an enterprise, it often results in less data security.

The Challenges of Patching

There are numerous challenges associated with patching that hamper adopters' security practices. Unfortunately, due to the urgency of some patches, administrators don't have much time for informed decision making or patch testing. Most major attacks tend to occur within hours of the release of a security patch. Upon release of a security patch, attackers reverse engineer the code, identify the vulnerability and subsequently develop and release exploits, hitting organizations before they are protected. Administrators need to act fast to safeguard their networks, while keeping in mind that deploying a faulty patch can result in significant downtime. A common pattern observed in the industry is worm creation following the patch availability. If a company is victim of a worm, it is likely that the business failed to exercise their duties properly to maintain their environment and thus protect customer's data.

Security patches are released frequently, so effective patching requires an ongoing commitment to timely response. Users may not know how to patch their systems, especially in the case of home users or smaller businesses. Applying a patch takes time and can sometimes break a system, rendering it unavailable for a period of time. While diligent patching is considered a best practice for software adopters, the costs associated with updating systems and the accompanying unavailability of systems forces IT to only provide maintenance at certain windows of time. Large companies usually don't allow system updates to be performed during periods such as the end of the quarter due to the potential impact on revenue. Unpatched systems increase the attack surface, making every adopter, to some degree, reliant on the patching practices of others. Add to this that pirated software is almost always unpatched and the attack surface is larger.

The ability of adopters to patch is affected by patch release policies and practices that vendors institute.

The question of when patches should be released is contentious. Some believe that releasing patches on a Friday is a poor choice since most adopters will not be able to deploy the fix promptly. Attackers, on the other hand, will work during the weekend to exploit vulnerabilities on unpatched computers. Vendors must also be sensitive to other countries' holidays and festivities. Microsoft releases security patches during the second Tuesday of the month. This date, also known as "Patch Tuesday," was chosen to avoid the beginning of the week (which is still the weekend in some time zones), but also to be far enough from the end of the week, allowing time for companies to resolve any problems that may arise due to the introduction of changes to the environment. While this allows system administrators to coordinate updates and plan accordingly, it also allows criminals to schedule their attack efforts. The term "Exploit Wednesday" has been coined by the media to describe all new assaults following Microsoft's update announcements. Patch coordination can be convenient to customers, but it also poses a danger by defining a window of exposure before the patch is released giving criminals a schedule for working on attacks.

Microsoft's Patch Tuesday has created unexpected difficulties for other software vendors. No other large software vendor has been able to conduct a similar patch release on the same day. Due to Microsoft's large market share, the number of important updates on the second Tuesday of the month can be overwhelming and often receives extensive media coverage. Vendors who have tried to schedule their own patch releases for the same date to simplify customers patch procedure have been accused of "hiding behind Microsoft" by releasing updates unnoticed by the media. Overwhelmed system administrators have also objected to this practice leaving the remaining vendors only with Wednesdays and Thursdays and the remaining Tuesdays of each month to release new patches.

There are also quality issues associated with patches. Users may not patch their systems immediately either because they find them too difficult to patch or the quality of the patch is not consistent enough that people can feel safe patching right away. From the vendor's perspective, if there is slow uptake of the patches by the end users, the pressure on vendors to develop the patch in less time is reduced. It might seem that if the vendors are given more time to patch for the vulnerabilities, then the quality of the patch will be better. Unfortunately, research shows that there has been only marginal benefit in the quality of the patches (August & Tunca, 2008).

As we know, the software industry is profit maximizing; a factor that some people believe creates disincentives for vendors to release patches. A case in point is the "Genuine Advantage" program launched by Microsoft in 2005. Genuine Advantage allowed users to download service packs on the condition of authentication of their Windows XP operating system. In essence, Genuine Advantage denied pirates the opportunity to patch. Critics contend that Microsoft was differentiating legitimate users from illegitimate users in hopes of converting some of the latter, thereby increasing revenue and protecting shareholder value. The unintended consequence was an increase in the number of unpatched hosts (an increase in the attack surface), exacerbating the security problem. The concern is that in protecting itself and its legal customers, Microsoft was in fact attempting to maximize its own welfare (profit) at the expense of all. This case demonstrates how patching, piracy, and vendor practices are entangled; piracy affects patching, and both are shaped by a variety of factors including market economics, local cultural norms and the diverse intellectual property policies of multiple societies (Business Software Alliance-International Data Corporation, 2008). Here we refer readers back to chapter one where Harter (quoting Ackoff, 1981) defined a mess as a "set of two or more interdependent problems (p. 52)." It is in this example that we clearly see how economic systems are interacting with technical systems and human systems in a way to produce emergent properties…we see "the mess".

Moving Forward

Toward the beginning of the chapter we discussed the interdependent nature of information systems and therefore the interdependent nature of information security risk. While adopting a cost benefit model is viewed as a best security practice, it is important to keep in mind that accurately measuring information security risk is quite difficult, as we discussed earlier. Therefore, determining what efforts should be made to invest in information security and predicating investments on expected benefits are considerable challenges.

In the section immediately before this one we alluded to the interdependence between vendors' patch decisions and adopters' patch practices on the state of security. We also noted that piracy, patching, market economics, local cultural norms, and intellectual property policy are intertwined issues. The field is beginning to see research studies that investigate the nature and context of this interdependence.

A study by Rahman and Kannan (2007) investigated whether vendors who restrict patches only to licensed users complement or substitute government efforts to enforce anti-piracy with respect to social welfare. They found that when anti-piracy efforts are high (when there are high levels of public policy) and the cost of developing a quality patch is high, the vendor does not benefit from restricting patches. In other words, once a certain level of government intervention is provided, it optimizes both vendor profit and social welfare to distribute the patch universally (to both legitimate and illegitimate users). A related study (August & Tunca, 2008) investigated the conditions under which a policy that allows only legitimate users to patch is optimal for the software vendor and social welfare. The conditions allowed for in this study were security risk, piracy enforcement, and piracy tendency. Their findings suggest that it is in vendor's interests to restrict patching to licensed users under the following conditions: (1) high security risk combined with low piracy enforcement, or (2) low piracy tendencies in the consumer population combined with high piracy enforcement levels. Regarding social welfare, the findings of August and Tunca (2008), which are counter to that of Rahman and Kannan (2007), suggest that when piracy enforcement is high, restricting patches to licensed users can be socially optimal. Despite these differences, what these studies reveal is the complexity of formulating optimal patching and piracy policy for users and vendors by accounting for software product characteristics, consumer market conditions, local cultural norms, and intellectual property policy. More work in this area is needed.

A loss of market value is a loss of economic welfare for the company and its shareholders. What is less clear is the potential impact of the vulnerability on the state of security and social welfare. The challenges in estimating costs and benefits (risk reduction) are not just important in order for organizations to make investment decisions, such measures are important for informing discussions of the overall state of security as a matter of social welfare and public policy.

Summary

From the discussion above, we can see that sound information security practices offer numerous benefits for adopters seeking to reduce software security harm and risk. While investing in good information security techniques can provide adopters an advantage, improper implementation of such practices remains an issue. Furthermore, due to highly interdependent nature of information systems, the implementation of such practices cannot address all of the harm and risk posed by insecure software. Despite best efforts to build, deploy and govern secure software, some portion of software vulnerabilities is inevitable, which brings us to the role of vulnerability disclosure.

VULNERABILITY DISCLOSURE

Vulnerability disclosure refers to the publication of information about a security problem. Questions about vulnerability disclosure include when, how, what, and to whom vulnerabilities should be disclosed. Vulnerabilities may be reported by full disclosure or by responsible disclosure. Full disclosure refers to a situation where information about how to detect and exploit the vulnerability is posted on public websites after discovery. In contrast, responsible disclosure describes the situation where vulnerability is first disclosed privately to a vendor, and the finder works jointly with the vendor to solve the problem. The vulnerability is made public only when a patch is available.

Full Disclosure

Full disclosure practitioners believe that publishing vulnerability information immediately after the vulnerability is discovered is desirable for a variety of reasons. Some full disclosure advocates support this practice on the premise that enhancing user and public awareness is critical as user action (or inaction) is an undeniable part of the security equation. By disclosing fully and immediately, users will patch systems thereby making us all more secure. A second rationale for full disclosure is that fixes will be produced faster because vendors are pressed to respond in order to protect their reputation and market share. A third justification for full disclosure is that the free flow of information may help other vendors to provide attack prevention solutions such as firewalls, antivirus software, and intrusion detection systems (IDS), which could take less time to produce compared to fixing fundamental architectural flaws in the vulnerable software.

Today's practice is that once the information about vulnerability is public, it is the vendor's responsibility to either confirm or deny the information. As the definitive authority on the product, this affirmation typically includes a rating of the severity of the vulnerability, a fix schedule, and a statement about the vulnerability of previous versions and similar products. Under the full disclosure model, the vulnerability is announced prior to a patch being available, therefore, whenever possible, the vendor should suggest a workaround for the problem, such as disabling the flawed functionality or blocking communication ports until a patch is available.

Some full disclosure advocates favor immediate release based on reducing the window of exposure. Others contend that it is irresponsible to disclose, discuss, or confirm security issues until a full investigation has occurred and any necessary patches or releases are available. The rationale for keeping the vulnerability secret is that immediate full disclosure provides detailed information to attackers before a defense mechanism is available for users. Some contend that attackers are able to develop better exploits and share those exploits among the attacker community, thereby increasing the potential for strong attacks. While it is possible to quantify the number of days it takes for vendors to fix a certain vulnerability that was fully disclosed, it is almost impossible to quantify the number of attacks that succeed due to the knowledge about unveiled breaches.

Given the potential for harm, vendors have attempted to sue finders who practice full disclosure. Alex Halderman, a Princeton PhD student, was threatened by SunnComm with a ten million dollar lawsuit for exposing a weakness in the Media Max CD3 product that allows a user to duplicate copyrighted material (Smith, 2003). SunnComm maintained that the disclosure affected the company's reputation and caused its market value to drop by more than $10 million. In this particular case, the student did not reverse engineer the product, but only used a well-known and documented OS feature to achieve the reported result. In essence, he described how the normal use of the operating system could cause undesirable results in the Media Max CD3 application. SunnComm eventually reversed the decision to sue the grad student. SunnComm CEO acknowledged his threat to file a lawsuit was a mistake and that "the long-term nature of the lawsuit and the emotional result of the lawsuit would obscure the issue, and it would develop a life of its own" (McCullagh, 2003).

Hostile vendor response to full disclosure can hinder hardening of products and can strain the relationship between software vendors and adopters. If vendors should bear responsibility for the security of their products, one wonders if rather than threatening Mr. Halderman with a law suit, the vendor should somehow reward him for going above and beyond the company's best efforts to find flaws during the test phase of the lifecycle and contributing to the enhancement of its product line? Was SunnComm's stiff reaction due to the harm caused by the flaw or due to pressure from the makers of copyrighted material?

Responsible Disclosure

Responsible disclosure intends to ameliorate some of the concerns raised regarding full disclosure. Under responsible disclosure, practitioners (or "finders") notify the vendor first to allow a reasonable timeframe to fix a problem. Once a fix is released, a finder may or may not publish full details about the vulnerability. Although vendors prefer not to give financial rewards to finders, it is common industry practice to publicly credit them for their work when a fix becomes available. Responsible disclosure aims to allow a vendor enough time to apply best engineering practices. These best practices improve both the quality of the fix and diminish the chance of introducing new flaws in the product. Solutions can be back ported to previous versions and fixes can be made available on internationalized versions of the product by the time the patch is announced.

While best engineering practices are desirable, they can significantly increase the time needed to produce a fix, thus increasing the window of exposure. Enterprise customers may not welcome frequent patches and do not always deploy them quickly. They often prefer fewer releases due to the cost of deployment and prefer installing a single patch that resolves several vulnerabilities (Viega, 2009).

Although many vendors are committed to excellence, others may delay security fixes in favor of revenue-generating feature enhancements and bug fixes. When faced with unacceptable delays, the finder is left with the dilemma of either trusting that the vendor is responding reasonably and acting in good faith, or demanding a shorter timeframe on behalf of the user community. For the finder, the ultimate weapon against negligent vendors is to threaten them with a full disclosure.

Once a fix is released, some finders publicize details of their findings. Unfortunately, the same contributions that ought to lead to improvements in security can be used to cause harm. According to Viega (2009), over 95% of the malware that leverages security flaws uses vulnerabilities whose details were published on the internet. The role of Good Samaritan and user advocate is suddenly challenged by the perception that finders are after self-promotion and financial gains from selling security assessments. According to this train of thought, it is not in the economic interests of finders to put off taking credit for finding vulnerabilities, even though users may be hurt.

Full vs. Responsible Disclosure: More to the Story

Clearly, the debate of full vs. responsible disclosure is current and multi-dimensional. According to Schneier (2007), responsible disclosure, by definition, requires secrecy, which in turn prohibits public debate about security. Inhibiting the free flow of information hurts security education, and security education leads to improvements. Information secrecy prevents citizens from accurately assessing their own risk and from making informed decisions about security. Other experts argue that when systems carry life-threatening flaws (such as a defect in an airport control system that could lead to an airplane crash,) public awareness is a necessity regardless of whether or not a fix is currently available.

Given the debate over which is the better approach to vulnerability disclosure, Cavusoglu, Cavusoglu and Raghunathan (2004) investigated how vulnerabilities should be disclosed in order to minimize the social loss. In this study, social loss was defined as the vendor's patch development cost and the damage and workaround costs incurred by adopters. The study looked at three disclosure models: full vendor disclosure, immediate public disclosure, and a hybrid approach. They found that none of the disclosure models is always optimal. Rather, the findings of this study suggest that the optimal approach to vulnerability disclosure is stochastic and the main determinants are the characteristics of the vulnerability (i.e., risk before and after disclosure), the cost structure of the software user population, and the vendor's incentives to develop a patch.

Arora, Telang and Xu (2008) examined how vulnerability disclosure policy can optimally balance the need to protect users while providing vendors with incentives to develop patches expeditiously. Their model suggests that the optimal disclosure policy depends upon the behavior of vendors, potential attackers, and users. When vendors do not internalize the entire user loss, they will release the patch later than what is in the best interest of users, unless they are threatened with disclosure.

Arora, Nandkumar and Telang (2006) investigated how attack propensity changes with the disclosure and patching of vulnerabilities. In contrast to the Cavusoglu et. al. (2004) study, this research sought to identify which policy (full instant disclosure regardless of patch availability vs. limited or no disclosure) is optimal based on reducing attack frequency over time. Findings suggest that patches do, in fact, provide crucial information to attackers, underscoring the need to think carefully about efficient and effective means for managing patch dissemination.

Studies such as these have the potential to provide important insight into the nuances of when, how, what, and to whom vulnerability information should be reported. As we can see from these studies, the real questions are not about full vs. responsible disclosure, but the conditions under which a particular disclosure policy may be better than another.

Approaches to Fix Flaws Discovered In-House

During the normal process of fixing defects and developing new application releases, software manufacturers occasionally find security flaws in their own products. Two common approaches for correcting flaws discovered in house are silent patching and responsible disclosure. Companies who follow the silent fix process resolve vulnerabilities in the product without public disclosure. Fixes are shipped with new releases of the product. Google follow this process to patch weaknesses on the Chrome web browser (Duebendorfer & Frei, 2009).

Vendors who implement silent fixes assert that the practice increases the difficulty of attacks as criminals are forced to apply sophisticated reverse engineering techniques to uncover details about the flaws. In the field, this argument is countered by noting that hackers are proficient in the art of reverse engineering. According to Duebendorfer and Frei (2009), silent updates force immediate updates for all users and therefore achieve the highest number of users with the latest patches installed. While conclusions are drawn from observing the percentage of updated browsers accessing Google over a period of time, the study makes no mention about how often the updates fail and break the browser. Due to the unavailability of information, silent fixes can hurt customers who depend on information (such as the severity of vulnerabilities) from software manufacturers to determine when to deploy patches and new releases.

The responsible disclosure process for internally discovered vulnerabilities is analogous to responsible disclosure of vulnerabilities found by outside researchers and customers. The only difference is that no one is publicly credited with the finding as companies consider it part of their job. It is believed that most large software vendors opt for responsible disclosure. Once again though, it is difficult to define a "reasonable timeframe to fix the problem". Given that no one but the software manufacturer knows of this vulnerability, the decision on timing rests solely with the software manufacturer.

Some believe that vendors who follow a responsible disclosure process tend to back port the fixes of internally discovered vulnerabilities to earlier product versions, while vendors who tend to use the silent fix process fix only the latest versions of the product. Practitioners of the silent fix philosophy argue that the process avoids costly coordination efforts related to responsible disclosure. They also assert that silent patching provides near instant updates and gives all users the latest version of products, which helps to cut the cost of customer service and product support, thereby enhancing social welfare. Critics of silent patching claim that the silent fix approach takes away customers' control of their environment. Patches can cause applications to malfunction. Without knowledge of updates, customers cannot evaluate how updates will affect their environment.

The Market for Vulnerabilities

On the premise that meaningful, high quality vulnerability research should be rewarded and that customers have a right to know, firsthand, about vulnerabilities that may impact revenues, companies such as iDefense and TippingPoint have emerged. These companies purchase vulnerabilities from finders. Once a vulnerability is tested and confirmed by iDefense, they notify their subscribers and appropriate software manufacturers about the finding. iDefense does not go public with the information and neither do any of the customers. Instead, iDefense assumes the finder's duty of communicating with the vendor and providing sufficient information to create the fix. Once the fix is out, iDefense pays the finder for the research. Some note that this phenomenon, the creation of a market to profit from software flaws, seems ethically questionable. If the normative ethical position is that moral agents ought to do what is in their own self-interest, developers working for software vendors may be enticed to purposely create flaws in their code and later sell them. Companies like iDefense and TippingPoint could inflate the market value of their subscription service by leaking vulnerability information to harm nonsubscribers. In addition, the motives behind customers who are buying these types of services are unknown; and, they may intend to profit from the flaw rather than to use the information to improve their security. Furthermore, introducing a "middle man" could delay problem resolution. On several occasions in the past, it took over one year for iDefense to report vulnerabilities to software manufacturers (Elf, 2004).

Summary

There are pros and cons associated with each of the approaches for the vulnerability disclosure as evident from the discussion above. However, it seems that the more we know about optimal vulnerability disclosure, the more we know what we don't know. What the chapter, thus far, shows us is that responsibility for harm and risk of software security flaws is a complex process with numerous parties, and various competing interests – i.e., it is a mess. We return now to our discussion of the common good. We outline key issues that especially challenge the effort to attaining the common good of software assurance. And finally, with the idea that "the law should conform to ethics, not the other way around" (Stallman, 1992, p. 1), we introduce the role of government with regard to responsibility for harm and risk of software security flaws.

The Common Good: The Role and Challenges of Government Intervention

In ethics, maximization or optimization is the concept of always doing the act that yields the greatest return ("Maximization", 2008); this is the ideal of the common good. Given that it is the *polis* that bears responsibility for the common good, the role and challenges of government intervention are timely and relevant.

One role for government is to enact public policy, laws, and regulations that seek to advance the common good and enhance social welfare. Laws and regulations are essentially rules that aim to induce people to do what we want them to do. Inducements can be positive or negative. Positive inducements, also called incentives, seek to make it easier and more rewarding for people to do what we want them to do. Deterrents, or negative inducements, seek to make it harder, or more costly, for people to do what we do not want them to do. We turn to a discussion of public policy and its role in responsibility for harm and risk of software security flaws.

Profit, Welfare, Laws and Software Security

As we know, the actions that each user, vendor, and adopter takes is influenced by multiple incentives and disincentives and produces several consequences for other users. Software vendors as profit maximizers patch their systems not because of social responsibility but rather because of the profit motive, i.e., the market measures and rewards companies by how much profit they can generate. Patching is only incidental to this goal.

For users, patching becomes a matter first of knowledgeability, and assuming full knowledge of the need to patch. Patching for users becomes a matter of how frustrated they are by unpatched software compared to their frustration with having to test and deploy yet another patch. Assuming the user frustration with unpatched software is greater; a vendor can decide whether the cost of possibly losing these users is worth the cost of creating the patch, and how to create patch deployment that decrease vendors' cost of patch efforts. Today, unregistered copies of Windows are not entitled to receive security patches. For this reason, most pirated copies of Windows are infected with viruses. This phenomenon threatens the security of all legal users, and Microsoft's reputation as a secure vendor. If sales decrease due to a perception that Windows is more prone to virus infections than its competitors, the company would be financially better off providing free security updates to all users, even those using pirated copies of windows.

A key question is how to balance the point of view of the profit maximizing vendor with the needs of adopters and users in a manner that is welfare maximizing. August and Tunca (2006) compared the status quo of consumer self-patching effects with three patching options: (1) mandatory patching, (2) patching rebates, and (3) usage taxes to determine the incentives each option and effects regarding profit maximization and welfare maximization. Further, they compared these patching options for proprietary versus open source software. It was observed that mandatory patching is not useful in the case of open source. In the case of proprietary software, contractually mandating consumers (option 1) to patch does not improve vendor profit and is usually not helpful in increasing the social welfare (August & Tunca, 2006). The primary reason for the ineffectiveness of mandatory patching is that the consumers are forced to commit to the potential costs when they purchase the software, which negatively influences their purchasing behavior. This observation suggests that the patching decision should be left to the consumers and other ways to improve the users patching behavior should be investigated.

Option 2 is to provide users with increased incentives to patch by offering rebates to patching customers. According to August and Tunca (2006), there are two way for determining the amount of rebate to be given to its customers. The first is for the rebate amount to be determined by the vendor and the second is for the rebate amount to be determined by a social planner (a decision maker who attempts to achieve a result that is in the best interest of all parties). In the case of vendor-determined rebates, August and Tunca (2006) found that when both the patching cost and the effective security risk are high, the vendor must price low to induce purchases. In such cases, by offering rebates, vendors can induce an increased patching population and increase the security of the product. On the other hand, when the expected security risk is low as compared to the patching costs, it becomes expensive for the vendor to incentivize consumers to patch and rebates can result in losses for the vendor. In the case of social planner-determined rebates, when the security risk is high and patching costs are high, under vendor's optimal pricing, the patching population is small. Therefore, forcing the vendor to assume part of the risk by paying a rebate to the patching consumers may increase social welfare. On the opposite side, if the cost of patching is low, forcing the vendor to offer a rebate can decrease the social welfare by inducing inefficient patching behavior.

Given that poor patching behavior by the users introduces security risks on the entire user population, August and Tunca (2006) also investigated whether a usage tax would drive a certain group of users of the usage pool, thereby increasing overall security. They found that imposing a tax decreases the vendor's optimal price, but the price plus the tax, i.e., the effective amount that the consumers have to pay to use the software is larger than the optimal vendor price with no tax. Therefore, they concluded that taxes neither increase vendor profits, nor increases social welfare for proprietary software. Interestingly, a usage tax is the best policy for open sources software except when costs and risk are low, where a rebate policy still prevails. While the findings of this study should be of interest to vendors, adopters, and policy makers, more research is needed.

Furthermore, we have to remember that software security is entangled with other issues of information security. "Hacking tools" such as Metasploit, Ice Pack, and L0phtCrack significantly lower the technical knowledge necessary for attackers to commit transgressions against software. With the aim of minimizing computer attacks, an amendment to the Computer Misuse Act was proposed in the United Kingdom to make it illegal to supply (i.e., create and distribute) software that is likely to be used to commit an offense. Therefore, policy analysis needs to look at the effects of policies that ban tools used by hackers, the reduction on cybercrime, and consequent effects on the state of software security.

Governments have also increased the enforcements associated with different computer related violations. Take for example, the punishments for the following computer intrusions. Samy Kamkar, the author of the MySpace worm (Kamkar, 2007) was sentenced to 3 years probation, 90 days of community service, and an undisclosed amount of restitutions. Computer hackers, Eric McCarty, breached the University of California's (USC) registration website (Lemos, 2006). McCarty reported the vulnerability to USC and to SecurityFocus. This unauthorized intrusion resulted in a penalty of probations, home detention, and restitution for McCarty. Policy analysis needs to look at the effects of enforcement policies on deterrence, and the consequent effects of the state of software security.

Challenges of Policy Solutions

The measure of an effective public policy is its ability to address a problem. By nature, public policies target a specific locus of control to serve as leverage to fix the problem. Applying public policy to software security will be a challenge because the responsibility for harm and risk of software security is a complex causal situation. Both the causes and the effects of software vulnerabilities are diffuse and many. In situations where causes and effects of social problems are diffuse and rooted in a complex organizational system, inducements that are narrowly applied, as is the case with most public policy, are unlikely to have significant impact. It does not mean that public policy will not be enacted. It will. What happens though, is that that narrowly created policy is enacted over time, gradually addressing portions, hopefully the most significant, of the problem while leaving other portions unaddressed.

It also happens that inducements have unintended consequences, sometimes hurting the very things one is trying to protect. An example of a law that has had unexpected side effects is the German "anti-hacker law", enacted in June 2007, to ban hacking tools from its territory (Blau, 2007). As a result of this law, several organizations moved overseas to host the forbidden content and launch attacks from outside Germany. The law made no exceptions for security professionals who perform security assessments, thus limiting the effectiveness of these firms. Another example is the Eric McCarty case mentioned earlier. McCarty accessed only 7 USC database records and reported the vulnerability to SecurityFocus.com. SecurityFocus.com, in turn, notified USC about the flaw through a responsible disclosure process (Lemos, 2006). Despite this fact, USC was obligated by law to notify all 275,000 individuals in the database and shut down their registration service for 2 weeks (Yang, 2006). The estimated cost to USC was $140,000, which became the value of the law suit against the 25 years old would-be-USC student. Clearly, McCarty broke the law, but were his acts malicious or unethical? Will punishments like this genuinely help to ensure society's safety and peacefulness in the future?

Other Possible Government Roles

Another point of leverage the U.S. government has is its buying power. The Federal Desktop Core Configuration (FDCC) mandate is an example of the use of leverage. The FDCC is an OMB (U.S. Office of Management and Budget) mandate implemented in February 2008. It requires all Federal Agencies to standardize the configuration of approximately 300 settings on each of their Windows XP and Vista computers. The reason for this standardization is to strengthen Federal IT security by reducing opportunities for hackers to access and exploit government computer systems. As a result, several large vendors such as Microsoft and Symantec had to adhere to a list of configuration settings considered secure. It is generally believed that employing this standard yielded considerable government savings. Numerous other security focused organizations have also benefited from this mandate by adopting FDCC in their own environments.

Concerns with vendors' security practices made the Government explore in new mandates. Based on lists of well known and well understood attack techniques, the state of New York created an application security procurement language document which attempts to make software makers liable for their work. The goal is to give consumers a means to fight back when a minimum standard of due care is not achieved. The effectiveness of this mandate remains to be seen.

Vulnerabilities in widely used open source components and protocols affect a large number of users and demand coordination with multiple parties. Another role for government in this emerging landscape may be as coordinator and mediator of vulnerability disclosures in such cases, as it did in the past with the Sendmail vulnerability (Palella, 2003).

The fast paced dynamics of the field may make some laws and government efforts obsolete. While the laws in some countries traditionally have approached software as a product much like a shirt or a book, the entire concept of software has evolved into something more like a service. In addition, the infancy of the software assurance field imposes a real challenge for governments to determine the right level of incentives to provide.

CONCLUSION

As we have seen from the discussion above, the different parties involved have their own set of responsibilities, weaknesses, and interests. On the one hand are vendors, who are motivated to maximize their profit at the expense of the degree of security built into their products; with a primary objective being to maximize their market share and gain competitive advantage by bringing new products into the market in each business cycle. Factors such as complexity and cost to deliver more secure products conflict with market forces, yet this state of conflict does not absolve vendors of some responsibility for harm and risk of software flaws. For making vendors more liable for their products, a number of suggestions have been put forward, such as giving incentives to those organizations that invest in good programming practices, handing penalties and taxes to those who have high vulnerability rates, and granting access to source code to enhance the security of the code.

Adopters, on the other hand, have their own share of issues to deal with in implementing security practices within their organizations. Although the incentives to invest in security are many, the real difficulty lies in its implementation. Security isn't a technical problem only, but it encompasses other aspects as well, incorrect configurations of the systems, insufficient firewalls rules, inept policies, patching issues, low levels of security culture among the staff are some of the many reasons behind the operational failures.

The hard part of the problem of responsibility for harm and risk of software flaws, though, stems from interdependent risk, as discussed at the onset of the chapter. Given the diffuse and polycentric nature of this problem, vulnerability disclosure policies and practices have become important mechanisms for attempting to "raise the tide". The two models for vulnerability disclosure are full disclosure and responsible disclosure. While pros and cons of full and responsible disclosure models have been identified, more research is needed to improve our understanding of the conditions under which different vulnerability disclosure policies are effective.

We have also seen that government is responsible for enacting public policy, laws, and regulations that seek to advance the common good and social welfare. One challenge is in striking an effective balance among the different parties responsible for harm and risk of software security flaws: vendors, adopters and users. Even then, there are unintended consequences, hurting the very things one is trying to protect. The interdependent nature of the risk makes it difficult to develop policies that address causes of risk. Interdependent risk implicates interdependent responsibility. The logic of collective action (Olson, 1971) is such that in small groups, where each member gets a substantial proportion of the total gain simply because there are few others in the group, a collective good can often be provided by the voluntary, self-interested action of the members of the group. However, in the case of software security, the existence of a large group is obvious. While we do not have clear answers, we believe the real challenge is in finding the point at which the benefit to the group from having the collective good exceeds the total cost by more than it exceeds the gain to one or more groups. Only then we can achieve the objective of welfare economic and common good to help society make better choices with regard to the use of the available resources.

ACKNOWLEDGMENT

We got useful comments on drafts of some of this material from Wesley Higaki, Robert Hoffman, Shelley Mahr and Jessica Johannes.

REFERENCES

Ackoff, R. (1981). *Creating the corporate future*. New York: John Wiley & Sons.

Addams, J. (1910). *Twenty years at hull house: With autobiographical notes*. New York: The MacMillan Company.

Akerlof, G. (1970). "The market for lemons": Quality, uncertainty and the market mechanism. *The Quarterly Journal of Economics*, *84*(3), 488–500. doi:10.2307/1879431

Anderson, R. (2001). Why information security is hard - An economic perspective. Retrieved from http://doi.ieeecomputersociety.org/10.1109/ACSAC.2001.991552

Anderson, R., & Moore, T. (2006). The economics of information security. *Science*, *314*, 611. doi:10.1126/science.1130992

Aristotle. (350 BC). *Politics* (B. Jowett, trans.). Retrieved from http://classics.mit.edu/Aristotle/politics.html

Arora, A., Caulkins, J. P., & Telang, R. (October, 2004). *Sell first, fix later: Impact of patching on software quality*. Working Paper Series, H. John Heinz III School of Public Policy and Management, Carnegie Mellon University, Pittsburgh, PA. Retrieved October 8, 2009 from http://ssrn.com/abstract=670285

Arora, A., Nandkumar, A., & Telang, R. (2006). Does information security attack frequency increase with vulnerability disclosure? An empirical analysis. *Information Systems Frontiers*, *8*, 350–362. doi:10.1007/s10796-006-9012-5

Arora, A., Telang, R., & Xu, H. (2008). Optimal policy for software vulnerability disclosure. *Management Science*, *54*(4), 642–656. doi:10.1287/mnsc.1070.0771

August, T., & Tunca, T. (2006). Network software security and user icentives. *Management Science*, *52*(11), 1703–1702. doi:10.1287/mnsc.1060.0568

August, T., & Tunca, T. (2008). Let the pirates patch? An economic analysis of software security patch restrictions. *Information Systems Research*, *19*(1), 48–70. doi:10.1287/isre.1070.0142

Blau, J. (2007, August). German antihacker law could backfire, critics warn. *InfoWorld Website*. Retrieved from http://www.infoworld.com/d/security-central/german-antihacker-law-could-backfire-critics-warn-439

Business Software Alliance-International Data Corporation. (2009). Sixth annual BSA-IDC global software - 08 piracy study. Retrieved September 6, 2009 from www.bsa.org

Cavusoglu, H., Cavusoglu, H., & Raghunathan, S. (2004, May). *How to disclose software vulnerabilities responsibly?* Paper presented at the Third Annual Workshop on Economics of Information Security (WEISO4), University of Minnesota, Minneapolis, MN. Retrieved from http://infosecon.net/workshop/slides/weis_4_3.ppt

Cavusoglu, H., Mishra, B., & Raghunathan, S. (2004). The effect of internet security breach announcements on market value: Capital market reactions for breached firms and internet security developers. *International Journal of Electronic Commerce*, *9*(1), 69–104.

Computer Misuse Act 1990. Retrieved from http://www.opsi.gov.uk/acts/acts1990/UKpga_19900018_en_1.htm

Computing Research Association. (2006). *Four grand challenges in trustworthy computing*. (Report Series) Retrieved from http://www.cra.org/reports/trustworthy.computing.pdf

Cusumano, M. A. (2004). Who is liable for bugs and security flaws in software? *Communications of the ACM*, *47*(3), 25–27. doi:10.1145/971617.971637

Duebendorfer, T., & Frei, S. (2009, May). *Why silent updates boost security*. Paper presented at CRITIS 2009 Critical Infrastructures Security Workshop, Bonn, Germany. Retrieved from http://www.techzoom.net/publications/silent-updates/

Elf, D. (2004). [Full–Disclosure] iDefense: solution or problem? Derkeiler. Retrieved May 7, 2009 from http://www.derkeiler.com/pdf/Mailing-Lists/Full-Disclosure/2004-07/0698.pdf

Garg, A., Curtis, J., & Halper, H. (2003). Quantifying the financial impact of IT security breaches. *Information Management & Computer Security*, *11*(2/3), 74–83. doi:10.1108/09685220310468646

Greenemeier, L. (2007, May). T.J. Maxx data theft likely due to wireless 'wardriving'. *Information Week*. Retrieved from http://www.eetimes.com/news/latest/showArticle.jhtml?articleID=199500574

Howard, M., & LeBlanc, D. (2003). *Writing secure code* (2nd ed.). Redmond, WA: Microsoft Press.

Howard, M., & Lipner, S. (2006). *The security development lifecycle*. Redmond, WA: Microsoft Press.

IT Governance Institute. (2006). *Information security governance: Guidance for boards of directors and executive management* (2nd ed.).

Just, R., Hueth, D., & Schmitz, A. (2005). *The welfare economics of public policy: A practical approach to project and policy evaluation*. Williston, VT: Edward Elgar Publishing.

Kamkar, S. (2007). *The MySpace Worm*. Presentation at the OWASP & WASC AppSec 2007 Conference. San Jose, CA. Retrieved from http://www.owasp.org/images/7/79/OWASP-WASCAppSec2007SanJose_SamyWorm.ppt

Lemos (2006, September). Security pro pleads guilty to USC breach. *Security Focus*. Retrieved from http://www.securityfocus.com/news/11411

Maximization. (2008, August 2). *Wikipedia*. Retrieved from http://en.wikipedia.org/wiki/Maximization

McCullagh, D. (2003, October). SunnComm won't sue grad student. *Cnet news* Retrieved from http://news.cnet.com/SunnComm-wont-sue-grad-student/2100-1027_3-5089448.html

Moor, J. (1985). What is computer ethics? *Metaphilosophy*, *16*(4), 266–275. doi:10.1111/j.1467-9973.1985.tb00173.x

Myers, G. (1979). *The art of software testing*. Hoboken, NJ: John Wiley and Sons.

Olson, M. (1971). *The logic of collective action. Public goods and the theory of groups*. Cambridge, MA: Harvard University Press.

Pagkalos, D. (2008, January). ScanAlert's "Hacker Safe" badge not so safe and PCI compliant. </XSSED> web site. Retrieved from http://www.xssed.com/news/55/ScanAlerts_Hacker_Safe_badge_not_so_safe_and_PCI_compliant/

Pirate Party. (2009). Retrieved November 29, 2009 from http://www.piratpartiet.se/international/english

Rahman, M., & Kannan, K. (2007, May). *The countervailing of restricted patch distribution: Economic and policy implications*. Paper presented at 2007 Workshop on Economics of Information Security, Pittsburgh, PA. Retrieved September 6, 2009 from http://weis2007.econinfosec.org/papers/45.pdf.

Schneier, B. (2007, January). Debating full disclosure. *Schneier blog site*. Retrieved from http://www.schneier.com/blog/archives/2007/01/debating_full_d.html

Schneier, B. (2008). *Software Makers Should Take Responsibility*. Retrieved September 27, 2009 from http://www.schneier.com/essay-228.html

Stallman, R. (1992, April). Why software should be free. GNU Operating Systems website. Retrieved from http://www.gnu.org/philosophy/shouldbefree.html

Stonebruner, G., Goguen, A., & Feringa, A. (2002). *Risk management guide for information technology systems* (NIST Publication No. 800-30). Retrieved from http://csrc.nist.gov/publications/nistpubs/800-30/sp800-30.pdf

Viega, J. (2009, January). Responsible Disclosure is Irresponsible. *O'Reilly Community web site*. Retrieved from http://broadcast.oreilly.com/2009/01/responsible-disclosure-is-irre.html

Wagner, S. (2005, May). Software quality economics for defect-detection techniques using failure prediction. In *Proceedings of the Third Workshop on Software Quality* St. Louis, Missouri, May, 2005.

Wagner, S. (2007, May). Using economics as basis for modeling and evaluating software quality. *First International Workshop on the Economics of Software and Computation*, Minneapolis, MN.

Yang (2006). *San Diego Computer Expert Charged with Hacking into U.S.C. Computer System Containing Student Applications*. (DOJ News Release 06-045). Retrieved from http://www.usdoj.gov/criminal/cybercrime/mccartyCharge.htm

Zheng, J., Williams, L., Nagappan, N., Snipes, W., Hudepohl, J., & Vouk, M. (2006). On the value of static analysis for fault detection in software. *IEEE Transactions on Software Security*, *32*(4), 240–253. doi:10.1109/TSE.2006.38

ADDITIONAL READING

Biancuzzi, F. (2006, September 5). Disclosure survey. *Security Focus, 1-3*. Retrieved from http://www.securityfocus.com/columnists/415

Gibson, N. (2007, July). 5 reasons restricting hacking is not like gun control. *builder.au*. Retrieved from http://digg.com/d1AUNU

Incentives for improving cybersecurity in the private sector: A cost-benefit perspective: Hearings before the Subcommittee on Emerging Threats, Cybersecurity, and Science and Technology of the House Committee on Homeland Security, 110th Cong. 1 (2007) (testimony of Dr. Lawrence A. Gordon): Retrieved July 12, 2009 from http://homeland.house.gov/SiteDocuments/20071031155020-22632.pdf

Krebs, B. (2008, April 3). Apple Issues QuickTime Update for Mac, Windows. *The Washington Post*. Retrieved from http://voices.washingtonpost.com/securityfix/2008/04/apple_issues_quicktime_update_1.html

Lemos, R. (2004, May). Sasser's toll likely stands at 500,000 infections. *Cnet news* Retrieved from http://news.cnet.com/Sassers-toll-likely-stands-at-500,000-infections/2100-7349_3-5205107.html

McLaghling, K. (2006, July). Symantec: Vista Beta Code Could Pose Security Risks. *Channel Web*. Retrieved from http://www.crn.com/security/190700005;jsessionid=FEEST2PC41ZSOQSNDLPSKHSCJUNN2JVN

Palella (2003). Vulnerability disclosure, The double edged sword. Retrieved from http://www.giac.org/certified_professionals/practicals/gsec/2855.php.

Smith, T. (2003, October). SunnComm to sue 'Shift key' student for $10m [White paper]. *The Register*. Retrieved from http://www.theregister.co.uk/2003/10/09/sunncomm_to_sue_shift_key/

Stanford Encyclopedia of Philosophy. (2009). *Jane Addams*. Retrieved from http://plato.stanford.edu/entries/addams-jane/

Stuttard, D. (2008, January). Business as usual. *PortSwigger.net web application security web site*. Retrieved from http://blog.portswigger.net/2008/01/business-as-usual.html

ENDNOTE

1 Regarding pareto improvements, it should be noted that there can be numerous pareto optimal alternatives. Pareto measures are descriptive theoretical measures, they describe what is or could be – and they do not describe what should be. The role of welfare economics is in making these options manifest and perceivable. The subjective evaluation of which option to choose given consideration of liberty, equity, justice and so on, is the role of the policy maker.

APPENDIX: DISCUSSION QUESTIONS

1. Which model yields more secure software: open source vs. proprietary software?
2. Does market share have any relation to vulnerabilities?
3. How do shipping and patch release deadlines affect software security?
4. What role could a professional body play in helping improve the industry?
5. Why have software vendors traditionally not been liable for their flaws as car companies?
6. What is the role of the end user license agreement?
7. What is the responsibility of your school (or any other educational institution or the educational system) for the harm and risk of software security flaws?
8. Who else is responsible and how?
9. Who should be responsible for software security flaws?
10. The authors refer to software vulnerabilities as externalities; what does this mean? Do you agree?
11. Is software a common good? Why or why not?
12. How are education/professional bodies responsible? Who else should be responsible? How should they be responsible?
13. How can we create disincentives for irresponsible security researchers (aka hackers)?
14. What do security researchers (hackers) get out of finding flaws? What do they do with the findings?
15. Who suffers as a result of software security flaws?
16. Does intent matter? For example: what if I get confidential information from Google - am I a hacker?
17. Are all hackers unethical?
18. Can a system be secure?
19. Is security a belief and vulnerability an idea (refer to the notion of beliefs and vulnerabilities as presented in chapter 1)?
20. Is the debate on 'who should be responsible' an obfuscation technique for never achieving security?
21. Assume there are many parties that are responsible for some aspect of software security – if you do your part, but the next person does not, would you feel the need to do something about this problem?

Chapter 7
Social/Ethical Issues in Predictive Insider Threat Monitoring

Frank L. Greitzer
Pacific Northwest National Laboratory, USA

Deborah A. Frincke
Pacific Northwest National Laboratory, USA

Mariah Zabriskie[1]
Pacific Northwest National Laboratory, USA

ABSTRACT

Combining traditionally monitored cybersecurity data with other kinds of organizational data is one option for inferring the motivations of individuals, which may in turn allow early prediction and mitigation of insider threats. While unproven, some researchers believe that this combination of data may yield better results than either cybersecurity or organizational data would in isolation. However, this nontraditional approach yields inevitable conflicts between security interests of the organization and privacy interests of individuals. There are many facets to debate. Should warning signs of a potential malicious insider be addressed before a malicious event has occurred to prevent harm to the organization and discourage the insider from violating the organization's rules? Would intervention violate employee trust or legal guidelines? What about the possibilities of misuse? Predictive approaches cannot be validated a priori; false accusations may harm the career of the accused; and collection/monitoring of certain types of data may adversely affect employee morale. In this chapter, we explore some of the social and ethical issues stemming from predictive insider threat monitoring and discuss ways that a predictive modeling approach brings to the forefront social and ethical issues that should be considered and resolved by stakeholders and communities of interest.

DOI: 10.4018/978-1-61692-245-0.ch007

INTRODUCTION

In this chapter, we explore some of the social/ethical and privacy issues that may arise from attempts to protect information assets from crimes (including but not limited to espionage and sabotage) perpetrated by employees and trusted "insiders." Espionage and sabotage involving computer networks are among the most pressing cybersecurity challenges that threaten government and private sector information infrastructures. Surveys, such as the 2004 e-Crime Watch Survey (CERT 2004), reveal that current employees are thought to pose the second-greatest cybersecurity threat (22%), exceeded only by hackers (40%). Categories such as former employees (6%), current/former service providers (4%), foreign entities, competitors, and the like are perceived as much less likely sources. The insider threat is manifested when individuals do not comply with established policies, whether the noncompliance results from malice (malicious insiders) or a disregard for security policies. The types of crimes and abuse associated with insider threats are significant; the most serious include espionage, sabotage, terrorism, embezzlement, extortion, bribery, and corruption. Malicious activities include an even broader range of exploits, such as copyright violations, negligent use of classified data, fraud, unauthorized access to sensitive information, and illicit communications with unauthorized recipients. The insider threat also includes unintentional actions by individuals who inadvertently or unknowingly provide access to outsiders, such as in phishing and other attacks. For the purposes of the present discussion, we shall limit our scope to crimes or attempted exploits by malicious insiders.

The "insider" is an individual presently or previously authorized to access an organization's information system, data, or network. In many organizations, these individuals knowingly accept a commensurate level of scrutiny from their organization, meant to deter or detect abuse of these privileges. Insiders represent an especially insidious threat to organizations if they are careless or malicious. As trusted employees, they are permitted by the organization to have access to information and systems that could compromise the organization if misused. In deliberately proffering trust, the organization also decides in advance whether the risk outweighs the advantages, and presumably could withdraw such trust if it so chooses.

"Insider threat" for our purposes refers to harmful acts that trusted insiders *might* carry out—for example, something that causes harm to the organization or an unauthorized act that benefits the individual. A U.S. Department of Defense (DoD) Inspector General report (1997) found that 87% of identified intruders into DoD information systems were either employees or others internal to the organization. More generally, recent studies of computer crime or "cybercrime" –such as the CERT *E-Crime Watch Surveys* (CERT, 2004, 2005, 2006, and 2007; see also Keeney et al., 2005) in both government and commercial sectors– reveal that the proportion of (reported) insider threat exploits has ranged from 31% in 2004 to 49% in 2007, and the financial impact and operating losses due to insider intrusions are increasing. Insider crimes are not only a financial concern for employers; they also yield societal costs in the form of short- to long-term physical and emotional pain, lost opportunities, and additional "protection" mechanisms that society puts in place to prevent, detect, and respond to such threats. These costs are borne by individuals and organizations. To the extent that predictive insider threat monitoring can reduce risks and costs to organizations and society, the greater the benefit to society in terms of capacity to invest in other priorities. This too, is part of the promise of predictive insider threat monitoring. We hope that this chapter will provide input for those seeking to begin, or continue, this conversation.

Figure 1. Assessing ability, opportunity, and motivation is a primary decision-making task underlying the threat analysis.

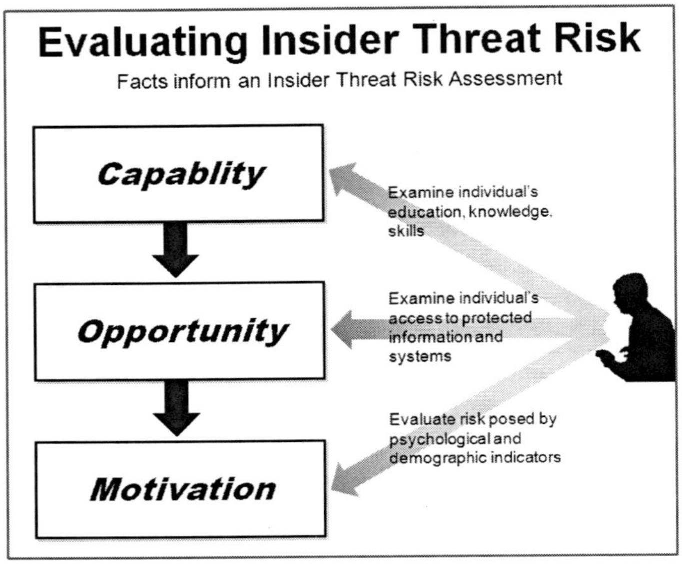

Threat Detection Process

With regard to insider threat, the current practice is largely reactive—attempting to identify a perpetrator of a crime after the event occurs—and focuses on forensic analyses of recorded computer activities to obtain evidence of the exploit (e.g., Gabriel son, Goertzel, Hoenicke, Kleiner, & Winograd, 2008). The security research community is investigating the feasibility of identifying potentially malicious insiders early, even before a malicious act has been committed, so as to prevent or mitigate harmful acts.

Identifying the warning signs of insider threats[2] prior to a full-blown event requires timely and complete communication and coordination of all the facts—some personal and confidential—between Security, Human Resources (HR), coworkers, and management. It might, for instance, require an analyst to put the pieces of information together and evaluate risk level for each employee whose behavior appears to involve some risk. The analyst would need to ascertain capacity (such as legitimate or apparent access sufficient to do harm and technical capability to do so), motivation to harm the organization, and decide if, in conjunction with the observed computer or organizational activities, further scrutiny is needed. Numerous next steps are possible. For instance, if the analyst decides that the risk is high, he or she could quickly alert the personnel manager and systems managers, and decide on appropriate mitigations. The initial decision-making task is to assess whether the individual has the ability, the opportunity, and the motivation to perform a malicious act as depicted in Figure 1. Note that error is possible at each stage of this process, and judgments are likely to be qualitative and based on observations available to the analyst, which will not necessarily be comprehensive.

BACKGROUND

There has been much research into the psychology and motivation of insiders, but the hard fact is that insider attacks are difficult to predict (Kramer, Heuer, & Crawford, 2005). Research aimed at prediction is still desirable, however, because of the potential advantages (Schultz, 2002). In describing case studies, Shaw and Fisher (2005, p. ix) noted that a common factor in insider espionage is that in most cases "damage could have been prevented by timely and effective action to address the anger, pain, anxiety, or psychological impairment of perpetrators, who exhibited signs of vulnerability or risk well in advance of the crime of abuse." Thus, as Schultz (2002) observes, an approach to prediction is to identify attack-related behaviors and symptoms—"indicators" that include deliberate markers, meaningful errors, preparatory behaviors, correlated usage patterns, verbal behavior and personality traits—from which "clues can be pieced together to predict and detect an attack." (Schultz, 2002, p. 526) Similarly, we believe that it is possible to combine traditionally monitored information security data (e.g., workstation/Internet activity) with other kinds of organizational and social data to infer the motivations of individuals and predict the actions that they are undertaking, which may allow early identification of high-risk individuals. But as Schultz observed when advocating this type of approach, while it is promising to synthesize and build upon critical models and findings concerning insider attacks, such approaches are unproven (Schultz, 2002). Certainly, predictions must be of high quality before they can be relied upon to direct mitigation. Improving prediction quality may involve may involve augmenting data captured by monitoring computer activities with data obtained from other observations, such as those typically kept in personnel files. The issues include both accuracy (beyond the scope of this chapter) and determining whether the methods used to predict or detect insiders are counterproductive. Proactive mitigation may be an advantage to the organization, and may also be an advantage to the individuals involved. However, it is possible that increased, invasive, or onerous scrutiny would exacerbate an already precarious situation, and lead to more—or more severe—malicious insider threat events than less invasive methods (which typically do not consider personnel data or at most consider personnel data through traditional management routes).[3]

This leads to the dilemma at the heart of this chapter. Should warning signs of a malicious insider be addressed before the abuse occurs? While each component of the required analysis is important, the task of identifying possible behavioral indicators through employee monitoring—largely a profiling activity—represents the most difficult and sensitive challenge. What data are appropriate for insider threat monitoring? Would intervention based on potentially useful data violate employee trust or legal guidelines? Predictions imply the potential for false accusations, which can affect the career of the accused, and collection/monitoring of certain types of data may adversely affect employee morale, which in turn may increase the likelihood of insider abuse. How can such competing interests be reconciled? What should be the path forward in light of such uncertainties?

DATA MONITORING CHALLENGES

Using research literature and case studies as a guide, we first describe a possible set of employee behavioral-monitoring data that may be collected. We also note practical considerations that have led to the evolution of a set of variables that will help identify possible precursors or indicators of potential insider abuse.

Types of Data

Numerous studies have been carried out to identify the psychological profiles that are consistent with insider threat and could serve as predictors. Many of these are case studies of individuals who have been convicted of espionage. Also, numerous papers and books, such as *Fighting Computer Crime* (Parker, 1998), have investigated in detail computer crime cases and include interviews with those who have been caught committing computer crimes and in many cases convicted in court. Interview studies and surveys (Gelles, 2005) of convicted spies, such as Project Slammer (1990)[4], have revealed behaviors, motivations, personality characteristics, and mindsets associated with this criminal behavior. The most-at-risk personality disorders in personnel security, and most prevalent among spies, are antisocial personality and narcissistic personality (Krofcheck & Gelles, 2005). This body of research may be summarized using general categories of "warning signs"—psychosocial/behavioral indicators—that might be observed before an employee actually commits an insider attack: anti-social personality disorder, ability, narcissism, personal stress, attitude, isolation, and suspicious behavior. In addition to these warning signs, some demographic indicators common to past instances of insider threat include (Krofcheck & Gelles, 2005):

- non-U.S. citizen,
- major life change,
- access to classified information,
- system administrator rights,
- high level of computer skills and knowledge,
- intermittent work history,
- Family/marriage issues,
- legal issues,
- credit/debt problems,
- past or current arrest/criminal activity, and
- strong interest in Blackhat community (see Wikipedia, 2009 for a Blackhat definition).

Organizations with more than 500 employees typically maintain information systems to collect and use organizational and employee data that enable payroll, benefits, reporting, and other activities. Two basic sources of internal employee data common to most large organizations are HR data and security data. An HR Information System, or HRIS, collects, maintains, and reports employee demographics and other data. Larger organizations typically have multiple systems, databases, and processes to manage employee data in addition to the main HRIS. Together, they form a rich repository of information about past, present, and potential employees. Data collected often include the following:

- national origin,
- Visa status, if a foreign national,
- results of background investigations, including credit, criminal, work history, and personal references,
- requests for personal, medical, and other leaves,
- education level,
- life events including birth, adoption, marriage, divorce, and death in the family,
- attendance records,
- performance evaluations,
- legal issues (e.g., garnished wages),
- disciplinary issues,
- complaints by or against the employee, and
- employment applications (including background check, references, education, and work history).

Organizations that handle classified and/or sensitive materials typically have some sort of security and/or cybersecurity department that tracks incidents and indicators in both personnel and electronic security. The security department may maintain the following information:

- legal issues (e.g., arrests),
- security clearance awarded (or denied),
- complaints by or against the employee,
- security incidents involving the employee,
- actual (or attempted) inappropriate internet or system access, and
- times and dates for facility access.

Based on the same research literature and case studies, other researchers (e.g., Band et al.,

2008) propose modeling approaches designed to exploit consistencies or patterns in precursors to insider attacks, *viz.*:

- the prevalence of both behavioral and technical precursors (such as computer use policies/rule violations),
- stressful events, including organizational sanctions, that are observable before and during the insider attack, and
- prevalence of certain personality predispositions, including serious mental disorders, personality problems, social skills, and a history of rule conflicts.

These patterns and precursors to insider espionage and sabotage incidents may be manifest in particular issues relating to financial debt and/or anger, where anger (disgruntlement) may be fueled by a need for attention, revenge, or ego satisfaction, among other issues. A critical question, of course, is how to observe and record such behavioral data?

Sources of Data

Not all organizations store employee data electronically; some of it is in hard copy notes or memos, while other information is "tribal knowledge" shared by staff and managers. Those organizations that do collect information electronically often do so in multiple systems that may or may not interface. Access to these data is a challenge faced by many organizations. Below, we discuss multiple sources of relevant data and potential indicators present in most large organizations. After describing the source in more detail, we give an example of how the source might provide indicators that predict risk of insider threat. Of particular concern, of course, is whether or not collection of the data in question presents legal, ethical, or privacy concerns. We briefly discuss potential legal/ethical/privacy barriers to using the data sources, if any; in the section that follows, we address those issues in more detail.

360 Profiler

A 360 Profiler is a survey tool used to evaluate an employee's traits, performance, work habits, and interpersonal style by gathering feedback from peers, subordinates, managers, and customers. It is most often used to evaluate managers and professional, exempt (salaried) staff. The responses regarding the employee are validated, analyzed, and reported back by psychological professionals and may be administered anonymously or semi-anonymously. The tool is useful in describing both the strengths and weaknesses of the employee, particularly as it relates to work relationships.

Example: A 360 Profiler is applied to all technical managers in a company. The profiler finds that one of the Computer Networking Group managers is viewed by his peers as being narcissistic, angry, and antisocial. The tool also indicates that his peers do not trust him. This case demonstrates someone with the ability to inflict threat (access to networks) and negative feedback regarding psychosocial indicators. An analyst might flag this individual as a "person of interest" for additional monitoring.

Performance Evaluation

An employee performance evaluation tool may be paper or electronic and is typically used annually or biannually to measure an employee's strengths, accomplishments, and needs for improvement. Typically, the manager seeks feedback from the employee's peers, subordinates, project managers, and customers. For exempt staff, a free-form narrative method is often used; for nonexempt staff, a standard numeric rating method is often used.

Example: An employee with access to classified information has received consecutive performance reviews that indicate interpersonal issues with other coworkers—he is known for narcissism, and feedback indicates that, although not the project manager, he seeks to control all aspects of a project. He was recently declined participation in a big project, and his manager noted in his evaluation that his performance has subsequently declined. An analyst might flag this person as potentially disgruntled (motive) with the ability (access to classified information) to become an insider threat.

Competency Tracking

Larger organizations often have a competency (or capability) tracking tool for workforce planning purposes. Each employee has an "inventory" of competencies or capabilities that records education, technical and soft skills (e.g., teamwork, relationship management, public speaking, etc.), and specializations. This tool could provide information regarding education and technical skills that indicate the ability of the employee to engage in cybersecurity events.

Example: An employee is a researcher in classified chemical warfare. His peers do not know that he has a computer engineering degree and that he considers himself an amateur hacker. When first hired, he was asked to complete a skills inventory; at that time, he indicated proficient skills as a system administrator and forensics expert in addition to his degree major. The employee's manager, who has access to the skills inventory for all of his staff, notices that the researcher has the ability and opportunity to be an insider threat. At that point, the manager should watch for motive and/or unusual computer activity from the researcher.

Disciplinary Incident Tracking

At some level, usually informal, an HR department tracks disciplinary actions to conduct trend reporting (e.g., escalating absenteeism may indicate a problem) and to make sure consequences are consistently applied (e.g., if two employees are both absent without justification five times in one month, they receive the same disciplinary action). A system like this usually records only serious infractions where the consequence from the manager is a formal written warning, suspension, or termination. Verbal warnings and coaching are typically not reflected as a disciplinary incident unless there is a persistent pattern of similar undesirable behavior.

Example: A helpdesk technician has been disciplined because task and project deadlines have been missed due to poor attendance. The technician has had few absences in the past—but within the past few months, she has been frequently missing work and showing up late. The manager is aware that her attitude has become poor and that she is not interacting well with her peers. When at work, she is constantly on the phone or on the computer doing nonwork-related activities. When the manager discusses expectations for improved performance, the technician angrily accuses him of picking on her and blames her performance problems on others in the department. She refuses to cooperate with the manager's requests. In this instance, an employee may have the motive (anger) and the ability (access to systems) to present risk. It would be wise of the manager and/or security personnel to monitor for unusual activity that might indicate inappropriate activity. (See also: Timecard Records, *below).*

Timecard Records

Excessive hours worked could indicate overreliance on one employee, relationship issues, work-related stress (nonexempt and exempt staff), or financial issues (nonexempt staff seeking overtime pay). In general, ongoing attendance issues may indicate a lack of loyalty to the employer, disregard for policy, or a sense of entitlement. Typically, staff with attendance issues have persistent, ongoing problems with adhering to policy. Sudden changes in attendance patterns may indicate health or personal issues and/or duress.

Example: See Disciplinary Incident Tracking, above, and Health Event Tracking, below.

Proximity Card Records

Many larger organizations have proximity cards (prox cards; also known as *access cards*) that allow entry into secured facilities. A time/date record is created when the employee uses the card to enter or leave the secured facility. Special attention may be paid to employees who are present at unusual hours or are attempting entry into an area where access has not been granted.

Example: An engineer whose regular hours are 8:00 a.m. to 4:00 p.m. has begun accessing a building after hours that is not his regular work location. There is little pattern to his visits—and the times are sporadic and well after others have likely gone home. Security notes the unusual activity and contacts the engineer's manager for more information.

Background Check/Public Records

Most companies conduct some form of background check before hiring an employee, and some perform random or regular post-hire screenings. The background process typically consists of checking for past criminal convictions,[5] evaluating credit history, interviewing references and past employers, drug tests, and validating past employment and education claims made by the individual. Federal security clearance processes are much more detailed than the general process used by most employers and also consider physical and mental health and other risk factors before awarding a clearance; they also prescribe timelines for regular rescreening.

Example: A skilled finalist for a position in the Finance Department submits to a background investigation. During the background check, the hiring manager learns that the candidate has significant credit problems. Although he indicated on his application that he was laid off from his last job, his former employer indicates he was terminated and is not eligible for rehire. The manager decides that hiring a financial professional (ability) with credit issues (motivation) into a position handling money (opportunity) who was not honest on his employment application (risk indicator) presents a potential risk for embezzlement. The candidate is ruled out and another candidate is selected for the position.

Security/Counterintelligence

Internal security personnel may peruse public arrest records to ascertain when employees have been charged with criminal activity. Employees with federal security clearances are required to report any arrest or similar legal activity to their manager and designated staff within their organization. Security may become aware of the activity at this point as well. The organization's security office may keep an internal tracking system that houses and can report staff complaints or concerns (i.e., reports of "shoulder surfing," unusual questions, access requests inappropriate for position). The security group may also manage reports regarding entry and exit times (*See Also*: *Proximity Card Records*, *above*). Generally, access to legal/arrest records or other personal information (financial records) is limited to employees with high-level security clearances or to cases in which there is sufficient suspicion to warrant such investigation.

Example: While perusing the county arrest records, an organization's security officer learns that an employee has been arrested for drug possession. Additional research indicates that although the employee has never been convicted, this is his second arrest for the same charge; and the first case was dismissed just 2 years prior. Knowing that this may indicate a substance abuse issue, that substance abuse clouds good judgment, and that prosecution is pending, the security officer concludes elevated risk and advises the employee's manager.

Use of Employee Assistance Program Services

Most large organizations contract with an independent Employee Assistance Program (EAP) provider to give confidential, personal services to employees. Most EAPs provide mental health and financial counseling, and some also provide community referrals to other types of providers (e.g., childcare, eldercare, etc.). The content of discussions between employees and EAP counselors is private. Information regarding an employee's use of EAP, and the type and date of service used by the employee, may or may not be available to the organization depending on the type of arrangement that is in place. Use of the EAP typically indicates one or more of the following: stress, duress, issues with coworkers, family issues, financial issues, and health and/or mental issues. [Legal note (see next section): While EAP records, if available, can be predictive of potential insider abuse, most organizations would opt *not* to include EAP data (which may reflect mental health issues) in analyses due to legal or privacy concerns.]

Example: A computer programmer seeks EAP services after notifying HR that her divorce has just been finalized. A few weeks later, she asks her manager for more hours, citing financial need. The manager reminds the computer programmer that she is a salaried employee and is not eligible for overtime. Later that month, she tells her manager that she plans to take a second job at a competing company on a contract basis to earn additional income. The manager tells the computer programmer that she can't take the job, citing conflict of interest. At this point, the employee tells the manager that she is using EAP services for both financial and mental counseling. The manager recognizes that, although she has not demonstrated performance issues, the computer programmer's current financial and personal issues, coupled with her ability and opportunity to engage in insider threat activity, present risk. While he trusts the employee and understands her situation, he keeps an eye on what types of systems and files she is accessing until he feels she is back on solid ground.

Use of Complaint Mechanism

It is usually common knowledge if an employee is in the habit of making frequent, unfounded, or frivolous complaints to HR or a similar dispute resolution office (e.g., Ombudsman, staff concerns, ethics or "whistleblower" hotline, etc.). This information is not typically stored electronically, and usually companies have a policy protecting employees from retaliation if they file a complaint. Employees who misuse these outlets may be using confidential mechanisms to seek revenge with peers, managers, or vendors. If the number and type of complaints were logged in a system for later analysis, the information might prove a significant indicator of workplace stress and/or anti-social personality issues. [Legal note (see next section): While employee complaint records can be predictive of potential insider abuse, most organizations would opt *not* to include such data in analyses due to legal or privacy concerns.]

Example: Jim, a disgruntled employee, has complained multiple times about a coworker that he thinks is seeking revenge. His concern is typically the same: Mary is the manager's "favorite" and is spreading rumors about him. After multiple investigations, his complaints are found to be without merit. Jim is angry; and accuses the manager, Mary, and the Ombudsman of retaliation. He transfers to a new manager who doesn't know the history. The new manager receives a report that shows Jim made frequent complaints and later sees Jim at a coworker's computer, which is unusual. Recognizing that there is now motive, and opportunity for inappropriate activity, the new manager consults security personnel.

Life-Event Tracking

Life events introduce stress resulting from a major change in the employee's life. Information regarding births, adoptions, deaths, divorces, and marriages are typically provided to HR in order to modify insurance benefits or request additional time off. Most organizations provide approved leave for these types of events. Although these individual events are not of concern, when considered in concert with other data, they may indicate potential financial and personal issues resulting from the event. [Legal note (see next section): However, there is concern that such personal factors are not within the purview of the employer, either for privacy or legal reasons. While tracking such events may be beneficial, we conclude that a more appropriate approach in most cases would be not to track life events, but instead to focus assessments on observable factors.] Thus, if a divorce leads to distress, we assume that the manager will identify manifestations of stress rather than relying on the tracking of personal events.

Health-Event Tracking

An employee may request short-term disability (STD) leave for serious personal mental and/or physical health issues including pregnancy and childbirth. Many organizations provide STD insurance coverage for full-time staff that pays up to 100% of the employee's salary for a period of time. If the health problem is persistent (e.g., exceeding 6 months), then the employee may request long-term disability (LTD). At this point, the employee is typically terminated as s/he is not likely to return and will receive a percentage of his or her working salary as a payment from the LTD insurance provider.

Eligible employees may also request unpaid family medical leave (FML) for personal health issues or for the care of an immediate family member, or in the event of childbirth or adoption. Access to this unpaid time off is governed by the national Family Medical Leave Act (FMLA); additional requirements may be imposed at the state level. Medical details of STD, LTD, or FML requests are confidential and are protected by law (see next section on considerations of law and justice).

Other types of health-related events may also be tracked. Employees who are under the influence of alcohol or drugs in the workplace, or who demonstrate strong emotional outbursts or erratic behavior, or who are otherwise unable to function can be referred by the employer to a retained medical provider for evaluation. The provider, not the employer or employee, determines whether the employee is fit for the workplace. If deemed unfit, the employee may be referred to a private health professional for treatment. The health professional may re-evaluate the employee before approval is given to return to work.

The availability of health event data for predictive monitoring varies with job category. Employees with federal security clearances are required to report major mental or physical issues. Employees without clearances are not required to disclose details except as needed for obtaining company benefits. [Legal note (see next section): While health records can be predictive of potential insider abuse, most organizations would opt *not* to include such data in analyses due to legal or privacy concerns.]

EXAMPLE: An employee in the Network Administration group has had increasingly disruptive verbal altercations with coworkers. It has reached the point that coworkers fear that their safety is threatened. Fact-finding reveals that the employee has instigated the altercations and that his behavior has become increasingly erratic. In a disciplinary meeting, the manager suspends the employee for engaging in harassing and intimidating behavior. The employee counters with accusations that coworkers are seeking revenge, that the manager is part of a conspiracy, and that he is going to "bring this place to its knees." The manager, concerned for the safety of all employees, requires the disruptive employee to obtain a psychological evaluation before returning to work. The manager later learns that the employee has been found to be unfit and is seeking mental health treatment. While the employee is out on STD for medical issues, past emails come to the manager's attention that indicate the employee was joking with friends about "messing with the network." When the employee returns to work, the manager does not immediately grant access to the network, recognizing that there may still be motive, ability, and opportunity for inappropriate activity.

In summary, we have described twelve sources of social/organizational (i.e., behavioral) data that appear to be relevant indicators or precursors of malicious insider activities. Some of these data sources (particularly the first seven examples) appear to present no particular *practical* issues regarding data collection because they are readily available, if not formally tracked, by managers and HR personnel; nevertheless, implementing a formal infrastructure for collecting and maintaining such data may lead to ethical and/or privacy concerns (to be addressed in the next section). Of equal concern are the last five data sources described above, not only due to possible ethical/privacy issues, but also potential legal issues. We shall turn now to discuss relevant considerations of law and justice, followed by a discussion of privacy/ethical considerations.

CONSIDERATIONS OF PRIVACY LAW AND ETHICS

Perspectives on Privacy of Citizenry

Issues of privacy in the IT age are a source of widespread debate and discussion among legal scholars, public advocacy groups, and social/political scientists. Fueling the debate is the availability of a variety of surveillance technologies that significantly enhance the ability to collect, analyze, and disseminate information about individuals, which creates concern for protecting individuals against intrusive governmental interference or access to personal or private information. At the broadest level of analysis that concerns public rights of and expectations for privacy, there is strong advocacy in fundamental principles embodied in the U.S. Constitution, and Bill of Rights that protect individual rights and limit the powers of federal government by preserving the liberty and autonomy of individuals.

In addition to restraints on the collection and use of information about individuals that derive from the U.S. Constitution and related legal doctrine, other governmental restraints have been expressed in state and federal statutes. Largely in response to increasing use by governments of electronic databases for administrative and statistical purposes in the 1960s, the following few decades saw a distinct increase in interest in policies and laws surrounding information privacy (Nissenbaum, 2004). Most notable is the Privacy Act of 1974, a federal law that applies to federal agencies, their contractors, and state or local agencies. The Privacy Act of 1974 dictates how records may be shared and for what purposes: Records may be used if they are not intended "to take any adverse financial, personnel, disciplinary, or other adverse action against Federal personnel" with the following exceptions: records may be used if "performed for foreign counterintelligence purposes or to produce background checks for security clearance of Federal personnel or Federal contractor personnel." (Privacy Act of 1974)

Other legislation passed in this period concerned credit reporting protections, privacy protections for individuals with disabilities, and privacy protection of medical records. The Fair Credit Reporting Act (FCRA) of 1970 dictates that if an employer makes an adverse personnel decision based on information obtained via a background check (i.e., credit report, work or education history, criminal record), the employer must notify the individual in writing, citing the reason for the adverse action. The individual has 30 days to respond and contest the information contained in the background check. This provision allows citizens the right to correct faulty information. Section 627 of this Act does provide for "Disclosures to Government Agencies for Counterterrorism Purposes." (15 USC § 1681, Public Law 90-321, 1970) In these instances, the individual will not be aware the information has been requested unless conducted as part of a federal security clearance process. In 2003, an amendment to the FCRA, the Fair and Accurate Credit Transactions Act of 2003 (FACTA), was enacted to allow employers to lawfully reuse the background check process during a workplace misconduct investigation without further consent from the employee (Fair Credit Reporting act, 2003).

The **Rehabilitation Act of 1973 requires** Federal contractors and subcontractors, who may ask applicants with disabilities to indicate their status when applying, to keep this information in a separate record from personnel records. "A pre-employment inquiry about a disability is allowed if required by another Federal law or regulation such as those applicable to disabled veterans and veterans of the Vietnam era. Pre-employment inquiries about disabilities may be necessary under such laws to identify applicants or clients with disabilities in order to provide them with required special services (US Equal Employment Opportunity Commission, 2008)." Organizations must take caution to not use information regarding the applicant's disability to presume how s/he may perform on the job. In 1990, additional legislation was enacted to protect privacy of individuals with disabilities. The **Americans with Disabilities Act (ADA), passed in 1990, protects employees** with physical and/or mental disabilities, either actual or perceived (US Department of Justice, 2009). Employers with more than 15 employees must comply with the Act, which prohibits discrimination in all employment practices, including job application procedures, hiring, firing, advancement, compensation, training, and other terms, conditions, and privileges of employment. It applies to recruitment, advertising, tenure, layoff, leave, fringe benefits, and all other employment-related activities (US Equal Employment Opportunity Commission, 2008). However, the employer is not required to hire or retain a disabled person in a position if there are threats to health or safety or if poor performance is documented.

The Health Insurance Portability and Accountability Act of 1996 (HIPAA) (US Department of Health and Human Services, 2009) comprises many components and has been amended as recently as 2003. Most relevant to employee privacy is the HIPAA "Privacy Rule" that limits how employers, as a quasi "covered entity" (Texas Workforce Commission, 2008) to health insurance carriers, may use patients' health information. For example, individually identifiable health information may not be used for purposes not related to health care, and covered entities may use protected information only for a specific purpose. If protected information is used, the patient must sign a specific authorization before that medical information may be related. HIPAA provides for limited use of medical information for narrow purposes related to law enforcement, as well as national defense and security (US Department of Health and Human Services, 2007).

A general theme of the privacy legislation noted above is the attempt by the federal government to protect employee privacy concerning data collected about their finances, health, and other attributes—acknowledging the need and value for such data collection while enacting safeguards that require such data to be maintained separately from personnel files and that it be subject to strict dissemination control limited for official use (e.g., in administering health care and other programs that benefit the employees). This legislation, as well as other state laws and even public sentiment, reflects the public concern expressed in metaphors like "Big Brother is watching" that derive from historical experiences of secret police surveillance (e.g., Agre, 1994).

From the foregoing discussion, we may conclude that the legal status of privacy and security issues is complicated and still evolving. While laws are useful for conveying minimal expectations, in many respects they are just that – minimums. Clearly minimal requirements are needed, but a society that sets low thresholds for privacy and security may not provide an environment that is sufficient for promoting liberty and autonomy. What is needed, of course, is a set of principles that can guide public deliberations as well as commercial practice relating to privacy. Nissenbaum (2004) identifies a set of principles in widespread use concerning (a) limitation of surveillance and use of information about citizens by agents of government, (b) restricting access to sensitive, personal, or private information, and (c) curtailing intrusions into places deemed private or personal (e.g., what people do in the privacy of their own homes should be shielded from surveillance). However, Nissenbaum argues that while this framework may serve as a benchmark for settling disputes, the application of these principles is not always obvious or clear: "Even when it is clear which of the three principles is relevant, it may not always be obvious precisely how to draw the relevant lines to determine whether or not that principle applies, particularly with precedent setting cases involving new applications of information technology." (Nissenbaum, 2004, p. 113).

As an alternative set of principles, Nissenbaum offers a *contextual integrity* framework as a universal account of what does and does not warrant restrictive, privacy-motivated measures. As she explains, "contexts are partly constituted by norms, which determine and govern key aspects such as roles, expectations, behaviors, and limits....Among the norms present in most contexts are ones that govern information... about people involved in the contexts." (p. 120). She defines contextual integrity in terms of two types of information norms: norms of appropriateness and norms of flow or distribution. According to Nissenbaum, in any given situation, a privacy violation is deemed to occur if either norms of appropriateness or norms of flow/distribution have been transgressed. The contextual integrity framework presumes a preference for the status quo, meaning that norms of appropriateness and flow are influenced by common practices, but that entrenched norms may be changed when they conflict with social, political, or moral values.

To understand how these norms apply, note that what is appropriate to share about an individual in the context of a friendship (which is largely open-ended) is different than what is appropriate in a classroom, which in turn differs from what is appropriate in a courtroom context (where norms of appropriateness regulate almost every piece of information presented). While few norms of appropriateness generally apply in friendships, norms of distribution clearly apply: Confidentiality of shared information between friends is important, and breach of confidentiality could call the friendship into question. Thus, personal information revealed in a particular context is always tagged with that context. As an example, it is common practice—and not a violation of norms of appropriateness and information flow—for online booksellers to maintain and analyze customer records electronically to facilitate targeting of marketing activities to the same customers. In contrast, if an online vendor provides information about consumer purchases to vendors of magazine subscriptions (without permission), this is considered a violation of norms of appropriateness *and* flow. In the final analysis, determinations of breaches of information privacy must take into account the roles of the parties acquiring the information and their capacity to affect the lives of the individuals about which the information might be shared. The determination therefore depends on whether the information practice causes harm, interferes with individuals' self-determination, or promotes inequalities in status, power, or wealth.

Perspectives on Workplace Privacy

A core concern is the tension between the needs or wishes of an organization to safeguard its assets through predictions related to insider threats and the privacy rights and expectations of individuals who use organizational resources, in particular, employees. The notion of privacy is generally characterized in terms of the right of individuals, groups, or institutions to determine for themselves when, how, and to what extent information about them is communicated. There is a fine line, situated in context, between what the organization needs to know and what is firmly in the realm of the employee's expectation of privacy. Few employees actually engage in activities that would constitute insider threat; the rest of the population consists of honest, hard-working staff who might be highly offended to learn they were being monitored, or who, even if they gave permission for monitoring to take place so as to obtain or keep their job, might consider that to be an objectionable requirement on the part of the employer.

Legal Concerns

With regard to the issue of workplace privacy, there is no single source of privacy law in the United States, but rather an incomplete patchwork that includes the U.S. Constitution (but the U.S. Constitution does not apply to the private sector unless the employer is acting as an agent of the government), the Fourth Amendment to the U.S. Constitution (protecting against unlawful search and seizure), State constitutions, and federal and state statutes (the reader is advised that many U.S. states have more restrictive laws and requirements too numerous to discuss here—see Smith, 2002 for a compilation of federal and state privacy laws). Workplace privacy has been a regularly contested area of law and policy. Originally considered a personal space of employees that is inviolate, the preponderance of opinion has shifted over time as public opinion, and more particularly, court decisions, have taken the position that ownership of servers by business organizations supersedes claims of privacy by employees who use computer systems as part of their jobs. This shift in presumption means that employers may routinely monitor employee e-mails and workstation activities (e.g., web-surfing). Although there are laws that prevent an employer from sharing intimate employee information with individuals outside the company, there are few restrictions on an employer's right to share it with people on the inside" (Lane, 2003, p. 261). Notice by the employer of such monitoring practices generally defeats an employee's "reasonable expectation of privacy (Biby v. Board of Regents, 2005)." Indeed, mere use of an employer's email system may mean an employee has no reasonable expectation of privacy in email; and even if the employee owns the computer and brings it into the workplace, this does not necessarily establish a reasonable expectation of privacy (United States v. Barrows, 2007). Thus, employers monitor employees' computer use by tracking the use of internet as well as internal information systems and, to a varying degree, by screening email metadata and contents. Surveys by the American Management Association show that the percentage of employers that conduct electronic monitoring of some type increased from 82% to 92% between 2001 and 2003. The percentage of employers that monitor email increased from 47% to 52% during that same time frame (AMA, 2001; AMA, 2003). It is widely acknowledged (Kelly, 1999) that employers have the right to monitor employee computer activities and to internally share personal employee data, although federal agencies can use this information only for job actions if "performed for foreign counterintelligence purposes or to produce background checks for security clearance of Federal personnel or Federal contractor personnel (Privacy Act of 1974)."

Nevertheless, the debate continues: the prevalence of employee monitoring and the current legal right of the employer to do so has resulted in heated debate and legal wrangling over personal privacy. The American Civil Liberties Union (ACLU) claims that "Electronic surveillance in the workplace is a major threat to your right to privacy (ACLU, 2003)." While acknowledging there are legitimate reasons a company may use technology to oversee some aspects of employee performance, they balk at "computer data banks [that] help employers track employees' past employment records, financial status and medical histories." The ACLU is actively seeking citizen and political support for state and/or federal workplace privacy legislation.[6] In the face of the continuing debate, there is a clear need for the U.S. government to undertake a broad, systematic review of national privacy laws and regulations (Waldo, Lin & Millett, 2007).

Trust

A fundamental concept underlying the issue of privacy and electronic workplace monitoring is trust. Trust has been described as the belief in, and willingness to depend upon, another party (Mayer, Davis & Schoorman, 1995). Tabak and Smith (2005) describe the implications for workplace monitoring from the perspective of trust initiation and formation between management and employees. From a theoretical perspective grounded in cognition and organizational behavior research, Tabak and Smith argue that both employees and managers develop trust in the workplace through a "sensemaking" process that interprets their current work experience (external information consisting of issues, events, objects, and individuals in the environment) in relation to previous work experience (in the form of existing knowledge structures or schemas), which influences individuals' disposition to trust. Tabak and Smith assert that the initiation of trust and subsequent trust formation affects managerial implementation of electronic monitoring policies and that these policies have implications for workplace privacy rights. Similarly, these same factors influence trust formation by employees, and management practices such as workplace monitoring are perceived by employees in ways that influence employee trust in and commitment to the organization.

From the employer's point of view, the cost and damage of one instance of sabotage or espionage may warrant monitoring all behavioral and demographic employee data available to anticipate and prevent incidents. Some organizations may formulate a monitoring policy based on beliefs that monitoring (either openly or otherwise) promotes productivity and affords better control over counterproductive employees; they may feel that this approach is justified because employers pay for employee time and own resources such as computer equipment and network connections. Critics of this perspective note that electronic workplace monitoring can increase employee stress, reduce commitment, and lower productivity (Brown, 1996). They also point out ethical implications relating to employee perceptions of their own privacy rights and the possible impacts on their sense of well-being and quality of work life (Rosenberg, 1999). Some privacy-rights advocates are concerned that potentially harmful information about individuals or their loved ones may be subject to unwanted intrusions. Extensive monitoring that is perceived as invasive may contribute to an employee's job dissatisfaction. Management intervention on suspected employee disgruntlement issues may actually increase an employee's frustration level (Shaw & Fischer, 2005). Moreover, false accusations that can arise from predictive approaches may affect the career of the accused. Complicating the situation further, inadequate attention and action by an employer can *increase* insider activity. Such influences on trust have been described as the "trust trap" (Band, Cappelli, Fischer, Moore, Shaw & Trzeciak, 2006).

The privacy and ethics debate is clearly a contentious issue that deserves more discussion by the research community and by stakeholders from government, industry, and the public. (Greitzer & Endicott-Popovsky [2008] took a first step in a forum discussion at a recent ACSAC meeting.) Employment is founded upon trust, which depends on the status of privacy, individual rights, rights of the organization, and the organization's power. While an organization may assert (and society may currently acknowledge) its right to conduct electronic workplace monitoring, there is the potential for negative backlash (reduced trust), particularly if the organization imposes monitoring surreptitiously or without advanced notice. If the process is fully disclosed and explained, as well as managed equitably, it may not be considered unfair by employees and the mutual trust relationship required for a healthy organization may remain intact.

Other Concerns

Other concerns that have been voiced about monitoring psychosocial factors of employees focus on possible negative effects on an employee's job security or performance evaluation during the early stages of monitoring. One particular concern is that in the course of monitoring psychosocial factors, a specific employee might be identified as one who presents elevated risk to the company. This might have a deleterious and unintended effect, even if subsequent analysis reveals no basis for suspicion. This is a disadvantage both for employee and employer. Indeed, if a manager handles this information poorly, it is possible that this could exacerbate the situation and lead to increased employee disgruntlement (Shaw & Fischer, 2005); hence the need for training, awareness and effective mitigation strategies. Note that unintended effects of proactive strategies are also possible when only traditional information sources are used—it is the predictive element, where estimations are made about possible future actions as opposed to traditional false positive concerns about detecting actions that have actually occurred, that creates the risk of this kind of error. There are precedents for safeguards against such unfair outcomes: e.g., as we noted above, the general direction of legislation on privacy, particularly regarding employee financial and health records, is to require storage of these data in separate repositories from personnel files. Any implemented use of prediction, regardless of the data source, should take this kind of error into consideration. Research into ways in which monitoring could be heightened without identifying a given employee is one useful component but is not sufficient by itself to fully address such concerns.

Implications

We suggest that researchers adopt as a best practice that data monitoring needed to inform a predictive (and behaviorally based) model should be completed openly and with proper privacy safeguards and should be based on actual behavior and events that are gathered in a similar fashion to the normal performance assessment process. The nature of the evaluation itself, which is necessary to collect the data that we are considering for insider threat monitoring and analysis, suggests that additional discussion and vetting of the process will be needed before it will be possible to establish an infrastructure for employee monitoring of this type. Performance reviews are generally acceptable when they are perceived to be administered fairly, perhaps also because they do not disrupt the established processes of an office, or because they are often defined as career development activity (rather than performance evaluation per se). If the standard practice of performance reviews is not considered an invasion of privacy, then might the related practice of assessing factors that may affect performance (such as stress, disgruntlement, etc.) also satisfy privacy criteria? From both an employee/career development perspective and considerations of workplace productivity and morale, it could be argued that enabling managers to assess motivational factors should bring about benefits to both the organization and the employees. As Fischer (2000) observed: "The chief conclusion drawn from several of the Slam-

Table 1. Sources of potential insider threat indicators

Name of Tool or Source	Description	Possible Ethical or Legal Barriers to *Internal* Use of Data for Threat Assessment
360 Profiler	Survey tool used to evaluate an employee's traits, performance, work habits, and interpersonal style by gathering feedback from peers, subordinates, managers, and customers	None
Performance Evaluation	Annual or biannual assessment of employee's accomplishments and career development	None
Competency Tracking	Inventory of employee competencies or capabilities that records education, technical, soft skills, and specializations.	None
Disciplinary Tracking	Database that records serious infractions that led to a formal written warning, suspension, or termination.	None
Timecard Records	Records of hours worked	None
Proxcard Records	Records of when an employee enters (or exits) certain areas that have "proximity" monitors	None
Background Check	Most companies conduct some form of background check before hiring an employee, and some perform random or regular post-hire screenings.	None
Security/Counterintelligence Data	Internal security personnel may proactively peruse public arrest records or other personal information (e.g., financial transactions) to ascertain when employees have been charged with criminal activity or to investigate possible suspicious activities.	Generally **not appropriate** except for staff who possess security clearances or when there is sufficient suspicion of possible illegal activity to warrant investigation by counterintelligence officer
Use of Employee Assistance Program (EAP)	EAP programs are typically available to provide confidential, personal services (such as mental health and financial counseling) to employees.	**Most organizations would not use EAP data due to legal or privacy concerns.**
Use of Employee Complaint Mechanism	Employee concerns resources such as Ombudsman, Staff Concerns, or "Whistleblower" Hotline	**Most organizations would not use such data due to legal or privacy concerns.**
Life-Event Tracking	Information regarding births, adoptions, deaths, divorces, and marriages are typically provided to HR in order to modify insurance benefits or request additional time off.	**Most organizations would not use such data due to legal or privacy concerns.**
Health-Event Tracking	Information regarding medical issues such as short-term or long-term disability, family medical leave, etc.	**Most organizations would not use such data due to legal or privacy concerns.**

mer reports is that had procedures been in place to help vulnerable employees deal with personal crisis, including an organizational climate supportive of co-worker intervention, much of this damage would have been prevented." (Fischer, 2000, p. 9). Of course, this also requires that (a) managers have appropriate skills to recognize potential problems and (b) they have requisite interpersonal skills and appropriate policies to mitigate problems. Broad, inclusive, deliberation on issues such as these is needed.

At the same time, it seems that incremental progress on predictive insider threat monitoring also has social merit. Given such, our work on a prototype has progressed. We summarized in table 1 the demographic, behavioral, or psychosocial data that can be used (in various combinations) to provide warning signs of malicious insider threats. One challenge is for the analyst in first finding the indicators, and once located, pulling them together for predictive purposes. Relevant data, although available in most large organizations, are not always readily or legally garnered for use. Beyond the mechanics of collecting the data, ever-present legal and ethical issues must be continuously revisited and weighed. We share how we have reasoned through legal and ethical issues to date.

Relevant legislation and judicial decisions described in the previous section lead to the conclusion that monitoring employee work activity, particularly *information technology/workstation activity*, is an acceptable practice from the legal perspective. This does not, of course, mean that such monitoring will be acceptable or effective in all contexts. Data sources used in monitoring that reflect behavioral or psychological/motivational factors still need to be examined with respect to both legal and privacy ethics status—i.e., behavioral indicators that are not eliminated on legal grounds should be examined using privacy ethics criteria such as the contextual integrity framework.

We attempted to engage in this type of analysis as we developed this research model; our analysis suggests that the first seven types of data sources described in the previous section (and listed in Table 1) are generally appropriate for use in a predictive insider threat monitoring system, as long as the data are stored separately from personnel records and used responsibly (following appropriateness and flow principles) to avoid harming innocent individuals. A final determination as to what is acceptable (and what is effective) regarding use of this model would need to be made on an organization-by-organization basis, with full participation by the corporate legal counsel and consideration of all ramifications with regard to issues discussed earlier in the chapter, as well as any country-specific rules. That said, our goal to was to identify data sources that provide a reasonable starting point when deciding what data might inform such a system.

The last five rows of the table represent data sources that, while likely to be predictive, are not appropriate on legal grounds, for most U.S. organizations as they appear in 2009, as described earlier in the chapter. These examples not only fall on questionable legal ground or are in fact illegal, but also would fail to meet privacy ethics scrutiny.[7]

Based on the above considerations, we then attempted to define a set of psychosocial indicators to complement workstation monitoring data in a predictive insider threat monitoring/mitigation framework that addresses behavioral indicators that we expect to be acceptable on legal and privacy/ethical grounds. This set of psychosocial indicators is described briefly in the next section.

PSYCHOSOCIAL DATA USED IN A PROTOTYPE PREDICTIVE MODEL

It is important to recognize that the organizational response to insider threat is not normally identical to its response to externally initiated attacks on computer information systems or infrastructures. The insider, by the definition used here, has legitimate access and legitimate reasons to be acting within the system, and those legitimate purposes may affect a wide variety of projects that may be entirely unrelated to the resource thought to be at risk. Further, when predictions are involved, there is not necessarily an existing violation to investigate or confirm. Even when actual organizational policy violations exist, there could be valid reasons for the violations. For example, the individual involved may have misunderstood the policy, bypassed policy to address a higher-level goal, or even have permission to perform an action that has not yet been recorded within the system. Thus, responses typically used to mitigate outsider attacks, such as cutting off access, are often inappropriate. As Schultz (2002, pp. 527-528) observes, the insider threat often involves working in close cooperation with other organizational functions such as human relations and the legal staff, and "clues concerning what exactly an internal attacker has done and the identity of the attacker itself are available through sources other than computers per se." Schultz goes on to observe that profiling suspected insiders "is proving to be one of the best ways of reverse engineering an insider attack.... Profiling suspected external attacks would in contrast almost always be a futile exercise."

Psychosocial Indicators

Greitzer et al. (2009) describe a predictive model for insider threat mitigation that includes an overall 'reasoner' that analyzes both workstation data and psychosocial data to infer indicators and behaviors that suggest possible insider threat risk. (The overall reasoner, including the predictive modeling approach for workstation data, is not discussed here; see Greitzer et al., 2009 for a more complete description.) The psychosocial component of the model is informed by research and case studies (e.g., Band et al., 2006); Gelles, 2005; Keeney et al., 2005; Krofcheck & Gelles, 2005; Moore et al., 2008; Parker, 2008; Shaw & Fisher, 2005; Schultz, 2002) that identify the role of psychosocial indicators of insider threat. While initial versions of the psychosocial component of the model attempted to follow the psychological research closely (e.g., identifying factors such as antisocial personality disorder, narcissism, etc.), it became apparent that a system designed to use evaluations by managers and HR experts would not be likely to provide reliable assessments of such psychological traits, especially because most organizations do not administer psychological or personality tests to their employees. Therefore, implementation of the psychosocial reasoning component of our model instead uses an observational/management reporting approach that would rely on personnel data and judgments that are likely to be available from management and HR staff. In particular, we developed a set of 12 indicators that could be described using examples or "proxies" that are more readily observed (Table 2)—we expect that such data can be derived from observations and reports by managers and HR professionals. In our judgment, these indicators reflect the psychological profiles and behaviors that have been observed in case studies to correlate with insider crime—e.g., personal predispositions that relate directly "to maladaptive reactions to stress, financial and personal needs leading to personal conflicts and rule violations, chronic disgruntlement, strong reactions to organizational sanctions, concealment of rule violations, and a propensity for escalation during work-related conflicts" (Band et al., 2006, p. 15 and Appendix G).

The component of the Greitzer et al. (2009) model implementing the reasoning about psychosocial indicators was developed by obtaining judgments from available HR experts on the prevalence and severity of different combinations of indicators that reflect different scenario cases. As revealed by this knowledge-engineering process, these psychosocial indicators contribute differentially to the judged level of psychosocial risk—*disgruntlement*, *difficulty accepting feedback*, *anger management issues*, *disengagement*, and *disregard for authority* have higher weights than other indicators, for example.

At this stage in the development of the model, the 12 indicators have been vetted with a limited set of HR experts with whom we have worked. Several points should be emphasized: (a) the indicators need to be empirically tested or vetted with larger samples of HR experts and managers to assess their validity, at least at a subjective level; (b) the judgments based on observations will necessarily always be subjective—there is no expectation that an objective test instrument will emerge from this research; (c) nevertheless, we believe that with appropriate training,

Table 2. Psychosocial indicators used in the predictive model

Indicator	Description
Disgruntlement	Employee observed to be dissatisfied in current position; chronic indications of discontent, such as strong negative feelings about being passed over for a promotion or being underpaid, undervalued; may have a poor fit with current job.
Accepting Feedback	The employee is observed to have a difficult time accepting criticism, tends to take criticism personally or becomes defensive when message is delivered. Employee has been observed being unwilling to acknowledge errors or admitting to mistakes; may attempt to cover up errors through lying or deceit.
Anger Management Issues	The employee often allows anger to get pent up inside; employee has trouble managing lingering emotional feelings of anger or rage. Holds strong grudges.
Disengagement	The employee keeps to self, is detached, withdrawn, and tends not to interact with individuals or groups; avoids meetings.
Disregard for Authority	The employee disregards rules, authority, or policies. Employee feels above the rules or that they only apply to others.
Performance	The employee has received a corrective action (below expectation performance review, verbal warning, written reprimand, suspension, termination) based on poor performance.
Stress	The employee appears to be under physical, mental, or emotional strain or tension that he/she has difficulty handling
Confrontational Behavior	Employee exhibits argumentative or aggressive behavior or is involved in bullying or intimidation
Personal Issues	Employee has difficulty keeping personal issues separate from work, and these issues interfere with work
Self-Centeredness	The employee disregards needs or wishes of others, concerned primarily with own interests and welfare.
Lack of Dependability	Employee is unable to keep commitments /promises; unworthy of trust.
Absenteeism	Employee has exhibited chronic unexplained absenteeism.

management and HR personnel would better understand the nature of the threat and the likely precursors or threat indicators that may be usefully reported to cybersecurity officers; (d) most importantly, the approach in predictive modeling is to provide "leads" for cybersecurity officers to pursue in advance of actual crimes, without which they would likely have little or no insight with which to select higher-risk "persons of interest" on which to focus analyses. For security analysis purposes, only cases where a manager is "highly concerned" about such factors or combinations of factors would be advanced in the predictive model to raise the level of concern or risk. As the risk level increases, so too would the level of monitoring and analysis on an individual increase.

The output of the psychosocial model feeds into a higher-level reasoner (along with workstation data monitored from network sensors) to derive the overall level of risk. Note that the collection regimen stops short of formally collecting information that relates to life events or personal data (medical and financial issues, divorce, arrest records, etc.), although the factors themselves (such as stress, anger management) that may be observed and reported may well derive from such events. There is also an assumption that the focus of the analysis is predictive and preventive. If the analysis yields more incriminating evidence that justifies additional data collection and evaluation, the process is expected to escalate and be transferred to counterintelligence or law enforcement personnel, who would not necessarily have the same legal and privacy restrictions.

Privacy Ethics Considerations of the Model

This chapter has been devoted largely to describing social/ethical issues in surveillance of employees as part of a comprehensive insider threat predictive modeling framework. As with any such discussion, many gray areas exist—changing social norms, regulations, and organizational customs mean that the appropriate choices will change over time. Our approach has been to vet the indicators and data sources selected for the model with HR personnel to discover whether there are any serious concerns based on privacy or ethical grounds, relating to either the welfare of the employee or of the employer. Of concern to the employer/employee relationship is the determination of what the organization needs to know and what is firmly in the realm of the employee's expectation of privacy and autonomy. Ethical and privacy considerations suggest that the use of personal information is unlikely to be appropriate or legal, regardless of its effectiveness in mitigating insider threat. This is particularly true in the case of medical information, where the employee's legal right to, and expectation of privacy supersedes the organization's interest in predicting potential insider threat. This restriction also applies to information related to an employee's use of an Employee Assistance Plan and an employee's life events such as birth, adoption, divorce, or marriage. Thus, any aspects of possible monitoring data that appear to have questionable or invasive aspects were eliminated from consideration by the model—this produced the final set of indicators in Table 2 that specifically omit strictly personal private information such as medical, financial, life event data, etc.

This implementation is a prototype that still requires careful vetting in broader contexts. Nevertheless, as a result of this process, we have some confidence that the psychosocial model presented here provides an implementation that satisfies privacy and ethics criteria, balancing the needs of the employer with the rights and welfare of employees. An appropriate next step from a research standpoint will be to look at a broader range of organizations to gain additional perspectives—and, as a practical matter; before adoption within an organization, discussion with internal stakeholders is paramount.

CHALLENGES TO PREDICTIVE MODELING OF INSIDER THREAT

It is not surprising that the insider threat was included on the list of eight problems on the 2005 INFOSEC (information security) Research Council Hard Problems List (INFOSEC Research Council, 2005) and that other hard problem lists also cite insider threat as an issue. Currently, early detection is considered state of the art with regard to insider-threat. Furthermore, early detection is hard (as evinced by so many malicious insiders who are identified years after their activities begin) leaving many open research questions. Focusing on prediction adds an even higher level of complexity to the task, from potential impact on employees to the development of testing models. In this section, we highlight elements of insider threat research that are exacerbated by use of predictive approaches.

Prediction is not detection. This point is crucial. Prediction often looks like detection, but attempting to use these approaches interchangeably can have very negative consequences, both from a scientific and a personnel perspective. We divide the major sources of confusion into four categories:

1. **The approach:** the methods used can be similar or even identical. Prediction, particularly prediction involving traditional cybersecurity data, often involves identification of stepping stone activities (precursors) used by a malicious insider, setting the groundwork for anticipated later activities. The methods used to identify these stepping stones are often similar or identical to those used to detect actual malicious events that are elements of an attack.
2. **Outcomes and goals:** preventing escalation versus detection of misuse. Because prediction as we define it is tied to likely precursor events and likely organizational indicators of policy violations or criminal

misconduct, our predictive approach may deter a potential insider from committing a significant policy violation or criminal act, through aggregating smaller misuse activities. This is a gray area. We choose to consider a method "predictive" if it allows us to discover a malicious insider's activities that could lead to a greater harm in the future. This includes activities that may in themselves involve bending or breaking organizational rules. The key for us is that the end goal of the malicious insider was not the breaking of those particular rules, but some future greater harm. Some of what is currently considered "low and slow" detection might, by our definition, be considered insider activity prediction. We would not consider a stealthy regular "low and slow" scan to be part of prediction by our definition, but we would consider a periodic checking of possibly weak administrator passwords to be predictive. The parallel might be that theft of a ream of office paper in itself is a violation of policy (detection), but if the theft is thought to be to aid copying of proprietary corporate information because it is occurring late after hours in a building with fast copiers, and is by a disgruntled employee, the intended outcome might be potential intellectual property theft (prediction).

3. **Interpreting false results:** different interpretation of false positives and false negatives. A predictive system, like a detection system, will produce false positives and false negatives. A false positive in a predictive system is one in which it is predicted that an employee is a malicious insider. This might in fact involve true detection of minor policy infractions as discussed in (B), but the prediction (that escalation was planned) is false. A false negative in a predictive system is one in which it is not predicted that an employee is a malicious insider. Again, true detection of minor policy infractions as in (B) might take place—but incorrectly, it was not predicted that these were part of an escalation.
4. **Interpreting positive results:** different interpretation of true positives and true negatives. Unlike detection, the categories of true positives and true negatives are difficult to discern and involve probabilities and a timing element. A true positive is a (correct) prediction that an insider is planning an escalation, but because the anticipated event is a future one, a "true positive" will have a confidence level associated as opposed to it being certain that a planned malicious act is in progress. One could only determine that the prediction was fully accurate by allowing the incident to run its course. Similarly, a "true negative" is at the opposite end of the spectrum from a "false positive." While in detection, a true negative indicates that there is no attack—nothing was uncovered because there was nothing to uncover—this is not true in prediction. In prediction, it is always possible that the "prediction" is made in advance of an insider's decision to begin malicious activity. Thus, a negative prediction could be accurate (and negative) at time t1, but this does not mean that at a time t1+n the prediction should become positive. Determining the earliest moment when prediction of malicious activity could be expected to occur (in other words, the earliest moment when a true positive or false negative becomes a possibility) is not likely to be decidable—it most certainly will be technology and data dependent.

There is no "ground truth." In some disciplines, it is possible to decide what is true and compare predictions against reality. However, for cybersecurity predictions, no standard metrics exist for measuring the success of insider threat monitoring (Gabrielson, 2008). One method is to continue observation of the potential insider to see what transpires; this may be an approach taken by law enforcement or counterintelligence, for instance.

The role of motivation: valid or malicious? It can be a challenge to distinguish among valid activities, minor violations, and malicious activities. The vast majority of observable computer/workstation behaviors are indistinguishable for normal/benign computer usage versus malicious actions. Minor violations are all too common, because individuals may accidentally attempt to access a protected file, or may deliberately work around an inconvenient security measure in order to achieve a higher organizational goal. Incorporating noncomputer-based psychosocial data in an analysis may perhaps help, on the assumption that such data will facilitate identifying features or patterns that better discriminate potential threats. Ethical judgment is necessary because of the potential harm that can result from false accusations. Still, assignment of motivation remains a murky area.

More data is not necessarily better data. Despite our suggestion that organizational data be integrated with cybersecurity and our belief that in some cases this will assist in detecting insiders, the hypothesis has not been thoroughly tested and it may not be possible to assess typical Bayesian models. Consider the difficulty of finding population base rates for any given organizational or behavioral factor, whether representative of the population at large, the population of a given organization, or a subgroup within the organization. The base rates of significant insider exploits are expected to be exceedingly small because the vast majority of employees are expected to be loyal and noncriminal members of the organization. Expert opinions about possible base rates of rare psychosocial factors can be seriously biased (e.g., Moore & Cain, 2007). On the other hand, because "ground truth" is unknown, the actual population rates of certain indicators may be somewhat higher than observed. Frank (1994) identified situations where additional data resulted in poorer performance rather than improved performance in intrusion detection systems; it is likely that prediction will have similar challenges.

Placing punishment before behavior. As mentioned earlier, the notion of false positives is problematic because recognizing precursors of a malicious exploit does not necessarily mean that a criminal act will take place. The nature of the organization's response to an identified "precursor" is fundamentally different from the response to the actual illegal act. An insider identified as a potential risk should be treated as a "person of interest" rather than a "suspect." While the intent of this paper is to use predictive metrics to prevent harm, quite often metrics have been used in negative ways. For instance, software metrics or productivity metrics are sometimes introduced for positive reasons, but have all too often been used to penalize employees (sometimes to the detriment of the organization's original goal). Great care and constant attention is likely to be needed by an organization's management, to ensure that the same harm is not done by insider predictions.

Differences in view. HR experts disagree about the amount of predicted risk to associate with individual psychosocial indicators, as well as with combinations of psychosocial indicators. This makes a predictive model difficult to develop or evaluate.

Need for training. The challenges described above indicate that analysts and managers must be carefully trained to use predictive data appropriately and ethically. No predictive system should be expected to perform more reliably than a human expert analyst. No tool deployment should depend only on an automated insider threat mitigation strategy. Human and automated resources should be integrated in such a way that the automated component helps to filter information and cue the human analyst about possible "persons of interest" to improve the speed, accuracy, and reliability of the overall system.

CONCLUSIONS AND FUTURE RESEARCH DIRECTIONS

In any potential security breach due to insider threat, three factors are present to varying degrees: the employee must have the ability, the opportunity, and the motivation to carry out the event. Various data points and indicators form a risk picture that may warrant preventive action.

Three clusters of information drive our discussion:

- Is the insider capable, motivated, and does s/he have the opportunity?
- Do we have unfavorable responses to high-risk indicators?
- Do we have a critical mass of low-risk, but unfavorable, responses to any of the indicators?

The question then becomes: Can an organization track and predict this ability, opportunity, and motivation, and at what point should an insider be closely monitored? To track indicators consistently, we believe that a single electronic-tracking system should be established. The system would aggregate weighted indicators and warn HR or Security personnel if a higher than normal risk is present in one or more employees. The technical details of such a system are beyond the scope of this chapter but have been described elsewhere (Greitzer et al., 2009). Such a system could become a powerful tool to predict and intervene in potential issues, especially in large organizations where managers are not always aware of details of their employees' personal lives and current issues.

We have described an approach aimed at integrating physical and psychosocial data into a predictive analysis framework for insider threat mitigation and associated privacy and ethical issues that arise from this framework. The research, which has been described elsewhere, has focused on the technical challenges inherent in this endeavor, while the need for increased attention to social, legal, and ethical issues has been promoted in earlier works (Greitzer & Endicott-Popovsky, 2008) and in this chapter. As the need for incorporation of psychosocial data in the analysis is increasingly acknowledged (Gabrielson et al., 2008), the discussion about social, ethical, and legal concerns grows in importance. Thus, the social discussion must continue and grow along with the technical research.

More formal approaches have described the effects of employee monitoring on security and factors such as employee trust in organizations, which may be considered as part of the overall discussion. System dynamics models (Band et al., 2006; Moore et al., 2008) might be useful here for capturing complex relationships and tradeoffs that an organization may face in defining levels of employee monitoring and other policy considerations. More research along these lines is needed. Greitzer et al. (2008) describes ongoing training workshops by the Computer Emergency Response Team (CERT) that also incorporate system dynamics modeling to help inform the process. Other ongoing research, funded by DoD, is aimed at applying serious game technology to accelerate learning about the behavioral indicators and precursors of insider threats. Such training and education efforts are also needed to help prevent insider threat, to educate stakeholders regarding the social, legal, and ethical issues, and to avoid misuse or liability in this field.

Anyone who has worked in a large organization has experienced the lack of consistent, accurate, and timely communication among multiple departments and individuals. Sometimes researchers assume that all information will be readily available in one location and that the manager or HR representative would know how and where to seek information and have time to do so. They would also have sufficient training to evaluate risk and know how to intervene to prevent an incident of insider threat. In the real world, though, there is no single source of this information, and it is not necessarily desirable to have it all in one place due to potential for abuse. Managers often supervise more than the recommended 10-12 employees (Window on State Government, 2003), most companies employ one HR representative for about 100-150 employees (Liebermann, 2009), and without the time, tools, and training to evaluate risk and intervene, it is more likely that a threat will go unnoticed if human observations are the only detection means. Thus, although adding automated support to the mix may seem desirable, it is important to realize that adding automated cyber security/insider threat analysis will not necessarily introduce more certainty nor will it necessarily improve the quality of the data being used. These issues will exist in an automated system just as they will exist in a human system. Such challenges are inherent in all computer systems that provide automated support to decision makers: users may become overly dependent on the automated aid, giving it a higher degree of confidence than warranted and deferring to its recommendations; at the other extreme, users may distrust automated aids, particularly if they don't understand how they work. A "joint cognitive system" or mixed-initiative system is most particularly appropriate for an application that monitors and predicts malicious insider activity because the state of technology and the need to safeguard privacy precludes a fully automated system. Therefore, our current work is also focusing on designing user interfaces and visualizations to support joint human-machine decision making in this context.

Insider threat remains a serious consideration for organizations and is likely to remain so. The U.S. courts have consistently upheld the employer's right to monitor emails, phone calls, and other transactions in the workplace (Liebermann, 2009). Employers and policymakers need to carefully balance current legal rights to use some employee information internally, against managing potentially negative impact on employee careers and morale. There is not, and likely will never be, a single clear-cut answer to this age-old tension between the needs of the many and the needs of the few. Still, we hope that this paper will provide a foundation for those seeking a place to begin, or continue, the conversation.

In this chapter, we have focused on psychosocial data monitoring for insider threat mitigation because these data, in particular, are especially sensitive from a privacy, legal, and ethical standpoint. We recognize that a complete predictive assessment is only possible through a monitoring approach that integrates psychosocial data and other cybersecurity data that are traditionally monitored by organizations. Within that context, we have briefly described a modeling approach and data collection criteria that we have adopted in a predictive model for insider threat mitigation. We have also attempted to outline the social/ethical issues that should be considered when developing, validating, and deploying such a model. We regard these social and ethical issues to be of equal importance as any technical challenge associated with creating or implementing a model. Clearly, public debate and further legal guidance are needed to resolve legal, ethical, and privacy issues of workplace monitoring. It is important for organizations to weigh potential benefits against the possible adverse effects that an insider threat detection and mitigation strategy could have on employees. It is also incumbent on the research community to maintain a focus on such debates.

It was our aim as information security researchers to talk through our thinking regarding these issues in a manner that it could serve the purpose of fostering an increase in such discussion – among policy makers, citizens, security researchers, organizations, and last, but not least, students, as they are the policy makers and security researchers of the future.

ACKNOWLEDGMENT

This research was conducted under the Pacific Northwest National Laboratory (PNNL) Information and Infrastructure Integrity Initiative (http://i4.pnl.gov) as Laboratory Directed Research and Development. The views and opinions of authors expressed herein do not necessarily state or reflect those of the United States Government or any agency thereof. PNNL is operated by Battelle Memorial Institute for the United States Department of Energy under Contract DE-AC05-76RL01830.

The authors wish to express thanks for comments by the Editor and reviewers; and deepest gratitude and appreciation in acknowledging the contributions of PNNL project team members Thomas E. Carroll, Sharon Eaton, Thomas Edgar, Lyndsey R. Franklin, Ryan E. Hohimer, Lars J. Kangas, Christine F. Noonan, and Patrick R. Paulson.

REFERENCES

Agre, P. E. (1994). Surveillance and capture: two models of privacy. *The Information Society*, *10*(2), 101–127. doi:10.1080/01972243.1994.9960162

American Civil Liberties Union (ACLU). (2003). *Privacy in America: Electronic monitoring.* Retrieved from htt p://www.aclu.org/privacy/workplace/15646res20031022.html

American Civil Liberties Union (ACLU). (2007). ACLU urges house to fix FISA legislation, warns against amnesty for telecom companies. *ACLU Newsroom*. Retrieved from http://www.aclu.org/safefree/general/31553prs20070905.html

American Management Association. *2001AMA survey: Workplace monitoring and surveillance.* Retrieved from http://www.amanet.org/research/pdfs/Email Policies Practices.pdf

American Management Association. *2003AMA survey: Email policies, rules and practices*. Retrieved from http://www.amanet.org/research/pdfs/Email Policies Practices.pdf

Band, D. R., Cappelli, D. M., Fischer, L. F., Moore, A. P., Shaw, E. D., & Trzeciak, R. F. (2006). *Comparing insider IT sabotage and espionage: A model-based analysis* (Technical Report CMU/SEI-2006-TR026026). Pittsburgh, PA: Carnegie-Mellon Software Engineering Institute.

Biby v. Board of Regents, 419 F.3d. 845 (8th Cir. 2005); and TBG Ins. Servs. Corp. v. Superior Court, 96 Cal. App. 4th 443, 452 (Cal. Ct. App. 2002).

Brown, W. S. (1996). Technology, workplace privacy, and personhood. *Journal of Business Ethics*, *15*, 1237–1248. doi:10.1007/BF00412822

CERT (Computer Emergency Response Team). (2004). *2004 E-crime watch survey ™: Summary of findings.* Retrieved from www.cert.org/archive/pdf/2004eCrimeWatchSummary.pdf

CERT (Computer Emergency Response Team). (2005). *2005 E-crime watch survey ™: Summary of findings.* Retrieved from http://www.cert.org/archive/pdf/ecrimesummary05.pdf

CERT (Computer Emergency Response Team). (2006). *2006 E-crime watch survey ™: Summary of findings.* Retrieved from http://www.cert.org/archive/pdf/ecrimesurvey06.pdf

CERT (Computer Emergency Response Team). (2007). *2007 E-crime watch survey ™: Summary of findings.* Retrieved from http://www.cert.org/archive/pdf/ecrimesummary07.pdf

Credit Reporting Act, F. 15 U.S.C. § 1681 et seq. (1970). Pub. L. No. 90-321, as amended. Retrieved from http://www.ftc.gov/os/statutes/031224fcra.pdf

DoD Office of the Inspector General. (1997). *DoD management of information assurance efforts to protect automated information systems (Technical Report No. PO 97-049)*. Washington, D.C.: U.S. Dept. of Defense.

Fair Credit Reporting Act. (2004a). Federal Trade Commission. Retrieved from http://www.ftc.gov/os/statutes/031224fcra.pdf

Federal Register. 69 (98):29061-29064. (2004b). Federal Trade Commission. Retrieved from http://www.ftc.gov/os/2004/05/040520factafrn.pdf

Fischer, L. F. (2000). Espionage: Why does it happen? *DoD Security Institute.* Retrieved from http://www.hanford.gov/oci/maindocs/ci_r_docs/whyhappens.pdf

Frank, J. (1994). Artificial intelligence and intrusion detection: Current and future directions. In *Proceedings of the 17th NCSC, Baltimore, MD.*

Gabrielson, B., Goertzel, K. M., Hoenicke, B., Kleiner, D., & Winograd, T. (2008). *The insider threat to information systems: A state-of-the-art report.* Herndon, VA: Information Assurance Technology Analysis Center (IATAC).

Gelles, M. (2005) Exploring the mind of the spy. In Online *Employees' Guide to Security Responsibilities: Treason 101.* Retrieved from Texas A&M University Research Foundation website: http://www.dss.mil/search-dir/training/csg/security/Treason/Mind.htm

Greitzer, F. L., & Endicott-Popovsky, B. (2008). Security and privacy in an expanding cyber world. Panel session at the Twenty-fourth *Annual Computer Security Applications Conference (ACSAC)*, Anaheim, CA.

Greitzer, F. L., Moore, A. P., Cappelli, D. M., Andrews, D. H., Carroll, L., & Hull, T. D. (2008). Combating the insider threat. *IEEE Security & Privacy, 6*(1), 61-64 (PNNL Report PNNL-SA-58061). Richland, WA: Pacific Northwest National Laboratory.

Greitzer, F. L., Paulson, P. R., Kangas, L. J., Franklin, L. R., Edgar, T. W., & Frincke, D. A. (2009). *Predictive modeling for insider threat mitigation* (PNNL Report PNNL-SA-65204). Richland, WA: Pacific Northwest National Laboratory.

INFOSEC Research Council. (2005). *Hard problems list.* Retrieved from http://www.infosec-research.org/docs_public/20051130-IRC-HPL-FINAL.pdf

Keeney, M., Kowalski, E., Cappelli, D., Moore, A., Shimeall, T., & Rogers, S. (2005). *Insider threat study: Computer system sabotage in critical infrastructure sectors.* Pittsburgh, PA: U.S. Secret Service and CERT Coordination Center, Carnegie Mellon Software Engineering Institute.

Kelly, M. (1999, December). Your boss may be monitoring your e-mail. *Salon.* Retrieved from http://www.salon.com/tech/feature/1999/12/08/email_monitoring/print.html

Kramer, L. A., Heuer, R. J., Jr., & Crawford, K. S. (2005). *Technological, social, and economic trends that are increasing U.S. vulnerability to insider espionage.* (Technical Report 05-10). Monterey, CA: Defense Personnel Security Research Center (PERSEREC).

Krofcheck, J. L., & Gelles, M. G. (2005). *Behavioral consultation in personnel security: Training and reference manual for personnel security professionals.* Fairfax, VA: Yarrow Associates.

Lane, F. S. III. (2003). *The naked employee: How technology is compromising workplace privacy* (p. 261). New York: American Management Association.

Liebermann, R. K. (2009, accessed). *How to right-size your HR resources: calibrating human resources to company size.* Retrieved from http://www.hrinsourcing.com/calibrating_hr.html

Mayer, R. C., Davis, J. H., & Schoorman, F. D. (1995). An integrative model of organizational trust. *Academy of Management Review, 20,* 709–734. doi:10.2307/258792

Moore, A. P., Cappelli, D. M., & Trzeciak, R. F. (2008). *The "Big Picture" of insider IT sabotage across U.S. critical infrastructures.* Pittsburgh, PA: Software Engineering Institute, Carnegie Mellon University.

Moore, D. A., & Cain, D. M. (2007). Overconfidence and underconfidence: When and why people underestimate (and overestimate) the competition. *Organizational Behavior and Human Decision Processes*, *103*, 197–213. doi:10.1016/j.obhdp.2006.09.002

Nissenbaum, H. (2004). Privacy as contextual integrity. *Washington Law Review (Seattle, Wash.)*, *79*(1), 119–158.

Parker, D. B. (1998). *Fighting computer crime: A new framework for protecting information*. New York: John Wiley & Sons, Inc.

Privacy Act of 1974, 5 USC. § 552a (1974). Pub. L. No. 93-579, as amended. Retrieved from http://www.usdoj.gov/opcl/privstat.htm

Rehabilitation Act of 1973, 29 U.S.C. §701 et seq. (1973). Public Law 93-112, as amended. http://www.dotcr.ost.dot.gov/documents/ycr/REHABACT.HTM

Rosenberg, R. S. (1999). The workplace on the verge of the 21st century. *Journal of Business Ethics*, *22*, 3–14. doi:10.1023/A:1006133732667

Schultz, E. E. (2002). A framework for understanding insider attacks. University of California-Berkeley Lab. Paper presented at Compsec 2002, London, England. Retrieved from http://www.itsec.gov.cn/webportal/download/2002-A%20framework%20for%20understanding%20and%20predicting%20insider%20attacks.pdf

Shaw, E. D., & Fischer, L. F. (2005). *Ten tales of betrayal: The threat to corporate infrastructures by information technology insiders. Report 1—Overview and general observation (*Technical Report 05-04). Monterey, CA: Defense Personnel Security Research Center (PERSEREC).

Smith, R. E. (2002). *Compilation of state and federal privacy laws*. Providence, RI: Privacy Journal.

Tabak, F., & Smith, W. P. (2005). Privacy and electronic monitoring in the workplace: A model of managerial cognition and relational trust development. *Employee Responsibilities and Rights Journal*, *17*(3), 173–189. doi:10.1007/s10672-005-6940-z

Texas Workforce Commission. (2008). HIPAA privacy rule – What employers need to know. Retrieved from http://www.twc.state.tx.us/news/efte/hipaa_basics.html

U. S. v. Barrows, 481 F. 3d1246 (10th Cir. 2007); and United States v. King, 509 F. 3d 1338 (11th Cir. 2007).

U.S. Central Intelligence Agency. (1990). Project SLAMMER Interim Report (U). Director of Central Intelligence/Intelligence Community Staff Memorandum ICS 0858-90, April 12, 1990. Retrieved October 22, 2009 from http://antipolygraph.org/documents/slammer-12-04-1990.pdf

U.S. Department of Health and Human Services. (2007). *Protecting the privacy of patients' health information.* Retrieved from http://www.hhs.gov/news/facts/privacy2007.html

U.S. Department of Health and Human Services. (2009). *Health information privacy.* Retrieved from http://www.hhs.gov/ocr/hipaa/

U.S. Department of Justice. (2009). Americans with Disabilities Act ADA home page. Retrieved from http://www.usdoj.gov/crt/ada/

U.S. Equal Employment Opportunity Commission. (2008). *Americans with disabilities act: Questions and answers.* Retreived from http://www.usdoj.gov/crt/ada/q%26aeng02.htm (last updated November 14, 2008).

Waldo, J., Lin, H. S., & Millett, L. I. (2007). *Engaging privacy and information technology in a digital age*. Washington, D.C.: The National Academies Press.

Wikipedia. (2009). Blackhat. Retrieved from http://en.wikipedia.org/wiki/Blackhat

Window on State Government. (2003). Reduce management costs in state government. Retrieved from http://www.cpa.state.tx.us/etexas2003/gg10.html

KEY TERMS AND DEFINITIONS

Cybersecurity: Policies, tools, methods, and individuals focused on protection of information technology and data from theft, corruption, or natural disaster, while allowing the information to remain accessible and productive for its intended users.

Employee Assistance Program (EAP): A program that provides confidential personal services to employees.

Human Resources Information System (HRIS): An information system that collects, maintains, and reports employee demographics and other data.

Insider: An individual currently or at one time authorized to access an organization's information system, data, or network.

Insider Threat: The potential for an authorized user to hinder resources or impede the mission of an organization.

Sensemaking: The largely cognitive activity of constructing a hypothetical mental model of the current situation and how it might evolve over time, the potential actions can be taken in response, and the projected outcomes of those responses.

Trust: The belief in, and willingness to depend upon, another party.

ENDNOTES

1. Now at Amazon.com
2. The phrase "insider threat" as opposed to "insider activity" is used deliberately here: a predictive approach means that the concern revolves around harmful acts that the insider *might* still carry out, not necessarily any that have already occurred.
3. Increased intrusiveness or severity of security measures may contribute to employee job dissatisfaction; management intervention on suspected employee disgruntlement issues may actually increase an employee's frustration level (Shaw & Fischer, 2005). At the opposite extreme, it is possible that inadequate attention and action can also feed and increase insider activity. One manifestation of this idea has been described as the "trust trap" in which the organization's trust in individuals increases over time, yielding a false sense of security because the trust leads to decreased vigilance toward the threat. This produces fewer discoveries of harmful actions, which in turn increases the organization's level of trust (Keeney et al., 2005; Band et al., 2006).
4. Project Slammer is a CIA-sponsored study of Americans convicted of espionage against the United States. A declassified interim report dated 14 April 1990 is available at: http://antipolygraph.org/documents/slammer-12-04-1990.shtml and http://antipolygraph.org/documents/slammer-12-04-1990.pdf.
5. Most companies review convictions, not arrests, subscribing to the standard that a person is innocent until proven otherwise.
6. The ACLU is also actively engaged in a similar privacy protection effort re: FISA http://www.aclu.org/safefree/general/31553prs20070905.html
7. Note that the potential needs of counterintelligence analysts or law enforcement personnel are not within the scope of the present employee monitoring discussion.

APPENDIX: DISCUSSION QUESTIONS

1. Discuss the ethical aspects of insider threat monitoring from a utilitarian, a virtue ethics, and a deontological ethics standpoint.
2. The chapter discusses the employer practice of monitoring employee e-mail and web surfing. Do you think that this monitoring is ethically justified? Why or why not? Under what circumstances might it be justified? Why?
3. Devise a fair usage policy for employee usage of computers for personal activities in the workplace. Your policy should describe acceptable activities and unacceptable activities. It should also include disciplinary actions for violators.
4. Do you agree with the notion that an employee has no reasonable expectation of privacy when he or she uses a personally owned computer in the workplace? Why or why not?
5. Discuss the notion of trust between an employer and an employee. Compare this to trust between two friends. Is there an assumption that trust exists at the beginning of either type of relationship? What factors might positively influence the level of trust? What factors might negatively influence the level of trust?
6. Is trust important in a workplace? Why or why not?
7. Is it ethical for employers to presume that employees are untrustworthy until proven otherwise? Why or why not?
8. Before an employer decides to use insider threat monitoring, should there be some quantifiable evidence (proof) that general patterns of past behavioral observations of employees of other companies is useful for predicting what current employees might do? Why or why not?
9. Do you think that insider threat monitoring would be more readily accepted in certain cultures? If so, which ones? Why?
10. Might your cultural norms influence your perception of whether insider threat monitoring is "ethical"? How so?
11. Do you think insider threat monitoring can alter cultural norms? Explain your position.
12. Discuss what you perceive to be the costs and benefits of insider threat monitoring. Please identify for whom it is a cost and benefit. What are the tradeoffs and for whom? Which is greater – costs or benefits?

Chapter 8
Behavioral Advertising Ethics

Aaron K. Massey
North Carolina State University, USA

Annie I. Antón
North Carolina State University, USA

ABSTRACT

Behavioral advertising is a method for targeting advertisements to individuals based on behavior profiles, which are created by tracking user behavior over a period of time. Individually targeted advertising can significantly improve the effectiveness of advertising. However, behavioral advertising may have serious implications for civil liberties such as privacy. In this chapter, we describe behavioral advertising ethics within the context of technological development, political and legal concerns, and traditional advertising practices. First, we discuss the developmental background of behavioral advertising technologies, focusing on web-based technologies and deep packet inspection. Then, we consider the ethical implications with a primary focus on privacy of behavioral advertising technologies. Next, we overview traditional market research approaches taken to advertising ethics. Following that, we discuss the legal ethics of behavioral advertising. Finally, we summarize these cross-disciplinary concerns and provide some discussion on points of interest for future research.

INTRODUCTION

Behavioral advertising is a method for targeting advertisements to individuals based on their actions. Market researchers construct behavior profiles by tracking user actions, such as purchases, recommendations, or reviews. Advertisers use an individual's behavior profile to tailor advertisements to that individual. An online behavior profile can be built by tracking the websites people visit on the Internet. The development of new behavioral advertising technologies, such as Deep Packet Inspection (DPI), makes the construction of behavior profiles possible in contexts where it was previously impractical. Behavioral advertising is currently a challenging public policy concern with interdisciplinary ethical implications as evidenced

DOI: 10.4018/978-1-61692-245-0.ch008

by recent efforts by the U.S. Federal Trade Commission (FTC) to encourage best practices.

New behavioral advertising technologies raise challenging ethical questions that this chapter seeks to address. How should consumers and advertisers approach the tradeoff of privacy for improved advertising effectiveness? What level of control over behavioral tracking should consumers have? Is first-party behavioral advertising more ethical than third-party behavioral advertising? Are there important ethical differences between web-based and network-based behavioral advertising? Is an opt-in default more ethical than an opt-out default? More specifically, who owns data regarding online behavior? How should traditional market research ethics affect behavioral advertising? Do current behavioral advertising technologies violate legislation or are they in some other way ethically dubious? We aim to clarify the scope and ethical implications of these questions.

Many of these ethical questions are civil liberty concerns. Civil liberties are rights in freedom. For example, the freedom of religion, freedom of speech, the right to keep and bear arms, the right to not be discriminated against, the right to a fair trial, and the right to privacy are all civil liberties. These freedoms limit government power and prevent governments from unduly intervening in the lives of citizens. Because many of the ethical issues regarding behavioral advertising ethics are fundamentally consumer privacy concerns, we have chosen this as a focus for this chapter.

Privacy is a particularly challenging ethical concern because it is inherently difficult to define. George Washington University Law Professor Dan Solove (2008) describes privacy as a "concept in disarray" (p. 1) that "[n]obody can articulate" (p. 1). Possibly the best-known definition of privacy comes from an 1890 law review article by Warren and Brandeis wherein they stated that privacy is "the right to be let alone" (Warren & Brandeis, p. 193, 1890). As data processing became more important Alan Westin (1967) recognized that being left alone was insufficient; he describes privacy as "the claim of individuals, groups, or institutions to determine for themselves when, how, and to what extent information about them is communicated to others" (p. 7). This recognizes that providing control to individuals is an important aspect of privacy. A more recent control-based definition by Jim Harper (2004) emphasizes even further the importance of the individual consumer. Harper (2004) calls privacy "the subjective condition that people experience when they have the power to control information about themselves" (p. 2). For the purposes of this chapter, we will assume Harper's control-based definition of privacy because it acknowledges both that privacy means different things to different people (i.e. that it is subjective) and that privacy involves an element of consumer control.

The FTC (2000a, 2000b) has voiced concerns that behavioral advertising violates consumer expectations of privacy. However, the difficulty of defining and valuing privacy hampers efforts to compare the economic benefits of behavioral advertising to the cost of constraining civil liberties (Solove, 2008; Szoka & Thierer, 2008). In an empirical study on the effectiveness of behavioral advertising,[1] Yan, Liu, Wang, Zhang, Jiang, and Chen (2009) reported that the information collected to construct a behavior profile can be used to improve advertising effectiveness[2] by at least 670% (Yan et al., 2009). This tension between powerful economic incentives and important civil liberties has resulted in scrutiny from the FTC (2000a, 2000b, 2007, 2009), U.S. Senate (Privacy Implications, 2008), and the U.S. House of Representatives (What Your Broadband Provider, 2008, Communications Networks, 2009).

Advertising-based business models are common on the Internet. The FTC (2000a) reported to Congress that Internet advertising revenues for 1996 totaled $301 million. By 2001, Internet advertising produced $7.2 billion in revenues (Internet Advertising Bureau [IAB], 2002). In 2007,

Internet advertising revenues had grown to $21.2 billion a year, with search-based advertising from companies like Google and Yahoo comprising 41% of that total (Internet Advertising Bureau, 2008). eMarketer (2007), a company that provides statistical research on e-business and online advertising, estimated that industry-wide spending on behavioral advertising techniques would grow from $220 million in 2005 to $3.8 billion in 2011, a 17-fold increase.

Developments in behavioral advertising technologies are driving the potentially explosive increase in its use. Behavioral advertising is a relatively new technique in the Internet advertising industry. Online advertisements were first targeted to consumers though advertisements that did not change based on the individual viewing the website. We refer to this practice as 'static advertising.' In static advertising, targeting was done based on the content of the website. If the website was about skiing, then the ads would be for products like ski jackets and particular ski lodges. However, some websites delivered primarily dynamic content, and for those sites static advertising is less effective.

Advertisers developed a new mechanism for targeting advertisements, called contextual advertising, based on the dynamic content of the website. In contextual advertising, information used to generate advertisements typically is not stored or linked to an individual. As a result, it is not necessary to generate or store individual behavioral profiles. Consider Google's Gmail service, which automatically scans the content of an email, determines the context of that email by identifying key words and phrases, and displays advertising previously determined to be related to that context. Although there was a firestorm of discussion amongst privacy advocates at the time (Electronic Privacy Information Center, 2004; World Privacy Forum, 2004), the debate has calmed down significantly since the details of the service became better understood. A computer algorithm determines the context of each message by scanning email contents and selects an ad to display. Google employees do not read email delivered to Gmail to generate these ads. Also, Google's Gmail service is voluntary. If someone remained concerned about their privacy after hearing how the service worked, they could avoid the potential privacy violation by simply using a different email service provider.

The remainder of this chapter is organized as follows. First, we provide some background on the developmental history and operation of behavioral advertising technologies with a specific focus on DPI. Following that, we discuss of the impact of technology ethics on behavioral advertising practices. Next, we describe the traditional market research approaches to advertising ethics because market research ethics has a long and rich history that provides interesting insights into the challenge of behavioral advertising (Blankenship, 1964; Tybout & Zaltman, 1974). Then, we discuss the legal implications of using DPI for behavioral advertising. Finally, we summarize the discussion and provide some thoughts on future research.

BACKGROUND

In this section, we describe the technical differences between first-party and third-party behavioral advertising, and detail specific web- and network-based technologies used to construct behavioral profiles online.

First-Party Behavioral Advertising

To start our discussion, consider the simplest form of behavioral advertising: an offline loyalty card program. Many businesses, such as supermarkets and bookstores, offer loyalty card programs to their customers. A loyalty card program allows a customer to trade personal information, such as their name, address, and shopping history, in exchange for discounts on products sold. The business can use the shopping history to produce individually targeted advertisements. For example, if a customer in a loyalty card program at a bookstore purchases three books on the American Revolution, then the bookstore could use this information to send coupons or other advertisements on U.S. history books to that customer. Most loyalty card programs are examples of first-party behavioral advertising.

In first-party behavioral advertising, the party displaying the advertising is also the party collecting the behavioral profile. First-party behavioral advertising can be accomplished through a multitude of techniques, including web-based techniques that could also be used by third-party advertisers. Amazon.com's recommendation service is a well-known example of first-party behavioral advertising. Amazon.com can collect the entire set of page links clicked on by registered, logged-in Amazon.com shoppers without being limited to the technologies on which a third-party advertiser would be forced to rely. The raw data is known as clickstream data, and it can be coalesced into a more concise behavioral profile through analysis and data mining. Amazon.com has patented their product recommendation analysis and data mining techniques (Wolverton, 2000). Amazon.com can use their behavior profiles to recommend other products to users. In addition to clickstream data, Amazon.com has access to customer wish lists, reviews, and ratings. This full access to customer data is only possible in first-party behavioral advertising systems. It is important to note that access to more data does not necessarily result in more effective advertising results. In fact, data analysis becomes harder as data sets change or grow in size and complexity.

Third-Party Behavioral Advertising

In third-party behavioral advertising, the party displaying the advertisement is different from the party collecting the behavior data and selecting which ad to display. Third-party behavioral advertising occurs when a web-based company partners with a dedicated advertising company that uses behavioral advertising techniques. The web-based company is the first party, the consumer is the second party, and the advertising company is the third party. In these partnerships, the third-party advertising company collects individuals' information to improve their targeting. Third-party advertisers use two broad techniques to construct behavior profiles: web-based or network-based. Each technique can be implemented with different underlying technologies. For example, cookies, web bugs, and local shared objects (LSO), also known as flash cookies, are technologies that can support web-based behavioral advertising. Advertising companies serving ads to many websites with these technologies can construct behavior profiles by tracking individuals as they surf from one website to another.

Currently, advertisers use two third-party behavioral advertising techniques to construct behavior profiles: web-based profiling and network-based profiling. Web-based techniques involve tracking behavior as users surf the Internet, but they are limited because advertisers can only collect information on websites to which they have access, such as those sites on which they advertise. More recently, Internet Service Providers (ISPs) have adapted network management techniques, like DPI, to do network-based profiling of their customers' behavior on the Internet. Network-based techniques are capable of building more detailed behavior profiles than web-based techniques because they have access to all online behavior rather than being limited to just web traffic. If this technology is widely adopted, then ISPs could operate as third-party advertising agencies. This would provide ISPs with an additional revenue source and improve the quality of broadband infrastructure, but it would also raise ethical concerns about pervasive surveillance of online activities affecting consumer privacy and free speech.

Web-Based Techniques

Web-based techniques for behavioral advertising involve tracking behavior as users surf the Internet. These techniques are limited because advertisers can only collect information on websites to which they have access, such as those sites where they advertise. The first web-based behavioral advertising technologies came in the form of browser cookies and web bugs (Federal Trade Commission [FTC], 2000a; FTC, 2000b). A browser cookie is a small file that contains information about the user and the user's session with a particular domain name and is stored on an Internet user's computer. Cookies are built into the Hypertext Transfer Protocol (HTTP), which is an application level protocol that runs on the Internet. Netscape began supporting cookies in 1994, and Microsoft's Internet Explorer began supporting cookies in 1995. Cookies can be used to identify or authenticate the user to the website, and can store session information such as the items currently in a user's electronic shopping cart for a particular domain.

Cookies loaded from the same domain as the website visited are called first-party cookies. When an advertisement on a webpage is hosted on a third-party server, cookies may be transferred by the HTTP request that loads the advertisement. These cookies are called third-party cookies. Domains can access only those cookies that they have previously set. For example, a cookie set by the domain www.example.com is only accessible to www.example.com. Most browsers allow users to set separate preferences for first-party and third-party cookies. Typical preferences include allowing cookies automatically, blocking cookies automatically, or prompting the user to choose whether to allow or block cookies as the user browses the web. In addition, users can install browser extensions for Firefox[3] like Adblock Plus[4] or NoScript[5] to prevent loading advertisements or the associated cookies.

Since cookies are the primary mechanism for identifying returning users, they can be used to differentiate between users desiring behaviorally targeted advertising and users desiring no targeted advertising. The former are called "opt-in" cookies, which indicate a desire to participate in information collection, and the latter are called "opt-out" cookies, which indicate a desire to avoid participation in information collection. There is no standard or industry-wide preference between opt-in and opt-out cookies. As a result, users may have both opt-in and opt-out cookies on their system at the same time. This can lead to challenges for individuals seeking to control their information collection because browsers only offer the ability to delete all cookies and anti-spyware programs often delete cookies (Swire & Antón, 2008). Individuals concerned about their privacy may prefer to keep opt-out cookies and delete opt-in cookies (Swire & Antón, 2008).

A web bug is fundamentally different from a cookie because it does not store data on the user's computer. Web bugs are typically tiny web graphics that are a single pixel in both height and width. They are included in the HTML for a website, but may be hosted on an advertising server. Web bugs usually match the background color of the website and, as a result, appear invisible to the Internet user. When the website is loaded, the advertising server can track all the sites for which a particular IP address requests a web bug image by logging the IP address of the Internet user's HTTP request for the web bug.

Web bugs may be used in tandem with cookies to increase the chances of collecting behavior information. Although web bugs cannot collect as much information as cookies, they are more difficult to block than cookies because browsers currently do not allow users to set preferences for blocking web bugs. Web bugs are third party images and do not need to use Javascript, and Javascript-blocking browser extensions, such as NoScript, may not be able to block web bugs.

Browser extensions attempting to block all advertising from third-party servers, such as Adblock Plus, may perform better.

Another important difference between cookies and web bugs is that web bugs can be used more easily to track users in HTML-formatted emails. An advertiser or spammer can verify that an email address is valid and active using a web bug. Consider the email address bob@example.com. To verify this email address, an advertiser could setup a web bug with an identifying filename, such as bob-at-example-dot-com.jpg, on a third-party server and include that image in an HTML formatted email sent to the email address. Assuming that bob@example.com is a valid, active email address and that the owner of that email address allows HTML-formatted email, then an HTTP request for the image will be made when the owner opens this email. The advertiser merely needs to record this request in his log files to determine whether both the timestamp and the email account are valid. It is important to note that web bugs do not work with email if the email client has been configured not to accept HTML-formatted email.

LSOs, also called flash cookies, are another technology for web-based behavioral advertising. LSOs are built into all versions of Adobe Flash Player—a common browser extension that supports audio, video, and online games. YouTube videos make use of Adobe Flash Player. Essentially, LSOs serve the same role in a flash-based setting as cookies in an HTTP-based setting, which is why they are sometimes called flash cookies. They are used to store settings, such as a volume preference, or keep track of session information, such as a score in a game, and they are only accessible to the same domain that created them. Although LSOs perform similar functions as cookies, user preferences for LSOs are set differently. Settings for LSOs are stored in the Adobe Flash Player Settings Manager and not in the standard browser preferences. Adobe has published documentation on their Settings Manager[6] and a walkthrough on how to manage and disable LSOs[7]. A browser extension that deletes LSOs, called Objection[8], is available for Firefox.

Through cookies, web bugs, and LSOs, third-party advertisers are able to compile behavioral profiles of Internet users. These profiles can include the content of the pages visited in a particular website, the amount of time the user spends on a particular page, any search terms the user enters for that site, and any purchases the user makes while on the site. This information can be tracked regardless of whether or not the user clicks on an advertisement.

Network-Based Techniques

Network-based techniques for behavioral advertising build behavior profiles from all network traffic rather than just web-based traffic. Network traffic is composed of discrete data packets sent through a layered set of protocols collectively known as the Internet Protocol suite. Layered protocols operate by abstracting away details to simplify the construction of a communications network. The Internet's layered network architecture enables encapsulated services starting with the hardware layer through the network layer up to the application layer. Each layer provides just enough information, in the form of a packet header, to complete the delivery of a packet. Packet headers are critical elements of network layering. They identify the source and destination for a particular packet at a particular layer. This identification is roughly similar to the routing information of an envelope sent through the postal system, which identifies the recipient's address and the sender's (return) address.

The concept of an envelope for real world postal mail is a common analogy for packet headers, but there are several inaccuracies with this analogy. First, packets may be wrapped in many packet headers with the outermost packet header being the one that represents the current layer. Second, as the packets are delivered, the packet headers are updated, removed, or altered as a part of the normal course of delivery. Finally, and perhaps most importantly, the contents of a packet are not invisible or hidden by a packet header. In regular mail, the envelope protects the contents of a message.

The delivery of packets according to their packet headers alone is the intended design of the Internet's layered protocols. Deep Packet Inspection is a label for a broad classification of technologies that inspect beyond the packet header to view the actual data being delivered. DPI techniques are called "deep" packet inspection because they look "deeper" into each packet to see past the header, glimpsing the actual data contained in the packet. By inspecting the packet's payload contents for all packets that an Internet user sends or receives, ISPs are able to generate a detailed behavioral profile from which targeted advertising can be constructed. In contrast to web cookie-based approaches, customers have no way to control DPI-based behavioral advertising with their browser preferences.

DPI ignores abstraction, which is a convenience of network protocol design. Looking at the data itself has been possible since the original design of the Internet, but the culture of the early Internet opposed violating abstraction in network design. Saltzer, Reed, and Clark (1984) describe the engineering efficiency gained by maintaining abstraction layers. This concept is called the end-to-end design principle (Salzer, Reed, & Clark, 1984). Essentially, the end-to-end design principle states that application design should be done at the endpoints in a communication system (Salzer, Reed, & Clark, 1984). For example, since all information transferred over the network is broken up in to packets, it is possible that the packets will arrive out of order. It is easier to let the endpoints correct the order of the packets than to construct the core of the network so that it ensures that packets arrive in the correct order. A single error in delivering a packet could cause delays due to the need to retransmit the packet. As a consequence, all subsequent packets would also be delayed.

The end-to-end principle links DPI to network neutrality, which is another highly debated ethical concern in network management. Network neutrality is difficult to define and actually comprises three separate ethical debates. First, network neutrality can describe an argument about tiered pricing schemes for end-users or for content providers. Second, network neutrality can describe a free speech argument about filtering content in the core of the network by blocking sensitive political, religious, racial, or sexual content. Finally, network neutrality can describe the argument about maintaining the culture of the end-to-end principle in networking. It is in this final argument that DPI and network neutrality are linked. If the culture of the end-to-end principle is not maintained, then end-users lose a measure of autonomy in their communications. As a result, the use of DPI involves a narrower set of ethical decisions than network neutrality.

The link between DPI and network neutrality exists because DPI technologies violate the end-to-end principle in two ways. First, DPI inspects beyond the packet header as packets are in transit for content analysis, classification, and collection. This type of application development in the core of the network violates the end-to-end principle. Second, in order to serve behaviorally targeted advertising, DPI inserts a fake web cookie into the packet streams of Internet users surfing the web. In non-DPI networks, the only way that a cookie can be placed on a user's browser is if the server at the other end of the communication placed it. However, in DPI networks, fake web cookies, which can be used as identifiers for third-party advertising services seeking to serve behaviorally targeted advertisements, must be placed on the user's browser by the ISP. This is a violation of the end-to-end principle as well because the cookie was generated in the core of the network by the end user's ISP rather than at the endpoint.

Since DPI refers to any technology that inspects the payload content of the packet rather than just the packet header, DPI techniques can be used for purposes other than advertising. For example, DPI can be used to filter spam, viruses, or malware out of the network by inspecting packets for identifying signatures. In addition, DPI can be used to improve quality of service by prioritizing packets for real-time media applications like streaming audio, streaming video, or VOIP (Voice Over Internet Protocol) telephony. These other uses of DPI could provide ISPs with an additional revenue stream without the need to collect personal information. For example, an ISP using DPI to improve the quality of streaming video from a particular domain, such as YouTube or ESPN, could charge customers an additional monthly fee to receive prioritized quality of service on these domains. Because these services are not advertising-based, we will not discuss their ethical implications other than to say that this use of DPI could be considered an unethical violation of network neutrality.

BEHAVIORAL ADVERTISING ETHICS

Ethics is the study of moral values. It is the authors' view that technology exists in an inherently value-free state[9]. For example, consider a hammer—if used to build a home, then the hammer serves an ethically valuable, or "good," purpose. If used as a weapon to attack an innocent person, then the hammer serves an ethically questionable, or "bad," purpose. The value-free nature holds for all forms of technology, and it has been recognized by several important computer technology organizations. For example, the Association for Computing Machinery (ACM), which the world's oldest scientific and educational computing society, states in their Code of Ethics (Association for Computing Machinery, 2009) that, "Because computer systems can become tools to harm as well as to benefit an organization, the leadership has the responsibility to clearly define appropriate and inappropriate uses of organizational computing resources" (Section 3.3, para. 1). Similarly, the IEEE Code of Ethics (Institute of Electrical and Electronics Engineers, 2006) seeks "to improve the understanding of technology, its appropriate application, and potential consequences" (Point 5) because the ethical values resulting from inherently value-free technologies are a result of human understanding and value-laden use of technology. In this section, we seek to comment on the value-based ethical concerns involved in the development and use of behavioral advertising technologies.

Value-Based Ethical Concerns in First-Party Behavioral Advertising

In first-party behavioral advertising, the party doing the advertising and collecting the profile is also the party being visited by the end user. Because the party collecting the information is also interested in selling products to that individual, the company has a vested interested in ensuring that the behavioral profile is secure, and that the end user has the ability to update or correct it. In short, first-party advertisers must be concerned about losing customers if their information practices do not satisfy the individuals to whom that information refers.

Third-party advertisers do not necessarily have the same level of economic interest because they operate as middlemen. They are concerned with improving their advertising effectiveness with accurate customer information, and they have an interest in keeping the information they collect secure to ensure that their competitors do not have access to it. However, third-party advertisers do not have the same level of concern about losing individual customers based on their information practices because their customers are other businesses rather than individuals.

First-party behavioral advertising is regarded by the FTC (2009) as "more likely to be consistent with consumer expectations, and less likely to lead to consumer harm than other forms of behavioral advertising" (p.26). Consumers can be made aware of a given sites' data collection practices via a web site's privacy policy. When data collection is conducted through cookies, consumers can control whether or not they wish to participate by directing their browser to accept or reject cookies from a given domain. This feature is common to all major browsers and can be configured without extensive technical knowledge.

Value-Based Ethical Concerns in Third-Party Behavioral Advertising

In third-party behavioral advertising, the party being visited by the end user is not the same as the party collecting behavior information or serving advertisements. While first-party behavioral advertising tracks an individual's behavior in a single domain, third-party behavioral advertising can track an individual's behavior across multiple websites. This could entail a third-party, generally an advertising company, setting a single cookie on the users' browser and accessing it as the user browses from website to website.

For example, if a ski lodge website were to support third-party behavioral advertising, then the site may attempt to set a cookie for a third party advertising company. If the user subsequently visits a different domain to book a travel package and that travel website hosted ads through the same advertising company, the advertising company would recognize the user and serve advertisements related to ski trips and ski lodges even if it was the user's first time visiting the subsequent travel site.

Both first- and third-party behavioral advertising allow Internet users some level of control over tracking if they depend on stored cookies for user identification. Modern browsers allow users to tailor how they want to manage cookies. As mentioned in the background section, individuals concerned about privacy often delete or actively manage the cookies stored on their browsers. However, this level of control is not afforded to individuals tracked though newer, non-cookie based technologies. For example, web bugs are often transparent and designed to be invisible from the end user's perspective. In addition, browsers and email clients do not commonly offer the ability to block web bugs.

The Ethics of Deep Packet Inspection Technology

Preserving the privacy of ISP customers is the primary ethical concern surrounding Deep Packet Inspection (DPI) technologies. DPI-based third-party behavioral advertising can be implemented in an undetectable fashion from the end user's perspective. If privacy is a desirable control-based right for end users of an ISP's services, then the ethical questions regarding behavioral advertising can be simply stated as follows, "Does the user have control over when their Internet usage is monitored by their ISP?" The answer to this, at least in part, is that customers have two clear technologies that provide them with control over their privacy: encryption and onion routing.

Strong encryption protocols like Secure Socket Layer (SSL), Transport Layer Security (TLS), and Pretty Good Privacy (PGP) can be used to prevent DPI technologies from being able to decipher the contents of the packet payload data. There are two problems with encryption as a means to protect end user privacy. First, encryption technologies require more processing power for servers. Providing encryption on a popular web server could prove to be prohibitively expensive or impractical, even for larger web-based organizations. Second, many websites simply do not support encryption at all. For these sites, the end user is still caught between using the service, being monitored by DPI technologies, or not using the service at all.

Onion routing is another means to protect privacy when using ISPs that employ DPI. Onion routing provides a bi-directional, private, encrypted tunnel for all Internet traffic (Reed, Syverson, & Goldschlag, 1998). Because of this tunnel, the web server cannot accurately identify the end user; it can only identify the end of the tunnel, called an exit node. The tunnel also prevents ISPs from determining the content of the traffic being delivered because the information is encrypted until it reaches the exit node. The name "onion routing" comes from the protocol's design, which calls for layers of encryption to hide user details.

In theory, onion routing seems to be the answer to the ethical concerns raised by DPI. In practice, onion routing introduces two important problems. First, servers that provide onion routing services cannot support the demand. The extra processing and bandwidth needed often painfully slow the available servers. A single onion router must support and encrypt all of an Internet end user's traffic to be effective. Such a design does not scale well to many thousands of users. Second, onion routers eventually have to decrypt the traffic that they are protecting. Onion routing is not end-to-end encryption; it merely provides source address anonymization in the segment of the route that deploys onion routing. For example, consider Bob, who is a New England Patriots fan living in Indianapolis, which hosts a rival team: the Indianapolis Colts. One day Bob decides to shop for Patriots apparel online. If Bob is using an onion router to protect his communication, then the onion router has to decrypt his Internet traffic at the exit node and pass it along to Bob's online store of choice. If Bob's browsing includes any unencrypted personal information, such as a username or credit card, then any router or server between the exit node and the online store at which Bob is shopping has a chance to identify Bob as a New England Patriots fan. Individuals desire better results from technology when seeking to control their privacy.

Market Research Ethics

Market research has a long history of addressing the ethical implications of advertising and should be a part of the behavioral advertising ethics discussion. Advertisers recognize that ethics has important relationships with the quality of market research data and ethical consumer protection concerns (Blankenship, 1964; Tybout & Zaltman, 1974; Warne, 1962). Tybout and Zaltman (1974) state, "an understanding of ethical issues involved in marketing research is essential for producing quality research" (p. 357). Many professional marketing organizations, including the American Marketing Association and the Market Research Society, maintain Codes of Ethics that should also impact any discussion of behavioral advertising. These Codes of Ethics discuss ethical practices for generating profiles of specific consumer groups through focus groups, interviews, and other traditional market research techniques. However, market researchers also recognize that a Code of Ethics is not enough. Blankenship (1964, p. 26) writes, "Codes alone cannot provide the answer. They can merely provide a few guideposts."

Market researchers seek to understand what people need, want, or believe for various purposes, including designing products, pricing products, improving product placement, and advertising. Marketers are tasked with determining what people want to buy despite the fact that many consumers do not know what they want. In an attempt to improve advertising results, the scope of advertising has expanded over time to include many sensitive areas of a person's life, such as education, family planning, and government (Tybout & Zaltman, 1974; Warne, 1962). Market research must be done carefully to ensure the quality and accuracy of the data while not violating individuals' rights.

Researchers use standard customer's rights as a guide to ensure ethical market research practices through surveys and interviews (Tybout & Zaltman, 1974). These rights are four-fold: the right to choose, the right to safety, the right to be informed, and the right to provide feedback and be heard. A consumer's right to choose is traditionally embodied as the choice to take a survey or participate in an interview (Tybout & Zaltman, 1974). Marketers have a strong incentive to allow the consumer to freely choose to participate in market research because they are concerned about the quality of the data obtained from a 'forced' interview or survey (Tybout & Zaltman, 1974). Although this seems straightforward, marketers could subtly trick consumers into participating in market research that they may otherwise decline. Tricks could include outright deception or more subtle psychological pressure to participate. Consumers who are 'forced' or otherwise pressured to provide information may be self-conscious or behave differently than they would otherwise.

In addition to the various methods to pressure participation, so-called unobtrusive measures could be used to collect data about consumers without informing them of the collection (Tybout & Zaltman, 1974). Imagine a door-to-door market researcher using the pretext of trying to determine a homeowner's opinion of vacuum cleaners. Once the researcher is allowed into the customer's home, he can learn all sorts of additional information about that homeowner, such as their taste in furniture, art, and lifestyle. If this information is recorded for marketing purposes without informing the customer, then that customer's right to choose has been violated.

In the case of DPI, there are at least two clear ways that an individual's right to choose may be violated. First, if an ISP has a monopoly in a particular market, the individual's right to choose is tied to their use of the Internet. Although the individual may wish to keep their web browsing habits to themselves, their wish to browse the web may be stronger. Second, in the initial pilot studies conducted by Comcast and NebuAd consumers were informed of the opportunity to opt-out of the pilot study through an obscure and easily disregarded notice (Anderson, 2008). The obscure nature of the notice itself may have violated the individual's right to be informed, and the policy may have violated the individual's right to choose by not ensuring that Comcast customers were freely choosing to take part. More importantly, the incentives are significantly different for DPI than for market research. Many consumers are completely unaware of the technology behind DPI or the types of information collected. In addition, individuals feel comfortable doing things online that they would not do in a traditional, real-world store. As a result, marketers may be more confident about the quality of the data and more inclined to use unobtrusive measures to obtain the data they need. After all, since individuals are unaware and intrinsically comfortable at their keyboards, the behavioral data they produce is likely to be high quality.

Tybout and Zaltman (1974) show the consumer right to safety in market research has at least three components: protection of anonymity, protection from undue stress, and protection from deception. Protection of anonymity safeguards the confidentiality of individuals' answers to sensitive questions, such as those regarding income, age, religion, or politics. Protection from undue stress is traditionally meant to protect individuals from potential psychological burdens. For example, if an individual with little knowledge of baking is asked a variety of questions about cake pans, then they may become distressed about their lack of cooking ability. Protection from deception ensures the consumers' ability to make informed choices regarding market research. It is particularly important given that DPI technologies can be used without alerting or informing consumers.

During the Senate Committee on Commerce, Science, and Transportation's hearings on behavioral advertising in 2008, one senator raised the question of how profiles were created in the days before Deep Packet Inspection (Privacy Implications, 2008). It is important to recognize that advertising firms made ethical decisions about the collection of customer profiles and purchasing habits for the purposes of targeting advertisements. Directed marketing companies have been collecting profiles for this purpose decades prior to the advent of DPI technologies. These profiles were combined into comprehensive lists that included the names, addresses, phone numbers, and other contact information for people with similar profiles. The fact that consumer mailing lists were created, bought, sold, and used for marketing purposes prior to the Internet does not directly justify the development or use of DPI, but it may provide insight that helps answer the ethical concerns raised by behavioral advertising.

Earlier directed marketing technology consisted of mailing lists and databases with contact information that did not contain enough information about individuals' preferences to target advertising behaviorally. Instead, directed marketing entailed classifying consumers into groups, such as "suburban middle class family" or "urban 20-somethings." Marketers sent specially designed marketing materials directly to the homes of individuals within these consumer groups. For example, an ad for a new bedroom set could be sent only to "suburban mothers" while an ad for football tickets could be sent specifically to "urban 20-something males."

Although this was more efficient than mailing advertisements to every household, directed marketing had relatively low response rates. It was driven by the 2% rule, which states that any of these marketing materials with a response rate of 2% or greater were worth the investment (Hughes, 1996). Most directed marketing campaigns resulted in 3-4% response rates, which meant that even a small change in effectiveness could result in relatively large economic benefits to the company (Department of Health Education and Welfare, 1973). Given these response rates, direct marketers were eager for any technology that might improve advertising effectiveness. In 1973, the Department of Health, Education, and Welfare voiced concerns that directed marketing needed "constructive publicity toward emphasizing the rights of the individual" to address citizens' civil liberties concerns (Department of Health Education and Welfare, Section IV, A Note on Mailing Lists, para. 9, 1973). In particular, the HEW report (Department of Health Education and Welfare, 1973) was concerned that citizens had little control over their private information was being used.

In many ways, the current discussion surrounding ethical principles for behavioral advertising mirrors the previous discussion regarding directed marketing. Just as directed marketing was more effective than random mass mailings, behavioral advertising is more effective than contextual or static online advertising. Randall Rothenberg, President and CEO of the Interactive Advertising Bureau, testified before the U.S. House Small Business Committee's Subcommittee on Regulations, Healthcare, and Trade that web-based advertising provides a significant improvement in effectiveness over traditional directed marketing because the interactive environment promotes an "ongoing, two-way engagement among consumers, their media, and the advertising" and "generates data on consumer interests, needs, and consumption patterns that makes advertising effectiveness far easier to measure" (Rothenberg, 2008). Although the technology has changed, the ethical questions remain strikingly similar: What consumer information should advertisers be allowed to collect and how should they collect it? What levels of notice, control, and access should consumers have? This history of market research ethics should not be ignored.

Legal Ethics

Whereas ethics is the study of moral values, the law is a codification of rules describing the particular values society desires to uphold and enforce. In the United States, the FTC is an independent government organization tasked with consumer protection. To protect consumer privacy, the FTC supports five principles, called the Fair Information Practice Principles. These principles are as follows: (1) Notice / Awareness, (2) Choice / Consent, (3) Access / Participation, (4) Integrity / Security, and (5) Enforcement / Redress. The first principle, Notice / Awareness, matches well with Tybout and Zaltman's (1974) "Right to be Informed" for market research subjects. The second principle, Choice / Consent, matches well with Tybout and Zaltman's (1974) "Right to Choose" for market research subjects. The fourth principle, Integrity / Security, matches well with Tybout and Zaltman's (1974) "Right to Safety" for market research subjects. The similarities between the Fair Information Practice Principles and consumer rights described by Tybout and Zaltman are examples of the FTC codifying ethical values.

The Federal Trade Commission (2000a, 2000b) first examined online profiling by holding a November 1999 workshop with network advertising companies. The Network Advertising Initiative (NAI), which was formed by several of these advertising companies, created self-regulatory principles for online profiling which the FTC (2000a, 2000b) supported. Continued public concern over behavioral advertising led the FTC (2007) to hold a November 2007 Town Hall workshop on behavioral advertising technologies. This workshop sought to develop guidelines for self-regulation of the industry (Federal Trade Commission, 2007).

In December of 2007, the FTC released its proposed self-regulatory principles for behavioral advertising, and requested additional comments to be submitted by following April. The next year the NAI (2008) revised their self-regulatory principles to ensure that "notice, choice, use limitation, access, reliability and security" (p. 3) were maintained. The FTC's four final self-regulatory principles were released in February 2009 and focus on (1) transparency and consumer control, (2) reasonable security and limited data retention for consumer data, (3) affirmative express consumer consent to material changes in existing policy, and (4) affirmative express consumer consent to the use of sensitive data for behavioral advertising (Federal Trade Comission, 2009). Key industry advertising and consumer protection groups, including the Internet Advertising Bureau, the Direct Marketing Association, and the Council of Better Business Bureaus, expanded on the FTC's principles to seven "Self-Regulatory Principles for Online Behavioral Advertising" (2009): consumer education, consumer control, transparency in the collection and use of data, security, consumer consent for material changes in policy, sensitive data handling, and accountability.

Despite the history of active participation from the government and many advertising companies, many scholars believe that self-regulation is not the answer. Chris Hoofnagle (2005), writing on behalf of the Electronic Privacy Information Center (EPIC), believes that privacy self-regulation principles still leave consumer privacy vulnerable and fail to educate consumers of the potential threats to their privacy. For example, Hoofnagle (2005) points out that opt-out policies are burdensome for consumers. Hoofnagle (2005) states that market forces have been "eroding both practices and expectations" (p. 15) regarding privacy and recommends that the FTC "abandon its faith in self-regulation" (p. 15). Other public interest organizations have taken a more moderate approach. For example, in 2008 the Center for Democracy and Technology (CDT) supported progress in self-regulation of privacy when responding to the NAI's 2008 principles, but also noted seven areas needing improvement. For example, the

CDT (2008) also takes issue with the use of opt-out choice mechanisms. More broadly, the CDT (2008) recommends independent third-party audits to ensure compliance to self-regulatory principles and foster accountability.

By May 2008, Charter Communications had partnered with a behavioral advertising company called NebuAd to run a pilot program using a new technology called DPI. Representatives Barton (R-TX) and Markey (D-MA) sent a letter to Charter Communications asking them to put the behavioral advertising pilot program on hold until the privacy concerns could be discussed (Barton and Markey, 2008). In July 2008, Representatives Dingell (D-MI), Barton, and Markey sent a letter to Embark CEO Tom Gerke seeking further information about a behavioral advertising technology test conducted in conjunction with NebuAd (Barton, Dingell, and Markey, 2008). Charter Communications is the third-largest cable operator in the U.S., and Embarq is the fourth-largest telephone carrier.

Eventually, both the U.S. Senate and House of Representatives decided to hold hearings to discuss the ownership of online behavior information, the legality of DPI itself, and Internet users' privacy concerns with comprehensive behavioral tracking. These hearings included testimony from Microsoft, Google, Facebook, the FTC, the Center for Democracy and Technology, and the Competitive Enterprise Institute (Privacy Implications, 2008; What Your Broadband Providers, 2008). Neither the Senate Committee hearings nor the House Committee hearings provided conclusive solutions to these concerns, but both committees promised to investigate the issue further.

Although neither the Senate Committee hearings nor the House Committee hearings provided conclusive answers to the questions raised, the advertising industry responded with significant changes. The CEOs of NebuAd and Adzilla, the two largest behavioral advertising companies in the United States, resigned from their positions under this extreme level of scrutiny (Hansell, 2008; Keane, 2008). Both NebuAd and Adzilla eventually closed their doors entirely leaving the U.S. without a DPI-based behavioral advertising business (Austin, 2009; Hansell, 2008; Keane, 2008). The largest remaining network-based behavioral advertising company in the world is Phorm, which operates in conjunction with British Telecom in the United Kingdom, but the European Commission is suing them for violations of European Union data protection laws (Wray, 2009). Google recently announced a web-based behavioral advertising service, but its impact remains to be seen (Helft, 2009).

Internet service providers are the only companies that are positioned to implement ISP-based behavioral advertising. As Paul Ohm points out, "Everything we say, hear, read, and do on the Internet passes first through their computers. If ISPs wanted, they could store it all, compiling a perfect transcript of our online lives" (Ohm, p. 1, 2009). Their position in the network puts ISPs in a unique and powerful position, but it does not put them beyond legislation and regulation.

Although Ohm's statement is theoretically true, Ohm also points out one practical problem that is important to the technology behind DPI. Compiling a perfect transcript of an individual's Internet use might be possible, but given the sheer amount of data that passes through an ISP's customer-facing routers, it would be technically infeasible to record all of this data in an easily accessible format. Normal routing of Internet traffic involves viewing the packet header to get routing information and not at the payload. No recording of information is necessary to deliver the packet. The construction of a complete profile of an individual's online behavior would require viewing and recording much larger amounts of data than contained in the packet header.

Ohm points out that Federal and State wiretapping laws, such as the federal Electronic Communications Privacy Act (ECPA), regulate packet-level surveillance, and it is possible that network-based behavioral advertising violates these laws (Ohm, 2009). The ECPA amended the federal law protecting the privacy of telephone conversations. Although the ECPA is perhaps better known for its protections of stored electronic communications, like emails stored by an ISP, these stored protections are much weaker than the protections provided to active communications, like packets sent while web surfing. Because DPI techniques inspect active communications, Ohm (2009) believes a strong case could be made that these techniques are already illegal.

The construction of complete end user profiles has been defended in some contexts as 'reasonable network management.' In particular, the United States Federal Trade Commission, which regulates ISPs' business practices, justified the use of DPI techniques as 'reasonable network management' because many ISPs use DPI to drop spam, viruses, and other malware. The legal ethics of this situation can be understood by the context of the situation. If a value-free technology can be used in one context (e.g. network security) as justifiably reasonable, nothing prevents the use of that same technology from being unethical in another context (e.g. marketing).

Nissenbaum (2004) discussed the importance of context to privacy law as an attempt to justify privacy as independent of property law. Privacy law and property law are historically intertwined because each is tied to the societal understanding of public and private contexts. Nissenbaum (2004) describes information as another context in which privacy laws apply. She outlines a framework, called "contextual integrity," that can be used to understand information privacy in spaces that would traditionally be considered public (Nissenbaum, 2004). In this framework, the distinction between public and private is made based on the context in which it is used rather than whether it is public or private, or even if it is gathered publically or privately (Nissenbaum, 2004). Using contextual integrity, Nissenbaum (2004, pp. 152-153) examines the privacy concerns involved in consumer profiling:

In the past, it was integral to the transaction between a merchant and a customer that the merchant would get to know what a customer purchased. Good - that is to say, competent - merchants, paying attention to what customers wanted, would provide stock accordingly. Although the online bookseller Amazon.com maintains and analyzes customer records electronically, using this information as a basis for marketing to those same customers seems not to be a significant departure from entrenched norms of appropriateness and flow. By contrast, the grocer who bombards shoppers with questions about other lifestyle choices—e.g., where they vacationed, what movies they recently viewed, what books they read, where their children attend school or college, and so on—does breach norms of appropriateness. The grocer who provides information about grocery purchases to vendors of magazine subscriptions or information brokers like Seisint and Axciom is responsible not only for breaches of norms of appropriateness but also norms of flow.

Nissenbaum's concept (2004) has already impacted the development of information systems. Barth, Datta, and Mitchell (2006) examined the use of contextual integrity to construct a framework for reasoning about access control and privacy policy frameworks. They validated their contextual integrity framework against information systems that must comply with laws and regulations (Barth, Datta, & Mitchell, 2006). Specifically, they evaluate information systems for compliance with the Health Insurance Portability and Accountability Act, the Children's Online Privacy Protection Act, and the Gramm-Leach-Bliley Act (Barth, Datta, & Mitchell, 2006). Although the contextual integrity framework may be limited to information systems, it certainly appears promising for use in analyzing the legal aspects of DPI.

Many unanswered legal questions about behavioral advertising remain. Congressional hearings have not yet conclusively determined whether behavioral advertising is in the public's best interest. The recent FTC self-regulatory rules have not yet impacted the industry, and scholars such as Hoofnagle do not believe they will. No conclusive case law exists that would clarify if DPI is a violation of existing wiretapping laws. Lawyers and lawmakers have not yet clearly defined the contexts for online privacy.

FUTURE RESEARCH DIRECTIONS

Behavioral advertising has the potential to improve sales and the consumer experience significantly, but it is still an under-researched area (Yan et al., 2009). Web-based behavioral advertising requires better control mechanisms for web bugs and LSOs. In particular, researchers should determine how to design a browser such that could provide end users the ability to set preference options to block web bugs and LSOs. Researchers also need to address the conflicts between opt-in and opt-out cookies. One promising solution may be recent browser extensions, such as the Targeted Advertising Cookie Opt-out (TACO) extension[10], that automatically restore opt-out cookies.

The most important area for future research in network-based behavioral advertising is the question of end user control over whether their Internet traffic is being monitored through DPI. Perhaps it is possible to provide users a technological solution that would allow them to control DPI. Finally, users could pursue a legal solution by pushing for new state or federal laws banning the use of DPI technologies by ISPs.

Focus is also needed on ways to provide end users choice regarding subjects that can be tracked. Providing a finer granularity of control would enable end users the ability to allow their ISP to build behavioral profiles regarding only certain types of marketing (e.g. furniture) while preventing more sensitive types of marketing (e.g. healthcare prescriptions). Although this level of control is more complex, if implemented on a per individual basis, it may provide a generic solution for communities that share relatively uniform norms of privacy. For example, this is the approach taken by Phorm to comply with the privacy norms of the United Kingdom.

Consumer notice and consumer education are a critical areas of future research needed to solve some of the ethical concerns of DPI technologies. If an ISP is profiling their customers, a control-based definition of privacy as the ethical standard calls for clear notification regarding what is being collected about them, how it is being collected, and what mechanisms they can use to control this process. Furthermore, consumers should be able to view, amend, or correct errors in these profiles. Providing these controls and assisting users in exercising them preserves end user privacy while allowing ISPs to make use of their valuable position in the Internet topography.

The effects of third party doctrine are another important area for future research. Third party doctrine is a legal interpretation of the Fourth Amendment of the U.S. Constitution, which protects citizens against unreasonable searches and seizures by the government. Third party doctrine states that individuals sharing information with third parties cannot make a Fourth Amendment claim of protection on that information. The ethics of third party doctrine extend beyond behavioral advertising, but under third party doctrine citizens could not use the Fourth Amendment to protect information shared with advertising companies using behavioral advertising technologies.

Finally, future research should also consider the effects of behavioral advertising on other civil liberties. For example, behavioral advertising technologies could be used as tools of discrimination because they can profile based on cultural or racial subjects. Similarly, if these technologies are used to profile religious subject matter, then there may be effects on freedom of religion. Behavioral advertising may also have a chilling effect on free speech because consumers may change the way they communicate when they know they are being profiled.

CONCLUSION

In this chapter we have discussed the ethics of behavioral advertising as they relate to consumer expectations of civil liberties, especially privacy. We began by describing behavioral advertising technologies and comparing them with earlier forms of advertising. Next, we then discussed previous market research ethics that provide insights into this ethical debate. Finally, we discussed the role of laws and regulations as a societal expression of ethically acceptable practices.

Although there are many difficult ethical questions about behavioral advertising, the role that advertising plays is incredibly important both in the economics of the Internet and more broadly in capitalist society. Advertising fueled the explosive growth of the Internet. Many products and services are offered free of charge to the end user. The company that provides the service makes money through advertisements included in these products and services. In addition, the cost of advertising is the overhead of matching consumers with producers in a capitalist economy. The lower this cost is, the more efficiently a capitalist economy performs. When consumers are able to find new and interesting products more easily while feeling confident about their privacy and producers are able to sell to everyone that truly wants their products, all players in the market win. There are real benefits to effective targeted online advertisements, but we must adequately address the ethical issues surrounding behavioral advertising.

REFERENCES

Anderson, N. (2008, July 23). Embarq: Don't all users read our 5,000 word privacy policy? *Ars Technica.* Retrieved May 24, 2009 from http://arstechnica.com/old/content/2008/07/embarq-dont-all-users-read-our-5000-word-privacy-policy.ars

Association for Computing Machinery. (2009). Code of ethics, Retrieved May 23, 2009 from http://www.acm.org/about/code-of-ethics

Austin, S. (2009, May 19). Turning out the lights: NebuAd. *Wall Street Journal Blogs*. Retrieved May 24, 2009 from http://blogs.wsj.com/venturecapital/2009/05/19/turning-out-the-lights-nebuad/

Barth, A., Datta, A., Mitchell, J. C., & Nissenbaum, H. (2006). Privacy and contextual integrity: Framework and applications. In *Proceedings of the 2006 IEEE Symposium on Security and Privacy* (pp. 184–198).

Barton, J., Dingell, J., & Markey, E. (2008, July 14). Letter to Tom Gerke, CEO of Embarq. Retrieved May 19, 2009 from http://markey.house.gov/index.php?option=com_content&task=view&id=3410&Itemid=141

Barton, J., & Markey, E. (2008, May 16). Letter to Neil Smit, CEO of Charter Communications. Retrieved May 19, 2009 from http://markey.house.gov/docs/telecomm/letter_charter_comm_privacy.pdf

Blankenship, A. B. (1964). Some aspects of ethics in marketing research. *JMR, Journal of Marketing Research*, *1*(2), 26–31. doi:10.2307/3149918

Center for Democracy and Technology. (2008). Response to the 2008 NAI principles: The network advertising initiative's self-regulatory code of conduct for online behavioral advertising. Retrieved September 16, 2009 from http://www.cdt.org/privacy/20081216_NAIresponse.pdf

Communications Networks and Consumer Privacy: Recent Developments: Hearing before Committee on Energy and Commerce, Subcommittee on Communications, Technology, and the Internet, House of Representatives, 111th Cong. 1. (2009).

Department of Health, Education, and Welfare [now Health and Human Services]. (1973). *Records, Computers and the rights of citizens, report of the secretary's advisory committee on automated personal data systems*. Retrieved from http://aspe.hhs.gov/DATACNCL/1973privacy/tocprefacemembers.htm

Electronic Privacy Information Center. (2004, August 18). Gmail Privacy Page. Retrieved May 23, 2009 from http://epic.org/privacy/gmail/faq.html

eMarketer. (2007). Behavioral Targeting: Advertising Gets Personal, Retrieved March 19, 2009 from http://www.emarketer.com/Report.aspx?code=emarketer_2000415

Federal Trade Commission. (2000a). *Online profiling: A report to congress (Part 1)*. Retrieved from http://www.ftc.gov/os/2000/06/onlineprofilingreportjune2000.pdf

Federal Trade Commission. (2000b). *Online profiling: A report to congress (Part 2): Recommendations*. Retrieved from http://www.ftc.gov/os/2000/07/onlineprofiling.pdf

Federal Trade Commission. (2007). *Online advertising and user privacy: Principles to guide the debate*. Retrieved March 19, 2009 from http://www.ftc.gov/os/2007/12/P859900stmt.pdf

Federal Trade Commission. (2009). *Federal Trade Commission staff report: self-regulatory principles for online behavioral advertising: tracking, targeting, and technology*. Retrieved from http://www.ftc.gov/os/2009/02/P085400behavadreport.pdf

Hansell, S. (2008, October 8). Adzilla, a would-be I.S.P. Snoop, quits U.S. market, *New York Times Bits Blog*. Retrieved from http://bits.blogs.nytimes.com/2008/10/09/adzilla-a-would-be-isp-snoop-abandons-us-for-asia/

Harper, J. (2004). Understanding privacy -- and the real threats to it. *Cato Policy Analysis*, *520*, 1–20.

Helft, M. (2009, March 11). Google to offer ads based on interests. *The New York Times*. Retrieved from http://www.nytimes.com/2009/03/11/technology/internet/11google.html

Hoofnagle, C. J. (2005). *Privacy self regulation: a decade of disappointment*. Available at SSRN: http://ssrn.com/abstract=650804 or DOI: 10.2139/ssrn.650804

Hughes, A. M. (1996). *The complete database marketer: Second-generation strategies and techniques for tapping the power of your customer database* (2nd ed.). New York: McGraw-Hill.

Institute of Electrical and Electronics Engineers. (2006). *Code of ethics*. Retrieved March 19, 2009 from http://www.ieee.org/web/membership/ethics/code_ethics.html

Internet Advertising Bureau. (2002). *Internet advertising revenue report: 2001 full year results*. Retrieved March 19, 2009 from http://www.iab.net/media/file/resources_adrevenue_pdf_IAB_PWC_2001Q4.pdf

Internet Advertising Bureau. (2008). *IAB internet advertising revenue report: 2007 full year results*. Retrieved March 19, 2009 from http://www.iab.net/media/file/IAB_PwC_2007_full_year.pdf

Keane, M. (2008, September 3). *Another nail in the NebuAd coffin: CEO steps down*. Retrieved March 19, 2009 from http://blog.wired.com/business/2008/09/another-nail-in.html

Network Advertising Initiative. (2008). *The network advertising initiative's self-regulatory code of conduct*. Retrieved September 16, 2009 from http://networkadvertising.org/networks/2008%20NAI%20Principles_final%20for%20Website.pdf

Nissenbaum, H. F. (2004). Privacy as contextual integrity. *Washington Law Review (Seattle, Wash.)*, *79*(1), 119–158.

Ohm, P. (2009). The rise and fall of invasive ISP surveillance. *University of Illinois Law Review.* (forthcoming). University of Colorado Law Legal Studies Research Paper No. 08-22. Available at SSRN: http://ssrn.com/abstract=1261344

Privacy Implications of Online Advertising: Hearing before Committee on Commerce, Science, and Technology. U.S. Senate, 110th Cong. 1 (2008).

Reed, M. G., Syverson, P. F., & Goldschlag, D. M. (1998). Anonymous connections and onion routing. *IEEE Journal on Selected Areas in Communications*, *16*(4), 482–494. doi:10.1109/49.668972

Rothenberg, R. (2008). *Testimony Before the Subcommittee on Regulations, Healthcare, and Trade Hearing on "The Impact of Online Advertising on Small Firms." Small Business Committee, U.* S. House of Representatives.

Saltzer, J. H., Reed, D. P., & Clark, D. D. (1984). End-to-end arguments in system design. *ACM Transactions on Computer Systems*, *2*(4), 277–288. doi:10.1145/357401.357402

Self-regulatory principles for online behavioral advertising. (2009) Retrieved September 16, 2009 from: http://www.iab.net/behavioral-advertising-principles

Solove, D. J. (2008). *Understanding privacy*. Boston, MA: Harvard University Press.

Swire, P. P., & Antón, A. I. (2008, April 10). Online behavioral advertising: Moving the discussion forward to possible self-regulatory principles. Testimony to the FTC. Retrieved March 19, 2009 from http://www.americanprogress.org/issues/2008/04/swire_anton_testimony.html

Szoka, B., & Thierer, A. (2008). Online advertising and user privacy: Principles to guide the debate. *Progress Snapshot*, *4*, 6.

Tybout, A. M., & Zaltman, G. (1974). Ethics in marketing research: Their practical relevance. *JMR, Journal of Marketing Research*, *11*(4), 357–368. doi:10.2307/3151282

Warne, C. E. (1962). Advertising – a critic's view. *Journal of Marketing*, *26*(4), 10–14. doi:10.2307/1248332

Warren, S. D., & Brandeis, L. D. (1890). The right to privacy. *Harvard Law Review*, *4*(193).

Westin, A. (1967). *Privacy and freedom*. New York: Atheneum.

What, Y. B. P. K. A. Y. W. U. *Deep Packet Inspection and Communications Laws and Policies: Hearing before the Committee on Energy and Commerce, Subcommittee on Telecommunications and the Internet, House of Representatives*, 110 Cong. 1 (2008).

Wolverton, T. (2000). Amazon snags patent for recommendation service, *CNET News*. Retrieved March 19, 2009 from http://news.cnet.com/2100-1017-241267.html

World Privacy Forum. (2004, April 6). An open letter to google regarding its proposed gmail service. Retrieved May 23, 2009 from http://www.worldprivacyforum.org/gmailrelease.pdf

Wray, R. (2009) Phorm: UK faces court for failing to enforce privacy laws. *The Guardian*. Retrieved May 24, 2009 from http://www.guardian.co.uk/business/2009/apr/14/phorm-privacy-data-protection-eu

Yan, J., Liu, N., Wang, G., Zhang, W., Jiang, Y., & Chen, Z. (2009). How much can behavioral targeting help online advertising? In *WWW '09: Proceedings of the 18th International Conference on World Wide Web* (pp. 261–270). New York, NY, USA.

KEY TERMS AND DEFINITIONS

Behavioral Advertising: A method for targeting advertising to individuals based on their actions.

Behavioral Profile: A profile of an individual's actions, interests, and demographics that can be used to tailor advertisements.

Cookie: A small file stored on a computer, or other web-browsing device, that can be used to identify returning users or store web browsing session information such as items stored in an online shopping cart.

Deep Packet Inspection (DPI): Any method of Internet routing or network management that involves using information in the packet payload instead of or in addition to the information in the packet header.

Local Shared Object (LSO): A small piece of information stored on a machine through Adobe Flash Player that can be used to identify a returning user or store web browsing session information such as the score on a flash-based game.

Web Bug: An image file loaded included on a web page or in an email for the sole purpose of tracking who loaded it an when it was loaded. Typically, web bugs are 1 pixel by 1 pixel transparent images.

ENDNOTES

1 Yan et al. refer to behavioral advertising as behavioral targeting.

2 The Click-Through Rate (CTR) commonly measures Internet advertising effectiveness; it is calculated as the number of times an ad is clicked compared to the number of times it is shown.

3 http://www.mozilla.com/en-US/products/firefox/

4 http://adblockplus.org/

5 http://noscript.net/

6 http://www.macromedia.com/support/documentation/en/flashplayer/help/settings_manager06.html

7 http://kb2.adobe.com/cps/526/52697ee8.html

8 http://objection.mozdev.org/

9 It is worth noting that some scholars would disagree with this statement and claim that ethical value is embedded during the design

APPENDIX: DISCUSSION QUESTIONS

1. Is opt-in or opt-out a more ethical default for cookies?
2. How can browsers support both opt-in and opt-out defaults when deleting cookies?
3. Should third-party cookies be treated differently than first-party cookies?
4. What is an ethical duration for the validity of cookies?
5. Would a more transparent standard for cookies improve user privacy? If so, how?
6. Do transparent web bugs violate notice/awareness?
7. Is the use of an image as a web bug a violation of the original purpose for which it was designed?
8. Web bugs are difficult to block, but they can only provide limited information. Does this make web bugs more or less fair than cookies?
9. Does the use of web bugs by spammers de-legitimize the use of web bugs by traditional advertisers?
10. How can an ISP provide customers notice regarding the use of DPI?
11. How can an ISP provide customers a choice regarding the use of DPI?
12. What types of information should be collected and used to generate profiles? How long should organizations keep this information?
13. Is it ethical to use DPI to detect and drop packets that contain viruses? In what ways is this different than advertising?
14. Cookies and DPI were originally developed for non-advertising purposes, but they have been found to be useful for advertising. Is it ethical to use technologies for a secondary purpose (i.e. for something that these technologies weren't originally designed to do)?
15. Should the companies be required to inform each consumer of the actual information they have and how they are using it?
    a. Would this solution scale knowing the large amount of notification data that would be sent to users?
    b. Is there an increased risk of identity theft by sending this information out?
    c. If so, is this an ethical issue?
16. Is it ethical that your information be collected without your knowledge and permission?
17. Who are the stakeholders' (individuals, corporations, and communities) in the discussion of behavioral advertising? Put yourself in the shoes of each stakeholder and describe your interests.
18. Should behavioral advertising be regulated? If so, how and by whom (self-regulation, standards, states, federal government)?
19. Consider what happens if some unintended entity were to acquire and sell behavioral advertising data? Who would be victims and why?
    a. Does this suggest that regulations, controls and policies and penalties be mandated? On whom and by whom?
20. Suggest a way of doing behavioral advertising without violating ethical principles?
21. Is DPI ethical?
    a. Should there be another way for ISPs to collect information without DPI?
22. Should Behavioral Advertising/DPI be limited to a subset of some user group or markets?
23. Is it ever ethical for a firm in a market relationship with a consumer to deceive the consumer?

Section 3
Emerging Issues and the Public Sector

Section 3
Introduction

Linda Morales
University of Houston Clear Lake, USA

Ethics in information security is rife with competing interests and difficult choices. Information systems strive for some sort of tolerable balance between competiong business concerns, between business concerns and social expectations, "between social costs and benefits"(as mentioned in Chapter 10), and between public goods and private interests. The concerns and demands are often contradictory, leaving us only unsatisfactory and unsettling choices. We are asked to choose between such things as privacy and transparency, confidentiality and accessibility, accountability and anonymity, the necessity for trade-offs being born out of our desire to improve our information systems and our society while at the same time protecting individual rights. Attributes of an "acceptable" solution are not easy to define or understand. So much depends on context, social expectation, profitability, and other motives.

There is no permanent security solution for any system, no holy grail to strive for. A "secure" system is an evolving beast. Each step in the evolution represents an unclear, and therefore, uneasy compromise among several ethical concerns. The rules and the technologies employed in each step are vulnerable to challenge and buffeted by conflict. The process is one of iterative improvement. We try a solution and hope it will hold for a few days or months. When it breaks, we tweak it to plug the leaks. Sometimes we have to abandon a solution and start afresh with new rules, new technologies. We can only hope that the path to a more secure system is like climbing a hill, instead of traversing a circle – that there is always improvement and that the path does not double back on itself, bringing us to a place we have already been which has proven to be insecure or unacceptable.

We see this evolutionary process at work in the next three chapters. The chapters deal with privacy in three different contexts. Chapter nine discusses ethical issues arising from the use of genetic information to determine appropriate dosage of medicines in the treatment of health conditions. Chapter 10 discusses attitudes, expectations and official policy regarding the protection of personal information accessible through government services that are available around the clock. These are "everyday" services such as medical benefits and income tax information. Chapter 11 analyzes data breach disclosure laws on a state-by-state basis in the US and discusses the need for federal policy to mandate data breach disclosure. At the center of this discussion of data breach disclosure laws is the issue of corporate responsibility, and the tension between the rights of the individual versus the business interests of the corporation.

Who can argue against the convenience of filing taxes or paying toll road charges on-line? The question is not whether these services are conveniences, the question is whether such conveniences are worth the potential of accompanying loss of privacy and increased vulnerability to fraud? Similarly, there is great value in knowing the right dosage of a medication. Is the health benefit worth the risk of personal genetic information stored in potentially vulnerable databases? Especially unwieldly is weighing immediate benefits against possible future costs, that may or may not come to bear. These questions have our collective attention today and will probably remain contentious for the foreseeable future. Not only is our attention focused on day-to-day services, we are concerned about fraud, and the privacy of our health-related information.

To add to the confusion, there are several interdependent co-evolutions taking place. Information systems themselves are evolving, but so are our notions of privacy and other rights. For instance, Chapter 10 observes that privacy is not a context-neutral concept. Information that might be considered sensitive in one setting may not be sensitive in another (Nissenbaum). Moreover, it may be more meaningful to view privacy as a collective right, rather than simply an individual right (Regan). This has legal ramifications, including the elevation of privacy to a loftier status, above the concerns of efficiency and security. Our understanding of other rights and requirements is changing as well. Chapter nine raises the question of ownership of genetic information – is it owned by the individual whose body it came from, or is it owned by research institutions that have extracted genetic information from a subject's body? There are many other ethical dilemmas that arise in the emerging field of pharmacogenomics, some of which can be addressed by guidelines used for other known ethical issues in medicine. There are other issues, however, that are unique to the field of pharmacogenomics and require further discussion and debate to understand. Many issues are not well understood, and it is likely that there are many other issues that are not yet evident. The chapter advises caution as the field progresses in order to protect the welfare of human subjects involved in pharmacogenetic studies.

Chapter 11 makes the point that as we are become "more organically interdependent on technology", our obligation to better understand technology becomes greater if we are to be participants in the control of the use of technology and its impact on our personal privacy, safety and the security of our personal data. As the use of social control mechanisms, such as public policy, increase in the field of information assurance and security, technologists also need to better understand public policy processes and outcomes. It is through these interdisciplinary understandings that we can better contemplate how technology affects the quality of human life and dignity – how we can use the creative power of man for the betterment of mankind.

REFERENCES

Ackoff, R. (1981). *Creating the corporate future.* New York: John Wiley & Sons.

Nissenbaum, H. (2004). Privacy as contextual integrity. *Washington Law Review, 79*(1), 119-157.

Regan, P. M. (1995). *Legislating privacy, technology, social values and public policy.* Chapel Hill, NC: University of North Carolina Press.

Chapter 9
Ethics, Privacy, and the Future of Genetic Information in Healthcare Information Assurance and Security

John A. Springer
Purdue University, USA

Jonathan Beever
Purdue University, USA

Nicolae Morar
Purdue University, USA

Jon E. Sprague
Ohio Northern University, USA

Michael D. Kane
Purdue University, USA

ABSTRACT

The risks associated with the misuse and abuse of genetic information are high, as the exploitation of an individual's genetic information represents the ultimate example of identity theft. Hence, as the frontline of defense, information assurance and security (IAS) practitioners must be intimately familiar with the multidimensional aspects surrounding the use of genetic information in healthcare. To achieve that aim, this chapter addresses the ethical, privacy, economic, and legal aspects of the future uses of genetic information in healthcare and discusses the impact of these uses on IAS. The reader gains an effective ethical framework in which to understand and evaluate the competing demands placed upon the IAS practitioners by the transformative utility of genomics.

DOI: 10.4018/978-1-61692-245-0.ch009

INTRODUCTION

Biotechnology and its related applications are advancing rapidly. As readers in the field of information assurance and security, you may wonder what biotechnology advancements have to do with information security. The intersection is clearly seen when one considers the fact that the human genome is made up of over 3 billion bits of *information*, where these bits are nucleotide base pairs. Viewed in this context, the human genome as information is slightly different in nature from other forms of personal information, such as a social security number, a credit card number, your name, your address, and so on. The difference is as follows. If an individual's social security or credit card number is compromised, she can get a new one – albeit not without some effort and cost. In fact, one can even get a new name. This is not the case with your genome. In this case, you are your information and always will be. Furthermore, the utility of this information could extend beyond your life. Your children and grandchildren are derived from your genome; they are information derivatives.

As such, consideration of the use and potential misuse of genetic information seems highly relevant to information assurance and security. We believe that IAS practitioners should be aware of the evolution of biotechnology and the consequent implications for the use of genetic information. Toward this end, this chapter discusses a particular area, known as pharmacogenomics, which is overviewed in the next section, and considers some of the ethical, privacy, economic, and legal aspects of the future uses of genetic and pharmacogenomic information in healthcare.

We begin with an overview of pharmacogenomics so that readers have a basic grounding. Next this chapter discusses the promise of technological innovation so that readers understand how advances are perceived as beneficial to society. Then we analyze ethics and genetic information, with a concentrated focus on ethics and pharmacogenomics. The analysis serves as a model demonstrating how critical ethical analysis of past innovations can serve to reveal whether or not there really is anything "ethically new" here. As you'll see, we conclude that with regard to pharmacogenomics, yes, there are a few novel challenges for consideration. Given that many ethical challenges are linked to public policy and social norms, we turn to discussion of how existing laws and social norms may or may not address/influence some of these challenges. Finally, we end by discussing implications for models of information assurance and security, bringing full circle the ramifications of biotechnology to information assurance and security.

Before we proceed to a discussion of background topics, let us highlight relevant information assurance and security concepts as these are some of the criteria by which we later evaluate the pertinent ethical issues that arise from the use of genetic information in healthcare. According to Bishop (2002) as well as Whitman and Mattord (2005), the fundamental IAS concepts include confidentiality (which includes privacy), integrity, availability, and evidence of trustworthiness. Confidentiality is the concealment of information or resources, and access control mechanisms help to enable confidentiality (Bishop, 2002); generally speaking, confidentiality has a close relationship with privacy (Whitman & Mattord, 2005). Privacy is a complex concept with many nuanced definitions (Schoeman, 1984); for our purposes, we delimit the definition of privacy to one's independent control over the public dissemination of one's personal information. Integrity, according to Bishop, refers to the trustworthiness of data or resources, and is usually operationalized in terms of preventing improper or unauthorized change. As such, integrity entails mechanisms that prevent modification or detection of the integrity of the data (Bishop, 2002). In tandem with confidentiality and integrity comes availability, which concerns access to the desired information or resources (Bishop, 2002); a classic example of not providing availability is a denial of service attack (Bishop, 2002). Lastly, evidence of trustworthiness concerns the assurance that a piece of information meets the security requirements expected by the user of the information, and as the phrase suggests, evidence must exist that supports this trust (Bishop, 2002). Together, these concepts (confidentiality, integrity, availability, and evidence of trustworthiness) form the basis of evaluation for the IAS professional as she or he encounters the ethical issues addressed later in this chapter.

BACKGROUND OF PHARMACOGENOMICS

Pharmacogenomics is the utilization of genomic markers – pieces of information used to identify and track genetic characteristics – to personalize prescription drug dosing and falls into the broader area of "personalized medicine". To elaborate, we need to provide a brief background in genetics – it's our aim to do this in a manner that is understandable by readers not steeped in a biology/genetics background.

The human genome, which is made up of over 3 billion bits of information (nucleotide base pairs), contains approximately 24,000 gene sequences. Furthermore, the human genome harbors over 1 million single nucleotide polymorphisms (SNPs). A SNP is a known location in the genome where a single base differs within the population. Therefore, SNPs are similar to genetic "mutations". The difference between a mutation and a SNP is that a mutation is known to be causal to a specific disease or disorder, whereas SNPs are simply seen as benign genomic differences among individuals. It is important to note that mutations and SNPs are not the same type of information when we classify information by its use. Currently, we are not using SNPs to predict a disease or disorder. Rather, the advances in biotechnology are exploring how SNPs can be used to predict and improve the outcomes of medicinal treatment, which we discuss in more detail later. But that is current day. Research is also underway that examines the role (if any) that certain SNPs play in the predisposition of specific diseases. As the medical community begins to derive predictive information about the future health of a patient from their DNA sample, the power of the utilization of genomic markers, as well as the associated liabilities, come into focus.

THE PROMISE OF PHARMACOGENOMICS

Health is essential to human flourishing. We all know first-hand the importance of health to quality of life; without health, matters of life, liberty, and pursuit of happiness seem less relevant. To understand why pharmacogenomic advances are being pursued, we need to take a closer look at how pharmocogenomics promises to contribute to human and social welfare.

SNPs associated with the genes that play a role in drug metabolism or drug action can be utilized to identify patients that may be at risk of experiencing an adverse drug reaction (ADR) when taking a specific medication. Adverse drug reactions can range from being relatively mild (e.g., headache), which sometimes causes patients to discontinue taking a needed medication (i.e., decreased compliance) to very serious and life threatening. Thus, one of the value propositions of this form of personalized medicine focuses on the potential it has to reduce the risk of adverse drug reactions in the population, increase dosing compliance and efficacy in the population. The implication is that by reducing risk of adverse drug reactions and increasing dosing compliance and efficacy, we will ultimately reduce healthcare costs. In other words, there is not only a quality of life motivation, there are economic and "healthcare outcome" benefits to utilizing a patient's DNA sample to support personalized prescription drug dosing.

The cost of ADRs is significant. According to a 1997 study (Classen, Pestotnik, & Evans), more than 770,000 patients die or sustain serious injury every year in hospitals from adverse drug reactions. It is likely higher now. Another study (Bates, Spell, and Cullen, 1997) found these ADRs were estimated to cost individual hospitals approximately $5.6 million per year and in terms of total health care dollars, ADRs were estimated to cost the U.S. health care system between $1.5 and $5.4 billion per year. While exact rates of ADRs are difficult to calculate, in 2000 it was estimated that adverse drug reactions accounted for 2% to 7% of hospital admissions (Thomas, Studdert, Burstin, Orev, Zeena, & Williams, 2000).

It is believed that patients who have experienced an ADR have longer and more costly hospital stays than those who do not. In a study funded by the Agency for Health Care Quality (AHRQ), it was found that patients with a serious adverse drug reaction had an average additional length of stay of 20 days ($38,007 in costs) and patients suffering from less severe ADRs had an average stay of 13 days ($22,474 in costs). These compare to patients with no ADR who had an average length of stay of 5 days and $6,320 in costs (Evans, Pestotnik, & Classen, 1992). Classen et al. (1997) found that patients who experienced an ADR were hospitalized on average one to five days longer than patients who did not, with an additional cost to the hospital of approximately $9,000. Bates et al. (1997) found on average an increase length of stay of 4.6 days and up to $4,680 in additional costs for patients with adverse drug reactions. Despite differences, the findings across all studies support the claim that adverse drug reactions are an area where medical costs could be reduced. This opportunity first received major attention with the release of the report by the Institute of Medicine entitled To Err is Human: Building a Safer Health System. This report, provided an in depth analysis into medication errors with the goal of building a better and safer health care system that limits mistakes and improves patient outcomes (Kohn, Corrigan, & Donald, 2000), and has been one catalyst for the advancements in pharmcogenomics.

An exemplary case study concerning the potential impact of pharmacogenomics on ADRs concerns the anticoagulant Warfarin. Warfarin is an anticoagulant (a blood thinner). This drug was initially put on the market as a pesticide – to kill mice and rats for example – and is still used for this purpose. In the early 1950s it was approved for use in humans given its effectiveness in preventing abnormal formation and migration of blood clots. Today, as many as 2 million patients a year may begin therapy with warfarin (Wu & Fuhlbrigge, 2009).

Treatment with warfarin is not without shortcomings. Many patients take weeks if not months to become stabilized on warfarin therapy. Research has found that warfarin was the third most common drug to cause a hospital admission due to an adverse drug reaction (Pirmohamed, James & Meaken, 2006). Another study found that bleeding complications associated with warfarin therapy were responsible for 29,000 emergency department visits per year (Wysowski, Nourjah, & Swartz, 2007). While the drug product itself is extremely inexpensive to purchase, the monitoring and follow-up can be very expensive.

For patients with two well known SNPs[1], there is a significantly elevated risk of inadvertent overdosing when the "normal" dose is administered. These patients have a decreased drug metabolism rate, resulting in drug levels in the body that exceed safe limits and a serious adverse drug reaction. In August of 2007, the U.S. Food and Drug Administration (FDA) updated their recommendations when prescribing warfarin to include consideration of genetic testing. The FDA product labeling therefore recommends SNP[2] screening for patients upon initiation of warfarin therapy.

A report by the AEI-Brookings Joint Center for Regulatory Studies suggested that testing for polymorphisms[3] would decrease health care spending in the U.S. by $1.1 billion annually

(Wu & Fuhlbrigge, 2009). Another report by economists at the FDA estimated that such testing before the initiation of warfarin therapy could save the U.S. healthcare system $1.1 billion annually, avoid 85,000 serious bleeding episodes, and prevent 17,000 strokes (Hughes & Pirmohamed, 2007). The report further suggested that 5% of all thromboembolic strokes (that is, a stroke caused by a blood clot in the brain) could be prevented by this type of genetic testing.

These data clearly suggest that pharmacogenomic testing before the initiation of warfarin therapy has the potential to provide substantial cost savings and improved patient outcomes.

Furthermore, there are many other medicinal drugs that will provide better and safer treatments if clinical genotyping is utilized to identify patients at higher risk of adverse drug reactions. The long term impact of personalized medicine on the therapeutics market will involve a greater diversity of medicinal drugs available to the healthcare community (reflecting the genetic diversity of the population), but will require genotype screening to insure a specific drug/dose is both safe and effective for an individual.

There are numerous potential advantages of obtaining genomic information through pharmacogenomic testing. However, there are also several questions that merit further deliberation, such as these. Will the public embrace pharmacogenomic testing or will there be backlash given concerns of privacy and discrimination? Will we find that SNPs can be used for disease and disorder prediction? If so, what might be the implications, advantages, and concerns? When? How? By whom? What is the potential for misuse of such information? Are existing laws and social norms sufficient to mitigate misuse? Are existing information assurance and security models robust enough to apply to genomic information? Clearly, this leaves a number of unknowns.

When challenged with new uncertainties, the question as to how move forward can be paramount. Frequently, moving forward requires careful consideration of past – a critical and analytical inventorying if you will. It is to this that we turn next.

ETHICS AND GENETIC INFORMATION

In the recent past, development of new biotechnologies utilizing genetic information, such as cloning of individual animals, the development of genetically modified organisms, or bio-enhancement utilizing nanotechnologies, has led to serious ethical concerns. These developments and subsequent concerns have given rise to the notion of "genetic exceptionalism" (Murray, 1997). As the phrase suggests, the key idea embodied in genetic exceptionalism is that genetic information is qualitatively different from other forms of health information. The predictive, personal, and familial nature of genetic information suggests that it has a unique status and should therefore be treated differently.

Advancements in biotechnology have led to the development and implementation of new genetic tests. The ethical problems have not been with use of genetic testing *per se* but, as mentioned earlier in this chapter, with the use and interpretation of the information obtained through genetic testing. Thus, as we discuss pharmacogenomic testing in the following section, keep in mind that we are referring to the information obtained through this particular type of testing.

Pharmacogenomics, a relatively new area in biotechnology, requires the development of new genetic testing. Given that past biotechnologies have been plagued with ethical concerns, contemporary pharmacogenomics likewise runs the risk of being so plagued. It would seem prudent, therefore, to take heed of the negative implications of the past and tread carefully when using the information derived from pharmacogenomic testing. Let us call this the "prudential argument" against pharmacogenomics.

What are the negative implications of such use? There are two common ways these implications may be morally evaluated. Either one may take a bottom-up approach, where individual cases lead to common ethical issues; or one may take a top-down approach, where ethical principles guide the evaluation of individual cases. The former is a type of inductive approach: in much the same way that we commonly expect the sun to rise tomorrow based on previous sunrises, so too do we expect similar moral outcomes from similar individual cases. The latter is a type of deductive approach: given the Law of Universal Gravitation for example, we are able to derive that if one drops a pen from her hand, then it will fall to the floor. Similarly, starting from ethical principles we can evaluate individual cases and decide whether they conform to those principles.

The incipiency of the field makes it difficult to utilize a bottom-up approach since there are not sufficiently relevant cases to evaluate. As such, our evaluation applies a top-down approach, utilizing a standard set of four ethical principles as defined by Beauchamp and Childress (2001). Evaluation of the prudential argument calls for us to determine whether the potential ethical issues arising with the development of pharmacogenomic testing and the use of information derived from this testing fulfill the moral requirements established by these four principles. Application of these four principles to the case of genetic testing for drug efficacy allows us to mark potential ethical hazards that can then be gone over with a finer-toothed ethical comb. We will first consider ethical issues with the development and implementation of genetic testing generally and then determine whether, and to what extent, pharmacogenomic faces these same issues.

Genomic Research and the Principle of Respect for Autonomy

According to Beauchamp and Childress (2001), the principle of respect for autonomy involves both negative and positive obligations (p. 64). They further explain that negative obligations require a "respectful *attitude*" (p. 63) that acknowledges "a person's right to hold views, to make choices, and to take actions based on personal values and beliefs" (*p. 63*). And, positive obligations require "respectful *action*" understood as an obligation "to build up or maintain others' capacities for autonomous choice while helping to allay fears in other conditions that destroys or disrupts their autonomous actions" (Beauchamp & Childress, p. 63). Given this principle, we can approach three major ethical issues regarding autonomy that appear in the literature: informed consent, privacy and confidentiality, and ownership of genetic information.

First, the debate around informed consent involves what information a researcher is obligated to provide to his or her human subjects concerning the term and conditions of the research project.[4] Traditional models of informed consent are in place to protect the autonomous choice of the human subject. The subject is allowed to weigh costs and benefits of his or her own voluntary participation in the research project based on sufficient disclosure of information concerning that project. In providing sufficient information to his human subject, the researcher fulfills both negative and positive obligations: he has taken a respectful attitude toward his subject's right to autonomous choice and has taken respectful actions to uphold and protect that autonomy. Genomic research, however, calls into question this model[5]. Why? Let us consider the following general example[6]. A genetic researcher wishes to verify a genetic link between risk for specific disease and a specific population of human subjects. To do so, he seeks informed consent from all the subjects of the group and completes the study. The results of this study prove his hypothesis: indeed, there is a correlation between the genetic variant in that population and the disease. With this result, the study population has increased to include not only all those participants who had given consent, but all members of the population who share that genetic variant. The researcher has failed his obligations to respect the autonomy of the community at large since some members of that population could suffer a type of group-based harm. Genomic research might also face this problem of a lack of community consent, understood as the consent of every individual affected by a study and not only each participant in the study.

Second, pharmacogenomic research, like all genetic research, faces problems of privacy and confidentiality: release of genetic information from pharmacogenomic research can lead to increases in psychological, economic, and social risk. There are abundant examples in the literature regarding psychological risk tied to the release of genetic information. If within a family unit the parents discover that they carry a genetic mutation linked to a specific disease (i.e., BRCA1, BRCA2 to breast cancer), the psychological well-being of the entire family including the children is negatively affected (Franklin, 2008). Moreover, the release of genetic information can lead to increased economic risk. For instance, a study published in 1996 based on 332 families affected by genetic diseases found that 22% of the subjects had been refused by a medical insurance corporation and 13% had been fired for infection risk (Lapham, Kozma & Weiss, 1996). Certainly, legislation passed by the United States Congress and signed into law in 2008, the Genetic Information Nondiscrimination Act (GINA, 2008), seeks to avoid these economic perils. Pharmacogenomic testing, however, may not be covered by GINA. GINA does not require that an insurance corporation, for example, cover a particular test or treatment. If pharmacogenomic testing proves that an individual has a difficult-to-treat genotype, they have no obligation to cover the necessary treatment. Hence economic risks based on this testing may be very real indeed. Moreover, we share Billing's idea that "legislation is not a panacea for genetic discrimination" (Billings, 2008, p. 806) in much the same way that legislation regarding previous forms of discrimination have ended neither racism nor sexism. Likewise, disclosure of information derived from pharmacogenomic tests could easily lead to increased social risk; i.e., the stigmatization of a population based on genetic difference.

Third, genetic researchers must be concerned with the ownership of genetic information. Should biotech companies be allowed to build and maintain large biobanks of genetic information? Who ultimately owns this information: the donor of the biological sample or the researcher analyzing that sample? This issue was brought to the public's attention with the case of John Moore in 1990 (Skloot, 2006). Moore, while being treated for a rare form of cancer, had his spleen removed. Researchers found what Eric Meslin (2008) has called an "incredibly cool cell line believed to be predictive of his genetically-mediated cancer", which they cloned and *patented*, without informing Moore. Interestingly, Moore lost the pending lawsuit concerning ownership of the patented cell line: the California Supreme Court ruled that an individual does not own the biological material of his or her own body removed and manipulated by researchers. However, in a following obiter dicta, Justice Mosk suggested that while the property rights decision was just, Moore may have legitimately argued that the researchers failed an obligation to protect his autonomy by not seeking his fully informed consent (Moore v. Regents of University of California 1990). Moore does not own biological or genetic products derived from his own biological or genetic material, but does have the right to be fully informed about the collection and use of that material. Pharmacogenomic testing will have to face these issues of ownership of genetic information in much the same way. Access to genomic information must be mediated against risk: financial interests should not override the researcher's moral and legal obligations to full disclosure both concerning the scope of the research project and the researcher's conflicts of interest.

On the topic of autonomy, the obvious concern for IAS professionals involves patients' confidentiality and privacy. Given our working definition of privacy that characterizes privacy as one's independent control over the public dissemination of one's personal information, one can see that independent control is based on the type of autonomy that we describe in this section. In the form of one's access to her or his own genetic information, availability is another consideration in this context for IAS professionals as is assurance; in this case, assurance concerns the trust that the patients have in the capacity of the underlying information system to maintain their ownership of their own genetic information. This is akin to the concern raised with electronic health records (EHRs) where the lack of trust in the security of the data may lead patients to conceal sensitive information (Layman, 2008).

Genomic Research and the Principles of Nonmaleficence and Beneficence

In much the same way that the principle of autonomy comprised both positive and negative obligations, so too, may we make the distinction between the positive principle of beneficence and the negative principle of nonmaleficence. However, just because a principle is negative does not likewise imply that the obligation it outputs should be fulfilled in a passive way. Nonmaleficence is the obligation "not to inflict evil or harm" (Beauchamp & Childress, 2001, p. 115). This is a negative principle that moves beyond a mere attitude of non-interference: it obligates us *not* to perform some action; i.e., it prohibits the actions of theft, of disablement, or of killing.

However, this is only one side of our obligations. As Beauchamp and Childress argue, "[m]orality requires not only that we treat persons autonomously and refrain from harming them, but also that we contribute to their welfare" (Beauchamp and Childress, 2001, p. 165). So, contributing to one's welfare falls under the principle of beneficence. This is a positive principle that requires us to prevent or remove evil or harm and promote good: we ought to proscribe benefits, protect interests, and promote welfare (Beauchamp and Childress, 2001, p. 114).

Genetic tests generally are tools utilized to assess the predisposition for some medical condition. As such, they per se cannot inflict harm. Recall the genetic test regarding BRCA1/BRCA2. It is not the information given by the test that causes psychological harm per se; rather, it is the limitations that that information imposes on your autonomous choice that causes harm. Apart from these psychological, economic, and social risks of harm outlined above, it would seem that whenever a genetic test is applied with no malicious intention it could not be done maleficently. However, this is only one side of the question. On the other side, we must ask whether genetic tests promote the welfare of the test recipient. Health is a good that promotes welfare and so whenever a genetic test is applied to increase health, it promotes welfare. Therefore, whenever genetic tests are applied to increase health, they are applied beneficently.

The concern related to assurance that we raise in the preceding section applies here in this section in a slightly different manner. Specifically, the lack of trust that the patients have in the capacity of the underlying information system to maintain their ownership of their own genetic information may lead patients to conceal sensitive information, and this concealment may have a negative impact, not only on their health, but on advances in biotechnology that contribute to collective welfare. Conversely, providing evidence of the trustworthiness of the system – which includes ensuring the integrity of the data – may positively impact patients' health by leading them to adopt and use the system, which in turn has implications for the collective.

Genomic Research and the Principle of Justice

There exist a wide variety of theories of justice – egalitarian, utilitarian, communitarian, libertarian, et cetera. As Beauchamp and Childress have argued, there is "no single theory of justice or system of distributing health care [that] is necessary or sufficient for constructive reflection on health policy" (2001, p. 272). However, all theories of justice share as a minimal requirement Aristotle's principle of formal justice: "treat like cases as like" (Aristotle, trans. 1984a, 1131a10-b15 & trans. 1984b, 1280 a8-15). Aristotle's statement implies that equals ought to be treated equally and unequal's ought to be treated unequally; however, it is a basic or formal principle in that it does not describe how this equality is to be determined. Each contemporary theory of justice that builds on Aristotle's minimal formal principle can play a role in our moral decision-making. It will suffice here to lay out several potential challenges of justice within the narrow scope of the formal principle – solutions to those principles are contingent on the more robust and particular theory of justice one accepts. In a biomedical context, issues of justice are commonly issues of fair and equitable distribution of resources.

Genomic testing faces several challenges in terms of justice. By delineating genetic differences in the population, genomic testing could support various forms of discrimination, each of which affects the equitable distribution of resources.[7]

First, the development of genomic testing brings with it risk of additional forms of discrimination. As we have argued, according to any theory of justice discrimination amongst equals is a moral wrong. Any third-party access to genetic information, including SNP references, has potential to lead to discrimination by a host of agents. Insurance companies, for instance, might increase rates given certain information linking a person's genetic variants to increased risk of disease or disorder. While federal legislation including the GINA of 2008 has taken steps to prevent just this sort of discrimination, it is still unclear whether further legislation is required to seal loopholes created by this new pharmacogenomic mapping technique. Additionally, discrimination by the potential connection of SNPs to race, ethnicity, or socio-economic class may lead to new forms of stereotypes based on new minority populations. If pharmacogenomic research provides evidence for correlation between a particular SNP and a particular drug given a particular set of research subjects, the researcher must consider the risk of discriminating against other individuals outside of the research group who might also benefit from the drug (Decamp & Buchanan, 2008, p. 544).

Second, if the future development of pharmaceuticals is driven by increases in the efficiency of some medical treatment for a given genetic population, it is easily foreseeable that whenever the population is sufficiently small in size or poor in resources, the economic incentive might not be available to drive drug research and production. Thus, some genotypes will be "orphaned." It seems that pharmacogenomic testing may lead to discrimination against any orphaned genotypes identified by this technology (Decamp & Buchanan, 2008, p. 541).

Clearly, genomic testing faces ethical dilemmas in terms of justice. Ultimately however, these questions of justice must be weighed pragmatically against increases of risk and cost, and threats against autonomy.

On the topic of justice, availability is the most important consideration in this context for IAS professionals. Layman (2008) raises the concern that EHRs fail to provide increased access for disadvantaged persons, and without access to their own genetic information, the same fate may befall disadvantaged persons in the area of pharmacogenomics. On the other hand, the possibility of discriminatory activities must lead the IAS professional to careful consideration of the ethical dimensions of providing such access.

The Ethical Implications of Pharmacogenomics

The ethical concerns presented in the sections above lend credence to the prudential argument: given both the continuity between pharmacogenomic testing and other types of biotechnologies and the ethical issues plaguing these other biotechnologies, we should be cautious in the development of pharmacogenomic testing. However, the soundness of this argument is based on a hidden premise; namely, that there is no significant difference between pharmacogenomic testing and other genetic testing. The truth of this premise can be called into question. A central difference is that pharmacogenomic testing, unlike other genetic testing, is not necessarily or even primarily associated with disease information/prediction but instead merely seeks out efficiency of treatment. In fact, Roses and others have noted that the "[e]thical, legal, and social implications for 'genetic tests' of single-gene mutational diseases should not automatically be assumed for other non-disease-specific applications simply because they are labeled imprecisely as 'genetic tests'" (Roses, 2000, p. 858). Pharmacogenomic tests are unique to genetic tests specifically because they do not predict disease. So perhaps the prudential argument fails: pharmacogenomic testing is sufficiently different that we can proceed unfettered.

Or can we? We should not automatically assume there are *no* possibilities to link information to disease. Some researchers maintain that some possibility remains that a genetic marker made available by pharmacogenomic testing could be linked to some disease predisposition, either environmentally or genetically mediated (Lindpaintner, 2001, p. 26; see also Lindpaintner, 2003; Schulte, Lomax, Ward, & Colligan, 1999).

We are left with the grounding that ethically-speaking, pharmacogenomic testing still seems to stand apart from other types of genetic testing, assuming we do not use genetic markers to predict disease. How then are we to define an ethical approach to pharmacogenomic research in the face of uncertainty? Let us consider how the unique status of pharmacogenomic testing affects the ethical issues we described above.

First, it has been suggested that pharmacogenomic testing leads to three major issues regarding the principle of respect for autonomy. Do these issues still hold if we consider pharmacogenomic testing a unique type of genomic testing? The first of these issues regarding autonomy, the problem of informed consent, still holds; however, it holds not only for pharmacogenomic research and genetic research but also for *all* research findings associated with a group. So the uniqueness of pharmacogenomic testing as a genomic test does not absolve the risk of infringing on the autonomy of all the members of the population who share some genetic variant. The second of these issues, related to privacy and confidentiality, greatly reduces the risk of psychological, economic, and social harms prevalent in other genetic testing precisely because pharmacogenomic testing does not predict disease. The psychological harm mentioned above is related to disease prediction. Merely determining efficient drug dosage does not bring with it these harms to the same degree. However, some economic and social risks could still persist. Consider that *ceteris paribus*, for an equally efficient treatment of some disease, a pharmacogenomic test reveals that an individual must take twice the dosage of some other individual. Here exists an economic risk: if the former individual does not have the economic means to afford the treatment, his choice of treatment will be limited; thus, his own autonomy will be limited as well. The third of these issues is related to biobanking. It seems hard to believe that the uniqueness of pharmacogenomic testing will remove all concern regarding biobanking. Even given this new premise, there will still be issues regarding storage, manipulation, and ownership of genomic information. For the ethical practice of pharmacogenomic testing, significant consideration of past informed consent failures is paramount. Despite pharmacogenomic testing not linking genetic information to disease and thereby avoiding the more significant harms of other genetic testing, it is nonetheless crucial to promote and respect the autonomy of the individual research subject.

Second, pharmacogenomic testing seems to fulfill the moral requirements of both of the principles of nonmaleficence and beneficence. This medical technique was developed specifically to prevent harm. By determining a link between specific single nucleopeptide polymorphisms and the level of absorption of various compounds introduced in the body, this research aims to prevent and reduce drug-adverse reactions: a serious problem with contemporary pharmacology (Kohn *et al.*, 2000; Neil & Craigie, 2004). Moreover, pharmacogenomic testing represents a potential major step forward in personalized medicine: not merely by ending one-size-fits-all medicine but by finding the maximally efficient and effective treatment dosage for a particular disease of a particular individual. In so doing, this medical technique supports the removal of harms by fitting the proper treatment to the individual: not only can the proper dosage of a particular drug avoid killing or harming the patient, but also can provide a sufficient amount of drug as an effective treatment. Overall, pharmacogenomic testing has potential to promote good by supporting the health of the individual. Since the health of individual leads to the general health of that individual's community, pharmacogenomic testing can support the overall health of the community.

Third, pharmacogenomic testing faces ethical challenges regarding discrimination and problems of orphan genotypes. These problems persist regardless of the unique status of pharmacogenomic testing among other genetic tests.[8]

Having considered the ethical implications of pharmacogenomics, it is now helpful to evaluate the current state of medical practice and existing laws as they concern genetic information and its use, and in doing so, to understand better the interplay between the ethical and legal dimensions of the use of genetic and pharmacogenomic information in healthcare. We do so in the following section.

EXISTING LAWS

The Edwin Smith Papyrus, which dates to the sixteenth century BC (Wilkins, 1992), is the earliest known recording of patient information and histories. The significance for us today is the recognition that medical records have been a common practice in the medical profession for centuries. Given advances in technology, i.e., the advent of internet[9] technologies, the emergence of mobile devices, and standards efforts such as Health Level Seven (HL7), health records are no longer only housed in paper-based form in storage cabinets in physicians' offices. Electronic health records are a common practice in most medical operations.

Electronic health records are viewed as having the potential to increase access to health care, improve the quality of care, and possibly decrease costs (Layman, 2008) – all important social values. While these are desirable outcomes, Layman (2008) points out that EHRs have not increased access for disadvantaged persons, improved the accuracy of records, nor positively impacted productivity. Furthermore, Layman (2008) discusses a multitude of other ethical issues concerning EHRs. Specifically, there may be a negative impact on a patient's autonomy when their health data are shared without their permission. Moreover, a "lack of confidence in the security of health data may induce patients to conceal sensitive information," and as a result, "their treatment may be compromised" (Layman, 2008). In response to concerns such as these, we have seen growth in legislation. One primary piece of legislation pertinent to electronic health records is the Health Information Portability and Accountability Act (HIPAA, 1996) – The goals of the HIPAA focus on five primary areas: individual control of one's medical information, boundaries on the use of medical information, privacy accountability, balance between the use of medical information for the public good at the expense of an individual's privacy, and the security of medical information (Whitman & Mattord, 2005). In addition to HIPAA, to date 32 states have enacted genetic privacy laws. These laws aim to protect genetic information beyond the measures taken in other laws such as HIPAA. That we need special laws to offer such protection for genetic information reflects a substantial shift in the public's awareness of their privacy needs as they relate to their genetic information. In essence, these laws suggest that genetic information is different than other information such as bank accounts and Social Security Numbers.

The state genetic privacy laws for the most part place restrictions on certain entities, such as insurers or employers, from carrying out given actions without the individual's consent. The actions that are restricted range as follows: performing or requiring a genetic test; obtaining or accessing genetic information; retaining genetic information; and disclosing genetic information. There is variation among the state laws. For example, 12 states require consent to perform or require a genetic test, 7 require consent to obtain or access genetic information, 8 require consent to retain genetic information, and 27 require consent to disclose genetic information. Five of the state laws specifically define genetic information as personal property and one includes DNA samples as personal property. Other elements in some of the genetic privacy laws are the provision for the individual to have personal access to his/her genetic information and a provision for penalties in the case of privacy violation. Clearly, there are divergences; 64% of the states have laws and these laws are notably varied. Detailed information on the criteria by state is available at the National Conference of State Legislatures website (www.ncsl.org). For our purposes, the important point is not how these laws differ among states, but that they do. These differences clearly demonstrate the differing views on socially accepted practice.

As discussed earlier, in addition to privacy issues, genetic information has implications for discrimination. To address this, there are a number of state laws that prohibit the use of genetic information when providing health insurance and separate state laws that pertain to the use of genetic information in employment decisions. Currently 48 states have laws that address genetics and health insurance anti-discrimination by placing restrictions on health insurers. In some states, the law pertains to individual insurance policies, in other states it pertains to group insurance policies, or both. These laws do not apply to employer-sponsored health insurance, which is under the purview of federal legislation. The types of restrictions found in these laws are: prohibit the use of genetic information to determine eligibility for insurance; prohibit the requirement of genetic testing in order to obtain insurance; prohibit the use of genetic information for risk classification and premium setting, and; prohibit the insurer from disclosing the genetic information without prior consent from the insured. Some states have only one restriction, where others include all four. Furthermore, some states have exceptions, such as allowing the use of genetic information for setting premiums when it benefits the individual. Summary detail can be found on the National Conference of State Legislatures website (www.ncsl.org).

To address employment discrimination, thirty-four states have laws that prohibit the use of genetic information in employment decisions. These laws make it illegal to discriminate when making employment decisions (hiring, firing, and terms or conditions of employment) based on the results of genetic information. The types of restrictions are prohibition from: requesting genetic information; requiring genetic information; performing a genetic test, and; obtaining genetic information from a genetic test. Not surprisingly, the prohibitions vary among states and detail can be found at www.ncsl.org.

At the federal level, several forces converged to lead to the passage of the aforementioned GINA in 2008. This act prohibits the use of genetic information in both insurance and employment decisions. GINA specifically addresses genetic information that is not sufficiently covered by HIPAA and seeks to address gaps and inconsistencies in the state laws. GINA provides a baseline level of protection to all U.S. citizens regardless of which state they reside in. By addressing the threat of discriminatory practices, GINA aims to assure patients that their genetic information is safe. This assurance is needed to increase the number of citizens who participate in genetic testing, as it is through such testing that the research community gathers the needed biomedical data to better understand and ultimately advance healthcare.

Critics of GINA note several outstanding concerns. First, GINA fails to rectify inconsistencies between state laws, leaving multistate entities responsible for complying with different regulations in each state. Second, GINA is overly broad leaving considerable room for interpretation. Third, GINA fails to prohibit insurers from using genetic information when establishing life, long-term care, and disability insurance; therefore, it does not go far enough in preventing discriminatory practices. And last, critics contend that GINA fails to allow us to use genetic information to its fullest potential by not requiring insurers to cover preventive care when a genetic test indicates that such care could prevent or minimize a health risk.

While it is common for societies to utilize public policy to address macroethical issues, it is prudent to keep in mind that laws, per se, cannot address all of the ethical issues society encounters. Science and technology forge ahead in a state of uncertainty. While today we do not think that SNPs can be used for disease prediction, we do not know that for certain. It also behooves us to be mindful that policy works at a much slower rate than technological innovation. Such implications are important for professionals where, in the face of uncertainty, complying with the law is a minimum expectation and acting in the best interests of society an ongoing aspiration. So, where does this leave us? What are the implications for information assurance and security?

IMPLICATIONS FOR INFORMATION ASSURANCE AND SECURITY

Probably the most profound implication for information assurance and security is seen by again focusing on the nature of genetic information, present and future. In reflecting on relevant laws, such as HIPAA and the varying genetic information laws, we can see that formal definitions of information have been enacted by legislative bodies. However, our working definitions of information are much more elusive, which suggests that the true nature of information is as a "moving target". Information is, and will continue to be, evolving. As evidence we offer this chapter as an assertion; biotechnological advancements are requiring students and practitioners in information assurance and security to expand their concepts and definitions of information to encompass the data derived from the ever-growing list of genetic tests.

And what of this type of information? What properties does it possess that perhaps characterize it in a manner that determines how it is to be assured and secured? According to researchers, genetic/genomic test information has unique characteristics that must be considered when determining appropriate protection (McGuire, Fisher, Cusenza, Hudson, Rothstein, McGraw, Matteson, Glaser, & Henley, 2008). These characteristics are as follows. Genetic information is especially unique – excepting identical twins, each individual has a unique genetic code. Genetic information is immutable – an individual's inherited information does not and, for the most part, cannot change. Genetic information has predictive capability and familial network effects – such information can be used to make predictions about oneself and one's family spanning generations. McGuire et al., (2008) also advise that given the relative novelty of genetic testing and genetic information, treating this field holistically is advisable. As such, they note several relevant, contextual factors. First, we have a history of misuse of genetic information to promote eugenics initiatives and obtain information about individuals for purposes of discrimination. Second, public opinions about the role and use of genetic information vary widely. Third, the technology is changing rapidly which exacerbates fear of further misuse and make public awareness even more challenging. And fourth, genetic information is getting increasingly easier to procure. Together, the characteristics of the information coupled with the context, highlights the need for models of confidentiality, integrity, availability, and evidence of trustworthiness that consider these relevant characteristics in a holistic manner that includes the ethical areas that we discuss earlier: autonomy, nonmaleficence/beneficence, and justice.

On the topic of autonomy, the obvious concern for IAS professionals involves patients' confidentiality and privacy. Since our working definition of privacy characterizes it as one's independent control over the public dissemination of one's personal information, it becomes clear that independent control is based on the type of autonomy that we describe in this section. In the form of one's access to her or his own genetic information, availability is another consideration in this context for IAS professionals as is assurance. In this case, assurance concerns the trust that the patients have in the capacity of the underlying information system to maintain their ownership of their own genetic information. This is akin to the concern raised with EHRs where the lack of trust in the security of the data may lead patients to conceal sensitive information.

The concern related to assurance that we raise in the preceding paragraph applies here in a slightly different manner. Specifically, the lack of trust that the patients have in the capacity of the underlying information system to maintain their ownership of their own genetic information may lead patients to conceal sensitive information, and this concealment may have a negative impact on their health. Conversely, providing evidence of the trustworthiness of the system – which includes ensuring the integrity of the data – may positively impact patients' health by leading them to adopt and use the system.

On the topic of justice, availability is the most important consideration in this context for IAS professionals. Layman (2008) raises the concern that EHRs fail to provide increased access for disadvantaged persons, and without access to their own genetic information, the same fate may befall disadvantaged persons in the area of pharmacogenomics. On the other hand, the possibility of discriminatory activities must lead the IAS professional to careful consideration of the ethical dimensions of providing such access.

CONCLUSION

We might reasonably conclude that there are significant differences between pharmacogenomic tests and other types of genetic testing. While other genomic tests are developed to predict disease, bringing with them a host of difficult moral quandaries, pharmacogenomic tests are developed to maximize drug efficacy. In so doing, pharmacogenomic testing attains a unique status among types of genomic tests and minimizes potential ethical risks involving the privacy of genetic information, the autonomy of the individual, and the just distribution of health resources related to these tests.

Those remaining risks, outlined above, must be weighed against the potential and actual benefits of pharmacogenomic research. Pharmacogenomics as an essential part of personalized medicine is an increasingly attractive target for the future of medical practice. Steps forward demand a pragmatic prudency that will allow researchers and research subjects to evaluate risk and weigh benefits throughout development and implementation.

The future of pharmacogenomic research success depends on a proactive approach to the careful analysis of potential ethical issues. Despite this minimization of the ethical risks inherent in other types of genomic testing, there remains potential for increased risk associated, not with the development of pharmacogenomic testing, but with its implementation. Continuing to think through potential issues with the implementation of this type of tests will promote not only the efficacy of pharmacogenomic research but also the safety of its development.

In fact, the implementation of pharmacogenomic testing will require the services of IAS practitioners, as the genetic and drug data that intersect in pharmacogenomics require an information system that ensures privacy and security (Kane et al., 2008). Thus, these practitioners will have no recourse but to encounter the ethical dilemmas addressed in this chapter. In keeping with the notion that acknowledgment of the problem is a critical early step in any problem solving exercise, we have endeavored to raise the reader's awareness so that she, as an expert in the IAS domain, will be equipped to ask the correct questions and to raise the appropriate concerns.

Fundamental to this awareness is, first, an acknowledgment of the possibility of genetic exceptionalism and, second, recognition of the irrevocable nature of losing one' genetic information. Furthermore, the IAS expert must have an understanding that the acknowledged possibility of genetic exceptionalism dictates a heightened need for ethical behavior. Questions surrounding ownership, nonmaleficence/beneficence, access, discrimination, and biobanking remain; and, these questions may grow more onerous as the science behind pharmacogenomics evolves. So too will the science behind disease prediction evolve, bringing its own, more troubling ethical issues and threatening to create, collaterally, a turbid perspective on the ethics of pharmacogenomics. As the protector and purveyor of assured genetic information, IAS practitioners must be ready to inform the debate and to formulate ethical responses as they encounter the misuses and abuses of genetic information.

REFERENCES

Aithal, G. P., Day, C. P., Kesteven, P. J., & Daly, A. K. (1998). Association of polymorphisms in cytochrome P450 CYP2C9 with warfarin dose requirement and risk of bleeding complications. *Lancet*, *353*, 717–719. doi:10.1016/S0140-6736(98)04474-2

Almarsdottir, A. B., Bjornsdottir, I., & Traulsen, J. M. (2005). A lay prescription for tailor-made drugs—focus group reflections on pharmacogenomics. *Health Policy (Amsterdam)*, *71*(2), 233–241. doi:10.1016/j.healthpol.2004.08.010

Aristotle,. (1984a). Nicomachean ethics. In Barnes, J. (Ed.), *The complete works of aristotle* (*Vol. II*, pp. 1729–1868). Princeton, NJ: Princeton University Press.

Aristotle,. (1984b). Politics. In Barnes, J. (Ed.), *The complete works of Aristotle* (*Vol. II*, pp. 1986–2130). Princeton, NJ: Princeton University Press.

Bates, D. W., Spell, N., & Cullen, D. J. (1997). The costs of adverse drug events in hospitalized patients. *Journal of the American Medical Association*, *277*(4), 307–311. doi:10.1001/jama.277.4.307

Beauchamp, T. L., & Childress, J. F. (2001). *Principles of biomedical ethics*. Oxford: Oxford University Press.

Bevan, J. L., Lynch, J. A., Dubriwny, T. N., Harris, T. M., Achter, P. J., & Reeder, A. L. (2003). Informed lay preferences for delivery of racially varied pharmacogenomics. *Genetics in Medicine*, *5*(5), 393–399. doi:10.1097/01.GIM.0000087989.12317.3F

Billings, P. R. (2008). Beyond GINA. *Nature*, *14*, 8.

Bishop, M. (2002). *Computer security: Art and science*. Boston, MA: Addison-Wesley.

Classen, D. C., Pestotnik, S. L., & Evans, R. S. (1997). Adverse drug events in hospitalized patients. *Journal of the American Medical Association*, *277*(4), 301–306. doi:10.1001/jama.277.4.301

Decamp, M., & Buchanan, A. (2007). Pharmacogenomics: Ethical and regulatory issues. In Steinbock, B. (Ed.), *The Oxford Handbook of Bioethics* (pp. 536–568). Oxford: Oxford University Press.

Evans, R. S., Pestotnik, S. L., & Classen, D. C. (1992). Prevention of adverse drug events through computerized surveillance. *The Annual Symposium on Computer Applications in Medical Care, 16*, 437-441.

Franklin, D. (2008). Family struggles with ambiguity of genetic testing. *All Things Considered, 12/30/2008*. Retrieved July 1, 2009 from http://www.npr.org/templates/story/story.php?storyId=98818197.

Genetic Information Nondiscrimination Act (GINA). (2008), Retrieved June 28, 2009 from http://www.govtrack.us/congress/ billtext.xpd?bill=h110-493.

Green, M. J., & Botkin, J. R. (2003). "Genetic exceptionalism" in medicine: Clarifying the differences between genetic and nongenetic tests. *Annals of Internal Medicine*, *138*, 7.

Health Insurance Portability and Accountability Act of 1996 (HIPAA). (1996). Retrieved July 10, 2009 from http://www.cms.hhs.gov/HIPAAGenInfo/Downloads/HIPAALaw.pdf

Health Level Seven (HL7). (2009). Retrieved from http://www.hl7.org/

Hippocrates. (4th Century B.C.). The oath by Hippocrates. Retrieved from http://classics.mit.edu/Hippocrates/hippooath.html

Hollon, T. (2000). NIH researchers receive cut-price BRCA test. *Nature Medicine*, *6*, 6. doi:10.1038/71545

Hughes, D. A., & Pirmohamed, M. (2007). Warfarin pharmacogenetics: Economic considerations. *Pharmacoeconmics*, *25*(11), 899–902. doi:10.2165/00019053-200725110-00001

Kane, M. D., Springer, J. A., & Sprague, J. E. (2008). Drug safety assurance through clinical genotyping: Near-term considerations for a system-wide implementation of personalized medicine. *Personalized Medicine*, *5*(4), 387–397. doi:10.2217/17410541.5.4.387

Katz, J. (2002). *The silent world of doctor and patient*. Baltimore, MD: The John Hopkins University Press.

Kohn, L. T., Corrigan, J., & Donald, M. S. (Eds.). (2000). *To err is human: Building a safer health system*. Washington, D.C.: National Academy Press.

Lapham, E. V., Kozma, C., & Weiss, J. O. (1996). Genetic discrimination: perspectives of consumers. *Science*, *274*, 5287. doi:10.1126/science.274.5287.621

Layman, E. J. (2008). Ethical issues and the electronic health record. *The Health Care Manager, 27*(2), 165–176.

Lee, C. R. (2005). Warfarin initiation and the potential role of genomic-guided dosing. *Clinical Medicine & Research, 3*(4), 205–206. doi:10.3121/cmr.3.4.205

Lindpaintner, K. (2001). Pharmacogenetics and the future of medical practice: conceptual considerations. *Pharmacogenetics Journal, 1*, 1.

Lindpaintner, K. (2003). Pharmacogenetics and the future of medical practice. *Journal of Molecular Medicine, 81*, 3.

McGuire, A., Fisher, R., Cusenza, P., Hudson, K., Rothstein, M., & McGraw, D. (2008). Confidentiality, privacy, and security of genetic and genomic test information in electronic health records: Points to consider. *Genetics in Medicine, 10*(7), 495–499. doi:10.1097/GIM.0b013e31817a8aaa

Meslin, E. (2008). *Ethical issues in constructing and using biobanks*. Bioethics seminar series, Purdue University. Retrieved April 1, 2008 from http://www.purdue.edu/bioethics/files/video/meslin_ bioethics.mov

Moore v. Regents of University of California. 51 Cal.3d 120 (Supreme Court of California 1990).

Murray, T. H. (1997). Genetic exceptionalism and "future diaries": Is genetic information different from other medical information. In Rothstein, M. A. (Ed.), *Genetic Secrets: Protecting Privacy and Confidentiality in the Genetic Era*. New Haven, CT: Yale University Press.

National Conference of State Legislatures. Retrieved September 28, 2009 from http://www.ncsl.org/Default.aspx?TabId=13489

Neil, D., & Craigie, J. (2004). The ethics of pharmacogenomics. *Monash Bioethics Review, 23*, 2.

Pirmohamed, M., James, S., & Meakin, S. (2006). Adverse drug reactions as a cause of admission to hospital: A systematic review and metaregression. *Chest, 129*, 1155–1166.

Roses, A. D. (2000). Pharmacogenetics and the practice of medicine. *Nature, 405*, 6788. doi:10.1038/35015728

Schoeman, F. (Ed.). (1984). *Philosophical dimensions of privacy: An anthology*. Cambridge, MA: Cambridge University Press. doi:10.1017/CBO9780511625138

Schulte, P. A., Lomax, G. P., Ward, E. M., & Colligan, M. J. (1999). Ethical issues in the use of genetic markers in occupational epidemiologic research. *Journal of Occupational and Environmental Medicine, 41*, 8. doi:10.1097/00043764-199908000-00005

Skloot, R. (2006, April 16). Taking the least of you. *The New York Times Magazine.* Retrieved from http://www.nytimes.com/2006/04/16/magazine/16tissue.html

Thomas, E. J., Studdert, D. M., Burstin, H. R., Orav, E. J., Zeena, T., & Williams, E. J. (2000). Incidence and types of adverse events and negligent care in Utah and Colorado. *Medical Care, 38*(3), 261–271. doi:10.1097/00005650-200003000-00003

Whitman, M. E., & Mattord, H. J. (2005). *Principles of information security*. Boston, MA: Thomson Course Technology.

Wilkins, R. H. (1992). *Neurosurgical Classics*. New York: Thieme Medical Publishers.

Woodcock, J., & Lesko, L. J. (2009). Pharmacogenetics – Tailoring treatment for the outliers. *The New England Journal of Medicine, 360*(8), 811–813. doi:10.1056/NEJMe0810630

Wu, A. C., & Fuhlbrigge, A. L. (2009). Economic evaluation of pharmacogenetic tests. *Clinical Pharmacology and Therapeutics*, *84*(2), 272–274. doi:10.1038/clpt.2008.127

Wysowski, D. K., Nourjah, P., & Swartz, L. (2007). Bleeding complications with warfarin use: A prevalant adverse effect resulting in regulatory action. *Archives of Internal Medicine*, *167*(13), 1414–1419. doi:10.1001/archinte.167.13.1414

ENDNOTES

1 Warfarin is predominantly metabolized by the oxidative enzyme "CYP2C9" (Aithal et al., 1998) and pharmacologically inhibits vitamin K epoxide reductase complex 1 (VKORC), which prevent the blood clotting cascade from forming clots (Lee, 2005). There are two SNPs in CYP2C9 that have a reduced capability for metabolizing warfarin, with 11% and 7% frequency in the Caucasian population for SNPs CYP2C9*2 and CYP2C9*3, respectively. Patients who are homozygous for these variant alleles (i.e. patients have two variant copies of the 2C9 gene) experience a 65% decrease in drug clearance rate and therefore have elevated plasma levels of the drug.

2 In particular, screening for CYP2C9 and VKORC

3 In CYP2C9 and VKORC1

4 There are stricter and more moderate views of the requirements for informed consent. Compare, for instance, Jay Katz's strict view (Katz, 2002) with Childress and Beauchamp, 2001.

5 Group-based harms are not concerns unique to pharmacogenetic or even to genetic research more generally (Decamp & Buchanan, 2007, p. 547).

6 An example commonly given in the literature is the Ashkenazi Jewish population. See Decamp and Buchanan, 2007, p. 544.

7 As a general concern that is not immediately relevant to IAS professionals, genomic testing faces the issue of access; namely, how do we most justly distribute access to a particular test? The obvious obstacle to just access to genetic testing is the price of the test. For instance, there is a patent on BRCA1 and BRCA2 testing held by Myriad Genetic Laboratories. Before cutting a deal with NIH, Myriad was charging up to $2580 for patient-requested analysis (Hollon, 2000, p. 610). Individuals who cannot afford that test or whose insurance companies will not cover that expense have no access to the BRCA testing. One might think that the mean price of these tests will decrease with the continued research and development of genetic testing; however, patenting and insurance obstacles will remain. Apart from the obvious economic questions of access, geographical questions of access must also be taken into consideration. Even if increases in availability of the test itself continue to develop, translation of that information will continue to require genetic counseling which may not be as equally distributed geographically.

8 As a general consideration beyond the realm of IAS, we ought to consider this question of access both in terms of future and present access. Consider the scenario of the future of pharmacogenomic testing: a pharmaceutical corporation develops a new drug to combat some disease. It is likely that, given technological innovation of pharmacogenomic testing, this corporation will develop and release such a test in tandem with the drug. Keeping the cost of this test within a range accessible to everyone who purchases the drug will help ensure that the drug itself remains on the market, avoiding the past problems of inefficiency and adverse reactions. Such

adverse reactions would cause the drug to be pulled from the market, imposing significant cost to the corporation. Thus in this future scenario, it seems that there is no question of access to the test per se, apart from questions of access (economic, geographical, etc) to the drug. However, the present status of pharmacogenomic testing is quite different from this utopian vision of the future. In the present, pharmacogenomic researchers continue to seek to develop tests for drugs currently available in trial or on the market. Assume that one such researcher has success. In this case, too, it seems that there would no problem of access to the test per se: it would be to the economic benefit of the corporation to make that test as widely available as possible, to prevent risk of adverse reaction or inefficient absorption. In both the present and future scenarios, there seem to be no problem of access to the test itself.

9 We use internet to denote both public (the Internet) and private interconnected networks.

APPENDIX: DISCUSSION QUESTIONS

1. What ethical risks might there be in the development of genomic testing?
2. Who should be allowed to see and use genetic genomic test results for what purpose and under what conditions?
3. What if our cultural ethos did not uphold privacy and instead all information was public?
4. Who are the stakeholders of genomic information?
5. Is there another way to analyze the "results" of the application of the four principles described in the chapter?
6. The conclusion suggests that the "Argument from prudence" is sound: we should move slowly. But even if we do, how are we to recognize moral pitfalls before jumping into them?
7. What special role do IAS professionals have in terms of the ethical treatment of genetic information?
8. Why are these four principles important?
9. What are the similarities and differences between the four principles presented in this chapter and the classical ethical theories presented in chapter two and what might that mean for considering ethical risks of pharmacogenomic testing for drug efficacy?
10. What is the requirement of system designers with regard to genomic information systems?
11. To implement the policy surrounding genetic testing, which approach is better? Top-down or bottom-up? What is your justification?
12. Should we uphold the individual's right to privacy over the public good of the portability of medical data?
13. What is the ethical relationship between genetic testing for disease prediction and pharmacogenomic testing?
14. Is it preferable to store just a person's SNPs or the person's more detailed genetic information for the purpose of pharmacogenomic testing for drug efficacy?
15. Is there another way to analyze the "results" of the application of these four principles?
16. Consider and compare the following two cases:
    a. A mother is diagnosed with a genetic predisposition for Parkinson's disease. Her daughter is deciding whether to get the test. What are the ethical risks associated with her diagnosis?
    b. A mother is diagnosed as needing a higher dose of heart medication. Her daughter is at risk of a similar heart condition as her mother. What are the ethical risks associated with pharmacogenomic testing to calculate appropriate drug dosage for her?
17. What are the advantages and disadvantages of pharmaceutical corporations as stakeholders in pharmacogenomic testing? Consider both that pharmaceutical companies may not produce drugs for "orphan genotypes" but also may reproduce orphaned drugs! How might this absolve access issues?

Chapter 10
Privacy and Public Access in the Light of E-Government:
The Case of Sweden

Elin Palm
The Royal Institute of Technology, Sweden

Misse Wester
The Royal Institute of Technology, Sweden

ABSTRACT

This chapter addresses the competing interests of privacy versus public access to information. The chapter explores the collective and individual value of privacy and public access in a manner that considers information at the macrosocial and macroethical level. By using Sweden as a case study, we exemplify the classic and irresolvable tension between issues of information availability and confidentiality, integrity, and privacy. Given that privacy and public access interests will constantly need to be rebalanced, we present the views of government officials due to their unique role in implementing this balance. We conclude with an analysis of the reasonableness of this conduct.

INTRODUCTION

Modern society is, to a large extent, dependent on services and applications based on Information and Communication Technology (ICT). The focus of this chapter is online services that governments offer citizens, which is sometimes described in terms of a shift to a "paperless government". One of the hopes for e-Government is that it will, if correctly used, increase transparency and civic involvement. This is an important aspiration. As a result of the European Union's (EU) e-Government strategy of April 2006, several programmes have been launched to promote a more efficient and easily accessible digital government. The extent to which individual member states offer on-line services, however, vary (UN, 2008).

In Sweden, ranked third on the United Nations' 2008 e-Government Readiness Index, a long-standing governmental goal has been to create the "24 hours authority" – an electronic service available 24 hours a day, 7 days a week, providing Swedish citizens access to public services

DOI: 10.4018/978-1-61692-245-0.ch010

and contact with all government authorities and agencies at all times. Although the encompassing e-Government has not been launched as planned, a significant number of governmental services are currently made available on-line. Increasingly, Swedish citizens rely on e-services for tax issues, pensions, parents' allowance and health insurance.

Although e-Government is seen as desirable for improving access to services, transparency, and civic involvement, projects aimed at establishing e-Government are typically considered difficult and include a large amount of risk (Heeks, 2006; Heeks & Stanforth, 2007). Most e-services are based on ICT and share the general vulnerabilities of the Internet infrastructure. That is, ICT enables new forms of classical crimes like fraud, novel crimes like hacking and identity theft, and controversial practices like data mining (Cavoukian, 1998; Tavani, 1999). The expanding field of on-line governmental service implies that an increasing amount of personal information is collected and transferred via channels that may be difficult to secure. Information security concerns, such as confidentiality, integrity, availability, and reliability of data pose serious challenges. The emerging e-service society increases the need for well functioning information security – both system security and security of personal data (Brey, 2007). Data protection requires both robust technical systems to protect the data and awareness of proper and ethically defensible ways of handling the information to be collected and processed.

The true challenge, as we see it, is not in ensuring access to e-services or in guaranteeing security. Rather, the challenge is finding and maintaining a proper balance between the social costs and benefits when securing e-governmental services and safeguarding the privacy of citizens. It is widely recognized in the field of information assurance and security that the most significant challenges are in implementation where information assurance and security must integrate technical, organizational, and policy countermeasures. Successful integration of technical and nontechnical information assurance and security countermeasures hinges on the knowledge levels and attitudes of decision makers. In this chapter we explore the issue of balance from an ethical perspective by focusing on the attitudes towards e-Government, privacy, and data protection among representatives of six Swedish governmental agencies. Those interviewed are professionals dealing with the security and privacy implications of e-services. Drawing from their expreriences we discuss the ethical aspects of reasonable use, access to, and control over personal data as, well as the task of balancing these interests.

The chapter is organized as follows. The next section provides a background to the discussion on ethical aspects of e-Government. Section three discusses benefits and risks attached to e-services and e-Government. Section four provides a brief inventory of prevailing privacy protection policies and legislation. Section five offers a philosophical basis for privacy protection. Section six discusses potential conflicts between privacy and data protection on the one hand, and the principles of transparency and public access to official documents on the other hand. Section seven analyzes conflicts between public access and privacy in relation to the findings from the empirical study on attitudes in government agencies. Section eight indicates future research directions. Section nine summarizes and concludes the issues discussed in this chapter.

BACKGROUND

e-Government can be defined as ICT-based services for public administration on a national or international level. As noted above, the European Union is advocating the development of e-Government. The 2006 Action Plan on e-Government requires EU Member States to commit themselves to inclusive e-Government objectives to:

ensure that by 2010 all citizens, including socially disadvantaged groups, become major beneficiaries of e-Government, and European public administrations deliver public information and services that are more easily accessible and increasingly trusted by the public, through innovative use of ICT, increasing awareness of the benefits of e-Government and improved skills and support for all users. (Commission of the European Communities, 2006a, p, 5)

It is believed that e-Government will facilitate the goals of the Lisbon Treaty, such as reducing barriers for services and mobility across Europe, facilitating the information flow, policy implementation and enhancing civic involvement. ICT and e-services are meant to modernize public administration within the EU. (Commission of the European Communities, 2006b) Yet, the aspirations for the effective use of ICT in Government are even greater. Today's imperative is to utilize the power and pervasiveness of ICT to level the playing field for all (United Nations, 2005), which is known as e-inclusion. e-inclusion is a "Socially Inclusive Governance Framework" that serves to reduce inequality of opportunity; by reducing the access-divide, e-inclusion seeks to promote the economic and social empowerment of all citizens.

The outcomes of e-services and e-Government, however, are still largely unexplored. For example, the option or consequence of *not* using modern technology to communicate with authorities is not fully explored. Does a lack of e-services actually hinder civic involvement? How? For whom? The drive towards technical development is sometimes motivated by a perceived "public demand". However, this "demand" in many cases is not properly investigated; and a public discussion on the risks and benefits has not influenced the technical development. It is against this background that we will explore potential conflicts between ideas of transparency, public access, and privacy.

BENEFITS AND RISKS WITH E-SERVICES

In this section, benefits and risks with e-services and e-Government are introduced. Certainly, e-services can be beneficial both to service users and service providers. e-Government implies easy access to vital services irrespective of time and location. Using the Internet to apply for sick-leave reimbursement or to declare taxes is obviously efficient and convenient. In particular, it has been emphasized that individuals with impaired mobility may gain substantially from not having to visit a government agency in person, and from not having to employ a proxy to conduct these tasks on their behalf. Governmental agencies benefit in terms of increased efficiency by saving time on reduced paper work and, in an ideal situation, by allowing for direct access and transparency. However, just as e-services are beneficial to service providers and service users, both parties are subject to risks.

The most common form of attacks directed towards on-line services and e-Government are Distributed-Denial-of-Service attacks (DDoS) (Mitrokotsa & Douligeris, 2004). A DDoS-attack is characterized by an attempt to prevent legitimate users from utilizing a service - a hacker may prevent legitimate users from accessing certain web-sites or on-line services. This can be done by "flooding" a website or network in order to disrupt network-traffic. The target may be an individual user, but are more often complex systems. One example is the Estonia cyber attacks 2007, when vital functions like on-line banking and media were disrupted and government and police websites were flooded and subjected to defacement. For individuals, identity theft is a risk when releasing personal information as this can be used by someone else (usually for the purpose of fraud or financial gain).

Service providers are responsible for the protection of the information they possess (see section on E-services and Legislation on Europe). In order for these systems to function, e-service systems require a large amount of potentially privacy sensitive information. For example, in order to utilize e-services, users typically create on-line profiles by providing person specific data such as social security number, name and address, financial and marital status. Another example pertains to sick leave - in order to qualify for sick-leave reimbursement, citizens are required to provide information regarding the reasons for, and duration of, sick leave. Inadequate information security (technical and/or organizational) may enable unauthorized parties to access, change or erase these, or any, data. As a consequence, government agencies may be prevented from fulfilling their duties and from providing their service. If information in electronic files or registers are unduly changed or erased, a government agency's decision to grant reimbursement may err if based on incorrect or incomplete information. Furthermore, a failure to maintain information security may undermine public trust in government agencies and their services. It would seem that in pursuit of a socially inclusive governance framework, that public distrust would be particularly troubling.

Risks attached to e-Government can be further exemplified by the Swedish National Audit Office's report stemming from a 2007 assessment of 11 Swedish government agencies information security work (Riksrevisionen, 2007). In this report, it was concluded that these 11 agencies fail to live up to norms and laws regulating information security, and lack systematic security work. For example, several failures to stifle virus attacks resulting in disrupted services were reported. Due to these attacks, government officials lacked access to information needed to make decisions. As a consequence, some services could not be provided adequately, and others were not provided at all. Serious incidents were also reported during changes from one ICT-system to another. Vital e-services had to shut down for up to two weeks and employees encountered difficulties in performing their daily tasks in the new systems. Weak protection of government web-pages had resulted in unauthorized parties gaining access to privacy-sensitive information and the opportunity to change the information (Riksrevisionen, 2007). The reasons for the agencies' failure to protect themselves were: underestimation of the value of information; poor knowledge of information security requirements; insecurity regarding responsibilities and low awareness about risks and threats. Furthermore, internal education of the employees and risk assessments were insufficient (Riksrevisionen, 2007).

E-GOVERNMENT AND LEGISLATION IN EUROPE

As can be seen from the discussion above, e-services carry several benefits. At the same time, such services require that the individual releases personal data. In the absence of proper information security - both technical and organizational – these data can be accessed by unauthorized persons, and e-services may becompromised. The following section provides an overview of current data and privacy protection within the European Union. Prevailing privacy protection legislation is a result of lengthy discussions on privacy invasive aspects of ICT that started in the early 1960s and 70s with the advent of mainframe computers and PCs (Moor, 1985, Bynum, 2008). That is, ICT has driven and shaped present privacy protection regimes.

As of yet, within the European Union there is no law that explicitly addresses e-Government issues. Rather, those issues are regulated *via* several directives like the Database Directive 96/9/EC, the Data Protection Directive 95/46/EC, the Data Protection in Electric Communications 2002/58/EC and the Privacy Protection in Telecommunication 97/66/EC. In addition, internationally accepted Information Security Standards, like ISO/IEC 27001:2005, apply to e-Government practices. The CIA triad – emphasizing the need to protect the core values of Confidentiality, Integrity, and

Availability – is an internationally recognized Information Security (IS) model also widely used in the European Union.

In what follows we offer a brief overview of the development of legislation relating to protection of privacy together with a description of different directives that apply to e-Government within the European Union.

Privacy Protection Regimes

In Europe, the right to privacy has been protected since the 1950s. The basis of European privacy protection legislation consists primarily of Article 12 of the Universal Declaration of Human Rights and Article 8 of the European Convention for Protection of Human Rights and Fundamental Freedoms (1950). Article 8 states that "Everyone has the right to respect for his private and family life, his home and his correspondence". It is important to note that privacy is interpreted in a wide sense as extending beyond private life. The broad interpretation is clearly visible in the Niemitz vs Germany case from 1992 where respect for private life is interpreted as including respect for relations in the semi-public context of work (Niemitz *vs* Germany, 16/12/1992-A-251).

In response to the emergence of electronic data processing, in the 1970s, national data protection laws were established starting with the Swedish Data Protection Act (PUL) in 1973. A decade later, a treaty for the protection of human rights in relation to the automated processing of personal data was passed (1981) and the Organization for Economic Cooperation and Development (OECD) developed a set of Guidelines on the Protection of Privacy and Transborder Flows of Personal Data (1980). These are often referred to as the Fair Information Principles (FIPs) regulating ways in which data may be collected, stored, and transferred. The Fair Information Principles appear either explicitly or implicitly within all respective regulations. According to FIPs, any organisation or authority must be held accountable for all the personal information held in its possession. Organizations and authorities should identify the purposes for which data are collected and processed and limit the collection of personal information to the amount necessary for the given purpose. Further, they should not use or disclose personal information for purposes other than those identified, except with the consent of the individual (the finality principle). Information should be retained only as long as necessary and should be kept accurate, complete and up-to-date. Personal information should be protected with appropriate security safeguards. Moreover, organizations are obliged to be open about their policies and practices and to allow data subjects access to their personal information (Bennett, 1992).

On the European level, one of the most important regulations is the previously mentioned EU-Directive 95/46/EC on the protection of individuals with regard to the processing of personal data and on the free movement of such data. It emphasizes that "Member States shall protect the fundamental rights and freedoms of natural persons, and in particular, their right to privacy with respect to the processing of personal data"(EU Directive 95/46/EC, Art 1). Additionally in Article13, exemptions and restrictions were formulated allowing member states;

to adopt legislative measures to restrict the scope of the obligations and rights when such a restriction constitutes a necessary measure to safeguard national security: defence, public security, the prevention, investigation, detection and prosecution of criminal offences, or of breaches of ethics for regulated professions; an important economic or financial interest of a Member State or of the European Union, including monetary, budgetary and taxation matters, the protection of the data subject or of the rights and freedoms of others. (EU Directive 95/46/EC, Art 13)

These efforts have been rather successful, although, there are substantial differences in their enforcement among European countries.

It deserves mentioning that, although closely related, the concepts of *privacy* and *data protection* are not identical. While privacy enjoys the status of a fundamental right, primarily protected by Article 8 European Convention on Human Rights, the concept of the protection of personal data contains basic principles to protect the data subject. The right to privacy is more comprehensive than the concept of data protection. The objective of the latter concept however, is not only to enhance privacy, but to guarantee other fundamental rights, such as the right not to be discriminated against. The basic rules on data protection are laid down in the general data protection framework 2001/45/EC on the protection of individuals with regard to the processing of personal data and the free movement of such data (the "Data Protection-regulation") and Directive 2002/58/EC concerning the processing of personal data and the protection of privacy in the electronic communications sector (Directive on Privacy and Electronic Communications).

Privacy Impact Assessments (PIAs) are increasingly used to safeguard privacy, both in the public and private sector, as are Privacy Compliance Audits and technical solutions like Privacy Enhancing Technologies. Although these assessments come in many forms, the main aim of PIAs is to anticipate and address potential issues relating to privacy that might be subject to intrusive practises. PIAs ensure that novel technology, routines, databases etc., comply with fair information practices. "Ultimately, a privacy impact assessment is a risk assessment tool for decision-makers that can address not only the legal, but also the moral and ethical, issues posed by whatever is being proposed" (Flaherty, 1989).

Whereas, the OECD-guidelines are recommendations, non-enforceable by law and PIAs are optional self-regulatory instruments, the EU directives are legally binding to all Member States. The 2002 Directive on Privacy and Electronic communications sets an enforceable legal framework that guarantees the individual's right to privacy (Council Directive, 2002). It introduces measures to be respected by any organization (including governments and businesses) handling personal data, covering both data protection and system security.

A PHILOSOPHICAL PERSPECTIVE ON PRIVACY

Having described legal and policy aspects of privacy, we will now move on to discuss the meaning and content of the concept of privacy from a normative perspective. Whereas information and communication technology develops quickly, it typically takes time for the legal framework to adjust to novel practices like e-services. A discussion of the ethical implications of such services in the context of the meaning and value of privacy may provide a basis for what aspects *should* be protected.

The start of the modern philosophical debate on privacy is typically attributed to the American lawyers Samuel Warren and Lawrence Brandeis' paper "The Right to Privacy" (1890), in which they advocate protection from novel forms of intrusion (at the time, by means of taking photographs) framed as a "right to be let alone". Today the theoretical literature on privacy is vast, containing various conceptualizations and investigations of the meaning and value of privacy (cf. Schoeman, 1992). It ranges from the 1970s reactions to the proliferation of personal computers and the novel possibilities of generating, processing and transmitting personal information (cf. Westin, 1963; Rachels, 1975; Fried, 1975; Thompson, 1975; Scanlon, 1975) to the past decade's discussions on privacy in public (Nissenbaum, 1998; Regan, 1995) and the shift from privacy framed as an individual interest to a collective good (Regan, 1995). Several explanations as to why privacy is valuable and why it should be protected are given;

autonomy (Scanlon, 1998; Rössler, 2005), dignity (Bloustein, 1964), intimacy (Gerstein, 1978; Inness, 1992; Cohen, 2002) and democracy (Lever, 2005) are but a few.

Some describe privacy as a matter of control over personal information (Parent, 1983), while others defend privacy as necessary for the development of interpersonal relationships (Fried, 1970; Rachels, 1975) or to control others' access to us (Gavison, 1980; Allen, 1988). Although some privacy scholars tend to tie the significance of privacy to one moral value, others suggest that privacy is important for several reasons. DeCew argues that privacy is necessary for an individual's control over (1) personal information, (2) others' access to such information, and (3) decision-making regarding one's private life. These aspects are essential for the individual to express herself, and for her to develop and differentiate relationships (DeCew, 1997). Recently, Herman Tavani (2007) has launched an alternative to the non-intrusion, seclusion, limitation, and control theories of privacy. Rather than siding with one of these aspects they are all united into the RALC-theory on privacy (restricted access/limited control).

The Content and Value of Privacy

What is perceived as privacy sensitive and why?

Race or ethnic origin, political or religious affiliation, membership in trade unions, medical records, and sexual preferences are examples of information that traditionally have been protected as sensitive. These have been considered sensitive for the reason that these data can be harmful to the data subject's interests (Elgesem, 1999). Recent studies however, indicate that information related to income, taxation and savings are generally perceived as more privacy sensitive than for instance ethnicity or religious beliefs (cf. Dayarathna, 2005, pp. 69-70).

In contrast to comparative privacy valuation, is the idea that what is viewed as privacy sensitive is not fixed. In the article "Privacy as Contextual Integrity" (2004), philosopher Helen Nissenbaum argues that privacy is a contextually dependent notion. That is, it is impossible to definitively pinpoint what is privacy sensitive. Rather, this changes over time and varies with cultures, situations, and between persons. In this view, privacy and privacy preferences are not static. On the contrary, they are highly dynamic. The one thing that remains constant about privacy is that it is marked by continuous change. Addressing privacy in this light requires looking at the shape, nature, and conditions of change.

One parameter that seems to influence privacy sensitivity, however, is that of reasonable alternatives and voluntariness. Whether I, myself decide to omit personal information, or am forced (directly or indirectly) to provide it, affects the degree to which I perceive data collection to be privacy invasive. Another important aspect of perceived privacy invasiveness is the relationship between the data subject and the agent/agency requesting the information. It matters whether the relationship is characterized by intimacy i.e., a friendship relation, or by principles like the vow of silence in the context of health care. Following Nissenbaum, all relationships and situations are surrounded by informal or explicit norms central for the type and amount of information exchanged (Nissenbaum, 2004, p.119). That is, individuals compartmentalize information depending on the relation to (and relevance for) the receiver. In order to secure privacy, it is necessary that these norms are respected when information is transferred from one context to another. Intimate and private information may be given to a partner, but not to an employer, a colleague, or even to a close friend. Information that an individual states to her doctor or psychologist - governed by the health care professional's vow of silence – may become sensitive if transferred to her employer. Whereas a sober alcoholic may be comfortable to reveal her history of alcohol abuse in the company of Anonymous Alcoholics, the same information may be sensitive if transferred to her employer (or employees if she holds a managerial position). Thus, context is vital to the definition of privacy.

Following Nissenbaum's line of reasoning, it can be argued that information viewed as trivial in one context can be perceived as sensitive when transferred to a new context. Hence, rather than trying to provide an inclusive list of privacy sensitive aspects, we should be concerned with whether information that is perceived as neutral in one setting may be privacy sensitive when transferred to another, under what conditions, and how.

Although we will not succeed in discussing all relevant aspects of privacy in this chapter, it is important to address the question of why the concept of privacy is valuable and why it matters. European privacy protection legislation typically rests on the idea that:

The right to privacy consists essentially in the right to live one's own life with a minimum of interference. It concerns private, family and home life, physical and moral integrity, honour and reputation, avoidance of being placed in a false light, non-revelation of irrelevant and embarrassing facts, unauthorised publication of private photographs, protection against misuse of private communications, protection from disclosure of information given or received by the individual confidentially. (Parliamentary Assembly, Resolution 428, 1970)

The essence of privacy is often described in terms of a private sphere exempted from disclosure that allows individuals to remain in control of themselves, their persons, relations and communication. It can be seen as a fundamental right of a person to be in control over her life – to live according to her values and not to be unduly influenced. This includes the ability to control – or at least influence – how she is viewed and portrayed by others.

This view has been elaborated on by philosopher Beate Rössler (2005) who argues that what should be treated as private can be divided in three aspects:

1. local privacy,
2. decisional privacy,
3. informational privacy.

Local privacy concerns the interests an individual has with respect to the contents of her home or dwelling. An individual's right to decide over her body and medical treatment are examples of decisional privacy. This aspect may for instance include an individual's reproductive rights i.e. to decide when, how and with whom to reproduce, and also the right *not* to know of her genetic disposition with respect to a non-curable disease like Alzheimer's. For a more detailed discussion on a right not to know", we suggest Häyry and Takkala, 2001. Informational privacy can be characterized by an individual's interest in having control over information about her sexual preferences, medical record, love letters, how she votes, and her academic grades. These aspects are typically well-protected. Less protected, yet privacy sensitive, is information regarding the recorded history of one's marriages, divorce proceedings, and number of children with different spouses, for example (Anderson, 2007, pp. 84-86).

Rössler (2005) defines privacy as the spatial and intellectual sphere that enables individuals to decide, in matters that concern them, to control who has access to information and data about them, and to establish and develop different kinds of relationships (p. 44). The reason we should secure privacy is that we thereby protect a more fundamental value, namely personal autonomy. Rössler further defines autonomy to be the individual's capacity to identify and spell out her life plan (to the extent that this is possible) and to govern her *persona*. Individuals must be able to control information from direct sensory access. i.e., what can be seen and heard by individuals passing by. In other words, there is a difference between information released by participating in public life and the personal data stored in registers. Control over these aspects is crucial for individuals' ability to influence how others perceive them and in order to develop relations to others e.g. by choosing the degree of confidentiality or intimacy (Rachels, 1975). Moreover, individuals must be able to withdraw from long-term or constant observation in order to avoid being unduly influenced by others' opinions about us (Foucault, 1979; Nagel, 2002; Williams, 1994) and to be able to define ourselves. Without this possibility, we risk being subject to "The Panoptic Effect" – internalizing others' opinions about us (Foucault, 1979; Gandy, 1993).

From a short-term perspective, a loss of privacy might lead an individual to adopt certain ways of behaving just because she thinks this is the way she is supposed to act so that others will approve. This is critical because democratic societies are built on the idea of self-aware and autonomous citizens. In the long run, "mainstreaming" citizens' behavior due to a lack of privacy, may turn out to prevent critical and dissenting behavior that is considered to be an important impulse for economic and societal development. This is in agreement with Priscilla Regan's argument for a "communal anchoring" of privacy based on the idea that people have a shared interested in privacy, and privacy is socially valuable (Regan, 1995, p. 213). That is, privacy is not only an individual interest, but also a collective interest. A failure to safeguard privacy implies the risk that citizens refrain from utilizing their democratic rights and liberties and from expressing their ideals. Her reason for ascribing privacy the legal status of a shared interest is a pragmatic one, based on the assumption that there is a better chance of securing privacy when it promotes the collective good of society. The traditional framing of privacy primarily as an individual right has resulted in privacy being superseded by concepts valued for the common goods like "efficiency" and "security".

In "The Limits of Privacy" (1999), Amitai Etzioni argues that the public interest in security is more important to a society than an individual's freedom of choice and privacy interests. Citizens should subordinate their personal interests in privacy to communal interests in social security - *summum bonum* (Etzioni, 1999; Etzioni & Marsh, 2003). This line of reasoning has been echoed after 9/11 attack on the Wold Trade Center, and the Madrid and London bombings that followed. The so-called war on terrorism has meant an unprecedented focus on security in the Western world (Imre, Mooney & Clarke, 2008) and often to the detriment of privacy. Allegedly security enhancing measures like body scans at airports (also called "naked machines"), and biometrics, like finger/hand and retina scans, typically imply privacy intrusions. Such measures are usually implemented without articulating when and how security is obtained (Dworkin, 2003).That is, those implementing this type of technology have seldom specified what threats the technology is supposed to reduce. Unless the notion of security is operationalized we will not know when security is obtained and whether the technology is efficient in protecting us. As a result, privacy may be sacrificed for a value or goal that has no clear endpoint.

PRIVACY, TRANSPARENCY AND PUBLIC ACCESS TO OFFICIAL DOCUMENTS

Privacy is not an absolute right. It must be viewed in relation to other rights and obligations, and balanced appropriately. In the following, we present a brief investigation of the relationship between transparency and public access to official documents on the one hand, and privacy and data protection on the other.

Transparency and public access to official documents have been recognized as fundamental rights. Fundamental rights are rights and liberties that all human beings are granted. The freedom of speech and thought, and the right to vote are some examples of human rights. The Universal Declaration of Human Rights (UDHR) from 1948 provides a full statement of these rights (United Nations, 1948) and Regulation EC/2001/1049 describes the right of citizens to obtain documents of the European Parliament, the Council, and the Commission. The objective of public access rules is to ensure *admittance* under the jurisdiction of the EU institutions and bodies, whereas the data protection regulation must guarantee the protection of personal information and data (European Data Protection Supervisor, 2005). Reasons for protection of transparency and public access to official documents are expressed in the Swedish principle of public access -"Offentlighetsprincipen". "To encourage the free exchange of opinion and availability of comprehensive information, every Swedish citizen shall be entitled to have free access to official documents" (Freedom of the Press Act, 1949, authors translation). Examples of situations where this right may conflict with other considerations can be found in several contexts such as the administration of employment procedures, requests for information about employees of certain official institutions, requests for information on participation in meetings organised by official institutions, and in complaint procedures. The right to access public records may be superseded in cases related to national security; defence and international relations; public safety; or the prevention, investigation and prosecution of criminal activities. It may also be circumscribed by privacy.

Whereas, on an EU-level, the notions of privacy and data protection have a history longer than that of transparency; Sweden has a long (but interrupted) history of public access to official documents, established in 1766. The principle is intended to guarantee an open society with free public access to information on the activities of Government and government authorities. It enables citizens both to follow the work of their representatives in government, and to control the types of individual information stored and used by government agencies. In 1949, this principle was embodied in the Freedom of the Press Act granting Swedish citizens the right to examine official documents at will.[1] This right obliges the receiving authority to register all incoming or outgoing official documents such as letters, official decisions, or reports. Swedish citizens have the right to make an annual request to receive all data stored about themselves from each governmental agency, and the right to amend those data if inaccurate, incomplete, or obsolete.

There are exceptions. For instance, official documents may be classified as secret if they contain information relating to public safety, personal or financial data about individual citizens, or crime prevention activities by public authorities. When classified as secret, individual citizen are denied access to the record, even if it is self-pertinent.

Until now we have discussed the risks and benefits of e-services, where possible invasions of privacy have been identified as one risk with the increased use of information and communication technology. The balance between public access to services must be balanced with adequate security measures. However, privacy seems to be a contextual concept that depends on what information is released, who can access it and for what purpose. The expansion of e-services and e-Government needs to be complemented with a view by those actors who collect, store and use personal information - the service providers.

SIX SWEDISH GOVERNMENTAL AGENCIES' VIEW ON E-SERVICES AND PRIVACY

The following discussion is based on interviews with representatives from six Swedish governmental agencies; the Swedish National Police, the Social Insurance Agency, the Swedish National Tax Board, the Swedish Road Administration, the Swedish Institute for Infectious Disease Control, and the Swedish Data Inspection Board (DI). These agencies were selected for this study because they all possess extensive registers containing information about Swedish citizens. They also provide on-line services. It deserves mentioning that the Swedish Data Inspection Board holds a particular status among the agencies interviewed due to its responsibility to uphold the Swedish Data Protection Act (PUL) (1998:204) by assessing the use (collection, storage, processing and transfer) of personal data in Sweden.

Aims and Methods

The interviews were conducted during 2008 – 2009 and all but one in a face-to-face meeting. One interview was conducted over the phone for because of time constraints. A total of seven interviews were conducted with individuals responsible for the technical and organizational security with information and communication technology used for e-services and e-Government at the different agencies. One of the interviewees was an IT forensics specialist with expertise in risks within this area. The two authors conducted the interviews jointly in most cases. All interviews were semi-structured, where the respondents were asked questions around three main areas:

1. Privacy and privacy protection;
2. Data protection and Information security standards (Are directives clear? Action-guiding?); and
3. The development of e-services and e-Government.

The interviews were tape-recorded, transcribed, and analyzed by the two authors independently. The results of these interviews are intended to illustrate some of the perceived benefits and difficulties associated with the increased uses of e-services and e-Government. The analysis is as follows: first the respondents' view of privacy is presented; second, issues relating to data handling and protection are discussed; and third, the notion of "public demand" is investigated.

Discussion

Privacy

When asked if there were any types of information not covered by the Data Protection Act or by other relevant laws or policies, but that the respondents felt should be protected, none of the respondents identified any such types of information. However, some of them pointed to a certain group of clients in need of extra, and previously unrecognized, privacy protection - namely those with *protected identities*. Here, protected identity refers to individuals whose personal data, for example, one's place of work, telephone number, name of children's school, or place of residence, are protected from public access. These are individuals that have not changed their identity, as is done under the witness protection program, but are shielded from public access. Examples of individuals in this group can be battered women or political activists. In order to better accommodate the special needs of this group, some of the agencies were currently educating their staff on how to safeguard information related to these individuals. It can be argued that e-services and e-Government would be extra beneficial to this group in the sense that they must not expose themselves when visiting a government agency. However, the vulnerability of this particular group reinforces the need for reliable information security – both physical and personal.

Respondents were also asked whether they had noticed any changes in how privacy has been perceived over time, and if so, in what ways. Even if the concept of privacy was not perceived directly to have changed over time, most respondents expressed that they did see a difference in perception among their users, with groups of older people more sceptical and resistant towards using the technology, than groups of younger people. This generational shift is not uncommon as younger users are usually quicker in adopting new technologies than older users.

We also asked about potential conflicts and difficulties in balancing privacy and public access to official documents in relation to the Swedish principle of public access. In reply, most respondents expressed frustration that the balance between the principle of public access to official documents and the individual's right to privacy is poorly regulated, and that the final decision is sometimes left to the individual employee handling the particular request. In its most extreme case, what constitutes privacy, and to some extent information security, is left to the individual administrator to decide. This not only raises the need for clearer regulation, but also the need for stricter internal policies and increased education of public administrators.

It was noted that e-services generate information that may be of interest to third parties. For example, a school transport provider in the phase of hiring a new school bus driver may be interested in the road administration's register on traffic violations by potential employees. Another situation might be that a local emergency response team is interested in the Institute for Infectious Disease's register on the number of people infected by a specific strain of virus in order to track the development of a pandemic. In these examples, information is perceived as valuable for a group of people or for society at large. It is important to understand whether the release of such information is effective in protecting the safety of the group and if so, how to allow access to sensitive data while at the same time minimizing harm to individual privacy.

Some of the agencies reported that the amount, type, and level of detail of information released, depends on how the request is made. For example, little personal information will be released if the request is made by a third party *via* e-mail. More information will be released if requested *via* regular mail. Moreover, records are released only as printed matter. They are not released electronically. Electronic transmission is allowed between agencies only in order to minimize the flow of electronic information. It is believed that data in electronic form can be more easily distributed, whereas distributing a printed version of the same material would require more effort and lessen the likelihood of abuse. This was perceived as a kind of check and balance as it will make the individual administrator more aware of what information they are asked to release, and allow the time to question whether this request is reasonable or not. Regarding external threats, however, some of the respondents mentioned that the risk of administrators being physically threatened by individuals wanting information was still perceived as a greater risk than the risk of being hacked.

As noted above, sound and well-anchored policies and unambiguous procedures are vital to assist individual administrators' decision-making including a means to refer the decisions to a higher administrator. This may improve the probability of appropriate conduct regarding data transfer to third parties. Of course, even the most well-intentioned policies and internal documents cannot fully prevent staff members from accessing information or distributing or selling it to a third party for personal gain. Moreover, in some cases, technical security systems have flaws that enable staff to access information that they should not have access to.

Data Protection

Some of the government officials we interviewed find the Swedish Data Protection Act (PUL) (1998:204), and internal policies for data protection sufficient to protect the privacy of their clients. Other respondents perceived legislation as unclear, lacking in guidance, and not adapted to the present day situation.

As we have noted earlier, data protection is of central importance when government agencies handle personal information. PUL states that those responsible for personal data must undertake adequate technical and organizational measures in order to safeguard the information processed. Information should not be stored longer than necessary to achieve the aim for which the data were collected. Also, the law states that sufficient information regarding the treatment of data must be given to the individual in order for her to be able to consent in an informed manner.

Some of the respondents voiced the opinion that the lack of what constitutes "sufficient" information or "longer than" leaves the law open for interpretation and renders compliance difficult. Some also claim that even though technical developments have resulted in more detailed information and increased the storage capacities; the overall purpose of data collection has not changed, making the law difficult to apply to the novel possibilities enabled by technology. Furthermore, many of the respondents express a worry that information may be stored because it is possible to do so rather than for reasons of actual need.

It was also explained that the standard procedure is that employees at government offices should only have access to information that is necessary to exercise their particular task. That is, administrators' access to data registers is controlled by the type of tasks that they perform. Yet, a fear was expressed, that when their job title or work tasks change, administrators' access rights are not always redefined appropriately. Rather, they may keep their old access rights and gain additional access to new domains. Moreover, it was argued that although Information Security contains physical security (system security) and personal security (the security of data subjects), the latter is less developed. Typically, resources are directed to the computer support group/technical division, rather than in the direction of education of employees (at all levels), assessments, and discussion within the government agency. This is consistent with the National Audit Office (Riksrevisionen) 2007 report, which states that IS often is seen as a purely technical issue, excluded from agencies' risk analyses, and forwarded to their IT-support sections (Riksrevisionen, 2007).What seems to be missing are internal discussions within the organizations regarding the value of privacy and information, education in balancing openness and privacy, as well as privacy and security.

Public Demand for E-Services?

A key point brought up during the interviews was that the respondents perceived an increased demand among their clients for access to on-line governmental services. Interviewees also noted that the perceived demand has driven the agencies – despite the risks in terms of information security – to investigate how to best make their services electronically available. However, little or no investigations have been undertaken to determine the extent of this demand. When asked if technical possibilities should motivate or promote changes in how agencies interact with their users, rather than a real and documented desire stemming from the users, most respondents expressed that they had not questioned this perceived demand, but that it might be a worthwhile endeavor to map the needs to their users.

Regardless if the demand is perceived or real; it seems to have significant impact and legitimizes the expansion of on-line services and e-Government. However, some of the respondents voiced the opinion that the demand probably would decline if the public knew more about the amount and type of information stored about them, the vulnerability of the systems, and possible consequences of linking databases. This lack of knowledge was seen as a reason to question public consent, at least in any meaningful sense of consent.

The Fair Information Principles state that data processing is legitimate if and only if the data subject has *consented unambiguously*. Despite these recommendations, in practice, most respondents felt that it is difficult to identify *how much* information is enough in order to ensure substantial consent. It was also noted that meaningful consent is difficult to achieve since the uses of the collected data could change over time – something that in theory would require a new consent in order to be justifiable. As noted earlier, in many cases information is stored because it is technically possible, and in case it will be needed later on. Again, the technical possibilities open for new and unclear areas, where legislation is lacking or unclear. One central aspect of informed consent is that in order for an act to be voluntary and ethically justifiable, it must be well-informed and freely conducted. In order for an act to be freely conducted, it is important that the agent have reasonable options to choose from. In order to be *sufficiently* informed, individuals need to know how their information will be used, now and in the future. However, the future consequences of personal information released *today* are difficult to foresee.

In many cases, e-service users have few reasonable options than to release personal information in order to utilize a certain e-service. This has an impact on the quality of informed consent often taken as a valid token of acceptance. Certainly it can be argued that nobody is forced – in any stronger sense of the word - to use e-services or e-Government. Considering what individuals gain from using e-services (in terms of easy access at all hours and not having to visit government offices in person), they have strong reasons to use these services and may downplay privacy concerns. From the perspective of equality, the case could be made that these services should be open to *all* citizens. And, in order to avoid a development where individuals abstain from privacy concerns in order to be able to utilize convenient and time-saving e-services, it is of central importance that no more information is asked for than what is absolutely necessary for the service in question.

FUTURE RESEARCH DIRECTIONS

From an ethical perspective, one may ask, what if anything is new about the privacy threats posed by e-services and e-Government? Arguably, the privacy concerns raised in relation to e-services and e-Government are by no means a novel phenomenon. What is new is the range and scope of data processing. Deborah Johnson (1993) has shown how technical developments in ICT has, in an unprecedented manner, enabled the collection and storage of vastly more information, the processing of this information on a more detailed level, and the possibility to transfer and share this information among actors. As previously noted, the user profiles created on-line, in order to utilize e-services, contain considerable information about an individual and unauthorized access is a significant threat to users' privacy. Inadequately protected, digital profiles may enable alien users to manipulate data and to combine information from different registers or profiles. Such combinations may be privacy sensitive in the way a "Digital persona" i.e. "a model of the individual established through the collection, storage and analysis of data about that person" (Clarke, 1994) may be constructed. The construction of digital personas may be sensitive for the reason that even if an individual voluntarily consents to provide information a, b, and c to various government agencies (e.g. by including this data in her on-line profiles), she may not necessarily consent to a third party's conclusions based on a + b + c (Palm, 2005). Issues of consent and the construction of digital identities in relation to e-Government are hence issues in need of further research.

This also raises the issue of contextual integrity, that information given in one context and for one purpose must be further explored. Even though there are many principles aimed at protecting the use of information, such as the Finality Principle, technical advances are taking place at an unprecedented scale. It can be argued that the purpose for collecting information is the same, i.e. for increasing availability, efficiency and transparency; there is a danger that the principles are too vague and not easily adaptable to new applications of the technologies. The impact on citizens – be it as consumers or users of governmental services – of the increased reliance on transmitting and storing potentially sensitive data, must be better documented. The increased transparency of, and involvement in, e-Government also needs to be fully investigated.

CONCLUSION

The rapid development of e-services and e-Government – seemingly driven by public demand - challenges privacy and information security. The shift from secluded ICT-environments to an open e-service environment is new to many governmental agencies; and, the increasing complexity has left security issues behind. The e-development has implied a move from protection of certain sensitive data to information in general.

Individuals are at risk of having their personal information handled in ways that violate their privacy, and hence, their capacity for directing their lives. As noted before, what is perceived of as privacy sensitive is subject to change over time and varies with different contexts. Information that an individual comfortably states within one context for a specific purpose, may be perceived of as privacy sensitive if transferred to another domain. She may be comfortable stating information a, b, and c; but, may be uncomfortable with an agent getting access to the combined information a + b + c (Palm, in Hansson and Palm, 2005). Certainly, if governmental agencies were required to respect each individual's personal understanding of what he or she perceives as privacy sensitive – they would be prevented from accomplishing their work efficiently.

Two things are important to remember however. First, according to Rössler (2005), privacy is needed for information that is relevant to an individual's personal autonomy. Not all information falls into this category. Second, context is important when determining the type of information to protect.

Nissenbaum (2004) states that context such as the home, the workspace, or a health care situation imply specific relationships such as professional relationships or private, which are governed by (more or less) explicit norms. And, it is of central importance that these relationships and norms are taken into consideration when information from one context is transferred to another context.

From the perspective of the government agency, it is important to recognize that the agencies handling personal information are at risk of being perceived as less credible and trustworthy if they fail to treat the information appropriately. Trust may be threatened, for example, in cases when the media requests information on celebrities' tax returns or personal information about politicians, such as unpaid parking tickets or time spent on sick-leave.

As always, technological development is ahead of ethically justifiable legislation. It takes time for ethical issues to be understood and for legislation to be passed to address new issues. In the interim, or in addition to new laws, we propose Mandatory Privacy Impact Assessments (PIAs) to ensure that privacy is properly considered. Certainly, such assessments entail monetary cost, but they provide significant benefits. Consideration of privacy concerns at an early stage in the design phase of systems is cheaper than having to bring the system into compliance at a later stage. Moreover, privacy enhancing technologies (PETs) could be systematically integrated into systems development. An important principle is that systems should collect data on a "need to know" rather than a "nice to know" basis. Unfortunately, system-level solutions are insufficient for satisfactory privacy protection. In addition, the role of the individual may be substantially strengthened by campaigns to educate the public about system security. Citizens need information regarding the risks and benefits of e-services in order to critically assess the value of such services and the societal reliance on electronic services. The obligation to educate must fall on the shoulders of those developing and using possibly privacy invasive ICT. As technological development enables more and more possibilities for gathering, storing, and processing personal information, emphasis must be put on finding technical ways to restrict the usage and the sharing of this data.

REFERENCES

Allen, A. (1988). *Uneasy access: Privacy for women in a free society*. Totowa, NJ: Rowman & Littlefield.

Anderson, S. A. (2008). Privacy without the right to privacy. *The Monist*, January, *91*(1).

Bennett, C. J. (1992). *Regulating privacy: Data protection and public policy in Europe and the United States*. Ithaca, NY: Cornell University Press.

Bloustein, E. (1964). Privacy as an aspect of human dignity: An answer to Dean Possner. *New York University Law Review*, *39*, 962–1007.

Brey, P. (2007). Ethical aspects of information security and privacy. In Petcovic, W., & Jonker, M. (Eds.), *Security and trust in modern data management* (pp. 21–36). New York: Springer. doi:10.1007/978-3-540-69861-6_3

Bynum, T. W. (2008). Norbert wiener and the rise of information ethics. In van den Hoven, J., & Weckert, J. (Eds.), *Information technology and moral philosophy* (pp. 8–25). Cambridge, MA: Cambridge University Press. doi:10.1017/CBO9780511498725.002

Cavoukian, A. (1998). Data mining: staking a claim on your privacy. *Information and Privacy Commissioner's Report*. Ontario, Canada.

Clarke, R. (1994). The digital persona and its application to data surveillance. *The Information Society*, *10*(2), 77–92. doi:10.1080/01972243.1994.9960160

Cohen, J. (2002). *Regulating intimacy: A new legal paradigm*. Princeton, NJ: Princeton University Press.

Commission of the European Communities. (2006a). *i2010 e-Government Action Plan: Accelerating e-Government in Europe for the Benefit of All* (COM 173 Final). The European Parliament.

Commission of the European communities. (2006b). *Interoperability for Pan-European e-Government Services* (COM 45 Final). The European Parliament.

Council Directive 95/46/EC of the European Parliament and of the Council of the European Union of 24 October 1995 on the protection of individuals with regard to the processing of personal data and on the free movement of such data. Retrieved from http:www.legaltext.ee/text/en/T5023.html

Council Directive 97/66/EC of the European Parliament and of the Council of the European Union of 15 December 1997 concerning the processing of personal data and the protection of privacy in the telecommunications sector. Retrieved from http:www.legaltext.ee/text/en/T5023.html

Council Directive 2002/58/EC of the European Parliament and of the Council of the European Union of 12 July 2002 concerning the processing of personal data and the protection of privacy in the electronic communications sector (Directive on privacy and electronic communications). Retrieved from http:brief.weburb.dk/archives/00000209/

Dayarathna, R. (2007). *Towards Comparing Personal Information Privacy Protection Measures* (Licentiate Thesis of Philosophy, Stockholm University, Sweden). Report series 07-018.

DeCew, J. (1997). *In pursuit of privacy: Law, ethics, and the rise of technology*. Ithaca, NY: Cornell University Press.

Dworkin, R. (2003). Terror & the attack on civil liberties. *The New York Review of Books*, *50*(7), 31.

European Data Protection Supervisor. Public access to documents and data protection, [Guideline],*Background Paper Series*, European Communities, Belgium, July 2005. Retrieved from http://www.edps.europa.eu/EDPSWEB/webdav/shared/Documents/EDPS/Publications/Papers/BackgroundP/05-07_BP_summary_EN.pdf

Elgesem, D. (1999). The structure of rights in Directive 95/46/EC on the protection of individuals with regard to processing of personal data and the free movement of such data. *Ethics and Information Technology*, *1*(4), 283–293. doi:10.1023/A:1010076422893

Etzioni, A. (1999). *The limits of privacy*. New York: Basic Books.

Etzioni, A., & Marsh, J. (2003). *Rights vs. public safety after 9/11*. Lanham, MD: Rowman & Littlefield.

European Convention on Human Rights (1950) The Universal Declaration of Human Rights and Article 8 of the European Convention for the Protection of Human Rights and Fundamental Freedoms, Rome, Retrieved from http://www.echr.coe.int/nr/rdonlyres/d5cc24a7-dc13-4318-b457-5c9014916d7a/0/englishanglais.pdf

Flaherty, D. H. (1989). *Protecting privacy in surveillance societies: The Federal Republic of Germany, Sweden, France, Canada, and the United States*. Chapel Hill, NC: University of North Carolina Press.

Foucault, M. (1995). *Discipline and punish: The birth of the prison*. New York: Vintage Books.

Freedom of the Press Act [Tryckfrihetsförordningen], Chapter 2, Article 1, 1949:105 (1949).

Fried, C. (1984). Privacy (a moral analysis). In Schoeman, F. (Ed.), *Philosophical dimensions of privacy: An anthology* (pp. 346–402). Cambridge, MA: Cambridge University Press. doi:10.1017/CBO9780511625138.008

Gandy, O. (1993). *The panoptic sort: A political economy of personal information*. Boulder, CO: Westview Press.

Gavison, R. (1980). Privacy and the limits of law. *The Yale Law Journal*, *8*, 421–471. doi:10.2307/795891

Gerstein, R. (1978). Intimacy and privacy. *Ethics*, *89*, 78–81. doi:10.1086/292105

Heeks, R. (2006). *Implementing and managing e-government – An international text*. London, England: SAGE.

Heeks, R., & Stanforth, C. (2007). Understanding e-government project trajectories from an actor-network perspective. *European Journal of Information Systems*, *16*(2), 165–177. doi:10.1057/palgrave.ejis.3000676

Häyry, M., & Takkala, T. (2001). Genetic information, rights, and autonomy. *Theoretical Medicine and Bioethics*, *22*(5), 403–414. doi:10.1023/A:1013097617552

Imre, R. T., Mooney, B., & Clarke, B. (2008). *Responding to terrorism:Political, philosophical and legal perspectives*. Aledershot, England: Ashgate Publishing.

Inness, J. C. (1992). *Privacy, intimacy and isolation*. Oxford: Oxford University Press.

Johnson, D. (1993). *Computer ethics*. Englewood Cliffs, NJ: Prentice Hall.

International Standards Organization. *ISO 27001 Information Security Management System Specification*. Retrieved from http://www.w3j.com/5/s3.koman.html.

Lever, A. (2005). Feminism, democracy and the right to privacy. *Minerva: An Internet. The Journal of Philosophy*, *9*, 1–31.

Mitrokotsa, C., & Douligeris, A. (2004). DDoS attacks and defense mechanisms: classification and state-of-the-art. *Computer Networks: The International Journal of Computer and Telecommunications Networking*, *44*(5), 643–666.

Moor, J. (1985). What is computer ethics? *Metaphilosophy*, *16*(4), 266–275. doi:10.1111/j.1467-9973.1985.tb00173.x

Nagel, T. (2002). *Concealment and exposure and other essays*. Oxford, England: Oxford University Press.

Niemitz v Germany (1992) Series A 251-B paras 29-33, Judgement of 16 December 1992, A-251. B, point 33.

Nissenbaum, H. (1998). Protecting privacy in an information age: The problem of privacy in public. *Law and Philosophy*, *17*(5-6), 559–596.

Nissenbaum, H. (2004). Privacy as contextual integrity. *Washington Law Review (Seattle, Wash.)*, *79*(1), 119–157.

OECD. (1980). *Guidelines on the protection of privacy and transborder flows of personal data*, 23 September 1980. Retrieved from http://www.oecd.org/document/20/0,2340, en_2649_33703_15589524_1_1_1_37409,00. html

Palm, E. (2005). The dimensions of privacy. In Hansson, S. O., & Palm, E. (Eds.), *The ethics of workplace privacy* (pp. 157–174). Peter Lang Publishing Company.

Parent, W. (1983). Privacy, morality and the law. *Philosophy & Public Affairs*, *12*, 269–288.

Parliamentary Council. (1970). *Resolution 428, Assembly of the Council of. Europe, Constitutional Assembly. 21 St Ordinary Session, 3 rd.* Part.

Rachels, J. (1975). Why privacy is important. *Philosophy & Public Affairs*, *4*(4), 323–333.

Regan, P. M. (1995). *Legislating privacy, technology, social values and public Policy*. Chapel Hill, NC: University of North Carolina Press.

Regulation 1049/2001/EC of the European Parliament and of the Council of the European Union of 30 May 2001 regarding public access to European Parliament, Council and Commission documents. Retrieved from http:www.euractiv.com/en/pa/access-document/article-117440

Riksrevisionen [National Audit Office] (2007) Regeringens styrning av informationssäkerhetsarbetet i den statliga förvaltningen,, [Government regulation of work on information security in the public administration] RiR 2007:10.

Rössler, B. (2005). *The value of privacy*. Cambridge, MA: Polity Press.

Scanlon, T. (1975). Thomson on privacy. *Philosophy & Public Affairs*, *4*(4), 315–322.

Scanlon, T. (1988). *What we owe to each other*. Cambridge, MA: Belknap Press.

Schoeman, F. (Ed.). (1984). *Privacy: Philosophical dimensions of literature. In philosophical dimensions of privacy: An anthology* (pp. 203–221). Cambridge, MA: Cambridge University Press. doi:10.1017/CBO9780511625138

Tavani, H. T. (1999). Informational privacy, data mining, and the internet. *Ethics and Information Technology*, *1*(2), 137–145. doi:10.1023/A:1010063528863

Tavani, H. T. (2007). Philosophical theories of privacy: implications for an adequate on-line privacy policy. *Metaphilosophy*, *38*(1), 1–22. doi:10.1111/j.1467-9973.2006.00474.x

Thompson, J. J. (1975). The right to privacy. *Philosophy & Public Affairs*, *4*(4), 295–314.

United Nations. (1948). *Adopted and proclaimed by General Assembly resolution 217 A (III) of 10 December 1948*. Universal Declaration of Human Rights.

United Nations. (2005). *UN global e-government readiness report 2005: From e-government to e-inclusion*, Department of Economic and Social Affairs Division for Public Administration and Development Management, UPAN 2005/14.

United Nations. (2008). UN *e-government survey 2008 – from e-government to connected governance. Retrieved from:*http://unpan1.un.org/intradoc/groups/public/documents/UN/UNPAN028607.pdf.

Warren, S. D., & Brandeis, L. D. (1890). The right to privacy. *Harvard Law Review*, *IV*(5), 1–23.

Westin, A. (1967). *Privacy and freedom*. New York: Atheneum.

ENDNOTE

1 All documents containing information related to a person of some kind: text, pictures or information stored e.g. in a computer. A document is classified as official if it has come into, was drawn up by or is in the keeping of a public authority with an exception for memoranda and draft decisions.

APPENDIX: DISCUSSION QUESTIONS

1. Discuss some of the risks to society and individuals posed by the increasing popularity of e-government services. Are any of these risks unique to e-government services? Rank the risks in order of relative danger.
2. Compare and contrast the core security concepts of confidentiality, integrity and availability in the context of e-government services. Give an example that illustrates each concept.
3. Discuss the concept of transparency in the context of e-government services. Give an example that illustrates this concept. In your opinion, should transparency by required? Why or why not?
4. Discuss the concept of e-inclusion in the context of e-government services. Describe a plan to ensure e-inclusion for senior citizens in e-government services. You should consider how to make e-services truly accessible, not just in the procedural or operational sense, but also in terms of user-friendliness and usability. Keep in mind that many seniors lack mobility and dexterity and may have other barriers to overcome. They are also more likely to be novice users of computers. Your plan should include an education component to inform seniors of the benefits of e-government services and should encourage their buy-in.
5. Discuss a plan to educate senior citizens about fraud and identity theft prevention. The plan should include education about how to mitigate other security threats to their personal information.
6. Discuss the similarities and differences between confidentiality and privacy. Give an example of each.
7. Discuss the concepts of personal autonomy and privacy as described in the chapter, and also discuss the concept of public good. Is there a conflict between these concepts? Explain.
8. An example of the loss of privacy for the benefit of common good is the airport security screening programs (triggered by events such as the September 11 attacks on the World Trade Center in New York City). Discuss ways of "operationalizing" security screenings, and ways to ensure transparency, fairness and the preservation of human dignity.
9. The chapter discusses the principle of informed consent as defined in the Fair Information Principles. The chapter states:

   > *"In order for an act to be freely conducted, it is important that the agent have reasonable options to choose from. In order to be sufficiently informed, individuals need to know how their information will be used, now and in the future. However, the future consequences of personal information released today are difficult to foresee."*

   Discuss the problems raised by the observation that "in many cases information is stored because it is technically possible, and in case it will be needed later on." Does this practice violate the principle of informed consent?
10. Visit a popular website and read its privacy policy. Is the privacy policy written in a way that can be understood by most website users? How can it be improved? What kinds of personal data are collected? What does the policy say about the company's use of personal data? Are users of the website asked to give informed consent for the use of their personal data? Is informed consent needed? Why or why not?

Chapter 11
Data Breach Disclosure:
A Policy Analysis

Melissa J. Dark
Purdue University, USA

ABSTRACT

As information technology has become more ubiquitous and pervasive, assurance and security concerns have escalated; in response, we have seen noticeable growth in public policy aimed at bolstering cybertrust. With this growth in public policy, questions regarding the effectiveness of these policies arise. This chapter focuses on policy analysis of the state data breach disclosure laws recently enacted in the United States. The state data breach disclosure laws were chosen for policy analysis for three reasons: the rapid policy growth (the United States have enacted 45 state laws in 6 years); this is the first instantiation of informational regulation for information security; and the importance of these laws to identity theft and privacy. The chapter begins with a brief history in order to provide context. Then, this chapter examines the way in which historical, political and institutional factors have shaped our current data breach disclosure policies, focusing on discovering how patterns of interaction influenced the legislative outcomes we see today. Finally, this chapter considers: action that may result from these policies; the action type(s) being targeted; alternatives that are being considered, and; potential outcomes of the existing and proposed alternative policies.

INTRODUCTION

Although advances in computing promise substantial benefits for individuals and society, trust in computing and communications is critical in order to realize such benefits. The hope for cybertrust is a society where trust enables technologies to support individual and societal needs without violating confidences and exacerbating public risks. Cybertrust, in part, depends upon software and hardware technologies upon which people can justifiably rely. However, the cybertrust vision requires looking beyond technical controls to consider how other forms of social control

DOI: 10.4018/978-1-61692-245-0.ch011

contribute to the state of cyber trust. This chapter focuses on public policy. While the chapter does not specifically use the word *ethics*, it should be noted that ethical issues and public policy are intimately intertwined. Policy is not formed in a moral vacuum; on the contrary, policy is inherently normative in that it prescribes, sometimes explicitly and often implicitly, what *should be*.

The increased reliance on and utilization of information technology in society has created the need for new regulation regarding the use and abuse of these systems. We see this clearly just by briefly inventorying some of the regulations that have been enacted to protect security and privacy.

- Freedom of Information Act (1966)
- Fair Credit Reporting Act (1970)
- Bank Secrecy Act (1970)
- Privacy Act (1974)
- Family Educational Rights and Privacy Act (FERPA) (1974)
- Right to Financial Privacy Act (1978)
- Foreign Intelligence Surveillance Act (1978)
- Electronic Communications Privacy Act (ECPA) (1986)
- Telephone Consumer Protection Act (1991)
- Communications Assistance for Law Enforcement Act (1994)
- Driver's Privacy Protection Act (1994)
- Health Insurance Portability and Accountability Act (HIPAA) (1996)
- Computer Fraud & Abuse Act (1996)
- Children's Online Privacy Protection Act (COPPA) (1998)
- Digital Millennium Copyright Act (1998)
- Gramm-Leach-Bliley Act (GLBA) (1999)
- USA PATRIOT Act (2001)
- Federal Information Security Management Act (2002)
- Fair and Accurate Credit Transactions Act (2003)
- CAN-SPAM Act (2003)
- 45 State Data Breach Disclosure Laws[1] law (2003-present)

Eight of these laws were enacted between 1966 and 1986, while the last thirteen items in the list have been enacted between 1991 and 2009. This is not an exhaustive list, but it is representative and shows the increasing growth in legislation. This chapter focuses on the 45 State Data Breach Disclosure laws enacted in United States between 2003-2009 – a mere six year time span. Data breach has become a policy concern due to the rise in identity theft crimes and the erosion of privacy.

Identity theft is the crime of obtaining and using another person's personal information in order to commit fraud. There are four types of identity theft: (1) financial – illegally using someone else's identity to obtain good and services, (2) criminal – posing as another person when apprehended for a crime, (3) identity cloning – using another person's information to assume his/her identity in daily life, and (4) business/commercial identity theft – using another business' name to obtain credit (Identity Theft Resource Center, 2008). Identity theft is a concern because of the escalating incidence and costs for individuals, companies, and our nation. It is estimated that there were 8.4 million U.S. adult victims of identity fraud in 2007 resulting in losses of $49.3 billion (Javelin Strategy and Research Survey, 2007). A study by the Ponemon Institute (2008) surveyed 35 U.S. organizations and found the total average cost of a data breach in 2007 was $202.00 per record breached. The Privacy Rights Clearinghouse maintains a chronology of data breaches (www.privacyrights.org) that includes data elements considered useful to identity thieves, such as Social Security numbers, account numbers, and driver's license numbers. According to this chronology, there were approximately 34,000,000 records breached in 2008 in the United States.[2] If the number of records breached and costs per breach in 2009 are commensurate with the 2008 costs, the estimated costs for data breaches 2009 will be $6,868,000,000 ($197 x

34,000,000). Clearly, identity theft and data breach are an economic concern.

Escalating data breach problems further erode privacy. However, unlike identity theft, which has a legal definition and can be quantified in terms of incidents, privacy has no single definition or meaning. Generically speaking, privacy is the condition of being left alone, out of public view, and being in control of one's personal information. From a policy perspective, privacy can be classified in two basic categories: the reductionist view and the coherentist view (Schoeman, 1984). From the reductionist perspective all privacy claims are reducible to claims of other sorts, for example, property rights and trespass. According to this view, there is no purpose for considering privacy as a distinct issue of concern – existing policy can be extended to address it. In contrast, coherentism suggests that privacy consists of a number of fundamental, integrated, and distinct concerns. This view does not dispute what is addressed elsewhere. Rather, the coherentist concern is that disparate privacy components interact with each other and with other social priorities so that the whole of privacy is more than the sum of its parts. In which case, existing policies will not suffice. For both reductionists and coherentists, privacy begins with control of information, which is the ability to determine for ourselves when, how, and to what extent information about us is communicated to others (Westin, 1967). But for coherentists, privacy cannot be restricted to this 'information flow' definition. Doing so relegates it to the status of a moral or legal right, which is insufficient. The coherentist notion is that privacy is a condition (i.e., a state or modifying circumstance) that is inextricably linked to other desirable human conditions, such as human dignity, intimacy, social relationships, and personhood. Viewing privacy is this manner positions it as a collective good in addition to an individual good.

Given that information security and privacy are becoming more important, as evidenced by the growth in public policy, policy analysis in this area is timely and relevant. Policy analysis aims to address questions such the following. What do governments choose to do or not to do? How effective are the proposed or enacted solutions to public problems? How are issues that affect large numbers of citizens introduced to the public arena? What are the historical, political, and institutional factors that shape the formulation of public policy? In light of the relationships among policies, which of various alternative policies will be most effective in achieving a given set of social goals? How can policy making be improved through research and analysis?

This chapter seeks to advance information security and privacy policy analysis by specifically examining the data breach disclosure laws recently enacted in the United States. The background section includes a brief history of these laws and serves to provide context. The laws are analyzed using an institutional analysis and development framework (Ostrom[3], 1999)[4], which is overviewed in section two. Then, historical, political, and institutional factors that shaped our current data breach disclosure policies are analyzed with a focus on how patterns of interaction influenced the legislative outcomes we see today. In this way, the chapter is retrospective; we see how questions of *what should be* have shaped the current policy landscape. Last, this chapter considers how these policies may structure action with an eye toward alternatives and outcomes. In this way, the chapter is prospective and serves to question *what should be* moving forward.

BACKGROUND

Given that the data breach disclosure laws aim to ameliorate identity theft and privacy concerns, we start with an overview of other legislation in these areas. The first U.S. law that specifically addressed identity theft was passed in 1998 – the Identity Theft and Assumption Deterrence Act. The law was passed in response to the dramatic rise in identity theft in the 1990s. Prior to this act, ID theft was not regulated per se.

With regard to privacy, there is no provision for privacy in the U.S. constitution. There is no independent privacy oversight agency in the United States, and the United States has no comprehensive privacy law. Instead, the United States has taken a sectoral approach to privacy regulation so that records held by third parties (such as financial and personal records at banks, educational and personal records at universities, membership and personal information at associations, medical and personal records at community hospitals) are generally not protected unless a legislature has enacted a specific law. As a result, we have a patchwork of laws enacted to address privacy and data security. These are outlined next, starting with the laws that pertain to the federal government, followed by laws that pertain to the private sector and finally, state laws.

Federal Laws

The Federal Trade Commission (FTC) Act was established by the Federal Trade Commission in 1914 with the purposes of promoting consumer protection and eliminating and preventing anti-competitive business practices. Jurisdiction of the FTC Act extends to a variety of entities. Section 5 of the FTC Act forbids unfair or deceptive practices in commerce, where unfair practices are defined as those that cause or will likely cause substantial injury to consumers. Section 5 of the Federal Trade Commission Act has been used with regard to privacy and security where companies have been accused of deceptive claims regarding use of personal information (e.g., Choicepoint). In 2003, the FTC Act was amended to include a provision regarding the privacy of consumers' credit data (the Fair and Accurate Transactions Act of 2003 - 15 U.S.C. 1681-1681x).

The Privacy Act of 1974 (5 U.S.C. 552a) governs the federal government's information privacy program. The intent of the Privacy Act is to balance the government's need to maintain information about individuals and the privacy rights of individuals. The Privacy Act protects individuals against unwarranted invasions of privacy stemming from federal agencies' collection, maintenance, use, and disclosure of personal information (U.S. Department of Justice, 2008). The act was passed by the United States Congress in response to revelations of privacy abuse during President Richard Nixon's administration. A second goal of the Privacy Act is to address potential abuses stemming from government's increasing use of computers to store and retrieve personal data. The Privacy Act focuses on four basic policy objectives:

1. To restrict the disclosure of personally identifiable records that are maintained by federal agencies.
2. To grant individuals increased rights of access to federal agency records that pertain to themselves.
3. To grant individuals the right to seek amendment of federal agency records maintained on themselves given evidence that the records are inaccurate, irrelevant, untimely, or incomplete.
4. To establish a code of "fair information practices" that requires federal agencies to comply with statutory norms regarding collection, maintenance, and dissemination of records.

The Privacy Act specifies that agencies will not disclose any record that is contained in a system of records by any means of communication to any person or to another agency without the prior written consent of the individual to whom the record pertains - barring exceptions such as law enforcement. The Privacy Act also mandates that each federal agency have in place an administrative and physical security system to prevent unauthorized release of personal records. While the Privacy Act also applies to records created by government contractors, it does not apply to private databases.

The Federal Information Security Management Act (44 U.S.C. 3544) (FISMA), enacted in 2002, is the principal law governing the information security program for the federal government. FISMA calls for agencies to develop, document, and implement agency-wide information security programs. This includes information systems used or operated by an agency or by a contractor of an agency. A goal of FISMA is to see that information security protections are commensurate with the risk and magnitude of harm resulting from unauthorized access, use, disclosure, disruption, modification, or destruction of information collected or maintained by or on behalf of the agency. FISMA requires procedures for detecting, reporting, and responding to security incidents. Notification of security incidents must be provided to a federal information security incident center, law enforcement, and relevant Offices of the Inspector General. The Office of Management and Budget Breach Notification Policy, issued in 2007, reemphasizes agencies' obligations under the Privacy Act and FISMA by outlining two new privacy requirements and five new security requirements, which include explicit requirements for breach notification.

The Veterans Affairs Information Security Act (38 U.S.C. 5722) was enacted in 2006 in response to the May, 2006 breach of 26.5 million veterans' personal data. The Veterans Affairs Information Security Act requires the Veterans Administration (VA) to implement agency-wide information security procedures to protect the VA's sensitive personal information and information systems. While the VA Secretary is expected to comply with FISMA, this act includes other requirements not in FISMA, which are not specified here due to the narrow scope of this law, i.e., it only applies to the VA.

Private Sector Laws

In addition to the laws that shape the behavior of federal agencies, a suite of information security and privacy laws apply to the private sector. The two main laws are the Health Insurance Portability and Accountability Act (42 U.S.C. 1320) of 1996 (HIPAA) and the Gramm-Leach-Bliley Act (15 U.S.C. 6801-6809), enacted in 1999 (GLBA). HIPAA requires health plans, health care clearinghouses, and health care providers to ensure the privacy of medical records and prohibits disclosure without patient consent. While HIPAA includes privacy provisions, it is important to note that the primary purpose of HIPAA was job mobility. According to Hinde (2003):

It was perceived that the disclosure of pre-existing medical conditions or claims to a new employer and that employer's health plan might discourage job mobility if those conditions were excluded by the new health plan insurer. Thus, the concept of providing privacy over identifiable information for those covered by the plan (p. 379).

The security standards that require health care entities to maintain administrative, technical, and physical safeguards to ensure the confidentiality, integrity, and availability of electronic "protected health information" were added to HIPAA in 2003.

The Gramm-Leach-Bliley Act pertains to financial institutions. The impetus for GLBA was to "modernize" financial services. This included the removal of regulations that prevented the merger of banks, stock brokerage companies, and insurance companies. These financial institutions regularly bought and sold information that many would consider private, including bank balances and account numbers. Therefore, the

removal of these regulations raised significant risks that these new financial institutions would have access to an incredible amount of personal information with no restrictions upon its use. Prior to GLBA, the insurance company that maintained your health records was distinct from the bank that mortgaged your house and the stockbroker that traded your stocks. Once these companies merged, however, they would have the ability to consolidate, analyze, and sell the personal details of their customers' lives. (EPIC, 2008).

GLBA requires financial institutions (businesses that are engaged in banking, insuring, stocks and bonds, financial advice, and investing) to safeguard the security and confidentiality of customer information, to protect against threats and hazards to the security or integrity of these records, and to provide customers with notice of privacy policies. Section 501 (b) of GLBA requires banking agencies to establish industry standards regarding security measures such as risk assessment, information security training, security testing, monitoring, and a response program for unauthorized access to customer information and customer notice. In this way, GLBA is considered self-regulatory because it calls for financial institutions to appoint an intermediary to determine best practices for information security and to monitor the performance of financial institutions against these industry standards.

State Data Breach Disclosure Laws

The most recent spate of activity is in the 45 state data breach disclosure laws. California was the first state to establish a data breach disclosure law in 2003; 10 other states enacted laws in 2005, 19 in 2006, eight in 2007, five in 2008, and two in 2009. Questions and concerns about the efficacy of these laws are many. All of these laws address three common elements: personal information definition, notification requirements, and notification procedures and timelines. However, the definitions of "personal information", "breach", "encryption", and "potential risk" are not consistent across the various state laws. This creates challenges for companies that operate in more than one state. The need to comply with multiple state laws can be cumbersome and costly. Thus far, we do not know if consumer notification is effective and under what circumstances. Given that the laws vary with regard to what is protected, to what degree, and when, consumer advocates fear that that lack of consistency diminishes the effectiveness of the laws. By allowing consumer rights to vary, consumers lose their power; by meaning many different things, these consumer protections mean no one thing. Questions also arise about the use of personal notification as a mitigation strategy. Is it effective, and if so, under what circumstances does it work? The next four sections discuss these definitions in greater detail highlighting the differences among the 45 state data breach disclosure laws.

Personal Information Definition

All of the data breach laws include a section that specifies the type of data that is subject to the breach law. All state laws cover a common set of data types. This includes an individual's first name or first initial and last name in combination with another identifying element, such as: (1) SSN; (2) DL number; (3) state ID number; (4) financial account number in combination with an access code, security code, or password; (5) credit card number in combination with an access code, security code, or password; or (6) debit card number in combination with an access code, security code, or password. However, this is where the commonality ends. Other data types covered in some states include checking account number, savings account number, personal identification number, electronic identification number, employer identification number, government issued ID number, routing code, digital signature, biometric data, fingerprints, account passwords (not in combination with other data), mother's maiden name, address, date of birth, medical information, DOT Photo Identification number, and telecommunications device. While there is consistency among states on six of the data items, there is variation on 17 other types of personal information that could be used to commit identity theft or other types of fraud.

Notification Requirements

Each data breach law includes a notification requirement that specifies the conditions under which covered entities[5] are required to disclose the breach; however, the details vary. Eighty percent of the laws require covered entities to provide a safe harbor for encrypted data. Safe harbor means that covered entities are exempt from having to disclose breaches when the data are encrypted. To make the situation even murkier, encryption standards are specified in some state laws (e.g., Maine, North Dakota, and Indiana), but not in other states (e.g., California, Arkansas, Louisiana, and Illinois). For those states where an encryption standard is specified, covered entities are expected to disclose if their encryption method does not meet the standard. In states that do not specify an encryption standard, covered entities are able to choose their own encryption method, which may or may not be "good enough". Some states (New York, North Carolina, and Pennsylvania) require that covered entities notify victims when encrypted data are breached and the encryption key has also been acquired.

In all 45 laws, the notification requirements describe the categories of covered entities. There are two broad categories: (1) entities that own or license computerized data, and (2) entities that maintain computerized data. Whereas all state laws apply to entities that own or license personal information, just over 50% of the state laws also apply to entities that maintain personal data. In general, covered entities are persons, agencies, and/or businesses that are required to provide notification; though in some states the law does not apply to state and local government agencies. For the most part, the state disclosure laws apply only to computerized data; however, the North Carolina and Wisconsin laws apply to paper records as well.

In all of the state data breach laws, the notification requirements define the trigger for notification. From this perspective, there are basically two types of laws: acquisition-based and risk-based. Acquisition-based laws require disclosure anytime the covered personal information has been acquired by an unauthorized person. Risk-based laws require notification only if there is "reasonable likelihood" of harm, injury, loss, or risk. It should be noted that "reasonable likelihood" is subject to interpretation. Twenty-two of the state laws are risk-based laws.

Notification Procedures and Timelines

All of the laws include a section that specifies the method of notification and the circumstances under which affected individuals are to be notified. The laws spell out the methods for notification, i.e., written notice, electronic notice, or telephone notice. All states allow for written notice; almost all allow for electronic notice, with the exception of North Dakota. Another anomaly is Indiana's provision for notification via facsimile.

Many state laws include a provision for substitute notice. Essentially this provision allows for email notification, website posting notification, or notification through statewide media based on a threshold. The threshold for when substitute notification is allowable is the cost of notification or the size of the affected class of residents. For example, a state may allow for substitute notification when the cost is expected to exceed $50,000 or the affected class of residents to be notified exceeds 100,000. There is considerable variation in the provision for substitute notification (some states do not provide for substitution), as well as variation in the threshold levels ranging from $25,000 to $250,000 for notification cost and 5,000 to 500,000 for persons affected.

A minority of states specify a time limit for notification. More state laws address the timeline vaguely as the "most expedient time possible" and "without unreasonable delay", where notification time can be affected by allowing the covered entity the opportunity to (a) determine the scope of the breach, and/or (b) restore system integrity, and/or (c) notify law enforcement. Law enforcement officials can then delay notification further if it is deemed that notification would impede an investigation or jeopardize national or homeland security.

Several states require notification of other parties besides the individuals directly affected by the breach. For example, in some states covered entities must notify consumer reporting agencies and state agencies such as the Attorney General, the State Police, the Department of Justice, the Consumer Protection Board, the Cyber Security and Critical Infrastructure Coordination Office, and so on. Most state laws require notification to consumer reporting agencies. The three national consumer reporting agencies are Equifax Credit Information Services, Inc.; Trans Union LLC; and Experian Information Solutions, Inc. However, there is variation among the states regarding the threshold at which notification beyond the consumer is required. For example, in Minnesota the covered entity must notify the consumer reporting agencies if the breach exceeds 500 state residents; in Georgia the threshold is 10,000.

Other

A minority of the state data breach notification laws include requirements for data protection and secure data destruction and disposal. When information security provisions are included, the law is transformed from being just a data breach disclosure law into also being an information security law. Many would contend that improving information security is perhaps the most essential part of reducing identity theft.

The state data breach disclosure laws vary with regard to penalties. Fewer than half of the states include stipulations for monetary penalties, and the amount of the penalty varies widely. Some states allow for private right of action against companies for breached data while other states rely solely on the State Attorney General's office for enforcement. For example, West Virginia specifies that no civil penalty shall exceed $150,000 per breach or series of breaches discovered in a single investigation. Alaska violators are liable to the state for a civil penalty of up to $500 for each state resident who was not notified, but the total civil penalty may not exceed $50,000. Rhode Island delimits the penalty to no more than $100 per occurrence and no more than $25,000 adjudged against a defendant.

State laws also vary in their protections to consumers. Fewer than 20% of the state laws include a provision for a security credit freeze, which prohibits credit agencies from releasing consumer credit information without the express authorization of the consumer. This provision shows that some states believe that part of the solution is to provide consumers with more ability to take action to protect themselves and information on how to do so. The disparity among states reflects, in part, differences in the perceived importance of consumer rights and education.

The patchwork of 45 state data breach notification laws presents challenges. Interstate businesses say that their firms have difficulty complying with dozens of state laws. Critics also contend that the potential volume of notifications is a concern. As notifications increase we risk consumer desensitization and could lead to consumers' inattention to the risk, which would be counterproductive.

Need for Change

The clarion call is that we are drowning under a myriad of different state data breach notification laws, thereby making a federal data breach notification law imperative. In response, a number of federal data breach notification bills have been introduced in the past four years. These include the following from the 109th Congress (GovTrack.us), which spanned 2005-06:

- **S. 115:** Notification of Risk to Personal Data Act
- **S. 116:** Privacy Act
- **S. 500:** Information Protection and Security Act
- **S. 751:** Notification of Risk to Personal Data Act
- **S. 768:** Comprehensive Identity Theft Prevention Act
- **S. 1216:** Financial Privacy Breach Notification Act
- **S. 1336:** Consumer Identity Protection and Security Act
- **S. 1408:** Identity Theft Protection Act
- **S. 1789:** Personal Data Privacy and Security Act
- **H.R. 1069:** Notification of Risk to Personal Data Act
- **H.R. 1080:** Information Protection and Security Act
- **H.R. 3140:** Consumer Data Security and Notification Act
- **H.R. 3997:** Data Accountability and Trust Act
- **H.R. 4129:** Data Accountability and Trust Act
- **H.R. 5318:** Cyber-Security Enhancement and Consumer Data Protection Act

While all of these bills are dead, the discussion of preemptive federal law continues. The Senate Judiciary Committee of 111th Congress is trying to move forward a cybersecurity bill (the Personal Data Security and Privacy Act of 2009) that includes data breach notification.

The debate continues as to the needs of business versus consumer groups. As business vies for a high threshold for notification due to notification costs time, money, and reputation, consumer groups contend that higher thresholds don't grant enough notice to consumers. Questions of what *should be* with regard to identity theft, privacy, and security remain salient.

POLICY ANALYSIS

We now turn to a discussion of the policy analysis. The discussion is divided into three parts. First we look at the analytic framework used in this chapter, Ostrom's Institutional Analysis and Development (IAD) framework, and its general principles. Then, in a retrospective analysis, we use the model to consider why and how we arrived at the development of the 45 existing data breach laws. The state of information assurance and security is shaped by historical and institutional factors and it behooves us to consider these factors. Finally, we explore the anticipated effects of these laws in a prospective analysis.

IAD Framework

The IAD framework is associated with the social theory of new institutionalism, which grew out of institutionalism. Institutionalism studies formal institutions, such as organizations, norms, laws, and markets. New institutionalism adds to this the study of how institutions operate in a context. In new institutionalism, institutions are abstractly defined as "shared concepts used by humans in repetitive situations organized by rules, norms and strategies" (Ostrom, 1999, p. 37). New institutionalism considers topics such as how individuals and groups construct institutions, how institutions function in practice, how institutions interact and affect each other, the effect that the sociological environment has on these interactions, and the effects of institutions on society. Institutions are both the entities themselves, as well as things (rules, norms, strategies) that shape the patterns of interaction across entities.

Figure 1. Institutional analysis and development framework (adapted from P. Sabatier, 1999).

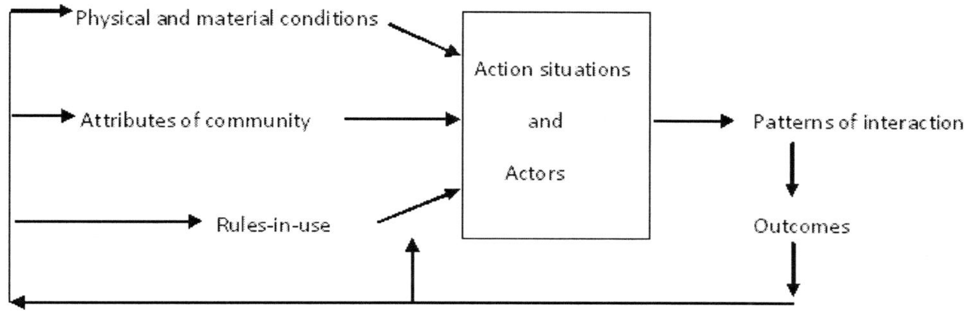

Interestingly, while these rules and norms are powerful, they are largely invisible, which makes identifying and measuring them hard to do (Ostrom, 1999). They can be described, but not precisely. This is relevant as readers will clearly see that this chapter uses qualitative descriptions to depict institutions in action, but we offer no quantitative measures. Readers should also keep in mind that all description of this type, by nature includes connotation, which cannot be avoided. After all, norms exist in us, not apart from us. Therefore, this chapter is subject to the author's bias. It is left to the readers to improve upon this work. It is incumbent on all who are interested in such research to be aware of, and guard against, personal biases where they may limit findings.

We begin discussion of the IAD framework (shown in Figure 1) with the action arena in the middle. The action arena includes the action situations and the actors. In describing the action situation(s), the analyst attempts to identify the relevant structures, i.e., those affecting the process of interest. This can include participants, allowable actions and linkages to outcomes, the level of control participants have over choice, information available to participants, and costs and benefits assigned to actions and outcomes. The analyst also identifies the pertinent actors. Actors are individuals and groups (entities) who take action, i.e., they behave in a manner to which they attach meaning, either subjective or instrumental. Moving to the right in figure 1, the IAD model includes outcomes. Outcomes are observed, inferred, and/or expected behaviors or results.

Action arenas can also be viewed as dependent variables. In this way, the analyst looks at how rules-in-use, attributes of community, and physical/material conditions influence the action arena. Rules-in-use are shared understandings about what is expected, required, and allowed in ordering relationships. Physical/material conditions refer to the characteristics of the states of the world as they shape action arenas. Clearly, what is expected or allowed may be conditioned by what is physically or materially possible. Likewise, rules-in-use might be shaped by physical conditions and vice versa. Attributes of community are nonphysical conditions that provide structure to the community. Attributes of community may or may not be shaped by physical conditions and can serve to influence rules-in-use and the utilization of physical conditions. Using the IAD model, one can also study how outcomes influence physical conditions, attributes of community, and rules-in-use. The IAD model assumes that social systems are continually constituted and reconstituted; in this way, both the systems and the models to analyze them are organic in their worldview.

The IAD model includes four levels of analysis: operational, collective, constitutional, and meta-constitutional. Any of the units (action situation, actors, patterns of interaction, outcomes, rules-in-use, attributes of community, and physical/materials conditions) could be identified at any, some, or all of the four levels of analysis. The analyst can, for example, consider the nested structure of rules within rules, i.e., how do the structures and rules of a constitutional government shape constitutional choice, and then how does that shape collective choice and operational rules and how do these influence the action arena? Or how does the action arena at a collective level interact in such a way as to influence attributes of community at the constitutional level, and what does this suggest for patterns of interaction or outcomes? The power of the model is in its general nature; any one use of the model (including this one) is not likely to include all units of analysis or all levels.

Readers should note that the IAD model does not prescribe how analysis is performed. The arrows are not meant to suggest that the analyst needs to work through the model in full, or from left to right. So, for example, an analyst can work from (1) the action arena to (2) outcomes in an effort to discern or predict patterns of interaction. Another alternative would be to work from (1) observed outcomes to (2) effects thereof on rules-in-use or attributes of community. Or the analyst can work across levels, e.g., investigating how do collective choice rules-in-use such as excludability and the free-rider problem influence what type of operational policy can be enacted? This is the power of this model, which is partly why it was chosen for this analysis.

The IAD model is especially useful for analyzing self-governing entities. The defining characteristic of a self-governing entity is that individuals influence the rules that structure their lives. More specifically, the members (or their representatives) of a self-governing entity participate in the development of the collective-choice and constitutional rules-in-use. Self-governing entities are complex, adaptive systems in that they are comprised of a large number of elements interacting in multiple ways; the interactions change the system, which shapes future interactions such that outcomes are hard to predict, and thus, considered emergent. Self-governing entities are polycentric where citizens organize multiple governing authorities and private arrangements at different scales. A constitutional government is a self-governing entity; the author contends that the Internet is also a self-governing socio-technical entity. Public policy in information assurance and security then is about how a polycentric system governs a polycentric system, which is the second reason why the IAD framework was selected for this research.

Retrospective Analysis

In the retrospective analysis, we consider the rules-in-use, attributes of community, and physical and material conditions that served to shape the policy actions we have seen until now. To date, public policy in information security and privacy in the United States has been largely incremental in nature. We can see from the patchwork of laws discussed earlier in this chapter that we have, thus far, resisted a coordinated, federal law that preempts existing legislation. Incrementalism is common in self-governing, polycentric entities. In policy analysis, incrementalism assumes (1) that the effects of seriality enhance outcomes by reducing uncertainty, and (2) enhanced consideration of context enhances outcomes. That the information age has introduced a number of uncertainties makes incrementalism especially relevant.

Stated more directly, and in connection to the IAD model, one of the rules-in-use is incrementalism. When there is a high degree of uncertainty, policy will be enacted incrementally. Thus, the plethora of laws we have is to be expected. While identity theft is nothing new, the magnitude of identity theft that we have experienced in the past decade is new. The global information infrastructure is in its infancy – we are still learning what people will and will not do in the electronic frontier. The Internet was never designed to serve the myriad of purposes for which it is being used, nor was it designed for billions of users. Through trial and error we are learning how laws that were crafted for the industrial era do, and do not, apply in the information age. We have yet to learn what new laws are needed as a result of information technologies. We have yet to learn how effective these laws will be.

During this period of transition, new communities are being formed and existing communities are being reshaped; as a result, behavioral norms are being renegotiated. Given the global nature of the Internet, it is reasonable to view these communities as more heterogeneous or, at a minimum, heterogeneous in new ways. Therefore, norms probably cannot be easily transported from based on existing communities; they will have to be established from the ground up, which is bound to take time. Additionally, because the technology is still new, scientists and engineers are still determining what actions are physically possible. Talented individuals around the world are working on technologies to help anonymize data, enhance privacy-preserving computation, and provide improved intrusion detection, but this takes time as well. Experience in all of these areas – rules-in-use, attributes of community, and physical/material conditions – will be gained through observation, involvement, and exposure.

Though we don't have much experience, there has been the need to take action. Identity theft is on the rise and citizens are concerned. Two of the core imperatives of the state are domestic order and legitimacy (Dryzek, Downes, Hunold, Schlosberg & Hernes, 2003). Yet, the existing federal and private sector laws are not sufficient to address the rising identity theft problem threatening domestic order, thereby forcing lawmakers to take action to ensure their perceived legitimacy. In response, federal laws have been amended, private sector laws are being tweaked, and a flurry of state laws have been enacted. To what can we attribute the incremental changes we have observed? Why do we have these laws as opposed to something else? To answer these questions, we turn to a discussion of openness and transparency, informational regulation, the infancy of the information industry, and federalism; and we further examine how rules-in-use, attributes of community, and physical/material conditions have intersected in each of these areas to produce the policies we have today.

Openness and Transparency

A democracy is founded on principles of openness and transparency. In 1933, Justice Louis D. Brandeis coined the powerful phrase "sunlight as disinfectant" in support of increasing openness and transparency in public policy. While laws that aim to ensure openness and transparency in government operations existed before 1933, Brandeis is responsible for the term 'Sunshine Laws'. The impetus behind sunshine laws is twofold. First, a thriving, open democracy depends on open access and citizen participation, thus the right-to-know is a constitutional and inherent right of American citizens. Second, a government that is of the people, for the people, and by the people asserts government subservience to the individual, which predicates freedom of information.

The Freedom of Information Act (FOIA), signed into law on July 4, 1966 by President Lyndon B. Johnson, is a sunshine law. FOIA allows for the full or partial disclosure of previously unreleased information and documents controlled by the United States government. The concept of "freedom of information" conveys a philosophy that values the advantages of increasing our ability to gather and send information, and clearly does not connote privacy as a positive right. This acts as a rule-in-use.

The Privacy Act of 1974 arrived eight years later as an amendment to the FOIA in response to Watergate and the abuse of privacy during the Nixon administration. The Privacy Act of 1974 was passed not to promote privacy, but to establish a code of fair information practice. It was also an attempt to limit the powers of government and was passed hastily during the final week of the 93rd Congress, which was in session from 1973-74. According to the U.S. Department of Justice,

no conference committee was convened to reconcile differences in the bills passed by the House and Senate. Instead, staffs of the respective committees—led by Senators Ervin and Percy, and Congressmen Moorhead and Erlenborn—prepared a final version of the bill that was ultimately enacted...the Act's imprecise language, limited legislative history, and somewhat outdated regulatory guidelines have rendered it a difficult statute to decipher and apply. (U.S. Department of Justice, 2008).

Moreover, even after more than twenty-five years of administrative and judicial analysis, numerous Privacy Act issues remain unresolved or unexplored. Adding to these interpretational difficulties is the fact that many Privacy Act cases are unpublished district court decisions.

This offers important insight into the historical context with regard to how information and privacy are embedded in the past and offers food for thought on how this norm has shaped our ongoing collective treatment of it coming forward. Through the enactment of FOIA in 1966, we see the push to enable information sharing as a result of mistrust in government. Eight years later we see The Privacy Act, which is reactive in nature and also reflective of distrust of government. Through these pieces of legislation we find two noteworthy threads. First is the value of freedom of information, wherein information belongs to and exists for the advancement of citizens and the common good. This is coupled with an interesting distrust of government powers, wherein stewardship cannot be entrusted to the polity. Privacy in the Privacy Act is not a positive right, but rather is a necessary provision subservient to limiting government powers.

Earlier it was noted that HIPAA was passed to enable job mobility and GLBA was passed to modernize the financial services industry. Again, we see in the context of these laws that privacy is secondary to another purpose. In HIPAA and GLBA, privacy is cast as a means to an end; in other words, privacy plays a functional or instrumental role. We need privacy because we need job mobility; we need privacy because we need to modernize financial services. Implicit is the message that if we did not need job mobility or financial services modernization, we would not need to concern ourselves with privacy. Even though privacy was cast as a functional need in both HIPAA and GLBA, the similarity ends there. These industry sectors have significantly different regulatory frameworks (Congressional Research Service, 2008). What we see in the security and privacy provisions in these laws is more reflective of the larger regulatory framework for these industries. The regulatory framework for these industries served as additional rules-in-use, shaping these laws.

Informational Regulation

Another phenomenon that is essential to understanding the U.S. data breach laws is informational regulation. Informational regulation has become a striking development in American law (Sunstein, 2006). To date, informational regulation has been applied in the environmental and health policy arenas. The fact that informational regulation has been applied to environmental and health policy is noteworthy. In the case of environmental policy, informational regulations has been used to protect aspects of the environment that are *common (or public) good* in nature, which by definition means that the private sector will not attend to them. A similar situation occurs in public health where the health of all citizens is both good for the individual as well as for the collective as a means and an end, i.e., it is a common or public good.

Informational regulation has two functions. First, it serves to inform people of potential risk exposure (Volokh, 2002) and serves as "sunlight", which we already discussed as the value of transparency. Second, it aims to change the behavior of risk creators (Volokh, 2002) and aims to exert pressure on entities to care for the common good. Informational regulation is useful in a polycentric policy arena where the problems that the policy is meant to address are attributable to multiple sources, the solutions require participation from multiple parties, and the nature of problems and solutions is dynamic; all of which necessitate that the policy must allow for adaptability. Clearly caring for the environment or health are polycentric policy areas. Environmental and health problems stem from multiple sources and ameliorating these types of problems takes ongoing involvement from multiple parties. The same is true for data security, identity protection, and privacy. Improved data security is possible only under conditions that shape the practices of numerous individuals and covered entities; therefore, policy that provides incentives for such change is, in theory, necessary. How does informational regulation work in practice?

Figure 2 shows the mechanistic view of informational regulation for data breach. We start with consumers. Informational regulation intends to provide warning information to consumers. In theory, by enhancing the knowledge level, consumers can perform a personalized risk assessment and make purchase decisions based on that assessment. The market decisions made by consumers intend to drive the less secure entities out of the market, thereby improving the state of security overtime. In addition, the enhanced knowledge levels will propel consumers to engage in other protective actions, such as active credit monitoring or a credit freeze. Consumer credit monitoring typically includes alerting the bank and credit card merchant, notifying the FTC, and/or contacting law enforcement. A credit freeze allows the consumer to lock their consumer credit report and scores. Once a consumer has locked their credit information, the lender or merchant cannot access it, which significantly lowers the likelihood that the merchant will issue credit. The benefit is that the thief is not likely to get credit in the consumers' name (so the law prevents a false positive, also called a Type II error). The downside is that this also impedes consumers from quickly getting credit in their name (a false negative or Type I error); note, that consumers can release the freeze, but it takes a few days and may jeopardize quick access to special loans and other purchase incentives. These proactive consumer measures will in theory also lead to improved security over time.

Informational regulation also aims to change the actions of producers. By engaging producers in providing information, informational regulation, in theory, reveals an entity's practices. This sends a signal to society that perhaps this entity cannot be trusted. The premise is that covered entities value their reputation. As such, they will act to improve their security in order to preserve their reputation and minimize associated costs, which could include the costs of the notification itself, as well as downtime costs, costs of remediation and recovery due to the breach, and the costs of lost business. Ideally, these two streams combine to improve data security, which in turn mitigates identity theft and enhanced privacy.

The premise of informational regulation is that (1) market mechanisms can be used to shape risk behavior, thereby reducing the need for command-and-control regulation, and (2) it enhances democratic processes and promotes individual autonomy. By providing data breach information to victims, individuals are empowered to make decisions based on quality (i.e., they can elect to purchase goods/services from a provider who offers enhanced information security and privacy), and market mechanisms will be fortified. A failure to provide complete and accurate market informa-

Figure 2. Informational regulation premise for data breach disclosure laws

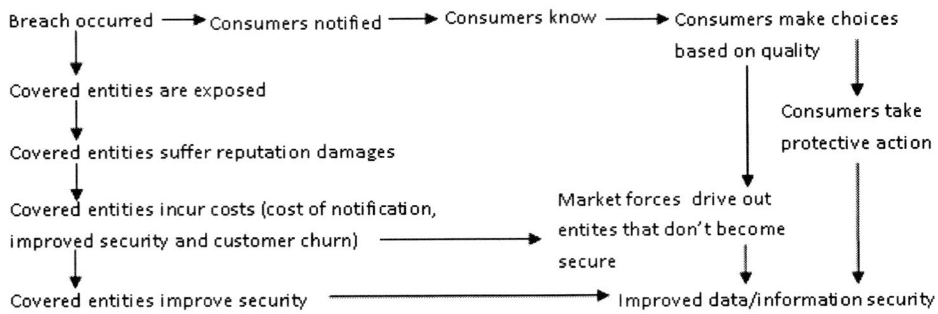

tion can impede the efficient allocation of goods and services and result in market failure, which is the driver for changing producers' behavior.

In theory, informational regulation allows more public monitoring of decisions, a norm already discussed. By forcing disclosure, more people are informed; and by informing more people, the quality and the quantity of public deliberation will improve, thereby enhancing the democratic processes that are vital for openness and transparency. In general, information disclosure rests on the normative belief that citizens have a right to know the risks to which they are exposed. This information promotes choice and autonomy, both of which are foundational to what some may consider the penultimate norm in American society: liberty (Renshaw, 2002).

In contrast to command-and-control regulation where the government sets and enforces standards, informational regulation is often less expensive. In the United States, we value efficient government and recent decades have seen an increased emphasis on downsizing the federal government. While it is not clear that command and control legislation would be effective in mitigating data breaches or in making data breach disclosure more effective, it is clear that a command and control approach is not politically efficacious at this point in time.

In summary, informational regulation has grown in areas where consumer protection, private sector practices, and risk converge. Examples include warning labels regarding mercury levels, nutrition labels disclosing fat contents, and notifications about the side effects of a given medication. That data security shares these same material features – consumer protection, private sector practices, and risk – has clearly contributed to adopting informational regulation as the model for data breach disclosure laws.

Infancy of the Information Industry and Federalism

Here we pick up a thread that was started earlier, namely our relative inexperience with the information age, and add a few contours. The information industry includes (1) industries that buy and sell information as a good or service, (2) certain service sectors that are especially information intensive, such as banking and legal services, (3) information dissemination sectors, such as telecommunications and broadcasting, and (4) producers of information processing devices, such as computers and software. The information industry is seen as a boon to the economy as information amplifies growth in more traditional industry sectors and the demand for information goods and services increases markedly. Because of this ends and means nature of information goods and services, the market is quite large and still emerging.

An example of emergence is the following relatively recent cascade of events: the Internet explosion; September 11, 2001; and the subsequent war on terror. These events converged to boost the data brokerage industry. Data brokerages are companies that collect and sell billions of private and public records containing individuals' personal information. Many of these companies also provide products and services, including identity verification, background screening, risk assessments, individual digital dossiers, and tools for analyzing data. Most data brokers sell data that they collect from public records (e.g., driver's license records, vehicle registration records, criminal records, voter registration records, property records, and occupational licensing records) or from warranty cards, credit applications, etc. In addition, data brokers purchase so-called "credit headers" from credit reporting agencies. Information on a credit header generally includes a person's Social Security number, address, phone numbers, and birth date (Congressional Research Service, 2007). Although some of the products and services provided by data brokers are currently subject to privacy and security protections aimed at credit reporting agencies and the financial industry under the Fair Credit Reporting Act (1971) and Gramm-Leach-Bliley Act (1999), many are not. Because the industry is relatively young, there is no history of oversight or self-regulation of the industry's practices, including the accuracy and handling of sensitive data, by an industry-sanctioned body.

Data brokerages are not the only unregulated entities. There are many other organizations that process, store, and transmit personal information: state and local agencies, public hospitals, departments of revenue and motor vehicles, courts at the state and local level, agencies that oversee elections, K-12 schools, school districts, post-secondary institutions, and business entities engaging in inter- and intrastate commerce. Most of these entities are not covered by HIPAA and GLBA (Congressional Budget Office, 2006) and have traditionally been governed through state law; hence the 45 state data breach laws discussed earlier. The suite of laws we have is in part a result of our lack of experience with information markets and partly a function of our need for legislation that spans the numerous and varied types of entities that process, store, and transmit personal information. A broad and amorphous social challenge such as information security and privacy is not only diffuse, it is emergent. Research has shown that in cases of open-access, common good resources (such as security and privacy), collective choice action arenas, i.e., those that improve opportunities for communication and public deliberation, result in better joint outcomes (Ostrom, 1999). The patchwork of data breach laws we have fit this profile – they aim to increase the communication and public deliberation.

In a federalist system, such as the United States, sovereignty is constitutionally divided between the federal government and the constituent states. The powers granted to the federal government in the United States are limited to the right to levy taxes, declare war, and regulate interstate and foreign commerce. The powers traditionally reserved by the states include public safety, public education, public health, transportation, and infrastructure. Of course, information security and privacy challenges permeate these state governed organizations too. While a federal, preemptive law might span all organizations and individuals, there is the possibility that it would erode state sovereignty and in the process alter the federal-state balance of power in unprecedented ways. The patchwork suite of laws we have can be partially attributed to a collective belief that this would be wrong.

In summary, this retrospective analysis provides nuanced insight into the present. Federal laws were enacted to delimit government powers and privacy was seen as necessary for that. Private industry sector laws were passed to innovate the private sector, and data security and privacy were included as functional means to that end. These federal and private sector laws reflect a general cultural norm in the United States of distrusting government while trusting in the private sector and market forces. Informational regulation was established as a form of legislation considered effective for issues that spanned consumer protection and risk, and where market mechanisms would/could work effectively, which is further evidence of pervasive trust in the private sector. Social and economic factors coupled with technological advancements are changing the landscape considerably. The problem is highly polycentric and emergent, and these conditions favor polycentric and incremental policy approaches. The resulting set of data breach laws put data security into the hands of citizens and organizations. In a society pillared by equity and freedom as ideals, and where there is no constitutional provision for privacy, the constant for deliberating the common good is through an open and representative process. This myriad of data security laws aims to serve the purpose of making explicit these individual preferences in a manner that allows all to translate these preferences into collective choice – the future of data security is contingent on us all.

Prospective Analysis

Because the data breach disclosure laws are so new, many of the interactions and outcomes are yet to be realized. Hence, this discussion is prospective in nature. First, we explore alternative policy configurations as a type of outcome. Then, we consider possible interactions and outcomes if these laws remain as they are today.

Alternative Policy Configurations

Alternative policies are not policy outcomes in the truest sense. Public policies don't intend to make more public policy. Rather, public policies intend to ameliorate a social problem or advance a social good. However, policy modifications frequently are the intermediate (incremental) outcome of policy making, especially in nascent issue areas embedded in self-governing action arenas. And so it is here that we begin.

The policy alternatives being considered vary according to how problems with the current policies are perceived. Embedded, either implicitly or explicitly, in the different criticisms are expectations for what outcomes the data breach disclosure policies aim to achieve and how. For sake of simplicity, the alternatives can be classified into two categories: (1) variations of existing laws using incremental approaches to 'fine-tune' the efficacy of the laws, and (2) introduce new laws, which could include comprehensive and preemptive federal legislation that is regulatory in nature and/or the application of tort liability to redress problems of negligent security. Some proposed alternatives are hybrid in that they include tweaking existing laws as well as the introduction of preemptive federal legislation with the caveat that when a state or industry sector law has higher requirements than the federal legislation, it shall prevail.

The first proposed alternative assumes that the premise of current laws is, for the most part, sound, but suggests that there are some minor flaws. However, there is considerable disagreement regarding how the existing laws are flawed. Some critics note that the outcome of data breach disclosure should be to motivate large-scale reporting so that data breaches and trends can be aggregated, which allows a more purposeful and defensive use of incident data. Those who advocate for large-scale data collection view the existing laws as "disclosure disincentives". This stems from two sources. First, breached entities view themselves as victims of attack and not deserving of reputational repercussions. Second, existing laws offer covered entities considerable discretion as to whether to disclose. Together, these factors result in underreporting of data breaches, which in turn constrains large-scale data collection regarding breaches.

The proposed policy solution is to modify the laws to make breach notification completely anonymous where breached entities report to an intermediary and not to consumers. Advocates of this approach contend that disclosing the locus of the breach to consumers is practically worthless; because consumers at this time generally either cannot, or choose not to, use this information for discriminatory purchasing, which is a premise of the legislation. Another benefit cited by advocates of anonymous disclosure is that it removes the requirement to postpone disclosure until law enforcement assures it will not conflict with an investigation, which enhances timely response to the breach. In summary, the net outcome gain of this alternative is viewed as increased and timelier disclosure. While advocates of this approach purport that we do not lose anything with this approach, for those who agree that data security is a polycentric problem needing polycentric solutions, omitting the consumer from participation may be viewed as undesirable at best and opaque and unparticipatory at worst.

The second incremental alternative is a coordinated response architecture, also called CRA (Schwartz and Janger, 2007). Advocates of this alternative agree that large-scale data collection on data breaches is needed, but contend that consumer notification needs to be amended, not eliminated. Their main concerns with the existing consumer notification practices are that (1) there are too many notifications, leading to consumer desensitization and (2) the information provided to consumers is unhelpful at best and befuddling at worst. In response, this group advocates for amendments to the data breach laws to include a CRA. The CRA is an intermediary agency with responsibility for (1) supervised delegation of the decision whether to give notice, (2) coordination and targeting of notices to other institutions and to customers, and (3) tailoring of notice content. Regarding notification to consumers, this policy alternative calls for a bifurcated notification scheme that includes notification to consumers based upon a *reasonable likelihood of harm or risk* and notification to the intermediary based upon a *reasonable likelihood of unauthorized access*. Under this policy alternative, the threshold for notification to the intermediary would be lower than the threshold for notification to the consumer; therefore breach information will be provided to the central intermediary while at the same time mitigating the concern of over-notification to consumers. The third policy change is that the CRA will play a role in mandating the inclusion (e.g., specific steps to take to place a credit freeze) or omission (e.g., marketing of security services that the breached entity is selling) of certain content in notification letters, so as to minimize consumer confusion and cynicism. Because the intermediary could potentially have tomes of personally identifiable information making it an attractive target, the policy would also call for establishment and implementation of data minimization principles for the CRA. Last, a recommended policy change would provide incentives for disclosure by offering companies a chance to avoid consumer notice through early reporting and cooperation, and a disincentive through a statutory fine of $500 for each failure to notify.

In contrast to tweaking existing laws, new laws are still being debated. For example, the discussion of a preemptive and uniform federal data security law continues. Proponents of this approach say that omnibus legislation provides for greater certainty in courts, reduces confusion and cost for entities that need to comply, and could provide for enhanced enforcement through private right to action. The difficulty in the uniform preemptive federal law is what it should include. Companies like the risk-based provision for notification, which reduces the burden on them, while consumer groups prefer the acquisition-based approach. Some companies, especially the smaller ones, prefer fewer information security requirements because they are costly and therefore more onerous for the smaller entities to incur. Small business advocates weigh in by noting that hefty information security requirements could be so costly as to disadvantage small companies from entering the market. Larger companies are generally less concerned with the information security requirements and more concerned with how to control for reputational damages from a massive data breach. Generally speaking, companies prefer less enforcement, while consumer groups advocate for more enforcement to include private action. The ultimate question for the policy makers is which action(s) to target given that no one law can strive toward them all.

Given that government regulations may not be enough, another alternative is tort liability. The reasoning is that applying common law rules to redress problems of negligent information security will motivate businesses to enact better policies and procedures, and comply with industry standards in a more effective manner than a one-size-fits-all government regulation could (Picanso, 2006). While not insurmountable, the following challenges would need to be addressed in order for tort law to protect personal data: determination of whether such a duty exists, defining a standard of care (no small feat given that emergent nature of security vulnerabilities), and accounting for intervening acts of third parties that would break the chain of causation.

Others support a mix and match set of alternatives. One example is a preemptive federal law in conjunction with tort laws and existing state laws, where the scope of preemption is fairly narrow. The justification is that such a policy mix would allow greater stringency, and therein sovereignty, in state laws as desired by states, but provide for certain requirements in a federal law in areas that are considered crucial to improving security. A few of the suggested requirements for a federal law are as follows. A federal law should specify an encryption standard and allow an exemption from disclosure when breached data are encrypted and standard compliant. According to advocates, this would entice more companies to use encryption and deter companies from purchasing inexpensive, ineffective encryption just for the sake of compliance. A federal law should mandate that all thresholds for disclosure be based on risk as opposed to acquisition, which would reduce over-notification and consequent desensitization.

Each of the alternatives offers a critique of the existing suite of laws. Each critique is grounded in a premise of what outcomes matter and each alternative offers a view on how policy can/should target actions in pursuit of these outcomes. However, another option is to make no policy change at this juncture. Here we turn to a discussion of anticipated interactions and outcomes of existing laws.

Interactions and Outcomes of Existing Data Breach Disclosure Laws

As previously mentioned, the IAD framework includes four nested levels of analysis: operational, collective, constitutional, and metaconstituional. Policy analysis at the operational level considers rules that affect day-to-day decisions made by participants. Policy processes at the operational level address issues of appropriation, provision, monitoring, and enforcement. The policy alternatives discussed above are at the operational level; for example, inserting an intermediary to allow large-scale collection of data breach information and trends to enhance monitoring. The collective-choice level is where decision-makers create rules to impact operational level activities and outcomes. Policy processes at the collective-choice level focus on policy-making and management. For, example, a group of farmers changing the way they share a water resource for irrigating their crops is a collective choice. The utilization of market forces for data breach and information security was a collective choice. The constitutional level includes rules to be used in crafting the set of collective-choice rules that in turn affect the set of operational rules. Policy processes at the constitutional level focus on policy formulation, governance, adjudication, and modification. For example, voting rules that specify how collective-choice members will be selected. The metaconstitutional level includes basic principles from which constitutional situations derive and affect all of the other levels. The metaconstitutional outcomes affect constitutional decision-making, which, in turn, shapes collective-choice decision-making, which, in turn, shapes operational decision-making. Here we consider possible interactions and outcomes of the existing data breach disclosure laws, first at the collective-choice level and then at the constitutional level.

Collective-Choice

The overriding collective-choice premise of the data breach disclosure laws is the use of market forces to stem the tide of data breach, which has implications for identity theft, information security, and privacy. Therefore, the significant question is whether informational regulation is the right model for regulation for this problem space. Will market forces work effectively or will citizens perceive that covered entities are victims too, and in that regard choose to not punish them by purchasing elsewhere? The dependencies presented in Figure 2 make many assumptions. The data breach laws assume that: consumers are notified, become knowledge and then take action; covered entities are exposed, suffer reputational loss, and incur costs, which motivate them to invest in information security; market forces drive entities that don't improve security out of the market; and the combined forces raise the tide of security. And as a result identity theft is mitigated and privacy improved. Is this the case?

As we know, policy in polycentric problem arenas is meant to address how multiple sources contribute to a dynamic problem. Thus, policy solutions require participation from multiple parties and must allow for adaptability. What do we know about the polycentric problem space? Data breach notification and data security are not the same thing. Data security and privacy are not the same thing. Privacy and identity theft are not the same thing. Identity theft and data breach are not the same thing. However, together they appear to constellate a polycentric problem arena.

While the premise that data breach is correlated to identity theft is plausible, a 2009 report by the American National Standards Institute (ANSI, 2009) looked at 166 studies investigating identity theft, data breach, identity theft protection, and information security. The ANSI report found several notable gaps in research. The research gaps range as follows: a lack of empirical research correlating data breach and identity theft; a lack of research investigating data traders' activities to consumers victimized by identity theft; a lack of studies on the efficacy of existing laws; and a lack of studies investigating whether and how information security solutions prevent identity theft. We need to know more about the relationship between data breach and identity theft if we want to evaluate data breach laws by their ability to reduce identity theft. If, on the other hand, there is little relationship between the data breach and identity theft, then it is not useful to evaluate the laws according to their impact on identity theft. If on the other hand there is a notable relationship, yet the laws do not seem to be mitigating identity theft, then we can be more certain that the laws are ineffective. The data breach disclosure laws assume that through the use of market forces the state of security will ultimately improve. The recent ANSI (2009) report notes that, as of now, there is no empirical basis to suggest the effectiveness of information security solutions correlate to identity theft and data breach. Again, knowing more about the interrelationships of the problem can inform policy analysis and future policy making.

Addressing questions such as these, however, is not easy. There are some existing studies that we can use. For example, the Javelin Strategy and Research Identity Fraud Survey Report (2008) includes measures such as consumer trust, intention to purchase in the future, and consumer credit monitoring. The Ponemon Institute study (2008) includes measures such as total cost, cost in different categories (e.g., cost of notification, cost of lost business, and cost by breach type). The concern is that while such sources exist, differences in terminology and research methodology have led to contradictory results. In response, a new cross-sectoral initiative called the Identity Management Standards Panel (IDSP) has been formed, the purpose of which is to reconcile disparities and create voluntary standards and guidelines, so that in the future we are better able to assess how well the marketplace is doing controlling identity crimes (American National Standards Institute, 2009). Progress in this regard is positive.

As we progress, a number of questions may be useful as we attempt to answer whether the marketplace is useful for fortifying information security and privacy and combating data breach and identity crimes. The data breach laws provide for notification exceptions, e.g., the notification thresholds and the fact that 50% of the laws do not pertain to covered entities that maintain data (both of which were discussed earlier). Therefore, the set of consumers who are notified is a subset of consumers whose data were breached. What is the size of this subset and what is the significance relative to utilizing a consumer market to drive change? The model assumes that once consumers are notified, they will be knowledgeable and this knowledge will lead to consumption choices based on quality. This assumes that consumers have complete information, can utilize this information effectively, and have well-ordered preferences. How complete is the information provided to consumers? What are the knowledge gain and the sufficiency of this knowledge gain? It is not clear that consumers have well-ordered preferences for data security over, for example, convenience and necessity. A citizen may receive notification from a retail store that his data were breached in a recent attack. However, the individual may value shopping at the store for its low prices and proximity more than it values changing retailers. Parents may receive notification that their child's school health records were breached. Clearly they cannot make a decision to "purchase schooling elsewhere". To what degree do citizens have well-ordered preferences? Can they, and do they, order their preferences thereby catalyzing market forces? Why or why not?

The data breach laws apply to a wide variety of covered entities, some of which are not in the private sector. How will the utilization of market forces to stimulate change impact entities such as local election boards, K-12 schools, non-profits and universities? What proportion of total data breaches occur in these types of covered entities? Can these types of entities find resources to invest in upgrading their information security? What repercussions are there if they do not upgrade their security?

Addressing collective action problems can be time consuming and costly. Given the dependencies, in order for collective choice problems to be meaningfully addressed, it is usually necessary to have a parallel effort to adapt constitutional institutions (Ostrom, Gardner, & Walker, 1994). We turn next to consider of interactions and outcomes at the constitutional level. Readers may wonder why this level not discussed first, given that it shapes the collective-choice and operational level interactions and outcomes. The reason is that this level is the most abstract. Often abstract ideas makes the most sense when viewed in relation to the more concrete as it is in the more concrete that the implications of the abstract become manifest and perceivable.

Constitutional

The United State is rooted in principles of democratic social order, distributed power, and active citizen participation. The citizens influence the rules that structure their lives and in this way the United States can be considered self-governing. A self-governing entity is one whose members participate in the development of many of the constitutional or collective-choice rules as they are expected to accept the legitimacy and appropriateness of these rules (Ostrom, 1990). Self-governing entities are complex, adaptive systems comprised of a large number of elements that interact in multiple ways, adapt in response to interaction, and emerge in sometimes unpredictable ways.

So far we talked about changes such as improving data breach laws to achieve outcomes such as reduction of consumer desensitization, large scale collection information about of data breaches, timely collection of data about breach incidents, and security for large companies, while exempting small entities. That all of these outcomes are of practical importance and worthy of deliberation seems undisputable. But it is the view of this author that privacy, security, identity theft, and data breaches disclosure are inherently good only in relation to citizens' lives and livelihood. The Internet is a complex socio-technical system with multiple actors, countless interactions, and myriad effects, many of which will never be truly "knowable". It seems doubtful that we will be able to "govern" the Internet and information systems. Still, that we need some form of governance that aims toward collective interests and common good is obvious. So we may ask ourselves questions about self-governance. How should we engage citizens in the constitution and reconstitution of establishing collective-choice and operational rules in this arena? How can we engage the myriad of organizations (covered entities) that own, license, or maintain computerized data?

Social issues we seek to improve range from efficient and effective healthcare to financial reform, privacy, and national security. Information pervades them all. It is here that we clearly see the tensions as we attempt to reconcile multiple competing interests. Information is the raw material of knowledge. Knowing enables national security. Knowing enables economic growth. Knowing can improve healthcare. Knowing is foundational to social welfare and domestic law and order. In this regard, information is "sunlight". In a society founded on principles of distributed power and active citizen participation, government accountability is paramount. Public officials in such systems are accountable for how their decisions are made and in whose interests. In order to achieve accountability, the preferences of citizens have to be available to decision makers. Seen in this light, the data breach disclosure laws may not be about using market forces to force covered entities to enhance their security. Instead, these laws are a mechanism for us to make our preferences regarding the myriad uses of information as ends and means more apparent to decision-makers. The data breach laws are an opportunity to raise our collective conscience about data breach, data security, information security, identity theft, and privacy so that we may use our human insight, reason, and vigilance to transform our structures in a way that: preserves self-governance first and foremost; advances the state of information security and privacy in support of other social goods like improved healthcare, economic growth, and national security; and contributes to a better understanding of the changing and elusive role of privacy in our lives.

In 2006, Bonner (p. 21) noted, "a sharp divide has been inserted between the potential meanings of privacy and its actual meaning in practice. Its potential has been left behind". Is privacy something more than an aggregation of other types of rights, e.g. property rights and trespass? Do we need privacy for reasons other than job mobility, improved healthcare, and restricting government power? Is privacy inextricably linked to other desirable human conditions such as human dignity, intimacy, social relationships, and personhood? How much do we value these conditions? How do we value these relative to improved healthcare, national security, economic growth, etc? Perhaps we should evaluate the outcomes of the data breach disclosure laws in regard to helping us more clearly see the costs and benefits of the freedom of information.

Recently the author was discussing privacy with a colleague where the statement was made that "privacy is dead". The logical malleability

(Moor, 1985) of the computer enables a market of one – entities can and do offer personalized goods and services based on our individual preferences. As consumers, we seem to like this. For all intents and purposes, privacy, as we knew it, is dead. Privacy today is based on the principle of one. My privacy will be different from yours. There is no given level of privacy that each of us should expect; instead the amount of privacy each of us has is what we claim for ourselves in short bursts of time. Privacy is a series of micro-states subject to rapid change, so that privacy is something that we have to continuously reclaim. Getting a populous to recognize this and continually practice it is a notable scaling up problem. Perhaps we should evaluate the outcomes of the data breach disclosure laws with regard to their impact on changing our collective conscience regarding this.

Finally, if principles of openness and transparency are vital for self-governance, should we even have an expectation of privacy, regardless of its merit for personhood? Is there an inherent contradiction? Ostrom notes that self-governance is always only a possibility and not a given (1990). Self-governance relies on a common understanding of the physical world we face and the trust and reciprocity of participants backed by their own willingness to monitor and enforce interpersonal commitments. Self-organization relies on smaller enclave to be productive in monitoring and enforcing. If, in the long run, the data breach disclosure laws amplify citizen participation in reconstitution of the macrostructure in a manner that support and encourages this self-organization, then they will have been highly effective.

In these more open, less-constrained situations, analysis is difficult. Interrelationships among institutions such as markets, legal systems, and social norms are highly complex and the effects are often unknowable. However, given the stakes, evaluation of the effect of the data breach disclosure laws on amplifying citizen participation and implications for self-governance seems to be the ultimate measure of the success of these policies.

CONCLUSION AND FUTURE RESEARCH

Information assurance and security is inherently normative, dealing with complex social and ethical issues such as data breach, identity theft, privacy, access, and ownership. Information assurance and security questions such as "How secure is *secure enough*?", "What *ought* this system do in order to preserve privacy?" and "To whom *should* access be granted?" are more than technical questions – necessitating that IAS professionals consider how technological, sociological, ideological, and ecological systems interrelate. We are becoming more organically interdependent on technology. As technology becomes more intimately a part of us, deliberation of the social control of technology grows in importance. If citizens are to influence their own future, they must know enough about technology to fulfill their role as citizens; they must be in a position to speak from knowledge because speaking from ignorance is a position of subservience; subservient individuals can never expect to control their own destiny (DeVore, 1984). Participatory control of this participatory technology is necessary. Therefore, IAS professionals need to work meaningfully toward educating users on the limitations of information technology systems and the complexities of this powerful, potentially benevolent, yet imperfect technology.

While individuals comprise the collective, the sum total of individual decisions is not necessarily the equivalent of a social decision. Information assurance and security professionals need to be aware of "social goals", how they are formed, and how social systems and human purpose are arrived at through the collective involvement of all citizens. And, this understanding needs to be brought to bear on the design, development, and control of technical systems. It was the intent of this chapter to analyze the policy landscape so that IAS students have a better understanding of the social context of information availability, information security, identity theft, data breach, and privacy. Enlightenment and knowledge regarding technology, society, and the relationship thereof to self-determination and self-governance is more important than ever before.

REFERENCES

American National Standards Institute (ANSI). (2009). *IDSP workshop report: Measuring identity theft.* Available at: http://webstore.ansi.org/identitytheft/

Bonner, B. (2006). The difficulty in establishing privacy rights in the face of public policy from nowhere. Saskatchewan Institute of Public Policy, *SIPP Public Policy Paper Number 43*. Retrieved from http://www.uregina.ca/sipp/documents/pdf/PPP%2043%20-%20Bonner.pdf

Congressional Budget Office. (2006). *CBO S. 1789 Personal data privacy and security act of 2005 cost estimate.* Retrieved July 20, 2009 from http://www.cbo.gov/doc.cfm?index=7161

Congressional Research Service. (2007). Data brokers: Background and industry overview. *CRS Report for Congress RS22137-070112*. Retrieved June 15, 2009 from http://opencrs.com/

Congressional Research Service. (2008). Federal information security and data breach notification laws. *CRS Report for Congress RS33199.* Retrieved June 15, 2009 from http://opencrs.com/

DeVore, P. (1984). *Technology: An introduction.* Worcester, MA: Davis Publication.

Dryzek, J., Downes, D., Hunold, C., Schlosberg, D., & Hernes, H. (2003). *Green states and social movements*. Oxford University Press. doi:10.1093/0199249024.001.0001

Electronic Privacy Information Center (EPIC). (2008). *The Graham-Leach-Bliley act.* Retrieved May 30, 2009 from http://epic.org/privacy/glba/

Fair Credit Reporting Act, at 15 U.S.C. § 1681 (1971).

Federal Trade Commission Act, 15 U.S.C. § 41-58 (1914).

GovTrack.us. Retrieved http://www.govtrack.us/congress/bill

Health Insurance Portability and Accountability Act, 42 U.S.C. § 1320 (1996).

Hinde, S. (2003). Privacy legislation: a comparison of the US and European approaches. *Computers & Security*, *22*(5), 378–387. doi:10.1016/S0167-4048(03)00503-0

Identity Theft Resource Center. (2008). Retrieved May 25, 2009 from www.idtheftcenter.org

Javelin Research. (2006). *Identity fraud survey report: 2006.* Javelin Strategy & Research. Retrieved May 8, 2009 from http://www.javelinstrategy.com/products/99DEBA/27/delivery.pdf

Javelin Research. (2007). *Identity fraud survey report: 2007.* Javelin Strategy & Research. Retrieved May 8, 2009 from http://www.javelinstrategy.com/uploads/701.R_2007IdentityFraudSurveyReport_Brochure.pdf

Javelin Research. (2008). *Identity fraud survey report: 2008.* Javelin Strategy & Research. Retrieved May 8, 2009 from http://www.idsafety.net/803.R_2008%20Identity%20Fraud%20Survey%20Report_Consumer%20Version.pdf

Lenard, T., & Rubin, P. (2005). An economic analysis of notification requirements for data security breaches. *Emory Law and Economics Research Paper No. 05-12*. Available at SSRN: http://ssrn.com/abstract=765845

Moor, J. (1985). What is computer ethics? *Metaphilosophy*, *16*(4), 266–275. doi:10.1111/j.1467-9973.1985.tb00173.x

Ostrom, E. (1990). *Governing the commons: The evolution of institutions for collective action*. New York: Cambridge University Press.

Ostrom, E. (1999). Institutional rational choice. An assessment of the institutional analysis and development framework. In Sabatier, P. (Ed.), *Theories of the policy process* (pp. 35–67). Boulder, CO: Westview Press.

Ostrom, E., Gardner, R., & Walker, J. (1994). *Rules, games, and common pool resources*. Ann Arbor, MI: The University of Michigan Press.

Personal Data Security and Privacy Act of 2009, S. 1490, 111th Congress (2009).

Picanso, K. (2006). Protecting information security under a uniform data breach notification law. *75. Fordham Law Review*, 355.

Ponemon Institute. (2008). *Consumers' report card on data breach notification*. Ponemon Institute Research Report. Retrieved May 15, 2009 from http://www.ponemon.org/local/upload/fckjail/generalcontent/18/file/Consumer%20Report%20Card%20Data%20Breach%20Noti%20Apr08.pdf

Ponemon Institute. (2008). *Fourth annual US cost of data breach study*. Ponemon Institute Research Report. Retrieved May 15, 2009 from http://www.ponemon.org/local/upload/fckjail/generalcontent/18/file/2008-2009%20US%20Cost%20of%20Data%20Breach%20Report%20Final.pdf

Privacy Rights Clearinghouse. (2008). *A chronology of data breaches*. Retrieved May 1, 2009 from http://www.privacyrights.org/ar/ChronDataBreaches.htm#1

Renshaw, K. (2002). Sounding alarms: Does informational regulation help or hinder environmentalism? *Environmental Law (Northwestern School of Law)*, *14*(3), 654–697.

Schoeman, F. (Ed.). (1984). *Philosophical dimensions of privacy: An anthology*. Cambridge, MA: Cambridge University Press. doi:10.1017/CBO9780511625138

Schwarz, P., & Janger, E. (2007). Notification of data breaches. *Michigan Law Review*, *105*, 913.

Sunstein, C. (1999). Informational regulation and information standing: Atkins and beyond. *University of Pennsylvania Law Review*, *147*(3), 613–675. doi:10.2307/3312719

U.S. Department of Justice. (2008). Available at: http://www.usdoj.gov/oip/04_7_1.html

Veterans Affairs Information Security Act, 38 U.S.C. § 5722 (2006).

Volokh, A. (2002). The pitfalls of the environmental right-to-know, *2002. Utah Law Review*, 805–841.

Westin, A. (1967). *Privacy and freedom*. New York: Atheneum.

ENDNOTES

1 The U.S. Virgin Islands, Puerto Rico and the District of Columbia have also enacted data breach disclosure laws.

2 It should be noted that in many reported breaches, the number of records breached is unknown. Thus the actual number is undisputedly higher.

3 Elinor Ostrom, an American Political Scientist, was awarded the Nobel Memorial Prize in Economic Science in 2009. She shares the award with Oliver Williamson.

4 This chapter provides a brief description of the Institutional Analysis and Development

model (IAD). For a more complete discussion of the IAD model, readers can turn to Elinor Ostrom books, two of which are – Governing the Commons: The Evolution of Institutions for Collective Action (New York: Cambridge University Press, 1990) or Institutional Incentives and Sustainable Development: Infrastructure Policies in Perspective (Boulder: Westview Press, 1993).

5 Covered entities are persons, agencies, and/or businesses that are required to provide notification and can include, for example, state and local agencies, public hospitals, departments of revenues and motor vehicles, courts at the state and local level, agencies that oversee elections, K-12 school districts, post-secondary institutions, and business entities engaging in inter and intrastate commerce not already covered by HIPAA and GLBA.

APPENDIX: DISCUSSION QUESTIONS

1. What is data breach?
2. What constitutes data breach?
3. What are the costs of data breach?
4. Who should bear these costs?
5. How can public policy be used to allocate costs to responsible parties?
6. What are the goals of the data breach disclosure laws?
7. Compare and contrast a few of the state laws? Might these laws conflict with each other?
8. How have historical factors and norms played a role in the data breach disclosure laws presented in this chapter?
9. Who is entitled to ask for information, in what context and why?
10. Once you have given your personal information out, what degree of control can you expect?
11. How can effective policy in information systems be developed, since public policies are always behind the technology?
12. What policy instruments are the best to use here? For example, might xxx be more appropriate?
13. Do data breach disclosure laws affect doing business in a state in good or bad ways? How?
14. What is the goal of data breach notification?
15. Would a continued state approach be more or less effective as compared to a federal law? Why?
16. What other approaches could be combined with public policies that may assist in bolstering citizen awareness and participation?
17. How could data breach notification be a more proactive process?
18. How detailed do and can we go to hold people or entities accountable for data breach?
19. How detailed should we go to hold people or entities accountable for data breach?
20. What are the pros and cons of sending data breach disclosure notices directly to citizens? Which entity do you think the data breach disclosure notices should be sent to and why?
21. Data breach notification is one attempt at accountability? What do you think are the pros and cons of this approach?
22. Compare and contrast the alternative policy configurations. Which you do think is optimal and why?
23. What could ethics do in helping prevent data breach?
24. What is the user's responsibility regarding data breach?
25. What are sunshine laws and how are the data breach laws a form of sunshine law?
26. In what ways do the data breach disclosure laws embody ideas in Mill's utilitarian ethics or Kant's deontological ethics?
27. How might the data breach laws influence entities the relationships between the covered entities and consumers?
28. What actions would you take immediately after you as an authority in your organization find out your customers' data have been breached? Compare and contrast these action plans?
29. Should organizations develop procedures to follow once a data breach occurs?
30. What kind of public policy might enable or motivate a company to do the right thing?
31. Is notification enough? Should entities be required to go beyond notification?

Afterword

Melissa J. Dark
Purdue University, USA

As technical systems become more capable, more pervasive, and more ubiquitous, their scope and power increases. In turn, questions surrounding technical means and human values become more relevant and pressing. As noted in the foreword, we are now in a fourth phase of development where consideration of how the technology affects the human life and dignity is central. Humans are part of a dynamic, organic system and computing and communications technologies have made us more connected and interrelated than ever before. The system is shaped by the presence and activity of each element in the system and each action alters, to some extent, the totality of the system. The more complex society becomes and the more sophisticated our adaptive and technical systems become, the greater the need for understanding these complexities; the greater the need for conceptualizing the power of technology – its potential for benevolence, and its limitations; the greater the need for conceptualizing the dynamics of interrelated systems for all levels of society; the greater the need for recognizing that the sum total of individual decisions will not necessarily be the equivalent of a social decision. While this book does have ready answers, it hopefully serves to identify relevant questions, such as these.

- How should technology be compatible with human needs?
- What macrostructures and relevant and how do these macrostructures co-adapt in pursuit of human flourishing?
- How do technology and sociological means function together to attain human goals?
- How do we structure social mechanisms in a manner that allows us to orient and utilize the power of our technical means?
- How do technology and technical means relate to individual freedom, equality, society, and human flourishing?
- How can fallible humans influence the means that structure their lives?

More importantly, this book asks you, the reader, to formulate your own questions and participate in the dialog. On the given that humans attain their fullest potential in a free society, such questions and questioning are more important than ever before; enlightenment regarding technology and its relationship to self-governance and well-being are more important than ever before.

Figure 1.

नमस्ते

Compilation of References

Ackoff, R. (1981). *Creating the corporate future*. New York: John Wiley & Sons.

Ackoff, R. (1986). *Management in small doses*. New York: John Wiley & Sons.

Act, C. (1976). 17 U.S.C. § 101-122 . *Pub., L*, 94–553.

Adams, J., & Rush, B. (2001). *The spur of fame: Dialogue of John Adams and Benjamin Rush, 1805 – 1813*. Indianapolis, IN: Liberty Fund.

Addams, J. (1910). *Twenty years at hull house: With autobiographical notes*. New York: The MacMillan Company.

Agre, P. E. (1994). Surveillance and capture: two models of privacy. *The Information Society*, *10*(2), 101–127. doi:10.1080/01972243.1994.9960162

Aithal, G. P., Day, C. P., Kesteven, P. J., & Daly, A. K. (1998). Association of polymorphisms in cytochrome P450 CYP2C9 with warfarin dose requirement and risk of bleeding complications. *Lancet*, *353*, 717–719. doi:10.1016/S0140-6736(98)04474-2

Akerlof, G. (1970). "The market for lemons": Quality, uncertainty and the market mechanism. *The Quarterly Journal of Economics*, *84*(3), 488–500. doi:10.2307/1879431

Allen, A. (1988). *Uneasy access: Privacy for women in a free society*. Totowa, NJ: Rowman & Littlefield.

Almarsdottir, A. B., Bjornsdottir, I., & Traulsen, J. M. (2005). A lay prescription for tailor-made drugs—focus group reflections on pharmacogenomics. *Health Policy (Amsterdam)*, *71*(2), 233–241. doi:10.1016/j.healthpol.2004.08.010

American Management Association. *2001AMA survey: Workplace monitoring and surveillance*. Retrieved from http://www.amanet.org/research/pdfs/Email Policies Practices.pdf

American Management Association. *2003AMA survey: Email policies, rules and practices*. Retrieved from http://www.amanet.org/research/pdfs/Email Policies Practices.pdf

American National Standards Institute (ANSI). (2009). *IDSP workshop report: Measuring identity theft*. Available at: http://webstore.ansi.org/identitytheft/

Anderson, R., & Moore, T. (2006). The economics of information security. *Science*, *314*, 611. doi:10.1126/science.1130992

Anderson, N. (2008, July 23). Embarq: Don't all users read our 5,000 word privacy policy? *Ars Technica*. Retrieved May 24, 2009 from http://arstechnica.com/old/content/2008/07/embarq-dont-all-users-read-our-5000-word-privacy-policy.ars

Anderson, R. (2001). Why information security is hard - An economic perspective. Retrieved from http://doi.ieeecomputersociety.org/10.1109/ACSAC.2001.991552

Anderson, S. A. (2008). Privacy without the right to privacy. *The Monist*, January, *91*(1).

Andrews, K. (2003). *Ethics in practice. Harvard business review on corporate ethics*. Boston, MA: Harvard Business School Press. (Original work published 1989)

Aristotle, . (1984a). Nicomachean ethics . In Barnes, J. (Ed.), *The complete works of aristotle* (*Vol. II*, pp. 1729–1868). Princeton, NJ: Princeton University Press.

Aristotle, . (1984b). Politics . In Barnes, J. (Ed.), *The complete works of Aristotle* (*Vol. II*, pp. 1986–2130). Princeton, NJ: Princeton University Press.

Arora, A., Nandkumar, A., & Telang, R. (2006). Does information security attack frequency increase with vulnerability disclosure? An empirical analysis. *Information Systems Frontiers*, *8*, 350–362. doi:10.1007/s10796-006-9012-5

Arora, A., Telang, R., & Xu, H. (2008). Optimal policy for software vulnerability disclosure. *Management Science*, *54*(4), 642–656. doi:10.1287/mnsc.1070.0771

Arora, A., Caulkins, J. P., & Telang, R. (October, 2004). *Sell first, fix later: Impact of patching on software quality*. Working Paper Series, H. John Heinz III School of Public Policy and Management, Carnegie Mellon University, Pittsburgh, PA. Retrieved October 8, 2009 from http://ssrn.com/abstract=670285

Association for Computing Machinery. (2009). Code of ethics, Retrieved May 23, 2009 from http://www.acm.org/about/code-of-ethics

August, T., & Tunca, T. (2006). Network software security and user icentives. *Management Science*, *52*(11), 1703–1702. doi:10.1287/mnsc.1060.0568

August, T., & Tunca, T. (2008). Let the pirates patch? An economic analysis of software security patch restrictions. *Information Systems Research*, *19*(1), 48–70. doi:10.1287/isre.1070.0142

Austin, S. (2009, May 19). Turning out the lights: NebuAd. *Wall Street Journal Blogs*. Retrieved May 24, 2009 from http://blogs.wsj.com/venturecapital/2009/05/19/turning-out-the-lights-nebuad/

Badaracco, J. (2003). *We don't need another hero. Harvard business review on corporate ethics*. Boston, MA: Harvard Business School Press. (Original work published 2001)

Band, D. R., Cappelli, D. M., Fischer, L. F., Moore, A. P., Shaw, E. D., & Trzeciak, R. F. (2006). *Comparing insider IT sabotage and espionage: A model-based analysis* (Technical Report CMU/SEI-2006-TR026026). Pittsburgh, PA: Carnegie-Mellon Software Engineering Institute.

Barth, A., Datta, A., Mitchell, J. C., & Nissenbaum, H. (2006). Privacy and contextual integrity: Framework and applications. In *Proceedings of the 2006 IEEE Symposium on Security and Privacy* (pp. 184–198).

Barton, J., & Markey, E. (2008, May 16). Letter to Neil Smit, CEO of Charter Communications. Retrieved May 19, 2009 from http://markey.house.gov/docs/telecomm/letter_charter_comm_privacy.pdf

Barton, J., Dingell, J., & Markey, E. (2008, July 14). Letter to Tom Gerke, CEO of Embarq. Retrieved May 19, 2009 from http://markey.house.gov/index.php?option=com_content&task=view&id=3410&Itemid=141

Basher, N., Mahanti, A., Mahanti, A., Williamson, C., & Arlitt, M. (2008). A comparative analysis of web and peer-to-peer traffic. In *Proceedings of the 2008 WWW Conference*. Beijing, China.

Bates, D. W., Spell, N., & Cullen, D. J. (1997). The costs of adverse drug events in hospitalized patients. *Journal of the American Medical Association*, *277*(4), 307–311. doi:10.1001/jama.277.4.307

Beauchamp, T. L., & Childress, J. F. (2001). *Principles of biomedical ethics*. Oxford: Oxford University Press.

Beckerman, R. (2008), Large Recording Companies v. The Defenseless: Some common sense solutions to the challenges of the RIAA litigations. *The Judges' Journal*, *47*(3).

Ben-Jacob, M. G. (2005). Integrating computer ethics across the curriculum: A case study. *Journal of Educational Technology & Society*, *8*(4), 198–204.

Bennett, C. J. (1992). *Regulating privacy: Data protection and public policy in Europe and the United States*. Ithaca, NY: Cornell University Press.

Bergson, H. (1949, 1955). *An introduction to metaphysics*. (T. Hulme, Trans.). Indianapolis, IN: Bobbs-Merrill.

Bergson, H. (1962). Time in the history of Western philosophy. In W. Barrett, & H. D. Aiken (Eds.), *Philosophy in the twentieth century* (A. Mitchell, Trans., Vol. 3, pp. 331-363). New York: Random House.

Berlin, I. (2000). The purpose of philosophy . In Berlin, I., & Hardy, H. (Eds.), *The power of ideas* (pp. 24–35). Princeton, NJ: Princeton University Press.

Bevan, J. L., Lynch, J. A., Dubriwny, T. N., Harris, T. M., Achter, P. J., & Reeder, A. L. (2003). Informed lay preferences for delivery of racially varied pharmacogenomics. *Genetics in Medicine*, *5*(5), 393–399. doi:10.1097/01.GIM.0000087989.12317.3F

Bhattacharjee, S., Lertwachara, K., Gopal, R., & Marsden, J. (2006). Impact of legal threats on online music sharing activity: An analysis of music industry legal actions. *The Journal of Law & Economics*, *49*(1), 91–114. doi:10.1086/501085

Biby v. Board of Regents, 419 F.3d. 845 (8th Cir. 2005); and TBG Ins. Servs. Corp. v. Superior Court, 96 Cal. App. 4th 443, 452 (Cal. Ct. App. 2002).

Billings, P. R. (2008). Beyond GINA. *Nature*, *14*, 8.

Bishop, M. (2002). *Computer security: Art and science*. Boston, MA: Addison-Wesley.

Blackburn, S. (2001). *Being good: A short introduction to ethics*. New York: Oxford University Press.

Blanchard, K., & Peale, N. V. (1991). *The power of ethical management*. New York: Fawcett Books.

Blankenship, A. B. (1964). Some aspects of ethics in marketing research. *JMR, Journal of Marketing Research*, *1*(2), 26–31. doi:10.2307/3149918

Blau, J. (2007, August). German antihacker law could backfire, critics warn. *InfoWorld Website*. Retrieved from http://www.infoworld.com/d/security-central/german-antihacker-law-could-backfire-critics-warn-439

Bloustein, E. (1964). Privacy as an aspect of human dignity: An answer to Dean Possner. *New York University Law Review*, *39*, 962–1007.

Bonner, B. (2006). The difficulty in establishing privacy rights in the face of public policy from nowhere. Saskatchewan Institute of Public Policy, *SIPP Public Policy Paper Number 43*. Retrieved from http://www.uregina.ca/sipp/documents/pdf/PPP%2043%20-%20Bonner.pdf

Boyle, J. (2008). *The public domain: Enclosing the commons of the mind*. New Haven, CT: Yale University Press.

Brey, P. (2007). Ethical aspects of information security and privacy . In Petcovic, W., & Jonker, M. (Eds.), *Security and trust in modern data management* (pp. 21–36). New York: Springer. doi:10.1007/978-3-540-69861-6_3

Brown, W. S. (1996). Technology, workplace privacy, and personhood. *Journal of Business Ethics*, *15*, 1237–1248. doi:10.1007/BF00412822

Business Software Alliance-International Data Corporation. (2009). Sixth annual BSA-IDC global software - 08 piracy study. Retrieved September 6, 2009 from www.bsa.org

Bynum, T. W. (2008). Norbert wiener and the rise of information ethics . In van den Hoven, J., & Weckert, J. (Eds.), *Information technology and moral philosophy* (pp. 8–25). Cambridge, MA: Cambridge University Press. doi:10.1017/CBO9780511498725.002

Cavoukian, A. (1998). Data mining: staking a claim on your privacy. *Information and Privacy Commissioner's Report*. Ontario, Canada.

Cavusoglu, H., Mishra, B., & Raghunathan, S. (2004). The effect of internet security breach announcements on market value: Capital market reactions for breached firms and internet security developers. *International Journal of Electronic Commerce*, *9*(1), 69–104.

Cavusoglu, H., Cavusoglu, H., & Raghunathan, S. (2004, May). *How to disclose software vulnerabilities responsibly?* Paper presented at the Third Annual Workshop on Economics of Information Security (WEISO4), University of Minnesota, Minneapolis, MN. Retrieved from http://infosecon.net/workshop/slides/weis_4_3.ppt

Center for Democracy and Technology. (2008). Response to the 2008 NAI principles: The network advertising initiative's self-regulatory code of conduct for online behavioral advertising. Retrieved September 16, 2009 from http://www.cdt.org/privacy/20081216_NAIresponse.pdf

CERT (Computer Emergency Response Team). (2004). *2004 E-crime watch survey ™: Summary of findings*. Retrieved from www.cert.org/archive/pdf/2004eCrimeWatchSummary.pdf

CERT (Computer Emergency Response Team). (2005). *2005 E-crime watch survey ™: Summary of findings*. Retrieved from http://www.cert.org/archive/pdf/ecrimesummary05.pdf

CERT (Computer Emergency Response Team). (2006). *2006 E-crime watch survey ™: Summary of findings*. Retrieved from http://www.cert.org/archive/pdf/ecrimesurvey06.pdf

CERT (Computer Emergency Response Team). (2007). *2007 E-crime watch survey ™: Summary of findings*. Retrieved from http://www.cert.org/archive/pdf/ecrimesummary07.pdf

Christin, N., & Chuang, J. (2005). A cost-based analysis of overlay routing geometries. In *Proceedings of IEEE INFOCOM'05* (Vol. 4., pp. 2566-2577). Miami, FL.

Christin, N., Weigend, A., & Chuang, J. (2005) Content availability, pollution, and poisoning in peer-to-peer file sharing networks. In *Proceedings of the Sixth ACM Conference on Electronic Commerce* (pp. 68-77). Vancouver, BC, Canada.

Clark, D., Wroclawski, J., Sollins, K., & Braden R. (2005). Tussle in cyberspace: Defining tomorrow's internet. *IEEE/ACM Transactions on Networking, 13*(3), 462-475.

Clarke, R. (1994). The digital persona and its application to data surveillance. *The Information Society*, *10*(2), 77–92. doi:10.1080/01972243.1994.9960160

Classen, D. C., Pestotnik, S. L., & Evans, R. S. (1997). Adverse drug events in hospitalized patients. *Journal of the American Medical Association*, *277*(4), 301–306. doi:10.1001/jama.277.4.301

Cohen, J. (2002). *Regulating intimacy: A new legal paradigm*. Princeton, NJ: Princeton University Press.

Communications Networks and Consumer Privacy: Recent Developments: Hearing before Committee on Energy and Commerce, Subcommittee on Communications, Technology, and the Internet, House of Representatives, 111th Cong. 1. (2009).

Computer Fraud and Abuse Act, 18 U.S.C. §1030 (1984).

Computer Misuse Act 1990. Retrieved from http://www.opsi.gov.uk/acts/acts1990/UKpga_19900018_en_1.htm

Computing Research Association. (2006). *Four grand challenges in trustworthy computing*. (Report Series) Retrieved from http://www.cra.org/reports/trustworthy.computing.pdf

Conger, S., & Loch, K. D. (1995). Ethics and computer use. *Communications of the ACM*, *38*(12), 30–32. doi:10.1145/219663.219676

Congressional Budget Office. (2006). *CBO S. 1789 Personal data privacy and security act of 2005 cost estimate*. Retrieved July 20, 2009 from http://www.cbo.gov/doc.cfm?index=7161

Congressional Research Service. (2007). Data brokers: Background and industry overview. *CRS Report for Congress RS22137-070112*. Retrieved June 15, 2009 from http://opencrs.com/

Congressional Research Service. (2008). Federal information security and data breach notification laws. *CRS Report for Congress RS33199*. Retrieved June 15, 2009 from http://opencrs.com/

Council Directive 2002/58/EC of the European Parliament and of the Council of the European Union of 12 July 2002 concerning the processing of personal data and the protection of privacy in the electronic communications sector (Directive on privacy and electronic communications). Retrieved from http:brief.weburb.dk/archives/00000209/

Council Directive 95/46/EC of the European Parliament and of the Council of the European Union of 24 October 1995 on the protection of individuals with regard to the processing of personal data and on the free movement of such data. Retrieved from http:www.legaltext.ee/text/en/T5023.html

Council Directive 97/66/EC of the European Parliament and of the Council of the European Union of 15 December 1997 concerning the processing of personal data and the protection of privacy in the telecommunications sector. Retrieved from http:www.legaltext.ee/text/en/T5023.html

Credit Reporting Act, F. 15 U.S.C. § 1681 et seq. (1970). Pub. L. No. 90-321, as amended. Retrieved from http://www.ftc.gov/os/statutes/031224fcra.pdf

Crisp, R. (2003). A defense of philosophical business ethics . In Shaw, W. (Ed.), *Ethics at work*. New York: Oxford University Press. (Original work published 1998)

Cusumano, M. A. (2004). Who is liable for bugs and security flaws in software? *Communications of the ACM*, *47*(3), 25–27. doi:10.1145/971617.971637

Dana, J., & Spier, K. (2001). Revenue sharing and vertical control in the video rental industry. *The Journal of Industrial Economics*, *49*(3), 223–245.

Dayarathna, R. (2007). *Towards Comparing Personal Information Privacy Protection Measures* (Licentiate Thesis of Philosophy, Stockholm University, Sweden). Report series 07-018.

Decamp, M., & Buchanan, A. (2007). Pharmacogenomics: Ethical and regulatory issues . In Steinbock, B. (Ed.), *The Oxford Handbook of Bioethics* (pp. 536–568). Oxford: Oxford University Press.

DeCew, J. (1997). *In pursuit of privacy: Law, ethics, and the rise of technology*. Ithaca, NY: Cornell University Press.

Department of Health, Education, and Welfare [now Health and Human Services]. (1973). *Records, Computers and the rights of citizens, report of the secretary's advisory committee on automated personal data systems*. Retrieved from http://aspe.hhs.gov/DATACNCL/1973privacy/tocprefacemembers.htm

DeVore, P. (1984). *Technology: An introduction*. Worcester, MA: Davis Publication.

Dewar. (1998). *The information age and the printing press*. Santa Monica, CA: Rand

Dinev, T., Goo, J., Hu, Q., & Nam, K. (2009). User behavior towards protective information technologies: the role of national cultural differences. *Information Systems Journal*, *19*, 391–412. doi:10.1111/j.1365-2575.2007.00289.x

DoD Office of the Inspector General. (1997). *DoD management of information assurance efforts to protect automated information systems (Technical Report No. PO 97-049)*. Washington, D.C.: U.S. Dept. of Defense.

Dryzek, J., Downes, D., Hunold, C., Schlosberg, D., & Hernes, H. (2003). *Green states and social movements*. Oxford University Press. doi:10.1093/0199249024.001.0001

Duebendorfer, T., & Frei, S. (2009, May). *Why silent updates boost security*. Paper presented at CRITIS 2009 Critical Infrastructures Security Workshop, Bonn, Germany. Retrieved from http://www.techzoom.net/publications/silent-updates/

Dworkin, R. (2003). Terror & the attack on civil liberties. *The New York Review of Books*, *50*(7), 31.

Easley, R. (2005). Ethical issues in the music industry response to innovation and piracy. *Journal of Business Ethics*, *62*, 163–168. doi:10.1007/s10551-005-0187-3

Eckersley, P., von Lohmann, F., & Schoen, S. (2007). Packet forgery by ISPs: A report on the Comcast affair. Electronic Frontier Foundation online report. Retrieved from http://www.eff.org/wp/packet-forgery-isps-report-comcast-affair.

EFF (Electronic Frontier Foundation). (2007). RIAA v. The People: Four years later. *Electronic Publication*. Retrieved August 2009 from http://w2.eff.org/IP/P2P/riaa_at_four.pdf

Electronic Privacy Information Center (EPIC). (2008). *The Graham-Leach-Bliley act*. Retrieved May 30, 2009 from http://epic.org/privacy/glba/

Electronic Privacy Information Center. (2004, August 18). Gmail Privacy Page. Retrieved May 23, 2009 from http://epic.org/privacy/gmail/faq.html

Elf, D. (2004). [Full–Disclosure] iDefense: solution or problem? Derkeiler. Retrieved May 7, 2009 from http://www.derkeiler.com/pdf/Mailing-Lists/Full-Disclosure/2004-07/0698.pdf

Elgesem, D. (1999). The structure of rights in Directive 95/46/EC on the protection of individuals with regard to processing of personal data and the free movement of such data. *Ethics and Information Technology*, *1*(4), 283–293. doi:10.1023/A:1010076422893

eMarketer. (2007). Behavioral Targeting: Advertising Gets Personal, Retrieved March 19, 2009 from http://www.emarketer.com/Report.aspx?code=emarketer_2000415

Erez, M., & Earley, P. C. (1993). *Culture, self-identity, and work*. New York: Oxford University Press.

Etzioni, A. (1999). *The limits of privacy*. New York: Basic Books.

Etzioni, A., & Marsh, J. (2003). *Rights vs. public safety after 9/11*. Lanham, MD: Rowman & Littlefield.

European Convention on Human Rights (1950) The Universal Declaration of Human Rights and Article 8 of the European Convention for the Protection of Human Rights and Fundamental Freedoms, Rome, Retrieved from http://www.echr.coe.int/nr/rdonlyres/d5cc24a7-dc13-4318-b457-5c9014916d7a/0/englishanglais.pdf

European Data Protection Supervisor. Public access to documents and data protection, [Guideline], *Background Paper Series*, European Communities, Belgium, July 2005. Retrieved from http://www.edps.europa.eu/EDPSWEB/webdav/shared/Documents/EDPS/Publications/Papers/BackgroundP/05-07_BP_summary_EN.pdf

Evans, R. S., Pestotnik, S. L., & Classen, D. C. (1992). Prevention of adverse drug events through computerized surveillance. *The Annual Symposium on Computer Applications in Medical Care, 16*, 437-441.

Fair Credit Reporting Act. (2004a). Federal Trade Commission. Retrieved from http://www.ftc.gov/os/statutes/031224fcra.pdf

Fair Credit Reporting Act, at 15 U.S.C. § 1681 (1971).

Federal Register. 69 (98):29061-29064. (2004b). Federal Trade Commission. Retrieved from http://www.ftc.gov/os/2004/05/040520factafrn.pdf

Federal Trade Commission Act, 15 U.S.C. § 41-58 (1914).

Federal Trade Commission. (2007). *Online advertising and user privacy: Principles to guide the debate.* Retrieved March 19, 2009 from http://www.ftc.gov/os/2007/12/P859900stmt.pdf

Federal Trade Commission. (2009). *Federal Trade Commission staff report: self-regulatory principles for online behavioral advertising: tracking, targeting, and technology.* Retrieved from http://www.ftc.gov/os/2009/02/P085400behavadreport.pdf

Feldman, M., Lai, K., Stoica, I., & Chuang, J. (2004). Robust incentive techniques for peer-to-peer networks. In Proceedings of the *Fifth ACM Conference on Electronic Commerce (EC'04)* (pp. 102-111). New York, NY.

Felten, E. W., & Halderman, J. A. (2006). Digital rights management, spyware, and security. *Security & Privacy, IEEE, 4*(1). Retrieved from http://ieeexplore.ieee.org/stamp/stamp.jsp?arnumber=1588821&isnumber=33481

Fischer, L. F. (2000). Espionage: Why does it happen? *DoD Security Institute*. Retrieved from http://www.hanford.gov/oci/maindocs/ci_r_docs/whyhappens.pdf

Flaherty, D. H. (1989). *Protecting privacy in surveillance societies: The Federal Republic of Germany, Sweden, France, Canada, and the United States*. Chapel Hill, NC: University of North Carolina Press.

Fleischmann, K. R., Robbins, R. W., & Wallace, W. A. (2009). Designing educational cases for intercultural information ethics: The importance of diversity, perspectives, palues, and Pluralism. *Journal of Education for Library and Information Science*, *50*(1), 4–14.

Fleischmann, K. R., & Wallace, W. A. (2005). A covenant with transparency: Opening the black box of models. *Communications of the ACM*, *48*(5), 93–97. doi:10.1145/1060710.1060715

Forster, E. M. (1951). *Two cheers for democracy*. New York, NY: Harcourt Brace and Company.

Frank, J. (1994). Artificial intelligence and intrusion detection: Current and future directions. In *Proceedings of the 17th NCSC, Baltimore, MD.*

Franklin, D. (2008). Family struggles with ambiguity of genetic testing. *All Things Considered, 12/30/2008*. Retrieved July 1, 2009 from http://www.npr.org/templates/story/story.php?storyId=98818197.

Freedom of the Press Act [Tryckfrihetsförordningen], Chapter 2, Article 1, 1949:105 (1949).

Fried, C. (1984). Privacy (a moral analysis) . In Schoeman, F. (Ed.), *Philosophical dimensions of privacy: An anthology* (pp. 346–402). Cambridge, MA: Cambridge University Press. doi:10.1017/CBO9780511625138.008

Gabrielson, B., Goertzel, K. M., Hoenicke, B., Kleiner, D., & Winograd, T. (2008). *The insider threat to information systems: A state-of-the-art report*. Herndon, VA: Information Assurance Technology Analysis Center (IATAC).

Gandy, O. (1993). *The panoptic sort: A political economy of personal information*. Boulder, CO: Westview Press.

Garg, A., Curtis, J., & Halper, H. (2003). Quantifying the financial impact of IT security breaches . *Information Management & Computer Security*, *11*(2/3), 74–83. doi:10.1108/09685220310468646

Gasset, J. O. (1984). *Historical reason* (Silver, P. W., Trans.). New York: W.W. Norton & Company.

Gasset, J. O. (2002). Ideas and beliefs. In J.O. Gasset, & J. Garcia-Gomez (Eds.). *What is knowledge* (J. Garcia-Gomez, Trans., pp. 175-203). Albany, NY: State University of New York Press.

Gassner, U. (2005). Copyright and digital media in a post-Napster world: International Supplement. Retrieved from SSRN: http://ssrn.com/abstract=655391 or DOI: 10.2139/ssrn.655391

Gavison, R. (1980). Privacy and the limits of law. *The Yale Law Journal*, *8*, 421–471. doi:10.2307/795891

Gelles, M. (2005) Exploring the mind of the spy. In Online *Employees' Guide to Security Responsibilities: Treason 101*. Retrieved from Texas A&M University Research Foundation website: http://www.dss.mil/search-dir/training/csg/security/Treason/Mind.htm

Genetic Information Nondiscrimination Act (GINA). (2008), Retrieved June 28, 2009 from http://www.govtrack.us/congress/ billtext.xpd?bill=h110-493.

Gerstein, R. (1978). Intimacy and privacy. *Ethics*, *89*, 78–81. doi:10.1086/292105

Golle, P., Leyton-Brown, K., Mironov, I., & Lillibridge, M. (2001). Incentives for sharing in peer-to-peer networks. In *Proceedings of the Second International Workshop on Electronic Commerce*. L. Fiege, G. Mühl, and U. G. Wilhelm (Eds.), Lecture Notes in Computer Science, Vol. 2232. (pp. 75-87). Springer-Verlag, London.

Good, N., & Krekelberg, A. (2003). Usability and privacy: A study of Kazaa P2P file-sharing. In *Proceedings of the ACM Symposium on Human Computer Interaction (CHI)*. Fort Lauderdale, FL, U.S.A.

Good, N., Dhamija, R., Grossklags, J., Thaw, D., Aronowitz, S., Mulligan, D., & Konstan, J. (2005). Stopping spyware at the gate: A user study of privacy, notice and spyware. In *Proceedings of the First Symposium on Usable Privacy and Security (SOUPS)*. Pittsburgh, PA, USA.

GovTrack.us. Retrieved http://www.govtrack.us/congress/bill

Green, M. J., & Botkin, J. R. (2003). "Genetic exceptionalism" in medicine: Clarifying the differences between genetic and nongenetic tests. *Annals of Internal Medicine*, *138*, 7.

Greenemeier, L. (2007, May). T.J. Maxx data theft likely due to wireless 'wardriving'. *Information Week.* Retrieved from http://www.eetimes.com/news/latest/showArticle.jhtml?articleID=199500574

Greitzer, F. L., & Endicott-Popovsky, B. (2008). Security and privacy in an expanding cyber world. Panel session at the Twenty-fourth *Annual Computer Security Applications Conference (ACSAC)*, Anaheim, CA.

Greitzer, F. L., Moore, A. P., Cappelli, D. M., Andrews, D. H., Carroll, L., & Hull, T. D. (2008). Combating the insider threat. *IEEE Security & Privacy, 6*(1), 61-64 (PNNL Report PNNL-SA-58061). Richland, WA: Pacific Northwest National Laboratory.

Greitzer, F. L., Paulson, P. R., Kangas, L. J., Franklin, L. R., Edgar, T. W., & Frincke, D. A. (2009). *Predictive modeling for insider threat mitigation* (PNNL Report PNNL-SA-65204). Richland, WA: Pacific Northwest National Laboratory.

Hale, J., & Manes, G. (2004) Method to inhibit the identification and retrieval of proprietary media via automated search engines. U.S. Patent number: 6732180. Filing date: Aug 8, 2000. Issue date: May 4, 2004

Hansell, S. (2008, October 8). Adzilla, a would-be I.S.P. Snoop, quits U.S. market, *New York Times Bits Blog.* Retrieved from http://bits.blogs.nytimes.com/2008/10/09/adzilla-a-would-be-isp-snoop-abandons-us-for-asia/

Harper, J. (2004). Understanding privacy -- and the real threats to it. *Cato Policy Analysis*, *520*, 1–20.

Harris, A. L. (2000). IS ethical attitudes among college students: A comparatives. In D. Colton, J. Caouette, B. Raggad (Eds.), *Proceedings of the Information Systems Education Conference 2000*: Vol. 17,§801. Retrieved from http://proc.isecon.org/2000/801/ISECON.2000.Harris.pdf

Hauptman, R. (1999). Ethics, information technology, and crisis . In Pourciau, L. (Ed.), *Ethics and electronic information in the twenty-first century.* West Lafayette, IN: Purdue University Press.

Häyry, M., & Takkala, T. (2001). Genetic information, rights, and autonomy. *Theoretical Medicine and Bioethics*, *22*(5), 403–414. doi:10.1023/A:1013097617552

Health Insurance Portability and Accountability Act of 1996 (HIPAA). (1996). Retrieved July 10, 2009 from http://www.cms.hhs.gov/HIPAAGenInfo/Downloads/HIPAALaw.pdf

Health Insurance Portability and Accountability Act, 42 U.S.C. § 1320 (1996).

Health Level Seven (HL7). (2009). Retrieved from http://www.hl7.org/

Heeks, R. (2006). *Implementing and managing e-government – An international text.* London, England: SAGE.

Heeks, R., & Stanforth, C. (2007). Understanding e-government project trajectories from an actor-network perspective. *European Journal of Information Systems*, *16*(2), 165–177. doi:10.1057/palgrave.ejis.3000676

Helft, M. (2009, March 11). Google to offer ads based on interests. *The New York Times.* Retrieved from http://www.nytimes.com/2009/03/11/technology/internet/11google.html

Herberg, W. (1986). *What is the moral crisis of our time?*The Intercollegiate Review.

Hillman, J. (1995). *Kinds of power: A guide to its intelligent uses.* New York: Currency Doubleday.

Hinde, S. (2003). Privacy legislation: a comparison of the US and European approaches. *Computers & Security*, *22*(5), 378–387. doi:10.1016/S0167-4048(03)00503-0

Hippocrates. (4th Century B.C.). The oath by Hippocrates. Retrieved from http://classics.mit.edu/Hippocrates/hippooath.html

Hofstede, G. (1980). *Culture's consequences: International differences in work-related values.* Newbury Park, CA: Sage.

Hofstede, G. (1991). *Cultures and organizations: Software of the mind.* London: McGraw-Hill.

Hollon, T. (2000). NIH researchers receive cut-price BRCA test. *Nature Medicine*, *6*, 6. doi:10.1038/71545

Hoofnagle, C. J. (2005). *Privacy self regulation: a decade of disappointment*. Available at SSRN: http://ssrn.com/abstract=650804 or DOI: 10.2139/ssrn.650804

Howard, M., & LeBlanc, D. (2003). *Writing secure code* (2nd ed.). Redmond, WA: Microsoft Press.

Howard, M., & Lipner, S. (2006). *The security development lifecycle*. Redmond, WA: Microsoft Press.

Hughes, A. M. (1996). *The complete database marketer: Second-generation strategies and techniques for tapping the power of your customer database* (2nd ed.). New York: McGraw-Hill.

Hughes, D. A., & Pirmohamed, M. (2007). Warfarin pharmacogenetics: Economic considerations. *Pharmacoeconmics*, *25*(11), 899–902. doi:10.2165/00019053-200725110-00001

Hyman, M., Skipper, R., & Tansey, R. (1990). Ethical codes are not enough. *Business Horizons*, *33*(2), 15–22. doi:10.1016/0007-6813(90)90004-U

Identity Theft Resource Center. (2008). Retrieved May 25, 2009 from www.idtheftcenter.org

Imre, R. T., Mooney, B., & Clarke, B. (2008). *Responding to terrorism:Political, philosophical and legal perspectives*. Aledershot, England: Ashgate Publishing.

INFOSEC Research Council. (2005). *Hard problems list*. Retrieved from http://www.infosec-research.org/docs_public/20051130-IRC-HPL-FINAL.pdf

Inness, J. C. (1992). *Privacy, intimacy and isolation*. Oxford: Oxford University Press.

Institute of Electrical and Electronics Engineers. (2006). *Code of ethics*. Retrieved March 19, 2009 from http://www.ieee.org/web/membership/ethics/code_ethics.html

International Standards Organization. *ISO 27001 Information Security Management System Specification*. Retrieved from http://www.w3j.com/5/s3.koman.html.

Internet Advertising Bureau. (2002). *Internet advertising revenue report: 2001 full year results*. Retrieved March 19, 2009 from http://www.iab.net/media/file/resources_ad-revenue_pdf_IAB_PWC_2001Q4.pdf

Internet Advertising Bureau. (2008). *IAB internet advertising revenue report: 2007 full year results*. Retrieved March 19, 2009 from http://www.iab.net/media/file/IAB_PwC_2007_full_year.pdf

Introna, L. (2007). Maintaining the reversibility of foldings: Making the ethics (politics) of information technology visible. *Ethics and Information Technology*, *9*, 11–25. doi:10.1007/s10676-006-9133-z

Isocrates, . (1929). *Isocrates II: On the peace. Areopagiticus. Against the Sophists. Antidosis. Panathenaicus* (Norlin, G., Trans.). Cambridge, MA: Harvard University Press.

IT Governance Institute. (2006). *Information security governance: Guidance forboards of directors and executive management* (2nd ed.).

Jaspers, K. (1997). *Nietzsche: An introduction to the understanding of his philosophical activity* (Wallraff, C., & Schmitz, F., Trans.). Baltimore, MD: Johns Hopkins University Press. (Original work published 1936)

Javelin Research. (2006). *Identity fraud survey report: 2006*. Javelin Strategy & Research. Retrieved May 8, 2009 from http://www.javelinstrategy.com/products/99DEBA/27/delivery.pdf

Javelin Research. (2007). *Identity fraud survey report: 2007*. Javelin Strategy & Research. Retrieved May 8, 2009 from http://www.javelinstrategy.com/uploads/701.R_2007IdentityFraudSurveyReport_Brochure.pdf

Javelin Research. (2008). *Identity fraud survey report: 2008*. Javelin Strategy & Research. Retrieved May 8, 2009 from http://www.idsafety.net/803.R_2008%20Identity%20Fraud%20Survey%20Report_Consumer%20Version.pdf

Johnson, D. (2001). *Computer ethics* (3rd ed.). Upper Saddle River, NJ: Prentice Hall. (Original work published 1985)

Johnson, D. (1993). *Computer ethics*. Englewood Cliffs, NJ: Prentice Hall.

Just, R., Hueth, D., & Schmitz, A. (2005). *The welfare economics of public policy: A practical approach to project and policy evaluation*. Williston, VT: Edward Elgar Publishing.

Kamira, R. (2007). Kaitiakitanga and health informatics: Introducing useful indigeneous concepts of governance in the health sector . In Dyson, L., Hendricks, M., & Grant, S. (Eds.), *Information technology and indigenous people*. Hershey, PA: Information Science Publishing.

Kamkar, S. (2007). *The MySpace Worm*. Presentation at the OWASP & WASC AppSec 2007 Conference. San Jose, CA. Retrieved from http://www.owasp.org/images/7/79/OWASP-WASCAppSec2007SanJose_SamyWorm.ppt

Kane, M. D., Springer, J. A., & Sprague, J. E. (2008). Drug safety assurance through clinical genotyping: Near-term considerations for a system-wide implementation of personalized medicine. *Personalized Medicine*, *5*(4), 387–397. doi:10.2217/17410541.5.4.387

Kant, I. (1993). *Grounding for the metaphysics of morals* (3rd ed.). (Ellington, J. W., Trans.). Indianapolis, IN: Hackett Publishing Company.

Kant, I. (1997). *Groundwork of the metaphysics of morals* (Gregor, M., Trans.). New York: Cambridge University Press. (Original work published 1785)

Karagiannis, T., Broido, A., Brownlee, N., Claffy, K. C., & Faloutsos, M. (2004). Is P2P dying or just hiding? In *Proceedings of IEEE Globecom 2004*. Dallas, TX, USA.

Karagiannis, T., Rodriguez, P., & Papagiannaki, K. (2005). Should internet service providers fear peer-assisted content distributions? In *Proceedings of the 2005 ACM/USENIX Internet Measurement Conference*. Berkeley, CA, USA

Katabi, D., Handley, M., & Rohrs, C. (2002). Congestion control for high bandwidth-delay product networks. In *Proceedings of the 2002 ACM SIGCOMM Conference*. Pittsburgh, PA, USA

Katz, J. (2002). *The silent world of doctor and patient*. Baltimore, MD: The John Hopkins University Press.

Keane, M. (2008, September 3). *Another nail in the NebuAd coffin: CEO steps down*. Retrieved March 19, 2009 from http://blog.wired.com/business/2008/09/another-nail-in.html

Keeney, M., Kowalski, E., Cappelli, D., Moore, A., Shimeall, T., & Rogers, S. (2005). *Insider threat study: Computer system sabotage in critical infrastructure sectors*. Pittsburgh, PA: U.S. Secret Service and CERT Coordination Center, Carnegie Mellon Software Engineering Institute.

Kegley, J. (1997). *Genuine individuals and genuine communities*. Nashville, TN: Vanderbilt University Press.

Kelly, M. (1999, December). Your boss may be monitoring your e-mail. *Salon*. Retrieved from http://www.salon.com/tech/feature/1999/12/08/email_monitoring/print.html

Kierkegaard, S. (2006). *Fear and trembling (Cambridge Texts in the History of Philosophy)* (Walsh, S., Trans.). New York: Cambridge University Press. (Original work published 1843)

Kim, D. (1999). *Introduction to systems thinking*. Waltham, MA: Pegasus Communications.

Kohn, L. T., Corrigan, J., & Donald, M. S. (Eds.). (2000). *To err is human: Building a safer health system*. Washington, D.C.: National Academy Press.

Kołakowski, L. (2001). *Bergson*. South Bend, IN: St. Augustine's Press.

Kramer, L. A., Heuer, R. J., Jr., & Crawford, K. S. (2005). *Technological, social, and economic trends that are increasing U.S. vulnerability to insider espionage*. (Technical Report 05-10). Monterey, CA: Defense Personnel Security Research Center (PERSEREC).

Krofcheck, J. L., & Gelles, M. G. (2005). *Behavioral consultation in personnel security: Training and reference manual for personnel security professionals*. Fairfax, VA: Yarrow Associates.

Lane, F. S. III. (2003). *The naked employee: How technology is compromising workplace privacy* (p. 261). New York: American Management Association.

Lapham, E. V., Kozma, C., & Weiss, J. O. (1996). Genetic discrimination: perspectives of consumers. *Science*, *274*, 5287. doi:10.1126/science.274.5287.621

Layman, E. J. (2008). Ethical issues and the electronic health record. *The Health Care Manager*, *27*(2), 165–176.

Lee, C. R. (2005). Warfarin initiation and the potential role of genomic-guided dosing. *Clinical Medicine & Research*, *3*(4), 205–206. doi:10.3121/cmr.3.4.205

Lemon, J. (2002) Resisting SYN flood DoS attacks with a SYN cache. In *Proceedings of USENIX BSDCON 2002*. San Francisco, CA.

Lemos (2006, September). Security pro pleads guilty to USC breach. *Security Focus*. Retrieved from http://www.securityfocus.com/news/11411

Lenard, T., & Rubin, P. (2005). An economic analysis of notification requirements for data security breaches. *Emory Law and Economics Research Paper No. 05-12*. Available at SSRN: http://ssrn.com/abstract=765845

Lever, A. (2005). Feminism, democracy and the right to privacy. *Minerva: An Internet . The Journal of Philosophy*, *9*, 1–31.

Levin, S., & Disher, J. (2004). System and methods for communicating over the Internet with geographically distributed devices of a decentralized network using transparent asymmetric return paths. U.S. Patent Application number 10/869,208, publication number 2005/0089014.

Liang, J., Kumar, R., Xi, Y., & Ross, K. (2005) Pollution in P2P filesharing systems. In *Proceedings of IEEE INFOCOM'05*, Miami, FL.

Liebermann, R. K. (2009, accessed). *How to right-size your HR resources: calibrating human resources to company size*. Retrieved from http://www.hrinsourcing.com/calibrating_hr.html

Liebowitz, S. (2006). File-sharing: Creative destruction or just plain destruction? Center for the Analysis of Property Rights Working Paper No. 04-03. Retrieved from SSRN: http://ssrn.com/abstract=646943 or DOI: 10.2139/ssrn.646943

Limitations on liability relating to material online. 17 U.S.C. § 512 (1998).

Lindpaintner, K. (2001). Pharmacogenetics and the future of medical practice: conceptual considerations. *Pharmacogenetics Journal*, *1*, 1.

Lindpaintner, K. (2003). Pharmacogenetics and the future of medical practice. *Journal of Molecular Medicine*, *81*, 3.

Lu, L.-C., Rose, G. M., & Blodgett, J. G. (1999). The effects of cultural dimensions on ethical decision making in marketing: An exploratory study. *Journal of Business Ethics*, *18*, 91–105. doi:10.1023/A:1006038012256

MacFarlane, A., Murphy, A. W., & Clerkin, P. (2006). Telemedicine services in the Republic of Ireland: An evolving policy context. *Health Policy (Amsterdam)*, *76*, 245–258. doi:10.1016/j.healthpol.2005.06.006

Machiavelli, N. (1991). *The prince* (Price, R., Trans.). New York: Cambridge University Press. (Original work published 1532)

MacIntyre, A. (1966). *A short history of ethics: A history of moral philosophy from the Homeric age to the twentieth century*. New York: Collier Books. doi:10.4324/9780203267523

Marshall, K. P. (1999). Has technology introduced new ethical problems? *Journal of Business Ethics*, *19*, 81–90. doi:10.1023/A:1006154023743

Mason, R. O. (1986). Four ethical issues of the information age. *Management Information Systems Quarterly*, *10*(1), 4–12. doi:10.2307/248873

Maximization. (2008, August 2). *Wikipedia*. Retrieved from http://en.wikipedia.org/wiki/Maximization

Mayer, R. C., Davis, J. H., & Schoorman, F. D. (1995). An integrative model of organizational trust. *Academy of Management Review*, *20*, 709–734. doi:10.2307/258792

Maymounkov, P., & Mazières, D. (2002) Kademlia: A peer-to-peer information system based on the XOR metric. In *Proceedings of the International Workshop on Peer-to-Peer Systems (IPTPS)*. Cambridge, MA.

McCullagh, D. (2003, October). SunnComm won't sue grad student. *Cnet news* Retrieved from http://news.cnet.com/SunnComm-wont-sue-grad-student/2100-1027_3-5089448.html

McGuire, A., Fisher, R., Cusenza, P., Hudson, K., Rothstein, M., & McGraw, D. (2008). Confidentiality, privacy, and security of genetic and genomic test information in electronic health records: Points to consider. *Genetics in Medicine*, *10*(7), 495–499. doi:10.1097/GIM.0b013e31817a8aaa

McNabb, R. (2007, March/April). Why you shouldn't be a person of principle. *Philosophy Now*, *60*, 26–29.

Meslin, E. (2008). *Ethical issues in constructing and using biobanks*. Bioethics seminar series, Purdue University. Retrieved April 1, 2008 from http://www.purdue.edu/bioethics/files/video/meslin_ bioethics.mov

Mill, J. S. (2001). *Utilitarianism* (2nd ed.). Indianapolis, IN: Hackett. (Original work published 1861)

Mill, J. S. (1979). *Utilitarianism* (Sher, G., Ed.). Indianapolis, IN: Hackett Publishing Company.

Millennium Copyright Act, D. (1998). 17 U.S.C. §§ 512, 1201–1205, 1301–1332; 28 U.S.C. § 4001 . *Pub., L*, 105–304.

Mitrakas, A. (2006). Information security and law in Europe: Risks checked? *Information & Communications Technology Law*, *15*(1), 33–53. doi:10.1080/13600830600557984

Mitrokotsa, C., & Douligeris, A. (2004). DDoS attacks and defense mechanisms: classification and state-of-the-art . *Computer Networks: The International Journal of Computer and Telecommunications Networking*, *44*(5), 643–666.

Moily, V. (2009). IT act will be amended to tackle cyber crime. *The Times of India*. Retrieved from http://timesofindia.indiatimes.com/news/india/IT-Act-will-be-amended-to-tackle-cyber-crime-Moily/articleshow/5048201.cms

Moor, J. (1985). What is computer ethics? *Metaphilosophy*, *16*(4), 266–275. doi:10.1111/j.1467-9973.1985.tb00173.x

Moore, A. P., Cappelli, D. M., & Trzeciak, R. F. (2008). *The "Big Picture" of insider IT sabotage across U.S. critical infrastructures*. Pittsburgh, PA: Software Engineering Institute, Carnegie Mellon University.

Moore, D. A., & Cain, D. M. (2007). Overconfidence and underconfidence: When and why people underestimate (and overestimate) the competition. *Organizational Behavior and Human Decision Processes*, *103*, 197–213. doi:10.1016/j.obhdp.2006.09.002

Moore v. Regents of University of California. 51 Cal.3d 120 (Supreme Court of California 1990).

Moore, J., Bland, W., Francis, S., King, N., Patterson, J., Srinivasan, U., & Widden, P. (2004) Interdiction of unauthorized copying in a decentralized network. U.S. Patent Application number 10/803,784, publication number 2005/0091167.

Murray, T. H. (1997). Genetic exceptionalism and "future diaries": Is genetic information different from other medical information . In Rothstein, M. A. (Ed.), *Genetic Secrets: Protecting Privacy and Confidentiality in the Genetic Era*. New Haven, CT: Yale University Press.

Myers, G. (1979). *The art of software testing*. Hoboken, NJ: John Wiley and Sons.

Nagel, T. (2002). *Concealment and exposure and other essays*. Oxford, England: Oxford University Press.

Nash, L. (2003). *Ethics without the sermon. Harvard business review on corporate ethics*. Boston, MA: Harvard Business School Press. (Original work published 1981)

National Conference of State Legislatures. Retrieved September 28, 2009 from http://www.ncsl.org/Default.aspx?TabId=13489

Neil, D., & Craigie, J. (2004). The ethics of pharmacogenomics. *Monash Bioethics Review*, *23*, 2.

Network Advertising Initiative. (2008). *The network advertising initiative's self-regulatory code of conduct*. Retrieved September 16, 2009 from http://networkadvertising.org/networks/2008%20NAI%20Principles_final%20for%20Website.pdf

Niemitz v Germany (1992) Series A 251-B paras 29-33, Judgement of 16 December 1992, A-251. B, point 33.

Nietzsche, F. (1980). *On the advantage and disadvantage of history for life* (Preuss, P., Trans.). Indianapolis, IN: Hackett Publishing. (Original work published 1874)

Nissenbaum, H. (2004). Privacy as contextual integrity. *Washington Law Review (Seattle, Wash.)*, *79*(1), 119–158.

Nissenbaum, H. (1998). Protecting privacy in an information age: The problem of privacy in public. *Law and Philosophy*, *17*(5-6), 559–596.

Nissenbaum, H. (2004). Privacy as contextual integrity. *Washington Law Review (Seattle, Wash.)*, *79*(1), 119–157.

Oberholzer-Gee, F., & Strumpf, K. (2007). The effect of file sharing on record sales: An empirical analysis. *The Journal of Political Economy*, *115*(1), 1–42. doi:10.1086/511995

OECD. (1980). *Guidelines on the protection of privacy and transborder flows of personal data*, 23 September 1980. Retrieved from http://www.oecd.org/document/20/0,2340,en_2649_33703_15589524_1_1_1_37409,00.html

Ohm, P. (2009). The rise and fall of invasive ISP surveillance. *University of Illinois Law Review.* (forthcoming). University of Colorado Law Legal Studies Research Paper No. 08-22. Available at SSRN: http://ssrn.com/abstract=1261344

Olson, M. (1971). *The logic of collective action. Public goods and the theory of groups*. Cambridge, MA: Harvard University Press.

Ortega y Gasset, J. (1961). *Meditations on Quixote* (Rugg, E., & Marin, D., Trans.). New York: W.W. Norton & Company.

Ortega y Gasset, J. (1957). *Man and people* (Trask, W., Trans.). New York: W.W. Norton & Co.

Ostrom, E. (1990). *Governing the commons: The evolution of institutions for collective action*. New York: Cambridge University Press.

Ostrom, E., Gardner, R., & Walker, J. (1994). *Rules, games, and common pool resources*. Ann Arbor, MI: The University of Michigan Press.

Ostrom, E. (1999). Institutional rational choice. An assessment of the institutional analysis and development framework . In Sabatier, P. (Ed.), *Theories of the policy process* (pp. 35–67). Boulder, CO: Westview Press.

Pagkalos, D. (2008, January). ScanAlert's "Hacker Safe" badge not so safe and PCI compliant. </XSSED> web site. Retrieved from http://www.xssed.com/news/55/ScanAlerts_Hacker_Safe_badge_not_so_safe_and_PCI_compliant/

Palm, E. (2005). The dimensions of privacy . In Hansson, S. O., & Palm, E. (Eds.), *The ethics of workplace privacy* (pp. 157–174). Peter Lang Publishing Company.

Paradice, D. B. (1990). Ethical attitudes of entry-level MIS personnel. *Information & Management*, *18*, 143–151. doi:10.1016/0378-7206(90)90068-S

Parent, W. (1983). Privacy, morality and the law. *Philosophy & Public Affairs*, *12*, 269–288.

Parker, D. B. (1998). *Fighting computer crime: A new framework for protecting information*. New York: John Wiley & Sons, Inc.

Parliamentary Council. (1970). *Resolution 428, Assembly of the Council of. Europe, Constitutional Assembly. 21 St Ordinary Session, 3 rd.* Part.

Peirce, C. S. (1955). *Philosophical writings of Peirce* (Buchler, J., Ed.). New York: Dover Publications, Inc.

Peirce, C. S. (1992). The fixation of belief . In Peirce, C. S., Houser, N., & Kloesel, C. (Eds.), *The essential Peirce* (*Vol. I*). Bloomington, IN: Indiana University Press. (Original work published 1877)

Personal Data Security and Privacy Act of 2009, S. 1490, 111th Congress (2009).

Picanso, K. (2006). Protecting information security under a uniform data breach notification law. *75 . Fordham Law Review*, 355.

Pirate Party. (2009). Retrieved November 29, 2009 from http://www.piratpartiet.se/international/english

Pirmohamed, M., James, S., & Meakin, S. (2006). Adverse drug reactions as a cause of admission to hospital: A systematic review and metaregression. *Chest*, *129*, 1155–1166.

Plato, . (2000). *The republic* (Jowett, B., Trans.). New York: Dover Publications.

Ponemon Institute. (2008). *Consumers' report card on data breach notification.* Ponemon Institute Research Report. Retrieved May 15, 2009 from http://www.ponemon.org/local/upload/fckjail/generalcontent/18/file/Consumer%20Report%20Card%20Data%20Breach%20Noti%20Apr08.pdf

Ponemon Institute. (2008). *Fourth annual US cost of data breach study*. Ponemon Institute Research Report. Retrieved May 15, 2009 from http://www.ponemon.org/local/upload/fckjail/generalcontent/18/file/2008-2009%20US%20Cost%20of%20Data%20Breach%20Report%20Final.pdf

Popkin, R., & Stroll, A. (1993). *Philosophy made simple* (2nd ed.). New York: Doubleday.

Privacy Act of 1974, 5 USC. § 552a (1974). Pub. L. No. 93-579, as amended. Retrieved from http://www.usdoj.gov/opcl/privstat.htm

Privacy Implications of Online Advertising: Hearing before Committee on Commerce, Science, and Technology. U.S. Senate, 110th Cong. 1 (2008).

Privacy Rights Clearinghouse. (2008). *A chronology of data breaches*. Retrieved May 1, 2009 from http://www.privacyrights.org/ar/ChronDataBreaches.htm#1

Rachels, J. (1975). Why privacy is important. *Philosophy & Public Affairs*, *4*(4), 323–333.

Rahman, M., & Kannan, K. (2007, May). *The countervailing of restricted patch distribution: Economic and policy implications*. Paper presented at 2007 Workshop on Economics of Information Security, Pittsburgh, PA. Retrieved September 6, 2009 from http://weis2007.econinfosec.org/papers/45.pdf.

Reed, M. G., Syverson, P. F., & Goldschlag, D. M. (1998). Anonymous connections and onion routing. *IEEE Journal on Selected Areas in Communications*, *16*(4), 482–494. doi:10.1109/49.668972

Regan, P. M. (1995). *Legislating privacy, technology, social values and public Policy*. Chapel Hill, NC: University of North Carolina Press.

Regulation 1049/2001/EC of the European Parliament and of the Council of the European Union of 30 May 2001 regarding public access to European Parliament, Council and Commission documents. Retrieved from http:www.euractiv.com/en/pa/access-document/article-117440

Rehabilitation Act of 1973, 29 U.S.C. §701 et seq. (1973). Public Law 93-112, as amended. http://www.dotcr.ost.dot.gov/documents/ycr/REHABACT.HTM

Reis, H. T., & Gable, S. L. (2000). Event-sampling and other methods for studying everyday experience . In Reis, H. T., & Judd, C. M. (Eds.), *Handbook of research methods in social and personality psychology* (pp. 190–222). Cambridge, MA: Cambridge University Press.

Renshaw, K. (2002). Sounding alarms: Does informational regulation help or hinder environmentalism? *Environmental Law (Northwestern School of Law)*, *14*(3), 654–697.

Rest, J. R. (1986). *Moral development: Advances in research and theory*. New York: Praeger.

Rest, J. (1994). Background theory and research . In Rest, J., & Narvaez, D. (Eds.), *Moral development in the professions* (pp. 1–26). Hillsdale, NJ: Lawrence Erlbaum Associates.

Riksrevisionen [National Audit Office] (2007) Regeringens styrning av informationssäkerhetsarbetet i den statliga förvaltningen,, [Government regulation of work on information security in the public administration] RiR 2007:10.

Robbins, R. W., Fleischmann, K. R., & Wallace, W. A. (2008). Computing and Information Ethics: Challenges, Education, and Research . In Luppicini, R., & Adell, R. (Eds.), *Handbook of research on technoethics* (pp. 391–408). Hershey, PA: IGI Global.

Roberts, P., Archer, B., & Baynes, K. (1992). *Modelling: The language of designing. Loughborough University of Technology, Department of Design and Technology*. Leicestershire, UK: Audio-Visual Services, Loughborough University.

Romme, A. G. (2003). Making a difference: Organization as design. *Organization Science*, *14*(5), 558–573. doi:10.1287/orsc.14.5.558.16769

Rosenberg, R. S. (1999). The workplace on the verge of the 21st century. *Journal of Business Ethics*, *22*, 3–14. doi:10.1023/A:1006133732667

Roses, A. D. (2000). Pharmacogenetics and the practice of medicine. *Nature*, *405*, 6788. doi:10.1038/35015728

Rössler, B. (2005). *The value of privacy*. Cambridge, MA: Polity Press.

Rothenberg, R. (2008). *Testimony Before the Subcommittee on Regulations, Healthcare, and Trade Hearing on "The Impact of Online Advertising on Small Firms." Small Business Committee, U.* S. House of Representatives.

Saltzer, J. H., Reed, D. P., & Clark, D. D. (1984). End-to-end arguments in system design. *ACM Transactions on Computer Systems*, *2*(4), 277–288. doi:10.1145/357401.357402

Scanlon, T. (1975). Thomson on privacy. *Philosophy & Public Affairs*, *4*(4), 315–322.

Scanlon, T. (1988). *What we owe to each other*. Cambridge, MA: Belknap Press.

Schneier, B. (2007, January). Debating full disclosure. *Schneier blog site*. Retrieved from http://www.schneier.com/blog/archives/2007/01/debating_full_d.html

Schneier, B. (2008). *Software Makers Should Take Responsibility*. Retrieved September 27, 2009 from http://www.schneier.com/essay-228.html

Schoeman, F. (Ed.). (1984). *Philosophical dimensions of privacy: An anthology*. Cambridge, MA: Cambridge University Press. doi:10.1017/CBO9780511625138

Schulte, P. A., Lomax, G. P., Ward, E. M., & Colligan, M. J. (1999). Ethical issues in the use of genetic markers in occupational epidemiologic research. *Journal of Occupational and Environmental Medicine*, *41*, 8. doi:10.1097/00043764-199908000-00005

Schultz, E. E. (2002). A framework for understanding insider attacks. University of California-Berkeley Lab. Paper presented at Compsec 2002, London, England. Retrieved from http://www.itsec.gov.cn/webportal/download/2002-A%20framework%20for%20understanding%20and%20predicting%20insider%20attacks.pdf

Schwarz, P., & Janger, E. (2007). Notification of data breaches. *Michigan Law Review*, *105*, 913.

Self-regulatory principles for online behavioral advertising. (2009) Retrieved September 16, 2009 from: http://www.iab.net/behavioral-advertisingprinciples

Shang, R. A., Chen, Y. C., & Chen, P. C. (2008). Ethical decisions about sharing music files in the P2P environment. *Journal of Business Ethics*, *80*(2), 349–365. doi:10.1007/s10551-007-9424-2

Shaw, E. D., & Fischer, L. F. (2005). *Ten tales of betrayal: The threat to corporate infrastructures by information technology insiders. Report 1—Overview and general observation (*Technical Report 05-04). Monterey, CA: Defense Personnel Security Research Center (PERSEREC).

Simmel, G. (1959). *Georg Simmel, 1858-1918* (Wolff, K. H., Trans.). Columbus, OH: Ohio State University Press.

Simon, H. (1973). Applying information technology to organization design. *Public Administration Review, 33*(3), 268–278. doi:10.2307/974804

Simon, H. (1981). *The sciences of the artificial* (2nd ed.). Cambridge, MA: MIT Press.

Simon, H. (1987). *Models of man—social and rational.* New York: Garland Publishing, Inc.

Singh, S., Cabraal, A., Demosthenous, C., Astbrink, G., & Furlong, M. (2007). Password sharing: Implications for security design based on social practice. In *CHI Proceedings 2007,* San Jose, CA.

Sitton, J. V. (2006). When the right to know and the right to privacy collide. *The Information Management Journal, 40*(5), 76–80.

Skloot, R. (2006, April 16). Taking the least of you. *The New York Times Magazine.* Retrieved from http://www.nytimes.com/2006/04/16/magazine/16tissue.html

Smith, R. E. (2002). *Compilation of state and federal privacy laws.* Providence, RI: Privacy Journal.

Solove, D. J. (2008). *Understanding privacy.* Boston, MA: Harvard University Press.

Spinello, R. (2003). *Case studies in information technology ethics* (2nd ed.). Upper Saddle River, NJ: Prentice Hall.

Stallman, R. (1992, April). Why software should be free. GNU Operating Systems website. Retrieved from http://www.gnu.org/philosophy/shouldbefree.html

Stonebruner, G., Goguen, A., & Feringa, A. (2002). *Risk management guide for information technology systems* (NIST Publication No. 800-30). Retrieved from http://csrc.nist.gov/publications/nistpubs/800-30/sp800-30.pdf

Sunstein, C. (1999). Informational regulation and information standing: Atkins and beyond. *University of Pennsylvania Law Review, 147*(3), 613–675. doi:10.2307/3312719

Swire, P. P., & Antón, A. I. (2008, April 10). Online behavioral advertising: Moving the discussion forward to possible self-regulatory principles. Testimony to the FTC. Retrieved March 19, 2009 from http://www.americanprogress.org/issues/2008/04/swire_anton_testimony.html

Szoka, B., & Thierer, A. (2008). Online advertising and user privacy: Principles to guide the debate. *Progress Snapshot, 4*, 6.

Tabak, F., & Smith, W. P. (2005). Privacy and electronic monitoring in the workplace: A model of managerial cognition and relational trust development. *Employee Responsibilities and Rights Journal, 17*(3), 173–189. doi:10.1007/s10672-005-6940-z

Taipale, K. (2003) Secondary liability on the internet: Towards a performative standard for constitutive responsibility. Center for Advanced Studies Working Paper No. 04-2003. Available at SSRN: http://ssrn.com/abstract=712101

Tavani, H. T. (1999). Informational privacy, data mining, and the internet. *Ethics and Information Technology, 1*(2), 137–145. doi:10.1023/A:1010063528863

Tavani, H. T. (2007). Philosophical theories of privacy: implications for an adequate on-line privacy policy. *Metaphilosophy, 38*(1), 1–22. doi:10.1111/j.1467-9973.2006.00474.x

Texas Workforce Commission. (2008). HIPAA privacy rule – What employers need to know. Retrieved from http://www.twc.state.tx.us/news/efte/hipaa_basics.html

Thomas, E. J., Studdert, D. M., Burstin, H. R., Orav, E. J., Zeena, T., & Williams, E. J. (2000). Incidence and types of adverse events and negligent care in Utah and Colorado. *Medical Care, 38*(3), 261–271. doi:10.1097/00005650-200003000-00003

Thompson, J. J. (1975). The right to privacy. *Philosophy & Public Affairs, 4*(4), 295–314.

Thorne, L., & Saunders, S. (2002). The socio-cultural embeddedness of individuals' ethical reasonin in organizations. *Journal of Business Ethics, 35*(1), 1–14. doi:10.1023/A:1012679026061

Toffler, A. (1981). *The third wave*. New York: Bantam.

Tybout, A. M., & Zaltman, G. (1974). Ethics in marketing research: Their practical relevance. *JMR, Journal of Marketing Research*, *11*(4), 357–368. doi:10.2307/3151282

U. S. v. Barrows, 481 F. 3d1246 (10th Cir. 2007); and United States v. King, 509 F. 3d 1338 (11th Cir. 2007).

U.S. Central Intelligence Agency. (1990). Project SLAMMER Interim Report (U). Director of Central Intelligence/ Intelligence Community Staff Memorandum ICS 0858-90, April 12, 1990. Retrieved October 22, 2009 from http://antipolygraph.org/documents/slammer-12-04-1990.pdf

U.S. Department of Health and Human Services. (2007). *Protecting the privacy of patients' health information.* Retrieved from http://www.hhs.gov/news/facts/privacy2007.html

U.S. Department of Health and Human Services. (2009). *Health information privacy.* Retrieved from http://www.hhs.gov/ocr/hipaa/

U.S. Department of Justice. (2008). Available at: http://www.usdoj.gov/oip/04_7_1.html

U.S. Department of Justice. (2009). Americans with Disabilities Act ADA home page. Retrieved from http://www.usdoj.gov/crt/ada/

U.S. Equal Employment Opportunity Commission. (2008). *Americans with disabilities act: Questions and answers*. Retrieved from http://www.usdoj.gov/crt/ada/q%26aeng02.htm (last updated November 14, 2008).

United Nations. (1948). *Adopted and proclaimed by General Assembly resolution 217 A (III) of 10 December 1948*. Universal Declaration of Human Rights.

United Nations. (2005). *UN global e-government readiness report 2005: From e-government to e-inclusion*, Department of Economic and Social Affairs Division for Public Administration and Development Management, UPAN 2005/14.

United Nations. (2008). UN *e-government survey 2008 – from e-government to connected governance. Retrieved from:*http://unpan1.un.org/intradoc/groups/public/documents/UN/UNPAN028607.pdf.

Veterans Affairs Information Security Act, 38 U.S.C. § 5722 (2006).

Viega, J. (2009, January). Responsible Disclosure is Irresponsible. *O'Reilly Community web site*. Retrieved from http://broadcast.oreilly.com/2009/01/responsible-disclosure-is-irre.html

Vitell, S. J., Paolillo, J. G. P., & Thomas, J. L. (2003). The perceived role of ethics and social responsibility: A study of marketing professionals. *Business Ethics Quarterly*, *13*(1), 63–86.

Volkema, R. (2004). Demographic, cultural, and economic predictors of perceived ethicality of negotiated behavior: A nine-country analysis. *Journal of Business Research*, *57*, 69–78. doi:10.1016/S0148-2963(02)00286-2

Volokh, A. (2002). The pitfalls of the environmental right-to-know, *2002 . Utah Law Review*, 805–841.

Wagner, S. (2005, May). Software quality economics for defect-detection techniques using failure prediction. In *Proceedings of the Third Workshop on Software Quality* St. Louis, Missouri, May, 2005.

Wagner, S. (2007, May). Using economics as basis for modeling and evaluating software quality. *First International Workshop on the Economics of Software and Computation*, Minneapolis, MN.

Waldo, J., Lin, H. S., & Millett, L. I. (2007). *Engaging privacy and information technology in a digital age.* Washington, D.C.: The National Academies Press.

Walsh, K., & Gün Sirer, E. (2006). Experience with an object reputation system for peer-to-peer filesharing. In *Proceedings of the Symposium on Networked System Design and Implementation.* San Jose, CA, USA.

Warne, C. E. (1962). Advertising – a critic's view. *Journal of Marketing*, *26*(4), 10–14. doi:10.2307/1248332

Warren, S. D., & Brandeis, L. D. (1890). The right to privacy. *Harvard Law Review*, *4*(193).

Westin, A. (1967). *Privacy and freedom*. New York: Atheneum.

What, Y. B. P. K. A. Y. W. U. *Deep Packet Inspection and Communications Laws and Policies: Hearing before the Committee on Energy and Commerce, Subcommittee on Telecommunications and the Internet, House of Representatives*, 110 Cong. 1 (2008).

Whitman, M. E., & Mattord, H. J. (2005). *Principles of information security*. Boston, MA: Thomson Course Technology.

Wikipedia. (2009). Blackhat. Retrieved from http://en.wikipedia.org/wiki/Blackhat

Wilkins, R. H. (1992). *Neurosurgical Classics*. New York: Thieme Medical Publishers.

Window on State Government. (2003). Reduce management costs in state government. Retrieved from http://www.cpa.state.tx.us/etexas2003/gg10.html

Wolverton, T. (2000). Amazon snags patent for recommendation service, *CNET News*. Retrieved March 19, 2009 from http://news.cnet.com/2100-1017-241267.html

Wood, W. A. (1993). Computer ethics and years of computer use. *Journal of Computer Information Systems*, *23*(4), 23–27.

Woodcock, J., & Lesko, L. J. (2009). Pharmacogenetics – Tailoring treatment for the outliers. *The New England Journal of Medicine*, *360*(8), 811–813. doi:10.1056/NEJMe0810630

World Privacy Forum. (2004, April 6). An open letter to google regarding its proposed gmail service. Retrieved May 23, 2009 from http://www.worldprivacyforum.org/gmailrelease.pdf

Wray, R. (2009) Phorm: UK faces court for failing to enforce privacy laws. *The Guardian*. Retrieved May 24, 2009 from http://www.guardian.co.uk/business/2009/apr/14/phorm-privacy-data-protection-eu

Wu, A. C., & Fuhlbrigge, A. L. (2009). Economic evaluation of pharmacogenetic tests. *Clinical Pharmacology and Therapeutics*, *84*(2), 272–274. doi:10.1038/clpt.2008.127

Wysowski, D. K., Nourjah, P., & Swartz, L. (2007). Bleeding complications with warfarin use: A prevalant adverse effect resulting in regulatory action. *Archives of Internal Medicine*, *167*(13), 1414–1419. doi:10.1001/archinte.167.13.1414

Yan, J., Liu, N., Wang, G., Zhang, W., Jiang, Y., & Chen, Z. (2009). How much can behavioral targeting help online advertising? In *WWW '09: Proceedings of the 18th International Conference on World Wide Web* (pp. 261–270). New York, NY, USA.

Yang (2006). *San Diego Computer Expert Charged with Hacking into U.S.C. Computer System Containing Student Applications*. (DOJ News Release 06-045). Retrieved from http://www.usdoj.gov/criminal/cybercrime/mccartyCharge.htm

Yankovic, A. M. (2006). *Don't Download this Song. On Straight Outta Lynwood* [CD]. Volcano.

Yar, M. (2005). The global 'epidemic' of movie 'piracy': crime-wave or social construction? *Media Culture & Society*, *27*(5), 677–696. doi:10.1177/0163443705055723

Zheng, J., Williams, L., Nagappan, N., Snipes, W., Hudepohl, J., & Vouk, M. (2006). On the value of static analysis for fault detection in software. *IEEE Transactions on Software Security*, *32*(4), 240–253. doi:10.1109/TSE.2006.38

About the Contributors

Melissa Jane Dark is a Professor in Computer and Information Technology and Associate Director for Educational Programs at CERIAS (the Center for Education and Research in Information Assurance and Security) at Purdue University. Her research interests focus on how to address the human aspects of information security problems. She investigates the utilization of education and public policy to shape the information security behaviors of people.

* * *

Annie I. Antón received the PhD degree in computer science from the Georgia Institute of Technology, Atlanta, in 1997. In 1998, she joined the faculty of North Carolina State University, Raleigh, where she is currently a professor, the founder and director of ThePrivacyPlace.org, and a member of the Cyber Defense Laboratory. Her research interests include software requirements engineering, information privacy and security policy, regulatory compliance, software evolution, and process improvement. She is a co chair of the Privacy Subcommittee of the ACM US Public Policy Committee. In 2009, she was recognized as a Distinguished Scientist by the ACM. She is a member of the CRA Board of Directors, IAPP, Sigma Xi, and the Data Privacy and Integrity Advisory Committee, US Department of Homeland Security. She is a senior member of the IEEE. She is a recipient of the US National Science Foundation Faculty Early Career Development (CAREER) Award.

Jonathan Beever is a doctoral student in the Department of Philosophy at Purdue University. He works primarily in applied ethics and bioethics but also has interests in continental philosophy, political philosophy, and semiotics. Jonathan is the co-founder of the Purdue Bioethics Seminar Series at Purdue University and has written on conflict of interest in medical decision-making, ethical publishing in science and engineering, the validity of nanoethics, and the environmental politics of French postmodernist Jean Baudrillard. His dissertation argues for a broadened scope of valuation in environmental ethics within the restraints of signification.

Hina Chaudhry is a PhD student in Information Security at the Center for Research in Information Assurance & Security (CERIAS) at Purdue University, Indiana,USA. Her research interests include security issues in Cloud Computing, Software Vulnerabilities and Information Security frameworks/models. Hina also holds a Masters in Information Systems from Middlesex University, UK. Prior to joining Purdue, Hina was a System Analyst with HCL Corporation, India where she supported multinational financial clients with their remote IT infrastructure.

Nicolas Christin is the Associate Director of the Information Networking Institute at Carnegie Mellon University, where he also serves as a faculty member. He is in addition a CyLab SysteM.S. Scientist, and (by courtesy) a faculty member in the Electrical and Computer Engineering department. He holds a Diplôme d'Ingénieur from École Centrale Lille, and M.S. and Ph.D. degrees in Computer Science from the University of Virginia. While in graduate school, he worked at Nortel's Advanced Technology Lab. Before joining Carnegie Mellon in 2005, he was a post-doctoral researcher in the School of Information at the University of California, Berkeley. He served for three years as resident faculty in the CyLab Japan program in Kobe (Japan), before returning to Carnegie Mellon's main campus in 2008. His research interests are in computer and information systeM.S. networks; most of his work is at the boundary of systeM.S. and policy research, with a slant toward security aspects. He has most recently focused on network security and its economics, incentive-compatible network topology design, and peer-to-peer security.

Joseph Ekstrom is Program Chair of the Information Technology program at Brigham Young University and an Associate Professor in that program. He received his BS, MS and PhD degrees from BYU in 1974, 1976, and 1992 respectively. After a 30 year career in industry as a software engineer and engineering manager, he joined the BYU faculty in 2001 to help create the new Information Technology Major. Dr. Ekstrom has been active in the definition of IT as a discipline and was one of the authors of the IEEE/ACM Information Technology Model Curriculum. His research interests include Information Assurance and Security curriculum, secure content storage and retrieval, and network security and management.

Deborah Frincke is a Chief Scientist at the Pacific Northwest National Laboratory. She has a PhD, MS and BS in Computer Science and a BS in Mathematics. As Initiative Lead for PNNL's Information and Infrastructure Integrity Initiative, she conducts research spanning a broad cross-section of computer security with an emphasis on infrastructure defense and computer security education. She has published over 80 articles and technical reports and is a charter member of the Department of Energy's cyber security grass roots community. She has been an Affiliate Professor with the University of Washington's information school (UW i-School) since December 2008. She is a member of several computer security editorial boards, the UW i-School Center for Cyber Security and Information Assurance advisory board, and the Idaho State NASA/EPSCOR Technical Advisory Committee. Before joining PNNL, Dr. Frincke was a professor at the University of Idaho, a co-founder and director of the University of Idaho Center for Secure and Dependable SysteM.S., and a co-founder of the TriGeo Network Security Company.

Cassio Goldschmidt is senior manager of the product security team under the Office of the CTO at Symantec Corporation. In this role he leads efforts across the company to ensure the secure development of software products. His responsibilities include managing Symantec's internal secure software development process, training, threat modeling and penetration testing. Cassio's background includes over 13 years of experience in the software industry. During the eight years he has been with Symantec, he has helped to architect, design and develop several top selling product releases, conducted numerous security classes, and coordinated various penetration tests. Cassio is also known for leading the OWASP chapter in Los Angeles. Cassio represents Symantec on the SAFECode technical committee and (ISC)2 in the development of the CSSLP certification. He holds a bachelor degree in computer science from PUC-RS, a masters degree in software engineering from SCU, and a masters of business administration from USC.

Frank L. Greitzer is a Chief Scientist at the Pacific Northwest National Laboratory. He holds a PhD in Mathematical Psychology and a BS in Mathematics. At PNNL he leads a Cognitive Informatics focus area that addresses human factors and social/behavioral science challenges through modeling and advanced engineering/computing approaches. He has over 30 years of applied research and development experience in cognitive psychology, human information processing, and user-centered design. His research interests include modeling human behavior to identify/predict malicious insider cyber activities, modeling socio-cultural factors as predictors of terrorist activities, and human-information interaction concepts for enhancing decision making in various information analysis domains. Other interests include evaluation methods and metrics for assessing effectiveness of decision aids, analysis methods and displays; and application of cognitive principles to improve training effectiveness and accelerate learning. Dr. Greitzer also is an adjunct faculty member at Washington State University-Tri-Cities, where he has taught courses in human-system interaction design and human factors.

Albert L. Harris (PhD, Georgia State University) is Professor of Information Systems at the Walker College of Business, Appalachian State University, and Editor-in-Chief of the Journal of Information Systems Education. He is Secretary of the AIS SIG-ED, International Association of Information Management (IAIM), and a member of the Board of Directors of AITP's Education Special Interest Group (EDSIG). He was a 2006 Fulbright Scholar to Portugal and a 2008-09 exchange Professor to the University of Angers in France. Dr. Harris is a Certified Information Systems Auditor and a Certified Management Consultant. He has consulted for numerous private and public organizations, both in the U.S. and abroad. Dr. Harris has traveled extensively and has used these experiences in his teaching and research. His research interests include IS education, IS ethics, and global IS/IT issues. He had co-edited a book and has over 90 publications as book chapters, journal articles, and in international and national conference proceedings.

Nathan Harter, prior to being admitted to the bar as an alumnus of the Indiana University School of Law, Nathan Harter was graduated from Butler University with departmental honors in both political science and philosophy. He then practiced law in southeastern Indiana, where he served as a city attorney and assistant prosecuting attorney. Harter is presently a professor of Organizational Leadership in the College of Technology at Purdue University and has been teaching non-traditional undergraduates since 1989. During his academic career, Harter was tenured in 1995 and was named a Welliver Faculty Summer Fellow at The Boeing Company in 2005. He has also served as chair of the scholarship section of the International Leadership Association.

Val Hawks is the Director of the School of Technology at Brigham Young University and an Associate Professor in the Manufacturing Engineering Program at BYU. He has a BS degree in Design Engineering Technology from BYU, an MS in Industrial Engineering from Lehigh University and PhD in Leadership Studies from Gonzaga. He has written several papers on topics in ethics and leadership as well as in his specific technical expertise are of quality systeM.S. His professional employment took him to Xerox Corporation in Rochester New York as a young engineer, then to Ben Franklin Technology Center in Bethlehem Pa. as a technical projects manager, before joining the faculty in the College of Engineering and Technology at BYU.

Michael Kane, PhD is an Associate Professor in the Department of Computer and Information Technology at Purdue University, as well as the Lead Genomic Scientist at the Bindley Bioscience Center at Discovery Park. Dr. Kane has a PhD in Molecular Pharmacology and over ten years experience in the pharmaceutical and biotechnology industry. His professional experience has produced 3 patents in the field of genomic technology development, as well as numerous publications in bioinformatics and genomics. He is recognized for his pioneering work in the development of methods for DNA detection, development of dedicated bioinformatics methods and software for DNA analysis, and utilization of genomic technologies in drug discovery and disease characterization.

Aaron Massey is a PhD candidate in the Computer Science department at North Carolina State University and a member of ThePrivacyPlace.org. His research interests include computer security, privacy, regulatory compliance, and managing legal requirements in software engineering. As a recipient of a 2008 Google Policy Fellowship, Aaron spent the summer of 2008 working with Jim Harper, Directory of Information Policy Studies at the Cato Institute. He is also the recipient of the 2008-2009 Walter H. Wilkinson Graduate Research Ethics Fellowship. Aaron earned a BS in Computer Engineering from Purdue University in 2003 and a MS in Computer Science from North Carolina State University in 2009. He is a student member of the Association of Computing Machinery, Institute of Electrical and Electronics Engineers, and International Association of Privacy Professionals. He is also a member of the ACM US Public Policy committee. Aaron is originally from Noblesville, IN.

Linda Morales is an Assistant Professor in the Computer Science Department at the University of Houston-Clear Lake. Her interests include algorithm design and analysis, approximation algorithms, networks, information security and information security ethics. She obtained her PhD in Computer Science for the University of Texas at Dallas. Prior to joining academia, she worked in the telecommunications industry for several years, where she specialized in network planning and the creation of wireless standards. She holds several patents in this area. She enjoys teaching, research and working with students.

Nicolae Morar is a PhD student in the Philosophy Department at Purdue University. He took his undergraduate degree in Philosophy in 2003-2004 from both 'Ecole de Philosophie et Théologie St Jean' and Lyon 3 'Jean Moulin' University (France) with a BA thesis on the foundations and critiques of Michel Foucault's Biopower. He received his Master Degree from Lyon 3 University in 2005 with a Master thesis on the stakes of reproductive medicine in the USA. He joined the PhD Program in Philosophy at Purdue University in 2006. As a recipient of the Puskas Fellowship in 2006, Nicolae initiated the Bioethics Lecture Series at Purdue. His primary interests are applied ethics, biopolitics (genetics and justice), and in recent Continental Philosophy: Foucault and Deleuze. He published articles in the Romanian Journal of Bioethics and has a contribution in a book Health Care, Autonomy, and Responsibility (NY, Zeta Books, 2009).

Elin Palm is a Post Doctoral Researcher at the Division of Philosophy, Royal Institute of Technology, Stockholm, Sweden. Her doctoral dissertation 'The Ethics of Workspace Surveillance' discusses ethical implications of surveillance technology in the context of work. Currently, she conducts research within the fields of Information and Communication Ethics and Intercultural Information Ethics.

Jon E. Sprague, RPh, PhD is Professor of Pharmacology and Dean at the Raabe College of Pharmacy, Ohio Northern University (ONU). Before returning to ONU, Dr. Sprague was Chair and Professor of Pharmacology at the Virginia College of Osteopathic Medicine at Virginia Tech University. He received his PhD in Pharmacology and Toxicology from Purdue University. His first faculty position was also held at Purdue. He then taught for 9 years at Ohio Northern University before he went to Virginia Tech. His research interests include studying the hyperthermic mechanisM.S. of the substituted amphetamines, namely 3,4-methylene¬dioxy-meth¬amphetamine (MDMA, Ecstasy). He and his wife (Aimee) have two young children; Emily (14) and Ryan (11).

John A. Springer, PhD, is an Assistant Professor in the Department of Computer and Information Technology at Purdue University and the Lead Scientist for High Performance Data Management SysteM.S. at the Bindley Bioscience Center at Discovery Park. His research interests involve the innovative use of database technology in bioinformatics, biomedical informatics, and advanced manufacturing; database management system performance and scalability; and novel methods for constraint specification and implementation in databases. His professional background includes stints at a global technology services consulting firm, a pharmaceutical company, and a start-up software company.

Misse Wester is a behavioral scientist, working as a researcher at the Division of Philosophy, The Royal Institute of Technology, Stockholm, Sweden. Her main research areas are risk perception, risk and crisis communication. Of particular interest are differences in perception relating to risk and benefit with new technologies, primarily between experts and lay people. She holds a PhD in psychology from Örebro University. This research was funded by the Swedish Civil Contingencies Agency under contract 1167/2007.

Dave Yates is an Assistant Professor in the College of Information Studies at the University of Maryland. Dr. Yates area of expertise is in social media and collaborative technologies, especially the privacy and security concerns of using these technologies. Dr. Yates is particularly interested in the privacy and security concerns that inhibit trust and information exchange in large-scale collaboration. His dissertation entitled "Technology support for virtual collaboration for innovation in synchronous and asynchronous interaction modes" won the Gerardine DeSanctis dissertation award at the 2007 annual meeting of the Academy of Management. A former Air Force officer, Dr. Yates has also been a consultant for both industry and government institutions in the areas of information security, and virtual collaboration.

Mariah Zabriskie is a certified Senior Professional in Human Resources with over a decade of progressive Human Resources experience at both Fortune 500 and non-profit organizations. MS Zabriskie earned a Bachelor's degree in Business Administration with a minor in Human Resources from Saint Leo University and a Master's degree in Sociology from Florida Atlantic University.

Index

Symbols

A

B

C

O

P

Q

R

S

Breinigsville, PA USA
24 September 2010

245912BV00002B/1/P

9 781616 922450